Image © Larry Macdougal - All Canada Photos. Oil Pumpjack in a Canola Field.

Contents

Acknowledgements

backroadmapbooks.com

#106 - 1500 Hartley Ave,
Coquitlam, BC, V3K 7A1
Toll Free: 1-877-520-5670
E-mail: info@backroadmapbooks.com

DIRECTORS	Russell Mussio, Wesley Mussio
VICE PRESIDENT	Chris Taylor
EDITOR-IN-CHIEF	Russell Mussio

GIS & CARTOGRAPHY TEAM

MANAGER	Andrew Allen
GIS SPECIALISTS	Farah Aghdam, Courtney Fry Dave Mancini, AJ Strawson
CARTOGRAPHERS	Aaron Dixon, Oliver Herz, Matthew Steblyna, Dale Tober

MARKETING & CREATIVE SERVICES

MANAGER	Nazli Faghihi
GRAPHIC DESIGN	Elisa Codazzi, Farnaz Faghihi, Nicole Larsen
CONTENT WRITERS	Sean Anderson, Kaan Eraslan, Leslie Bryant-McLean, Jay Hoare, Fernanda Fukamati, Colin Hughes, Mike Manyk, Linda Aksomitis, Trent Ernst
SALES	Basilio Bagnato, Chris Taylor
ADMINISTRATION	Shaun Filipenko, Jo-ana Maki

COVER PHOTO

LOCATION	Near Somerset, Manitoba (5/B2)
PHOTOGRAPHER(S)	Dave Reede, All Canada Photos

Library and Archives Canada Cataloguing in Publication

Mussio, Russell

Manitoba backroad mapbook [cartographic material] :
outdoor recreation guide / [editor, Russell Mussio]. --3rd ed.

(Backroad mapbooks) Includes index.

ISBN 978-1-897225-55-4

1. Recreation areas--Manitoba--Maps. 2. Outdoor recreation--
Manitoba--Guidebooks. 3. Manitoba--Maps. 4. Manitoba--Guidebooks.
I. Title. II. Series: Backroad mapbooks

G1156.E63E76 2010   796.5097127   C2010-904423-1

Copyright © 2015 Mussio Ventures Ltd.

Acknowledgements

We want to thank the many, many people who have helped over the years and with this updated edition, notably the dedicated and talented people at Mussio Ventures Ltd. This is a hat off to the talented research and writing team of Sean Anderson, Leslie Bryant-McLean, Jay Hoare, Colin Hughes, and Mike Manyk who spent countless hours digging up new places to visit and enjoy. This, coupled with the work of Colette and Trent Ernst, Linda Aksomitis and others before, has created a wealth of information found only in this book. We also want to thank the many mappers, graphics, marketing and sales, and technical support people in our growing company. Thank you Farah Aghdam, Andrew Allen, Basilio Bagnato, Elisa Codazzi, Aaron Dixon, Kaan Eraslan, Farnaz Faghihi, Nazli Faghihi, Shaun Filipenko, Courtney Fry, Fernanda Fukamati, Oliver Herz, Jo-ana Maki, David Mancini, Nicole Larsen, Matthew Steblyna, AJ Strawson, Chris Taylor, and Dale Tober for putting together the most comprehensive guidebook available for Manitoba.

This edition saw many contributors. Notably Northern Alberta has benefited from the road and resource information provided by Robert Coutts and the fine folks at Skybase Geomatic Solutions. We would also like to mention Paul Catt of Watt Mountain Wanderers for his help in and around Mackenzie County. Thanks also to all of our readers who have provided updates and/or tracks and waypoints in our track sharing program with the Backroad GPS Maps. With so much information being moved to the internet, we find we are not talking to as many people as we used to. But to all those who provide that information, we thank you for sharing. Although the names are many, we would like to note a few of the people who have provided more than their fair share of updates. Thanks again to Mike Bylsma, Dave Janzen, Gerard Lachapelle, Ken Sawich and Tom Jansing. If you do find errors or omissions or would just like to see a more accurate trail or road, please send your note or tracks to updates@backroadmapbooks.com.

Map contributors come from all reaches including Federal, Provincial and Municipal Government sources. We would like to express our gratitude to the many helpful map providers including but not limited to Alberta TrailNet Society, Alberta Snowmobile Association, Altalis, Alberta Municipal Data Sharing Partnership , GeoBase©, Natural Resources Canada, the Environment and Sustainable Resource Development, and Travel Alberta. Note the maps may contain information licensed under the Open Government Licence - County of Grande Prairie.

Finally we would like to thank Allison, Devon, Jasper, Madison, Nancy and Penny Mussio for their continued support of the Backroad Mapbooks Series. As our family grows, it becomes increasingly more challenging to break away from it all to explore our beautiful country.

Sincerely,

Russell and Wesley Mussio

Disclaimer

Backroad Mapbooks does not warrant that the backroads, paddling routes and trails indicated in this Mapbook are passable nor does it claim that the Mapbook is completely accurate. Therefore, please be careful when using this or any source to plan and carry out your outdoor recreation activity.

Please note that traveling on logging roads, river routes and trails is inherently dangerous, and without limiting the generality of the foregoing, you may encounter poor road conditions, unexpected traffic, poor visibility, and low or no road/trail maintenance. Please use extreme caution when traveling logging roads and trails.

Please refer to the Fishing and Hunting Regulations for closures and restrictions. It is your responsibility to know when and where closures and restrictions apply.

Help Us Help You

A comprehensive resource such as Backroad Mapbooks for Northern Alberta could not be put together without a great deal of help and support. Despite our best efforts to ensure that everything is accurate, errors do occur. If you see any errors or omissions, please continue to let us know.   All updates will be posted on our web site: www.backroadmapbooks.com

Please contact us at:

Backroad Mapbooks

#106- 1500 Hartley Ave, Coquitlam, BC, V3K 7A1

P: 604-521-6277 | F: 604-521-6260 | Toll Free 1-877-520-5670

Email: updates@backroadmapbooks.com

Website: www.backroadmapbooks.com

Introduction
Northern Alberta

Welcome to the new and improved Third Edition of the Backroad Mapbook for Northern Alberta!

In addition to significantly updating our road and trail networks, and adding countless new recreational opportunities on the maps and in the written section, we have responded to popular demand by enhancing our oil and gas resource information. Whether you live or play up north, the Backroad Mapbook will help you get to where you want to go.

As you travel the expanse of Northern Alberta, the landscape cascades from the jagged Rocky Mountains in the south, to gentler, sloping ranges in the north. Farther east you will discover Canada's northernmost prairie which tumbles into the majestic boreal forest of the north. Explore the ancient Canadian Shield as you journey on to Lake Athabasca in the northeast.

The region boasts Grande Prairie and Fort McMurray as its largest centres. Grande Prairie sits in the west, in the heart of the northern prairie. It is an active metropolis of over 55,000 and growing every year. Built upon agriculture and logging, the city's recent growth stems from oil and gas discovery. In the east, Fort McMurray has an economy founded on the extraction of oil and gas, primarily from its oil sands. The population of Fort Mac has boomed to over 76,000 over the last decade – and it shows no sign of stopping.

If you seek peace and solitude, you will find it in Northern Alberta. Known to some as "Canada's outback," the wild north stretches with untamed wilderness from sweeping grasslands to pristine lakes and rivers. Thanks to the wide range of formalized recreational amenities in parks and campgrounds, you can enjoy the land of Northern Alberta to its fullest.

Paddle through some of the country's greatest touring rivers that flow through the region. Just make sure to plan properly as these trips can last weeks or even months. If you want to navigate like an early explorer, follow the Trans Canada Trail through established trails and historic routes. Or mount your ATV or snowmobile and cruise the miles of backroads and cutlines.

For those on the hunt, the vast forests and lakes of Northern Alberta teem with wildlife. You will spot many moose, herds of elk, a bear or two and scores of deer while driving around the backroads. Anglers revel in the abundance of walleye in Lesser Slave Lake and rainbow trout throughout lakes in the region that provide some of Canada's best fishing opportunities.

The Backroad Mapbook will equip you with all you need to explore to explore the vast and bountiful land of Northern Alberta. For the armchair traveller, it will transport you to remote and wild places just waiting for you to visit someday. So sit back, or pack up, and let us guide you.

BACKROAD HISTORY

The Backroad Mapbook idea came into existence when Wesley and Russell Mussio were out exploring. They had several books and a few maps to try to find their way through the maze of logging roads around southern BC. The brothers were getting very frustrated trying to find their way and eventually gave up. Not to be outdone, the two ambitious brothers started brainstorming. Eventually the Backroad Mapbook idea was born.

They published their first book in January 1994 and it quickly sold out. Rather than simply reprinting it, they listened to the feedback of customers and made several alterations that helped improve the book. This formula of continuing to make the product better carries on today and has helped establish the Backroad Mapbook series as the top selling outdoor recreation guidebook series in the country. From the tiny beginnings in that Vancouver apartment with maps strewn all over the walls, to one of the most sought-after outdoor products in the country, the Backroad Mapbook series has truly come a long way.

Legend

Scale Bar

Scale 1:250 000 1 Centimetre = 2.5 Kilometres

2km   0km   4km   8km   12km

Scale 1:500 000 1 Centimetre = 5 Kilometres

4km   0km   8km   16km   20km

Scale 1:750 000 1 Centimetre = 7.5 Kilometres

7km   0km   14km   28km

Map Information

Elevation Bar:

- over 2000m
- 1750m-2000m
- 1500-1750m
- 1250-1500m
- 1000-1250m
- 750-1000m
- 500-750m
- 250-500m
- 0-250m

Map Projection:
Universal Transverse Mercator Zone 12

Map Datum:
North American Datum 1983 (NAD 83)

Area Indicators:

National / Provincial Parks	City
Conservation / Natural Area / Recreation Area	First Nations
Air Weapons Range / DND / Mining / Petroleum Area / Restricted Area	Water
Swamps	Intermittent Lakes

Contour Lines:

20m Intervals	100m Intervals
1000m Intervals	500m Intervals

Contour Intervals approximately 20m or approximately 100m (see map for details)

Visit backroadmapbooks.com to see tutorials on how to use different elements of our Legend.

Line and Area Classifications:

- Freeways
- Highways
- Secondary Highways
- Arterial Paved Roads
- Rural Paved Roads
- Local Paved Roads
- Forest Service / Main Industry Roads
- Active Industry Roads (2wd)
- Other Industry Roads (2wd / 4wd)
- Unclassified / 4wd Roads
- Deactivated Roads
- Railways

- Trans Canada Trail
- Long Distance Trail
- Snowmobile Trails
- Motorized Trails ATV/OHV/Snowmobile
- Developed Trail
- Routes (Undeveloped Trails)
- Ferry Routes
- Lake / River Paddling Routes
- Powerlines
- Pipelines
- Cut / Seismic Lines
- Township/Range Grid
- WMU - Wildlife Management Zone

Recreational Activities:

- ATV
- Boat Launch
- Beach
- Campsite / Limited Facilities
- RV Campsite / Trailer Park
- Campsite (back country / water access only)
- Canoe Access Put-in / Take-out
- Cross Country Skiing / Back Country Ski Touring
- Cycling
- Downhill Skiing
- Golf Course
- Hang-gliding
- Hiking
- Horseback Riding

- Interpretive Trail
- Horseback Riding
- Motorbiking
- Paddling (canoe-kayak)
- Picnic Site
- Portage
- P50m Portage Distance
- Rock Climbing
- Snowmobiling
- Snowmobile Trans Canada Route
- Snowshoeing
- Staging Area
- Trailhead
- Wildlife Viewing
- Windsurfing

Miscellaneous:

- Anchorage
- Airport / Airstrip
- Arrow / Location Pointer
- Cabin / Chalet / Hut / Shelter
- Compressor
- Dam
- Ferry
- Fire Lookout / Viewpoint
- Float Plane Landing
- Gate
- Gas Plant
- Highway: Primary
- Highway: Secondary
- Highway Interchange
- Historic Site / National

- Marsh
- Microwave Tower
- Mine Site
- Parking
- Pictograph
- Point of Interest
- Ranger Station
- Refinery / Well Disposal
- Resort
- Viewpoint / Forestry Lookout (abandoned)
- Visitor Information Centre
- Waterfalls
- Wilderness Area / Wildlife Area / Wildlife Reserve
- Weigh Scale
- Work Camp

Navigating
Your Backroad Mapbook Outdoor Recreation Guide

Introduction

This section has many valuable planning tools such as information on Travel/Tourism & Visitor Centres. One of the main tools will be your Legend.

Topographic Maps

This section starts with the Map Key for the region. Use our Topographic Maps and Insets to guide you to your Adventure destination.

Service Directory

Find details on some of the best Accommodations, Sales/Services and Tours/Guides in the area to help select the one that is the right fit with your travel style and needs.

Adventures

For each activity and experience this section will help you plan your trip and ensure you get the best experience of working with our maps and all of the great features.

Index

A full index of the guides' contents is included with page numbers and map coordinates for easy reference. Other tools included are Important Numbers, a Distance Chart and an Advertiser List.

YOUR *BRMB* EXPERIENCE

*Each of our Backroad Mapbooks is filled with amazing experiences that show you how to enjoy the outdoors and create unforgettable memories. Visit **backroadmapbooks.com** for our other great products, tips & tutorials, features and updates to further enhance your outdoor experiences.*

FORT McMURRAY
TOURISM

FORT McMURRAY AND THE WOOD BUFFALO REGION

NORTHERN STRONG!

In partnership with

Travel Alberta
Canada

REGIONAL MUNICIPALITY
OF WOOD BUFFALO

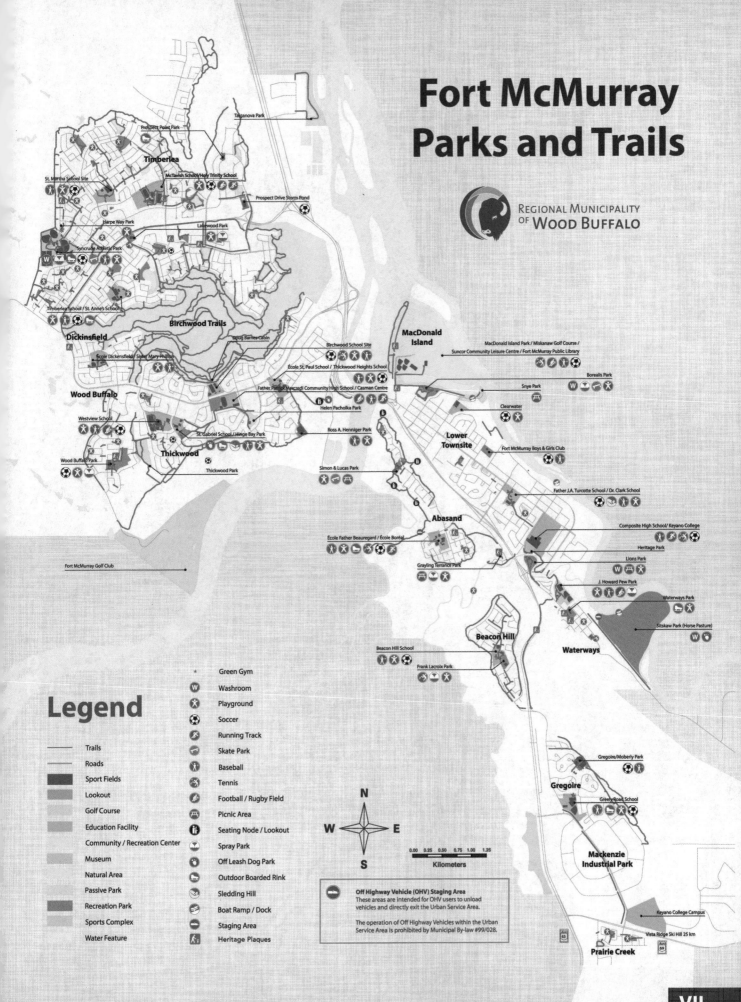

Fort McMurray Parks and Trails

REGIONAL MUNICIPALITY OF WOOD BUFFALO

Legend

- Trails
- Roads
- Sport Fields
- Lookout
- Golf Course
- Education Facility
- Community / Recreation Center
- Museum
- Natural Area
- Passive Park
- Recreation Park
- Sports Complex
- Water Feature

- ★ Green Gym
- Washroom
- Playground
- Soccer
- Running Track
- Skate Park
- Baseball
- Tennis
- Football / Rugby Field
- Picnic Area
- Seating Node / Lookout
- Spray Park
- Off Leash Dog Park
- Outdoor Boarded Rink
- Sledding Hill
- Boat Ramp / Dock
- Staging Area
- Heritage Plaques

Off Highway Vehicle (OHV) Staging Area
These areas are intended for OHV users to unload vehicles and directly exit the Urban Service Area.

The operation of Off Highway Vehicles within the Urban Service Area is prohibited by Municipal By-law #99/028.

Kilometers
0.00 0.25 0.50 0.75 1.00 1.25

Map Labels

Taiganova Park
Prospect Point Park
Timberlea
McTavish School/Holy Trinity School
St. Martha School Site
Prospect Drive Storm Pond
Harpe Way Park
Lakewood Park
Syncrude Athletic Park
Timberlea School / St. Anne's School
Birchwood Trails
Dickinsfield
Doug Barnes Cabin
Birchwood School Site
MacDonald Island
MacDonald Island Park / Miskanaw Golf Course / Suncor Community Leisure Centre / Fort McMurray Public Library
École Dickensfield / Sister Mary Phillip
École St. Paul School / Thickwood Heights School
Borealis Park
Snye Park
Wood Buffalo
Father Patrick Mercredi Community High School / Casman Centre
Clearwater
Lower Townsite
Westview School
Helen Pacholka Park
Fort McMurray Boys & Girls Club
St. Gabriel School / Hinge Bay Park
Ross A. Henniger Park
Thickwood
Father J.A. Turcotte School / Dr. Clark School
Wood Buffalo Park
Thickwood Park
Simon & Lucas Park
Composite High School/ Keyano College
Abasand
Heritage Park
Lions Park
École Father Beauregard / École Boréal
Fort McMurray Golf Club
J. Howard Pew Park
Grayling Terrace Park
Waterways Park
Sitskaw Park (Horse Pasture)
Beacon Hill School
Beacon Hill
Waterways
Frank Lacroix Park
Gregoire/Moberly Park
Gregoire
Greely Road School
Mackenzie Industrial Park
Keyano College Campus
Vista Ridge Ski Hill 25 km
Prairie Creek

VII

Map Key
Northern Alberta

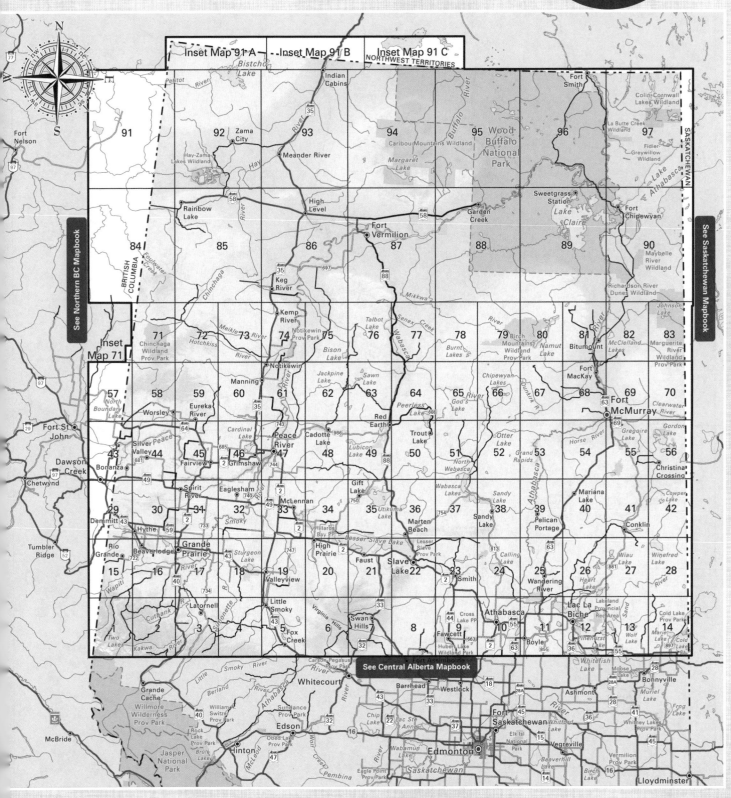

See Northern BC Mapbook

See Saskatchewan Mapbook

See Central Alberta Mapbook

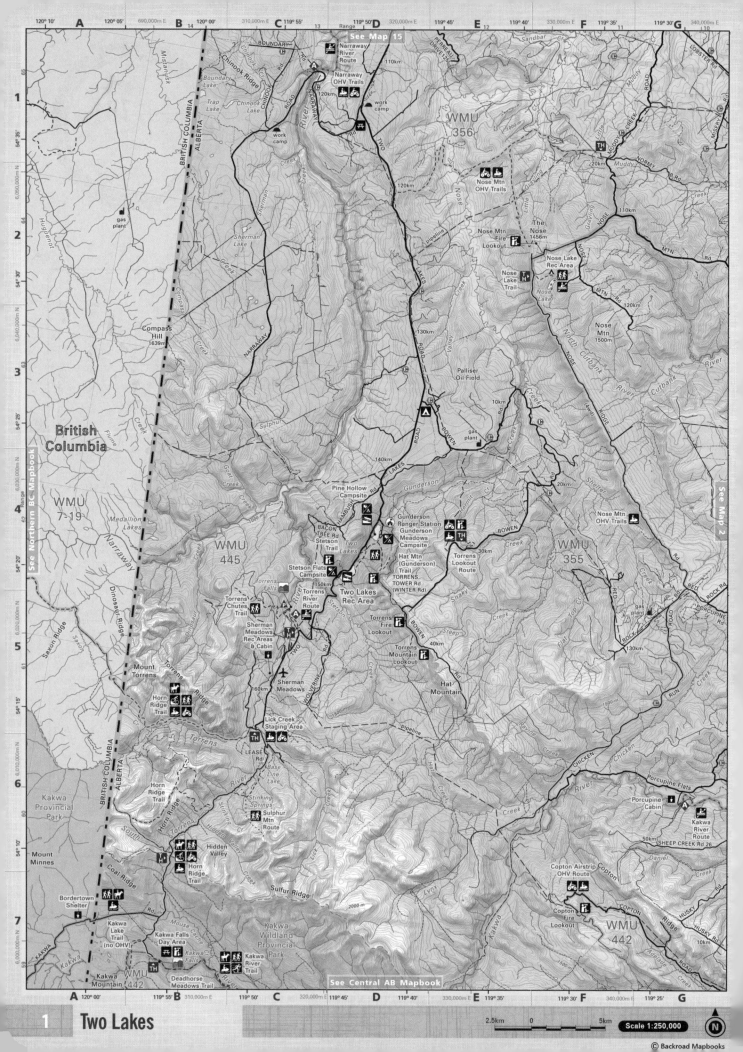

British Columbia

Kakwa Provincial Park

Two Lakes

Scale 1:250,000

© Backroad Mapbooks

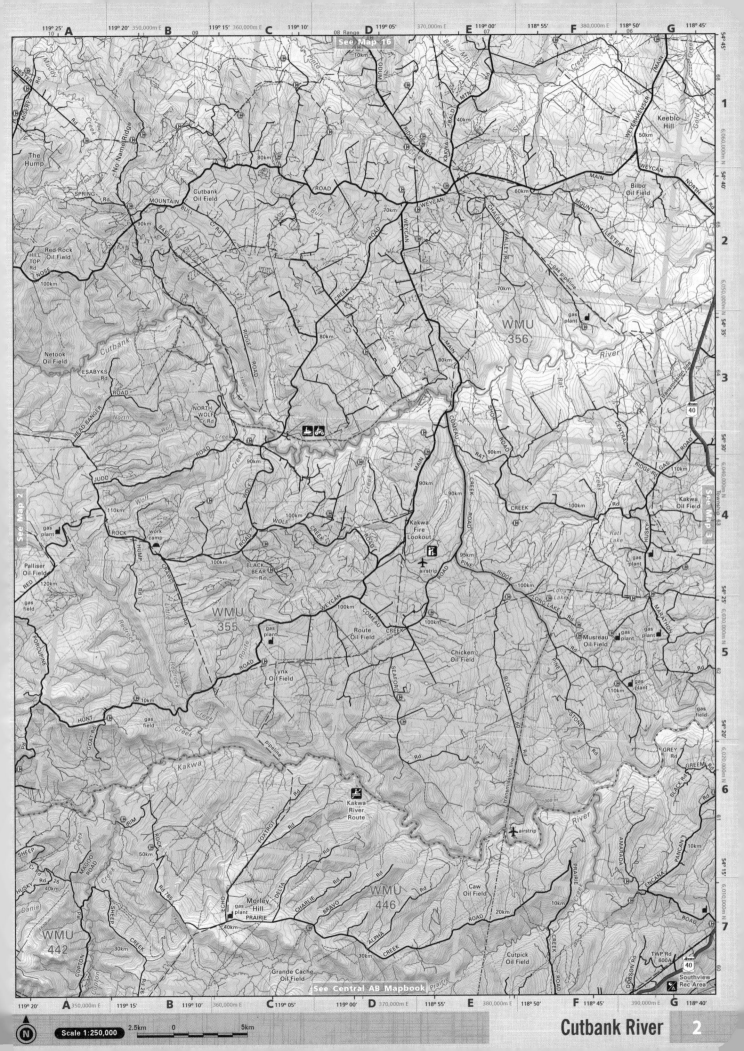

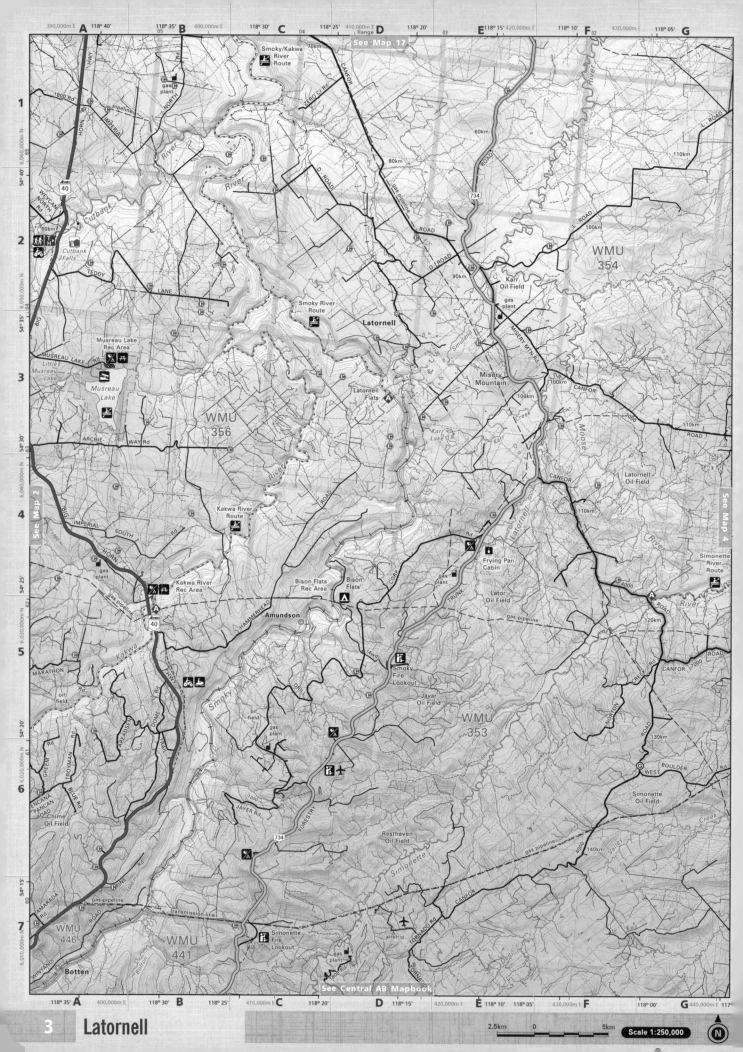

See Map 2
See Map 4

3 Latornell

2.5km 0 5km   Scale 1:250,000   N

Scale 1:250,000

Simonette River

4

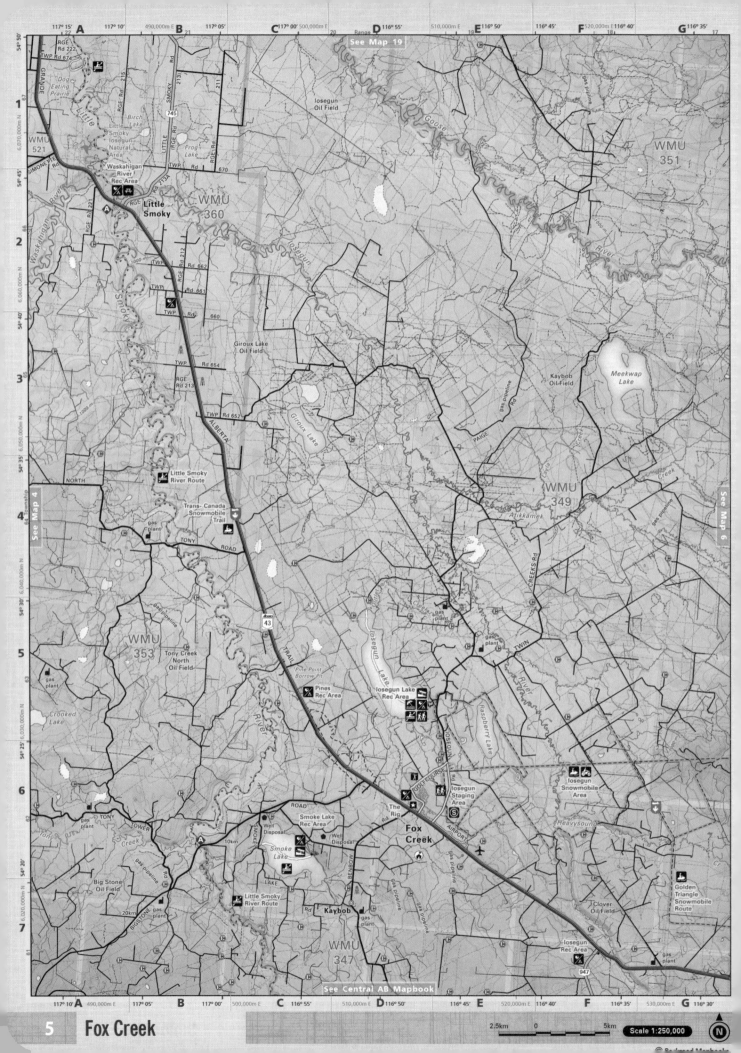

See Map 4

See Map 6

Little Smoky

WMU 521

WMU 351

WMU 360

WMU 349

WMU 353

Iosegun Oil Field

Giroux Lake Oil Field

Kaybob Oil Field

Meekwap Lake

Little Smoky River Route

Trans-Canada Snowmobile Trail

Tony Creek North Oil Field

Pine Point Borrow Pit

Pines Rec Area

Iosegun Lake Rec Area

Iosegun Snowmobile Area

Crooked Lake

Smoke Lake Rec Area

Well Disposal

Well Disposal

Smoke Lake

Fox Creek

Iosegun Staging Area

The Rig

Big Stone Oil Field

Little Smoky River Route

Kaybob

Golden Triangle Snowmobile Route

Clover Oil Field

Iosegun Rec Area

WMU 347

See Central AB Mapbook

2.5km 0 5km   Scale 1:250,000   N

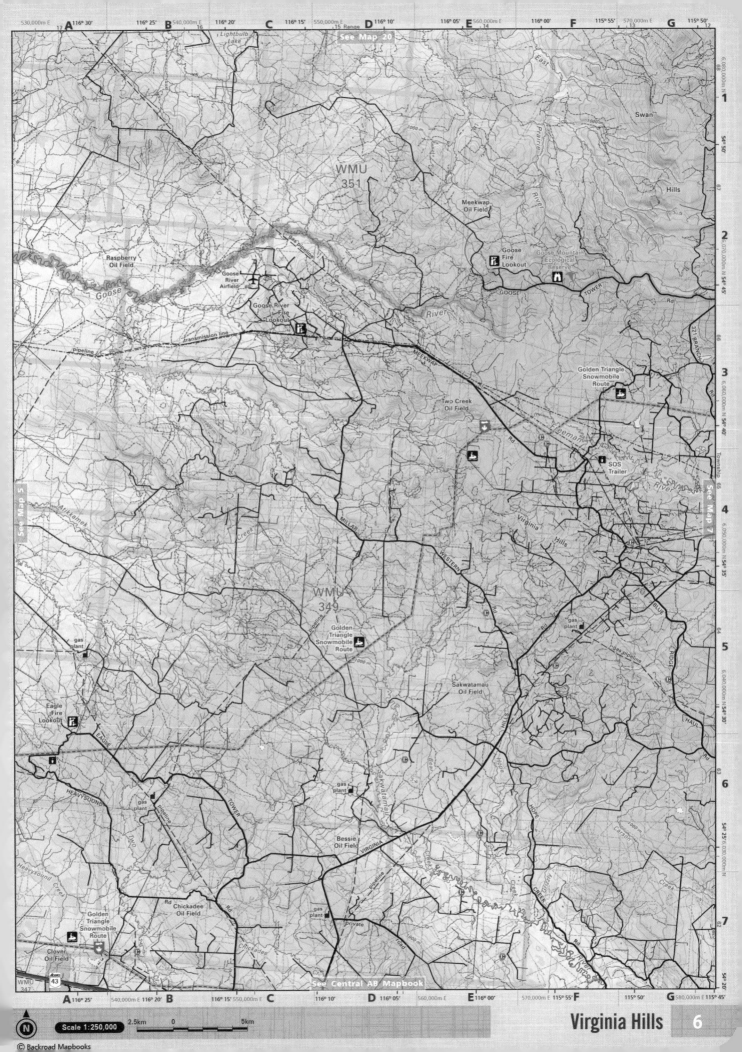

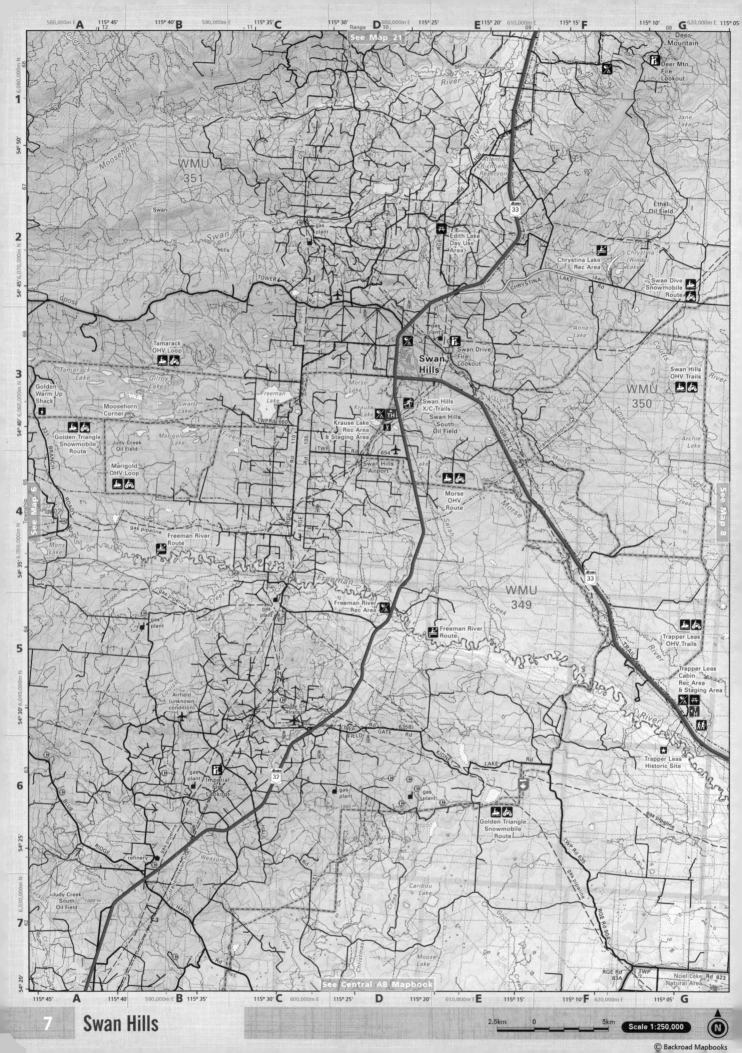

WMU 351

WMU 350

WMU 349

Swan Hills

Deer Mountain

Deer Mtn Fire Lookout

Ethel Oil Field

Chrystina Lake Rec Area

Swan Dive Snowmobile Route

Swan Hills OHV Trails

Golden Warm Up Shack

Tamarack OHV Loop

Moosehorn Corner

Golden Triangle Snowmobile Route

Judy Creek Oil Field

Marigold OHV Loop

Edith Lake Day Use Area

Swan Drive Fire Lookout

Krause Lake Rec Area & Staging Area

Swan Hills X/C Trails

Swan Hills South Oil Field

Swan Hills Airport

Morse OHV Route

Freeman River Route

Freeman River Rec Area

Freeman River Route

Trapper Leas OHV Trails

Trapper Leas Cabin Rec Area & Staging Area

Trapper Leas Historic Site

Airfield (unknown condition)

Judy Cr Airstrip

Imperial Fire Lookout

Golden Triangle Snowmobile Route

refinery

Judy Creek South Oil Field

Noel Lake Natural Area

See Map 6

See Map 8

7 Swan Hills

2.5km 0 5km

Scale 1:250,000

© Backroad Mapbooks

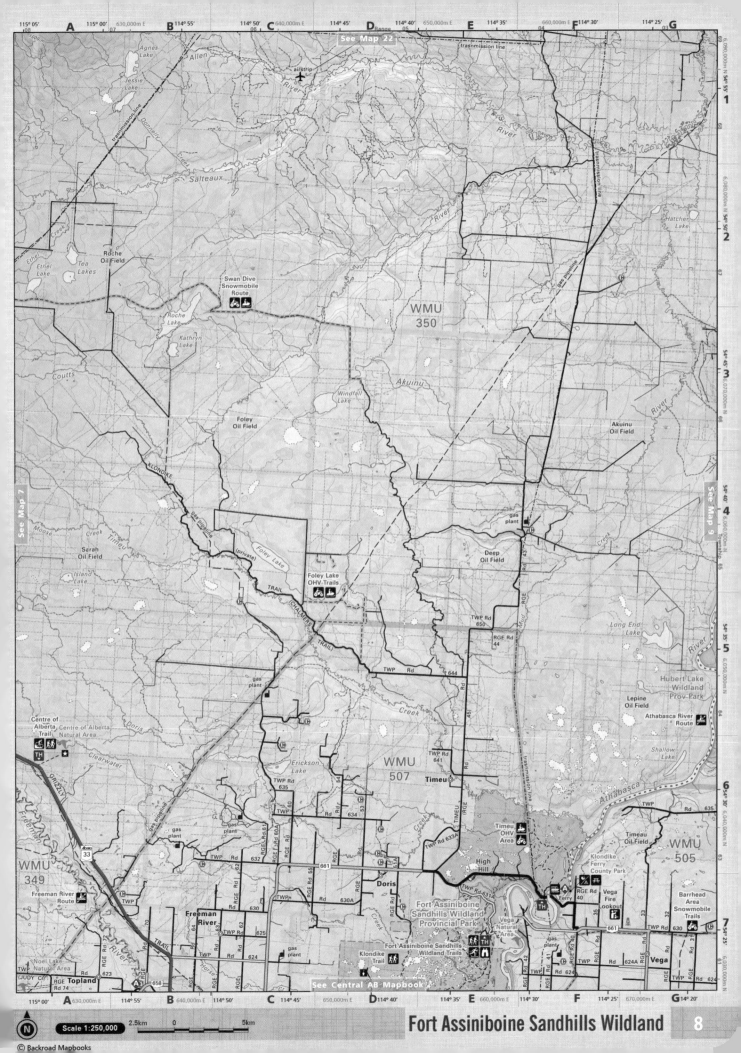

Fort Assiniboine Sandhills Wildland

8

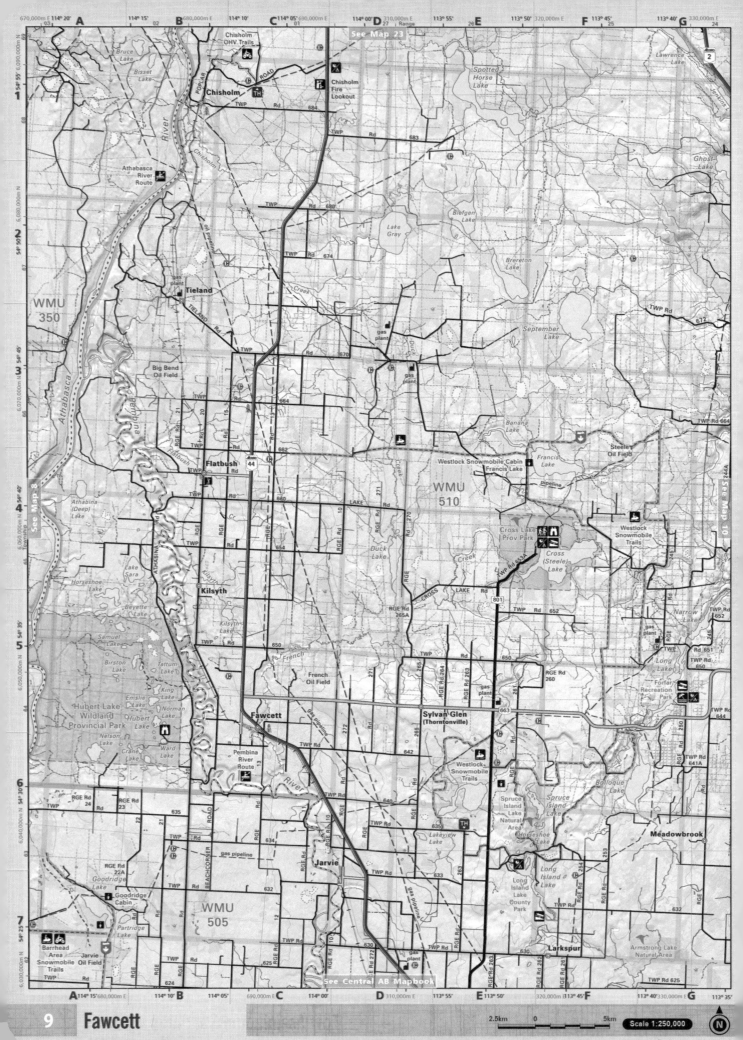

See Central AB Mapbook

Scale 1:250,000

© Backroad Mapbooks

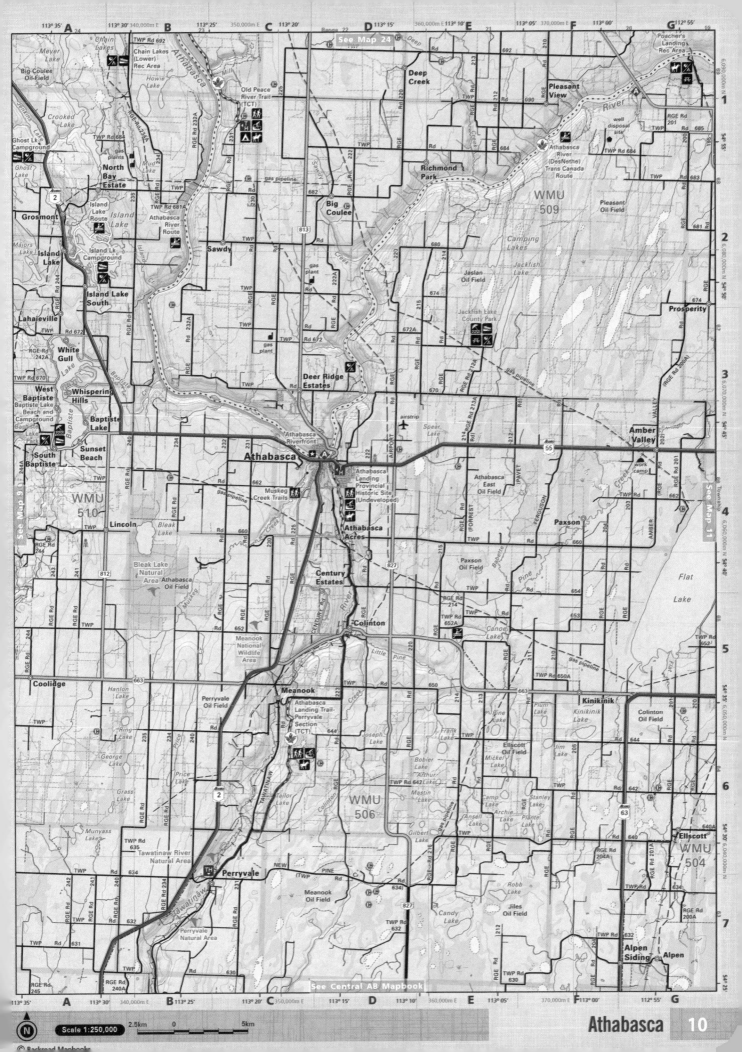

Scale 1:250,000   2.5km   0   5km

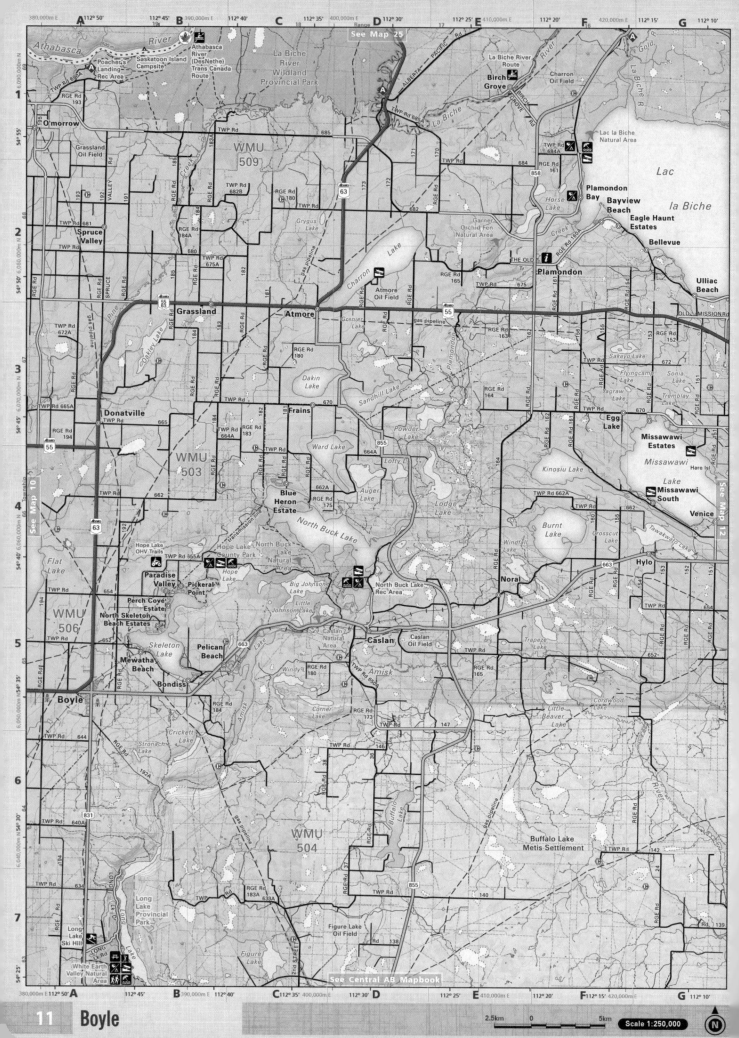

Scale 1:250,000

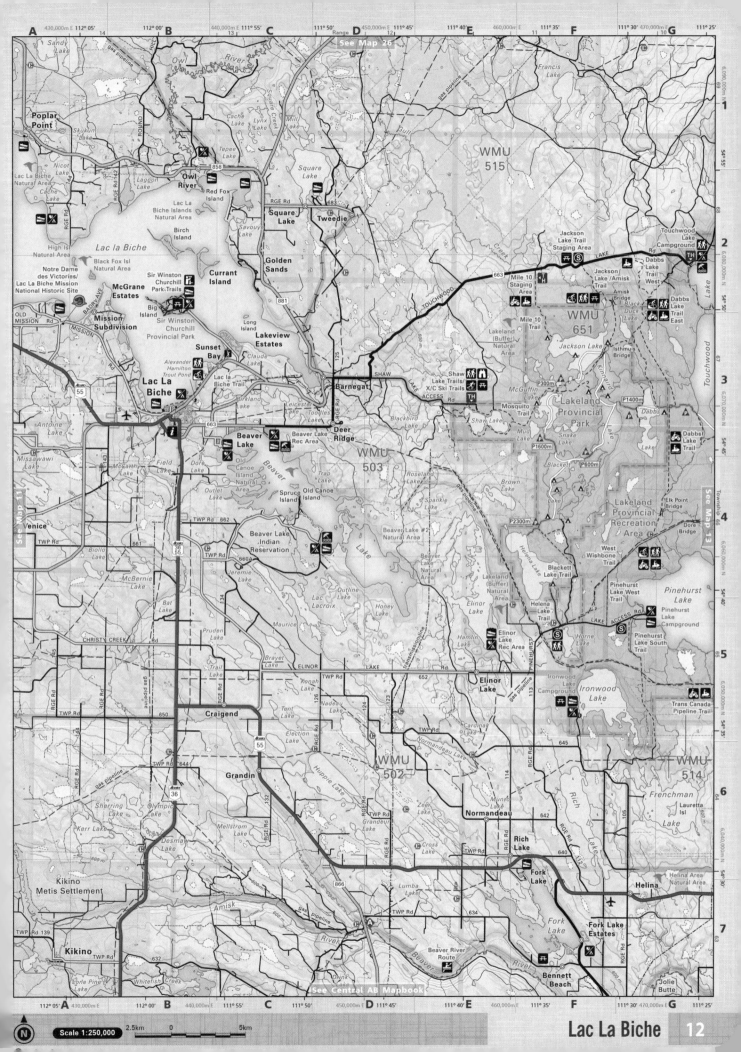

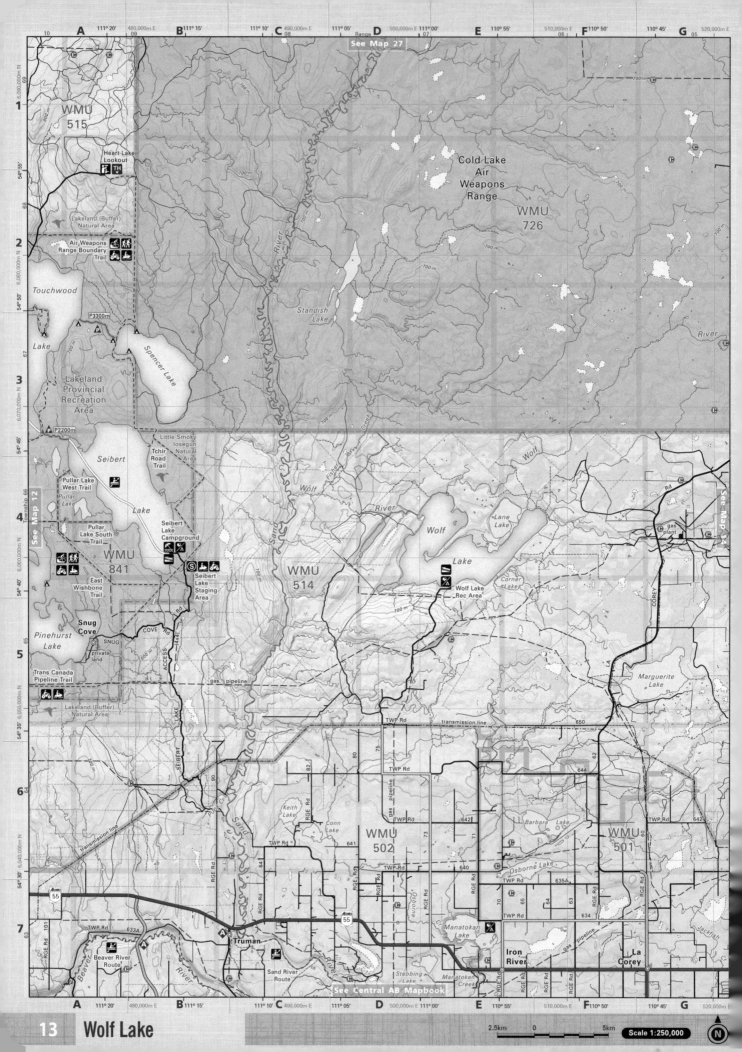

WMU 515

Heart Lake Lookout

Lakeland (Buffer) Natural Area

Air Weapons Range Boundary Trail

Cold Lake Air Weapons Range

WMU 726

Touchwood Lake

Standish Lake

River

Spencer Lake

Lakeland Provincial Recreation Area

Little Smoky Iosegun Natural Area

Tchir Road Trail

Seibert

Pullar Lake West Trail

Pullar Lake

Pullar Lake South Trail

Seibert Lake Campground

Seibert Lake

WMU 841

East Wishbone Trail

Seibert Lake Staging Area

Wolf

River

Wolf

Wolf Lake

Lane Lake

WMU 514

gas plant

Corner Lake

COREY

Wolf Lake Rec Area

Snug Cove

ACCESS Rd

COVE Rd

4x4

SNUG

private land

Pinehurst Lake

Marguerite Lake

Trans Canada Pipeline Trail

Lakeland (Buffer) Natural Area

gas pipeline

SEIBERT LAKE Rd

TWP Rd

transmission line

650

644

642

Keith Lake

Conn Lake

gas pipeline

Barbara Lake

WMU 502

TWP Rd

Osborne Lake

WMU 501

641

640

635A

634

transmission line

55

TWP Rd

633A

Truman

55

Beaver River Route

Sand River Route

Manatokan Lake

Iron River

La Corey

Stebbing Lake

Manatokan Creek

See Central AB Mapbook

See Map 12

See Map 14

13   Wolf Lake

2.5km   0   5km   Scale 1:250,000

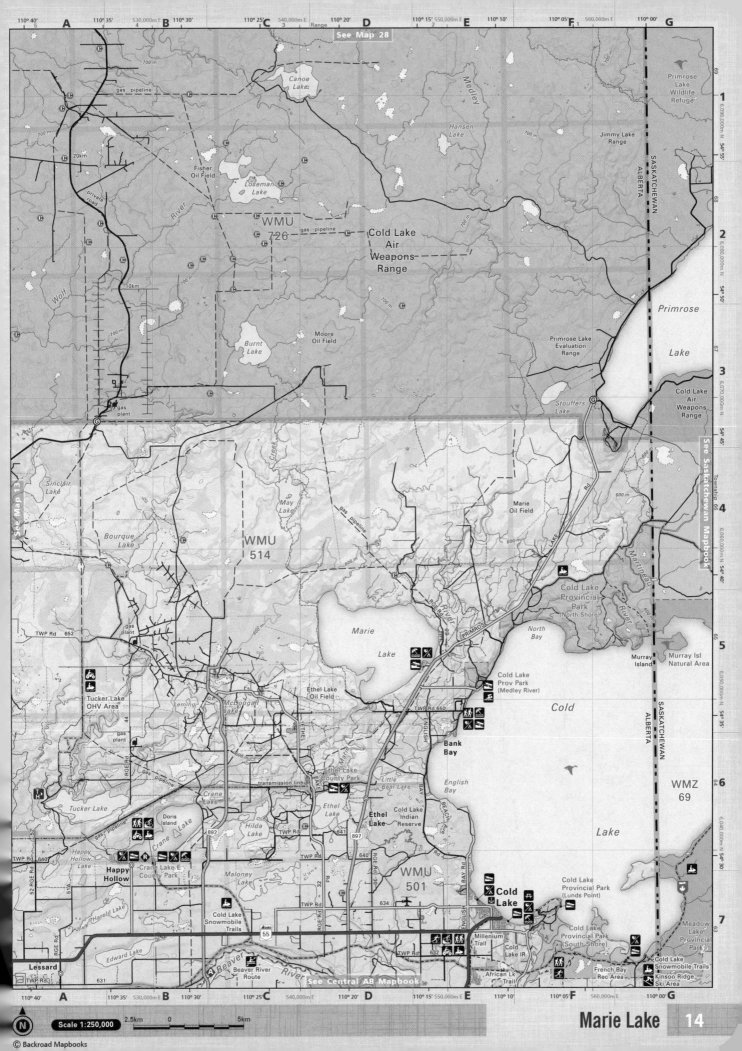

Primrose
Lake
Wildlife
Refuge

Canoe
Lake

Medley

Hansen
Lake

Jimmy Lake
Range

700 m

gas pipeline

Fisher
Oil Field

Loseman
Lake

**WMU
726**

gas pipeline

Cold Lake
Air
Weapons
Range

Wolf

Primrose

Lake

Burnt
Lake

Moore
Oil Field

Primrose Lake
Evaluation
Range

Cold Lake
Air
Weapons
Range

gas plant

Stouffers
Lake

See Saskatchewan Mapbook

Creek

Marie
Oil Field

600 m

See Map 13

Sinclair
Lake

May
Lake

gas pipeline

**WMU
514**

Bourque
Lake

600 m

Cold Lake
Provincial
Park
(North Shore)

Murray Isl
Natural Area

Murray
Island

TWP Rd 652

gas
plant

Marie

Lake

North
Bay

Cold Lake
Prov Park
(Medley River)

Cold

Tucker Lake
OHV Area

Leming

McDougall
Lake

Ethel Lake
Oil Field

gas
plant

TWP Rd 650

Bank
Bay

gas pipeline

Lake

Tucker Lake

Crane
Lake

transmission line

Ethel Lake
County Park

Little
Bear Lake

English
Bay

Doris Island

Crane Lake

Hilda
Lake

Ethel
Lake

Ethel
Lake

Cold Lake
Indian Reserve

**WMZ
69**

Happy
Hollow
Lake

892

Ethel

Maloney
Lake

897

641

TWP Rd

640

**WMU
501**

Cold Lake
Provincial Park
(Lunds Point)

TWP Rd 640

52 RGE Rd

51A

Happy
Hollow

Crane Lake E
County Park

634

**Cold
Lake**

Cold Lake
Snowmobile Trails

55

632

TWP Rd

Cold Lake
Provincial Park
(South Shore)

Harold Lake

Edward Lake

631

Beaver River
Route

Millenium
Trail

Cold
Lake IR

French Bay
Rec Area

Meadow
Lake
Provincial
Park

Lessard

TWP Rd

Beaver

River

See Central AB Mapbook

African Lk
Trail

Cold Lake
Snowmobile Trails

Kinsoo Ridge
Ski Area

Scale 1:250,000

2.5km　　0　　5km

© Backroad Mapbooks

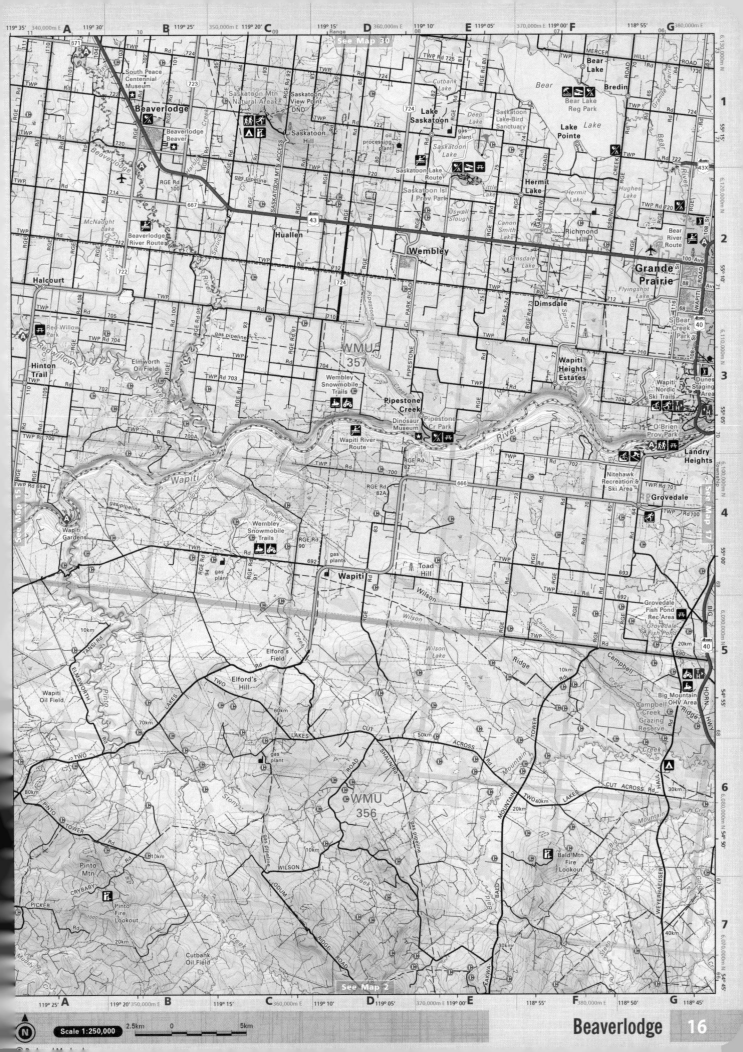

Scale 1:250,000

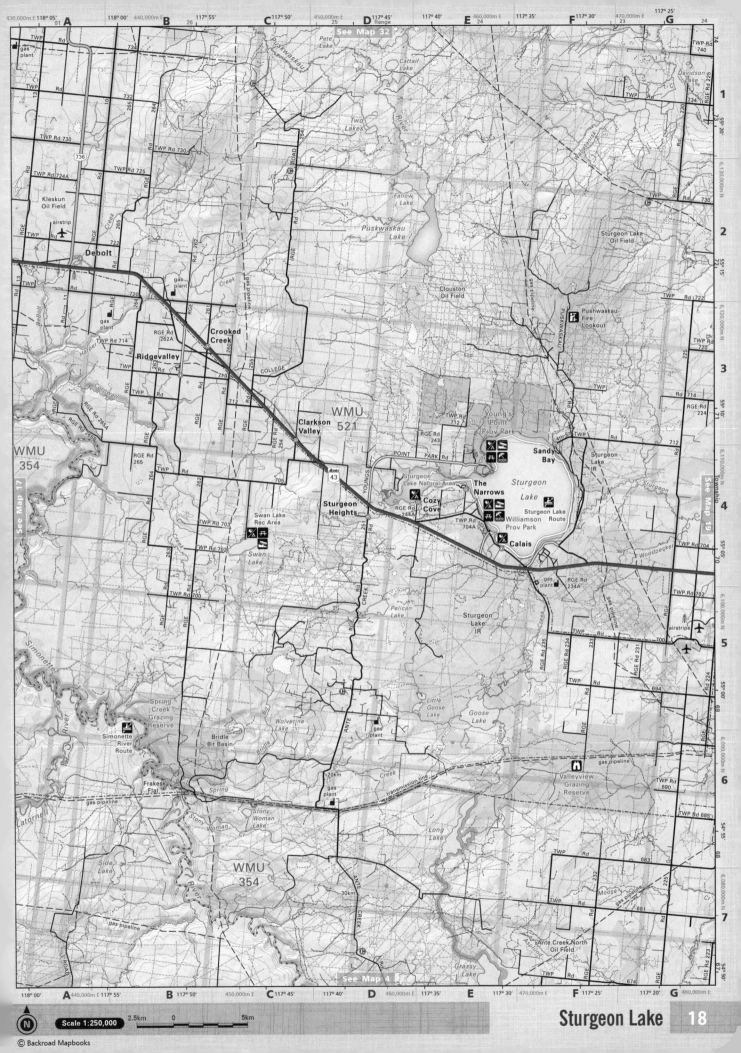

Scale 1:250,000

© Backroad Mapbooks

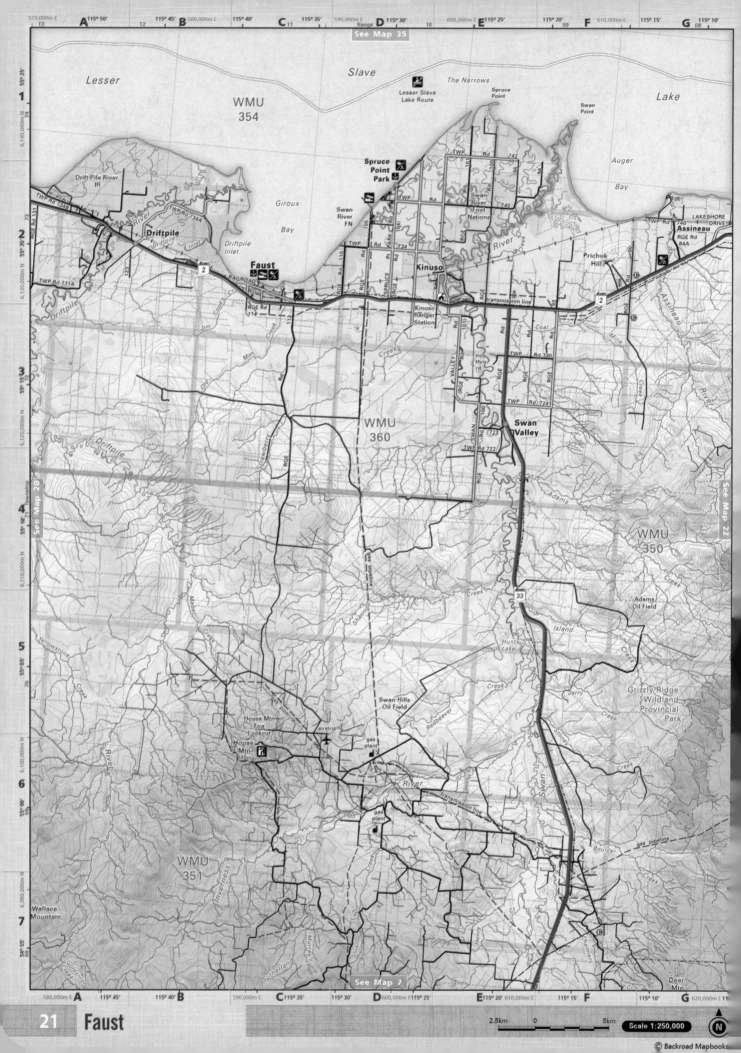

Scale 1:250,000

© Backroad Mapbooks

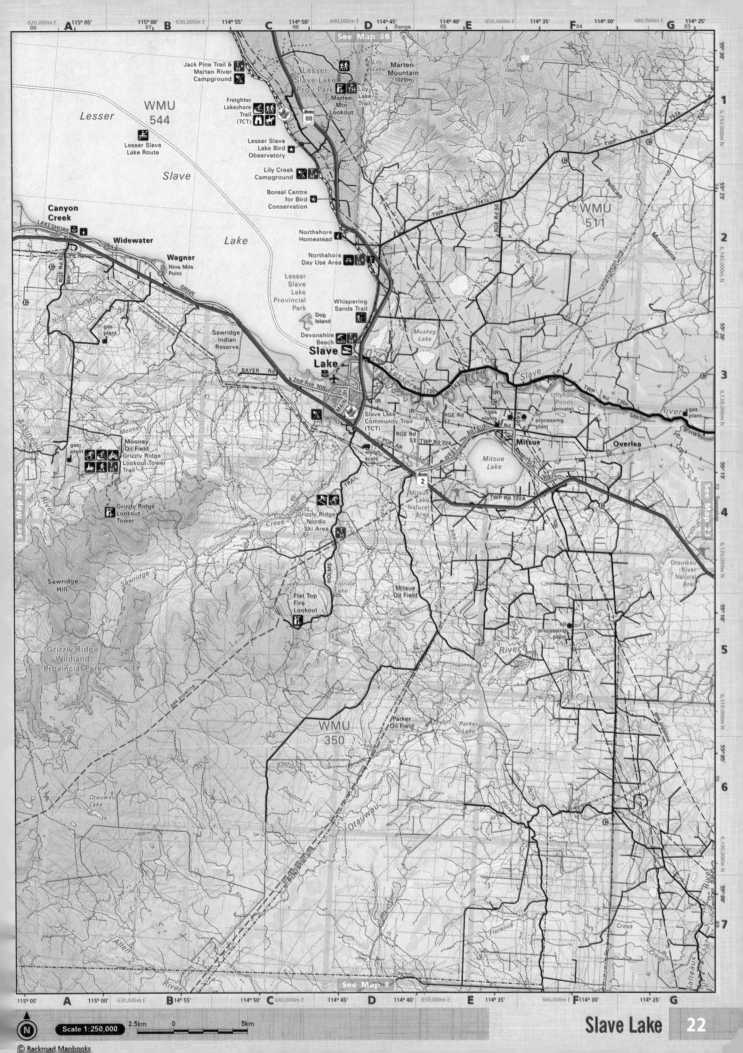

Scale 1:250,000

2.5km   0   5km

© Backroad Mapbooks

Scale 1:250,000

© Backroad Mapbooks

Marten Hills
Oil Field

TWP Rd 751A

gas plant

airstrip

ROCK ISL
Lk Rd

Tanasiuk
Rec Area

Rock
Island
Lake

813

Otter-Orloff
Lakes Wildland
Provincial Park

Orloff
Lake

Otter
Lake

WMU
511

TWP Rd 734

Rock Isl Lake
Fire
Lookout

pipeline

Francis
Oil Field

airstrip

Cherpeta
Oil Field

WMU
516

Amadou
Lake

Nipin
Oil Field

Amadou
Oil Field

Calling
Lake

IR

TWP Rd 724A

TWP Rd 724A

724A

Calling Lake West
Oil Field

gas pipeline

Calling
Lake

work
camp

Calling
Lake

MOOSE
St

Old Peace
River Trail
(TCT)

Quinn Creek
Campsite
37km

Tomato
Oil Field

Calling Lake
Provincial Park

Calling

River

Athabasca

Tomato Creek
Campsite
27km

Athabasca
River
Route

Canal
Oil Field

Calling Lake South
Oil Field

gas plant

RGE Rd 199A

Calling
River

Tomato

Creek

gas pipeline

Bouvier
Oil Field

WMU
510

gas
plant

813

gas
plant

Gambler
Oil Field

WMU
509

Old Peace
River Trail
(TCT)

TWP Rd
700

RGE Rd
235

RGE Rd 235A

River

Deep

Creek

RGE Rd
210

Meyer
Lake

Chain
Lakes

Chain Lakes
(Lower)
Rec Area

TWP Rd
692

RGE Rd
214

RGE Rd
212

RGE
Rd

RGE Rd
205

RGE Rd
203A

See Map 23
See Map 25

N

Scale 1:250,000   2.5km   0   5km

© Backroad Mapbooks

Calling Lake   24

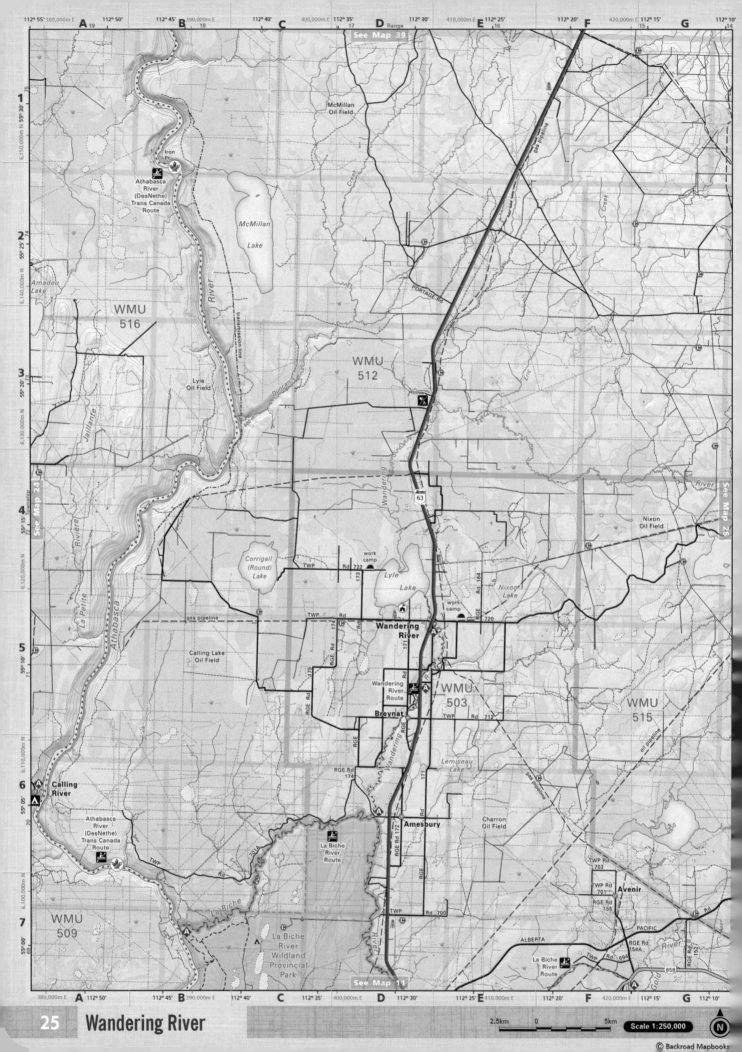

WMU
516

WMU
512

WMU
503

WMU
515

WMU
509

Scale 1:250,000

© Backroad Mapbooks

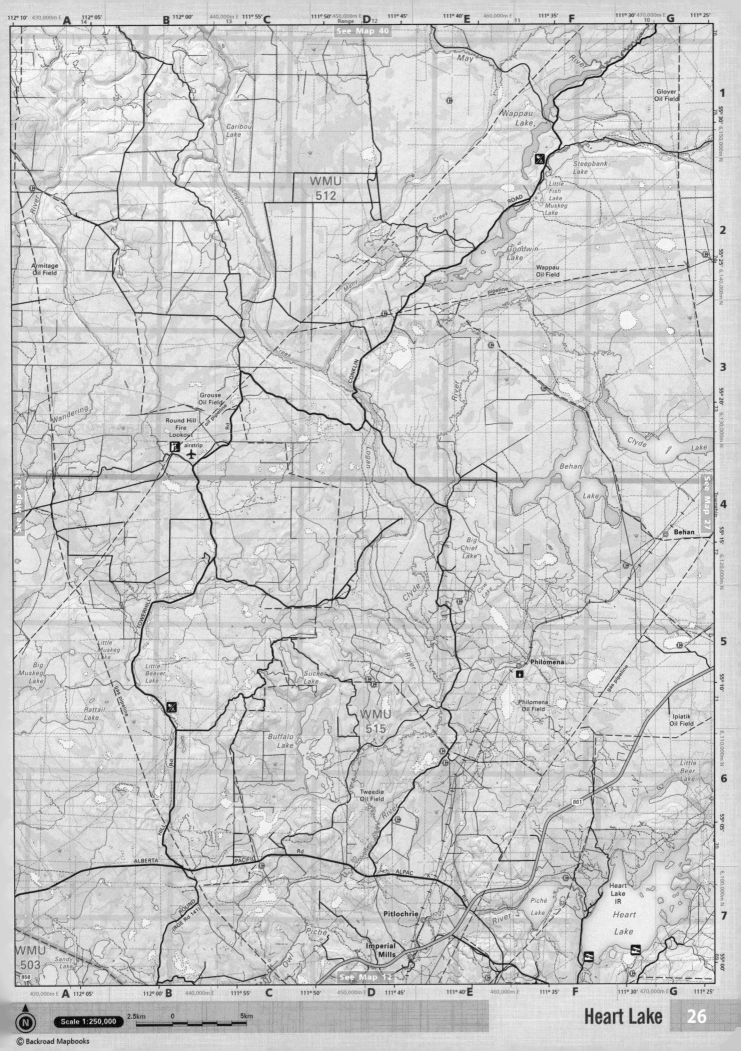

WMU 512

WMU 515

WMU 503

See Map 25

See Map 27

See Map 12

May River

Wappau Lake

Steepbank Lake

Little Fish Lake

Muskeg Lake

Glover Oil Field

Goodwin Lake

Wappau Oil Field

Caribou Lake

Armitage Oil Field

Grouse Oil Field

Round Hill Fire Lookout

airstrip

Wandering

Behan Lake

Clyde Lake

Behan

Big Chief Lake

Cow Lake

Philomena

Philomena Oil Field

Ipiatik Oil Field

Little Muskeg Lake

Little Beaver Lake

Sucker Lake

Buffalo Lake

Big Muskeg Lake

Rattail Lake

Tweedie Oil Field

Little Bear Lake

Pitlochrie

Piché Lake

Heart Lake IR

Heart Lake

Imperial Mills

Sandy Lake

881

858

ALBERTA PACIFIC

ROUND IRGE Rd 141

ALPAC

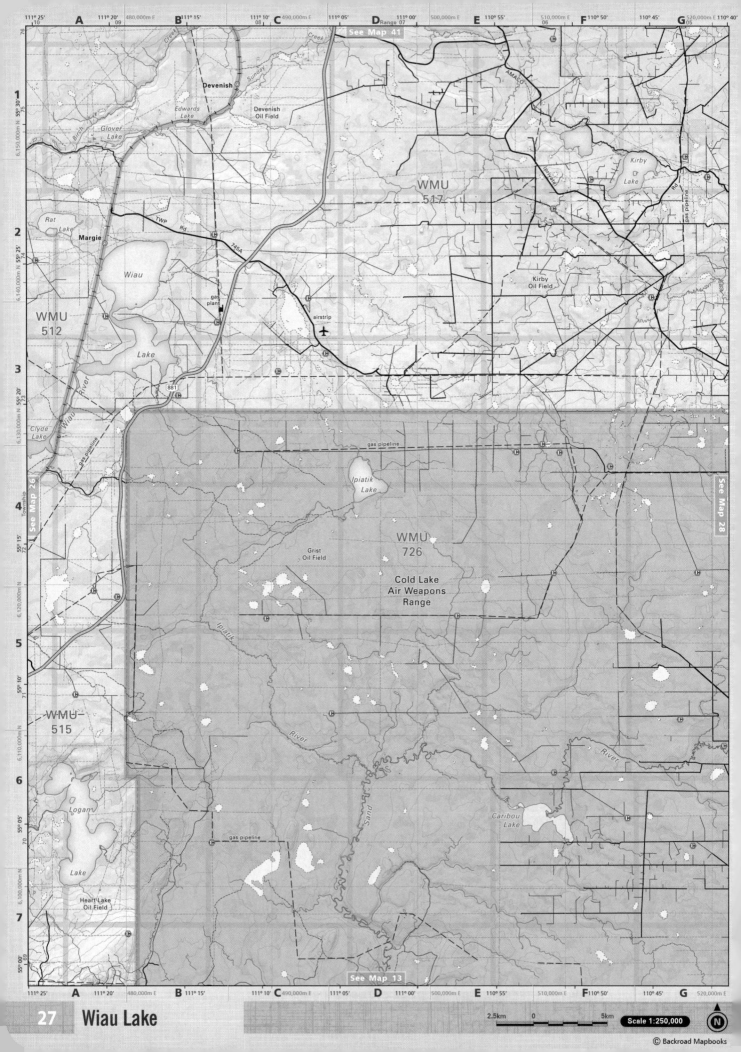

Scale 1:250,000

© Backroad Mapbooks

See Map 42

See Map 27

See Saskatchewan Mapbook

See Map 14

Winefred
Lake

Winefred
Lake Route

Winefred
Fire
Lookout

WMU
517

WMU
726

WMZ
73

Saskatchewan

Cold Lake
Air Weapons
Range

Cold Lake
Air Weapons
Range

Grist
Lake

Royemma
Lake

Taskam
Creek

Nisbet
Lake

Underwood
Lake

Tamarack
Lake

Scheltens
Lake

Primrose Lake
Wildlife Refuge

Fisher
Oil Field

AMACO
(private)
Rd

Fairstrip

Fairstrip

Sandy

River

Grist Creek

Dillon

River

Candel

Neath

Creek

Foster

Creek

Victor

Creek

River

Sand

River

40km

30km

ALBERTA

SASKATCHEWAN

ALBERTA

SASKATCHEWAN

Range

Township

Scale 1:250,000   2.5km   0   5km

N

Winefred Lake   28

© Backroad Mapbooks

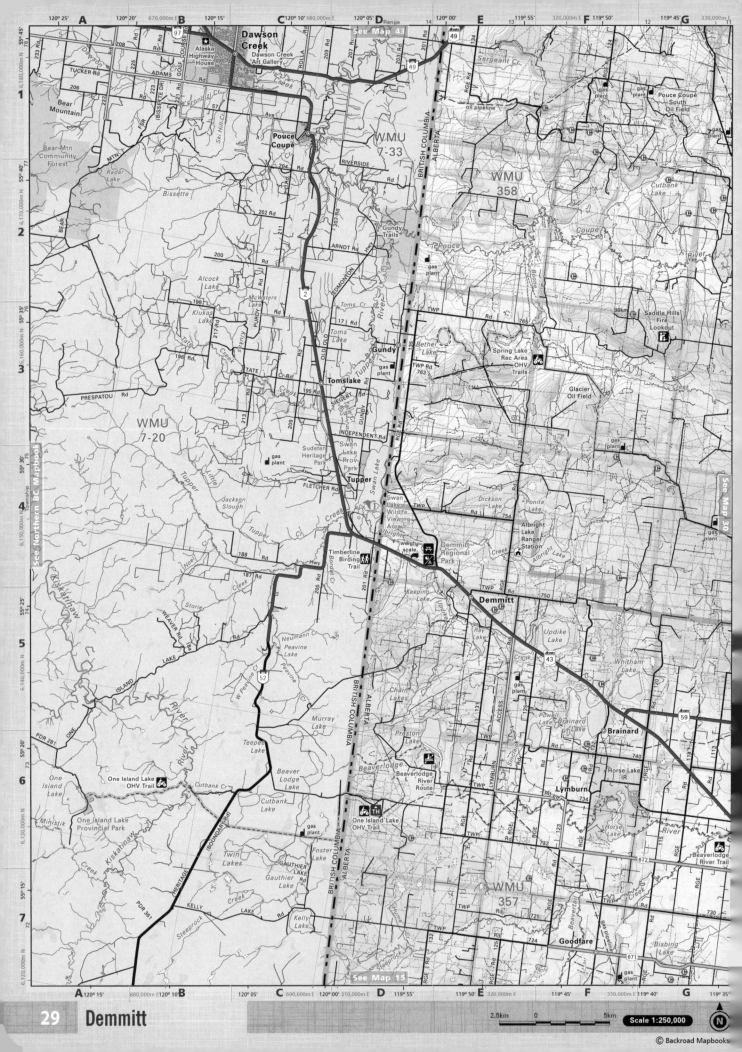

Scale 1:250,000

© Backroad Mapbooks

© Backroad Mapbooks

Scale 1:250,000

2.5km   0   5km

WMU 522

WMU 523

WMU 521

See Map 31

See Map 33

See Map 18

Peace River Wildland Prov. Park

Peace Valley Grazing Reserve

North Eaglesham Grazing Reserve

Eaglesham

Tangent

Codesa

Eaglesham Oil Field

Cindy Oil Field

Codesa Ranger Station (closed)

Four Mile Cr. Grazing Reserve

Smoky River Route

Watino

Culp

Girouxville Oil Field

Little Smoky River Route

North Goodwin Grazing Reserve

Whitemud Creek

Muddyshore Lake

Mountain Lake

Water Hen Lake

Smoky River Route

Smoky River Route

Wanham Grazing Reserve

Smoky River Wildland Prov. Park

Peace River Route

Camp Island

Long Island

Scale 1:250,000

2.5km   0   5km

© Backroad Mapbooks

Eaglesham 32

Scale 1:250,000

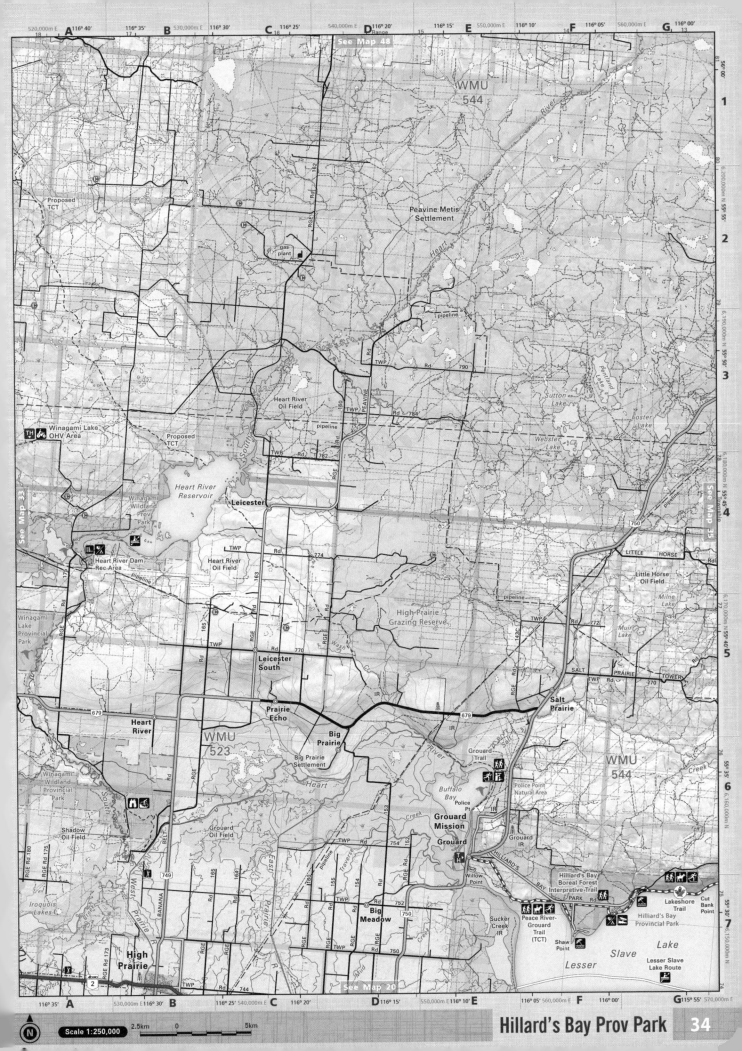

WMU
544

Peavine Metis
Settlement

gas plant

Heart River
Oil Field

pipeline

Heart
River

Sutton
Lake

Webster
Lake

Foster
Lake

Pantland
Lake

Winagami Lake
OHV Area

Proposed
TCT

Heart River
Reservoir

Winagami
Wildland
Prov
Park

Leicester

Heart River Dam
Rec Area

pipeline

High Prairie
Grazing Reserve

LITTLE
HORSE

Little Horse
Oil Field

Milne
Lake

Muir
Lake

Winagami
Lake
Provincial
Park

Heart River
Oil Field

Leicester
South

Prairie
Echo

Big
Prairie

WMU
523

Heart
River

Winagami
Wildland
Provincial
Park

Shadow
Oil Field

Big Prairie
Settlement

Grouard
Oil Field

Salt
Prairie

PRAIRIE

TOWER

WMU
544

Grouard
Trail

Buffalo
Bay

Police Point
Natural Area

Police
Pt

Grouard
Mission

Grouard

Grouard
IR

Creek

Willow
Point

Hilliard's Bay
Boreal Forest
Interpretive Trail

Lakeshore
Trail

Cut
Bank
Point

Iroquois
Lakes

Big
Meadow

Sucker
Creek
IR

Peace River-
Grouard
Trail
(TCT)

Shaw
Point

Hilliard's Bay
Provincial Park

High
Prairie

2

Lesser

Slave

Lake

Lesser Slave
Lake Route

RGE Rd 180 RGE Rd 175 RGE Rd 173

Scale 1:250,000   2.5km   0   5km

Hilliard's Bay Prov Park   34

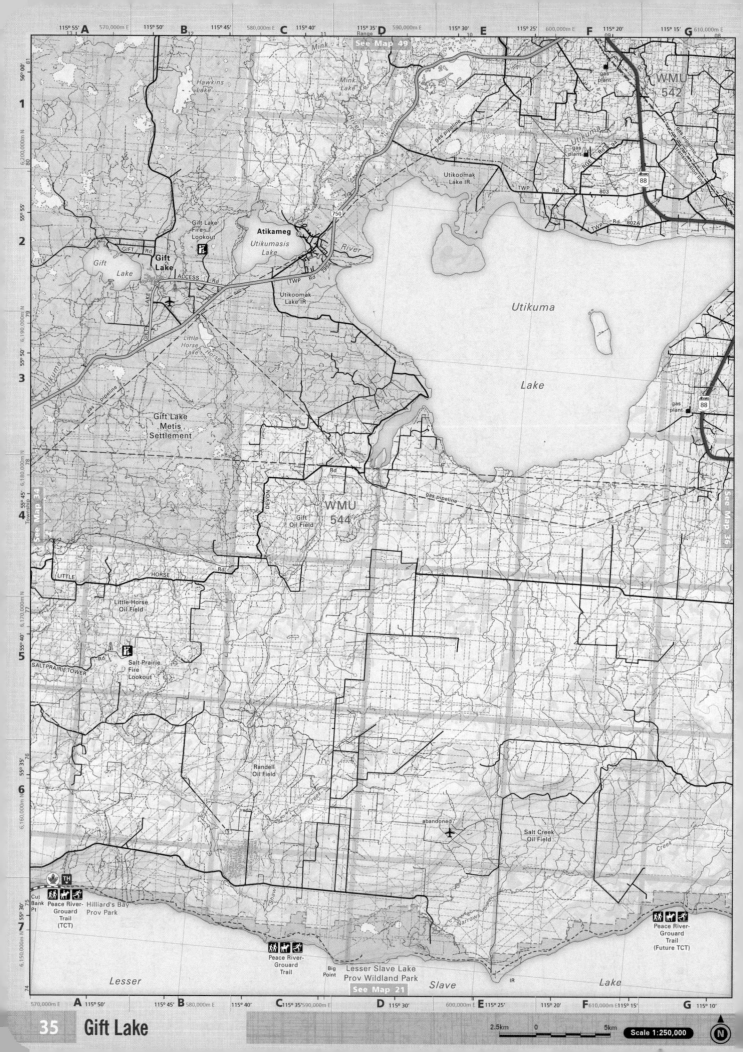

Gift Lake

Scale 1:250,000

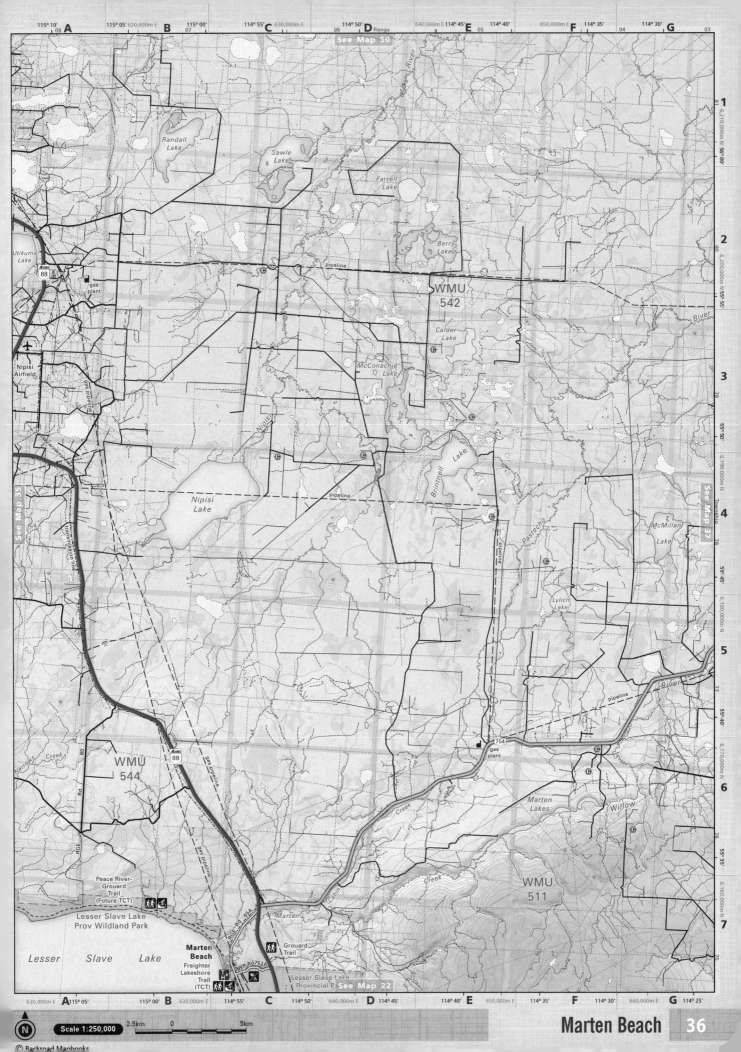

Utikuma
Lake

gas
plant

Nipisi
Airfield

Randall
Lake

Sawle
Lake

Farrell
Lake

Berry
Lake

WMU
542

Calder
Lake

McConachie
Lake

Brintnell
Lake

Pastecho

McMillan
Lake

Nipisi
Lake

pipeline

Pipeline

Lylich
Lake

754
gas
plant

River

pipeline

Marten
Lakes

Willow

WMU
544

WMU
511

Narrows
Creek

Peace River-
Grouard Trail
(Future TCT)

Lesser Slave Lake
Prov Wildland Park

Marten
Beach

Freighter
Lakeshore
Trail
(TCT)

Grouard
Trail

Lesser Slave Lake
Provincial P.

Lesser   Slave   Lake

Cabin

Creek

Creek

Marten

gas pipeline

transmission line

gas pipeline

Nipisi

RGE Rd 69A

TWP Rd 752A

Scale 1:250,000

2.5km   0   5km

© Backroad Mapbooks

See Map 51

North

Wabasca

Lake

Godin
Lake

River

Wabasca River
Route

North
Wabasca
Rec Area

WMU
518

Pastecho

McLeod Lake

Weaver Lake

Wabasca-
Desmarais

work
camps

gas
plant
work
camp

Hoole
Oil Field

WMU
542

Sander Lake

Desmarais
Oil Field

Bigstone
Cree
Nation

754

airstrip

IR

WMU
516

Pastecho
Lake

Mistehae
Lake

pipeline

pipeline

YELLOWKNEE Rd

CATTLEMAN
Dr

CEE TOO Dr

Wabasca
Indian
Reserve

South

Wabasca

Lake

McMullen
Lake

River

Doucette Fire
Lookout

DOUCETTE

754

WMU
511

Mistehae
Oil Field

pipeline

pipeline

Sandy Lake
Fire
Lookout

LOOKOUT Rd

DOUCETTE

Rd

pipeline

Horse

Willow

pipeline

Creek

Pelican
Oil Field

Doucette
Oil Field

powerline

gas
plant

Mountain

Pelican

SHAUNB

TWP Rd 754A

See Map 23

See Map 36

See Map 38

37 Wabasca Lakes

2.5km 0 5km Scale 1:250,000

N

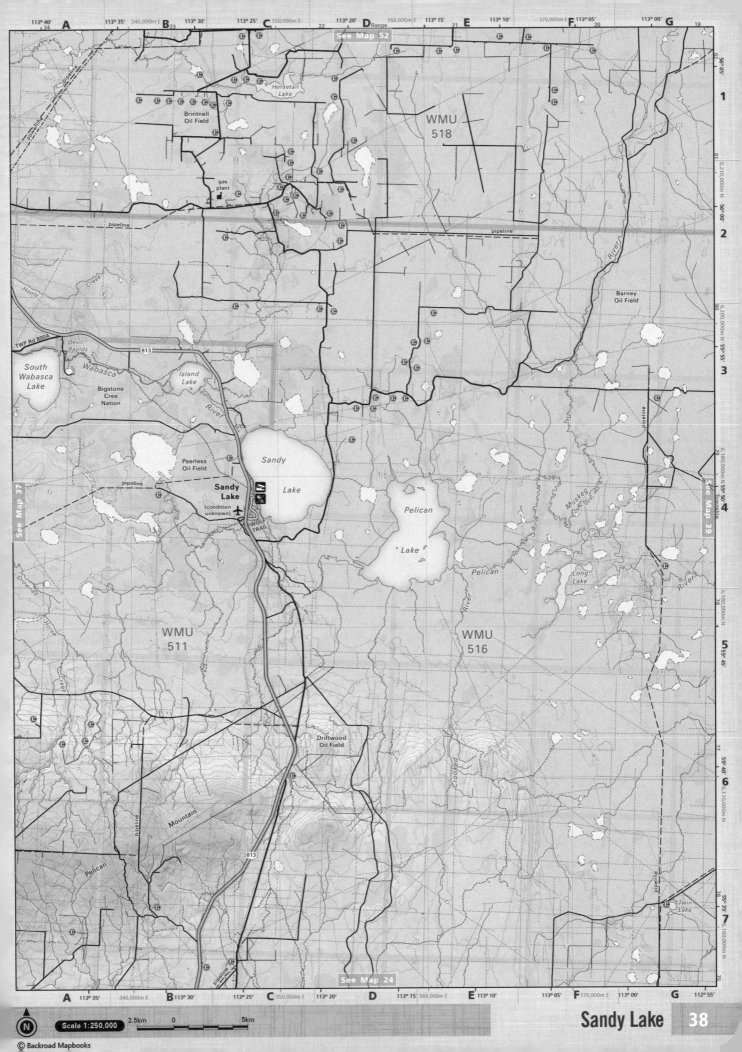

WMU
518

Brintnell
Oil Field

Horsetail
Lake

gas
plant

pipeline

pipeline

pipeline

Barney
Oil Field

113° 40'
113° 35' 340,000m E 113° 30' 113° 25' 350,000m E 113° 20' 360,000m E 113° 15' 113° 10' 370,000m E 113° 05' 113° 00'

Creek

Hoole

TWP Rd 800A

Devil
Rapids

813

Wabasca

South
Wabasca
Lake

Bigstone
Cree
Nation

Island
Lake

River

Peerless
Oil Field

pipeline

Sandy
Lake

Sandy
Lake
(condition
unknown)

WOLF
TRAIL

Pelican
Lake

Pelican

Muskeg

Long
Lake

River

River

Pelican

WMU
511

WMU
516

Driftwood
Oil Field

Crooked

Mountain

Horse

Creek

Drowned

pipeline

813

pipeline

pipeline

Twin
Lake

A 113° 35' 340,000m E B 113° 30' 113° 25' C 350,000m E 113° 20' D 113° 15' 360,000m E E 113° 10' 113° 05' F 370,000m E 113° 00' G 112° 55'

N

Scale 1:250,000   2.5km   0   5km

Sandy Lake **38**

© Backroad Mapbooks

Map labels:

Top border (left to right):
380,000m E · 112° 55' · A · 19 · 112° 50' · B · 18 · 112° 45' · C · 112° 40' · 400,000m E · 17 · D · 112° 35' Range · See Map 53 · 112° 30' · E · 410,000m E · 112° 25' · 16 · F · 112° 20' 420,000m E · 15 · 112° 15' · G · 14

WMU 518

WMU 519

House Oil Field

Rapides du Joli Fou

Athabasca River (DesNethe) Trans Canada Route

Loon Creek

Boivin

House

Dreoart Creek

See Map 38

Stony Rapids

Pelican Rapids

River

airstrip (abandoned)

Agnes Lake

Crow Lake Provincial Park

Crow Lake Eco Res

Crow Lake

Pelican Portage

Portage Oil Field

WMU 512

WMU 516

Upper Wells Cabin

See Map 40

River

RGE Rd 151A

gas plant

775A

63

TWP Rd

Athabasca River (DesNethe) Trans Canada Route

Manny Oil Field

Parallel

Pipeline

Athabasca

Pipeline

63

May Hill

May Hill Fire Lookout

See Map 25

Left border (top to bottom):
56° 05' · 82 · 81 · 56° 00' · 6,210,000m N · 2 · 55° 55' · 80 · 3 · 6,190,000m N · 79 · 55° 50' · Township 38 · 4 · 6,180,000m N · 78 · 55° 45' · 5 · 77 · 55° 40' · 6,170,000m N · 6 · 76 · 55° 35' · 7 · 6,160,000m N · 75

Bottom border (left to right):
380,000m E · 112° 50' · A · B · 390,000m E · 112° 45' · 112° 40' · C · 400,000m E · 112° 35' · D · 112° 30' · 410,000m E · 112° 25' · E · F · 112° 20' · 420,000m E · 112° 15' · G · 112° 10'

2.5km 0 5km   Scale 1:250,000   N

© Backroad Mapbooks

Scale 1:250,000 2.5km 0 5km

Ⓝ © Backroad Mapbooks

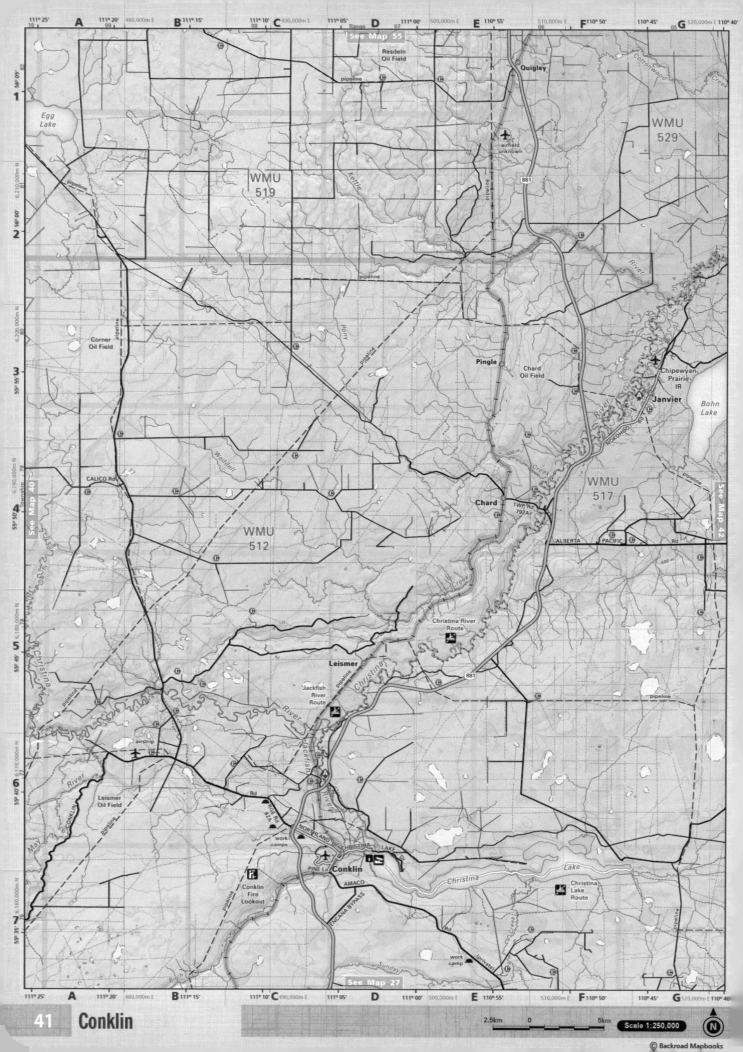

Egg
Lake

Resdeln
Oil Field

pipeline

Quigley

airfield
unknown

WMU
529

WMU
519

881

Cottonwood

River

Corner
Oil Field

pipeline

pipeline

pony

pipeline

Pingle

Chard
Oil Field

Chipewyan
Prairie
IR

Janvier

Bohn
Lake

Waddell

CALICO Rd

Creek

Chard

TWP Rd
792A

NOKOHOO Rd

WMU
517

See Map 40

WMU
512

ALBERTA

PACIFIC

Rd

Christina

Christina River
Route

See Map 42

Creek

pipeline

Leismer

881

pipeline

Christina

Jackfish
River Route

River

pipeline

airstrip

Leismer
Oil Field

River

May

CONKLIN

pipeline

Rd

RG Rd 82A

work
camps

NORTHLAND Dr

CHRISTINA LAKE Dr

Conklin

Lake

Christina

Christina
Lake
Route

PINE Ln

Conklin Fire
Lookout

AMACO

ENCANA BYPASS

Rd

Sunday

Birch

work
camp

(private)

2.5km   0   5km   Scale 1:250,000   N

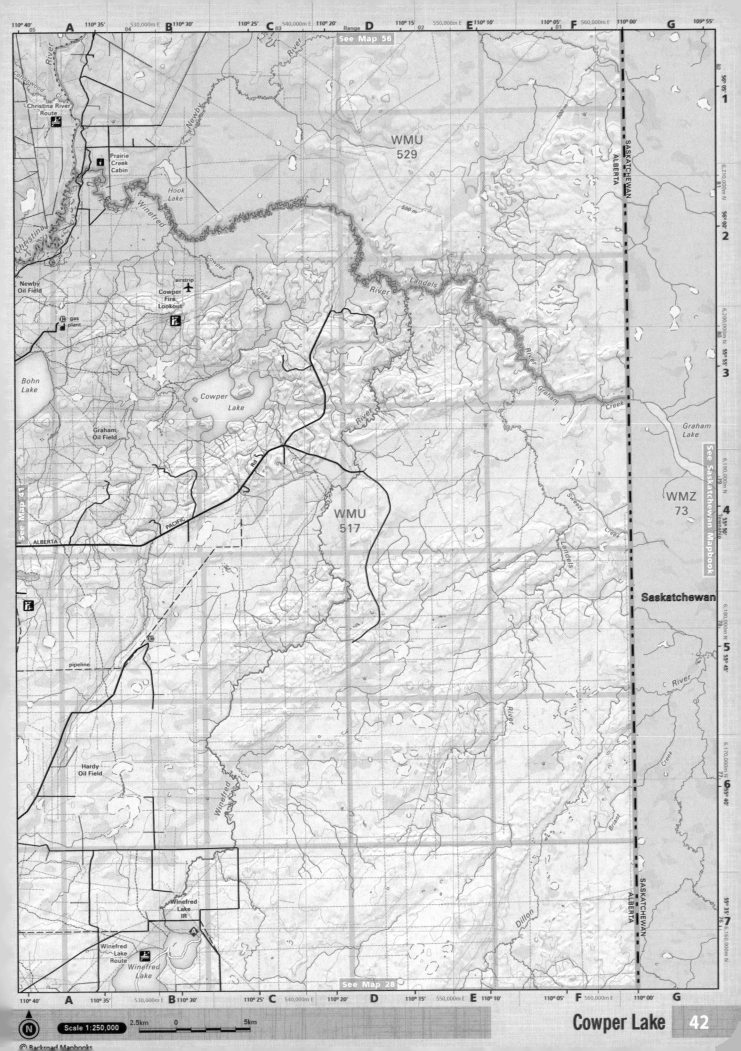

WMU
529

500 m

See Map 41

ALBERTA

WMU
517

See Saskatchewan Mapbook

WMZ
73

Saskatchewan

SASKATCHEWAN
ALBERTA

Christina River
Route

Prairie
Creek
Cabin

Hook
Lake

Newby Oil Field

airstrip

Cowper
Fire
Lookout

gas
plant

Bohn
Lake

Cowper
Lake

Graham Oil Field

Graham
Lake

Hardy
Oil Field

pipeline

Winefred Lake
IR

Winefred
Lake
Route

Winefred
Lake

Scale 1:250,000   2.5km   0   5km

Cowper Lake 42

© Backroad Mapbooks

Scale 1:250,000

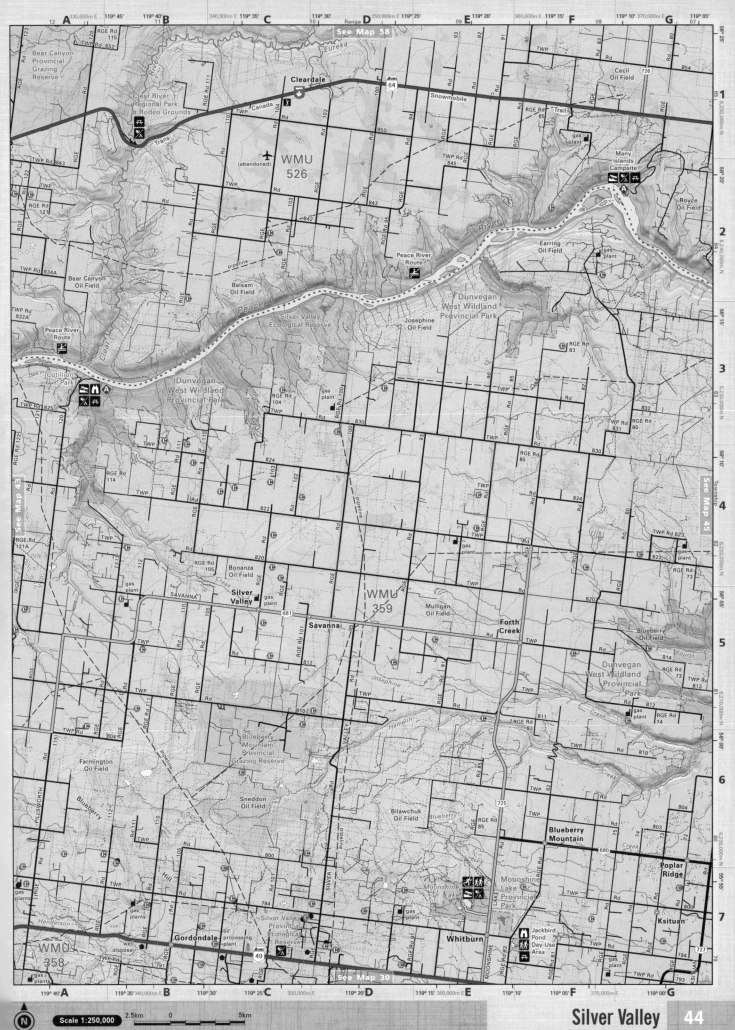

See Map 43

See Map 45

WMU
526

WMU
359

WMU
358

Bear Canyon
Provincial Grazing
Reserve

Clear River
Regional Park
& Rodeo Grounds

Cleardale

(abandoned)

Bear Canyon
Oil Field

Balsam
Oil Field

Silver Valley
Ecological Reserve

Peace River
Route

Peace River
Route

Josephine
Oil Field

Dunvegan
West Wildland
Provincial Park

Dunvegan
West Wildland
Provincial Park

Earring
Oil Field

Royce
Oil Field

Cecil
Oil Field

Many
Islands
Campsite

gas
plant

gas
plant

Cotillion
Park

Bonanza
Oil Field

gas
plant

Silver
Valley

Savanna

SAVANNA

gas
plant

gas
plant

Mulligan
Oil Field

Forth
Creek

Blueberry
Oil Field

Dunvegan
West Wildland
Provincial
Park

gas
plant

Blueberry
Mountain
Provincial
Grazing
Reserve

Farmington
Oil Field

Sneddon
Oil Field

Bilawchuk
Oil Field

Moonshine
Lake

Moonshine
Lake
Provincial
Park

Blueberry
Mountain

Poplar
Ridge

gas
plants

gas
plants

Gordondale

oil
processing
plant

well
disposal

Silver Valley
Provincial
Ecological
Reserve

gas
plant

Whitburn

Jackbird
Pond
Day-Use
Area

Ksituan

gas
plants

See Map 30

Scale 1:250,000   2.5km   0   5km

Silver Valley 44

Scale 1:250,000

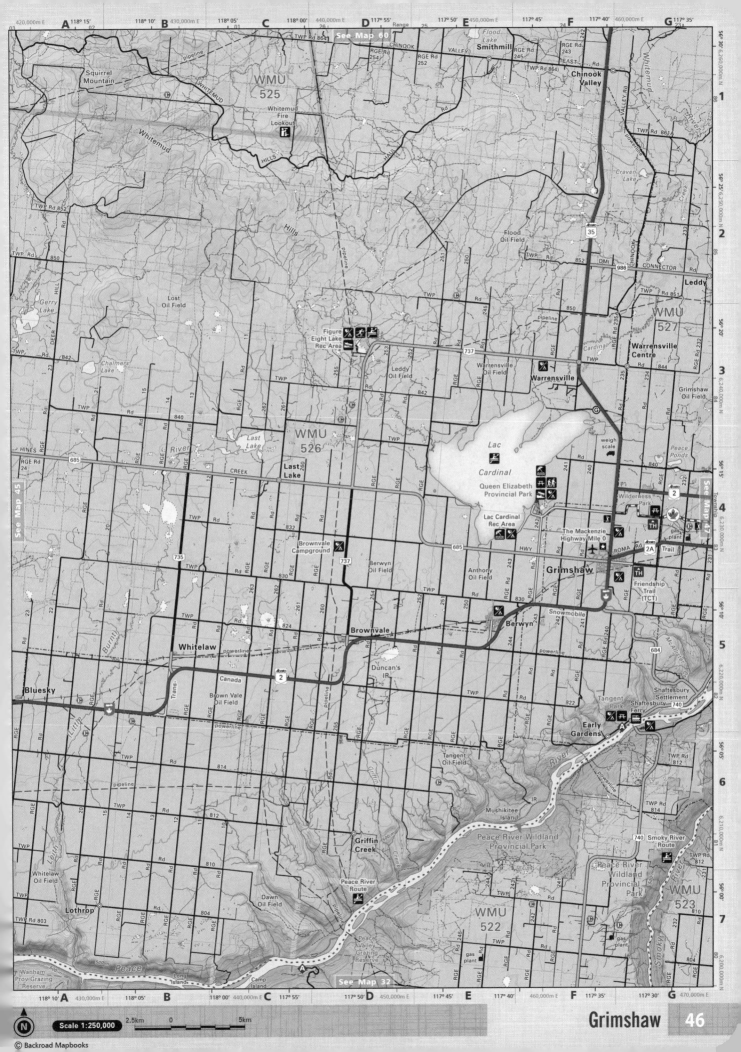

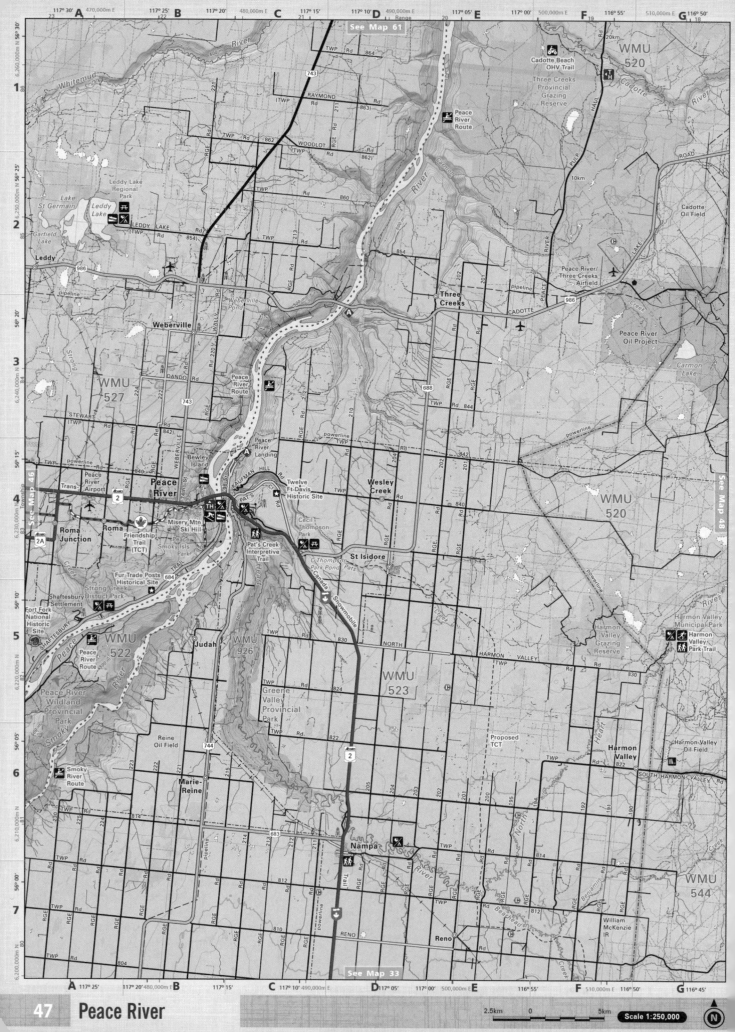

Scale 1:250,000

2.5km 0 5km

© Backroad Mapbooks

WMU
523

gas
plant

Woodland
Cree IR

986

CADOTTE
LAKE

Simon
Lakes

Simon
Lakes

Otter River

HAIG

Golden
Lake

Ochre Cr

IR

LAKE

Marten

Marten
River

Pipeline

986

Woodland
Cree IR

Little
Buffalo
Lookout

Little
Buffalo
(L'Hirondelle)

Little
Buffalo
Lake

Cadotte
Lake

Peace River
Oil Project

Nampa
Oil Field

WMU
520

River

Cadotte

Pipeline

Slave
Oil Field

Lubicon
Lake

See Map 47

gas
plant

Cliffdale
Oil Field

Cadotte
Fire
Lookout

powerline

gas
plant

See Map 49

Lemmy
Lake

North

Heart

River

South

River

Seal
Lake

Rd

Harmon
Valley
Oil Field

Walrus
Oil Field

HARMON

VALLEY

Heart

SOUTH

Benjamin

Creek

Dawson
Oil Field

WMU
544

Kimiwan
Fire
Lookout

Peavine
Metis
Settlement

See Map 34

N

Scale 1:250,000   2.5km   0   5km

Cadotte Lake   48

© Backroad Mapbooks

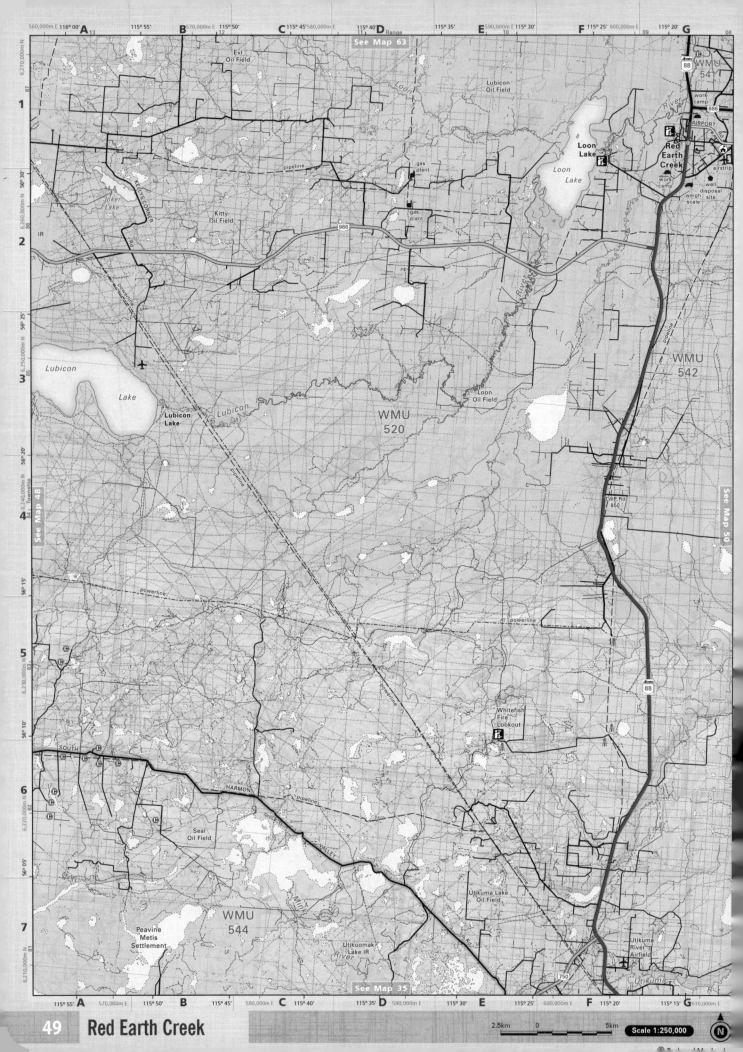

See Map 63

Evi
Oil Field

Loon

Lubicon
Oil Field

WMU
541

work
camp

686

AIRPORT

1

pipeline

gas
plant

986

Loon
Lake

Loon
Lake

Red
Earth
Creek

airstrip

well
disposal
site

work
camp

weigh
scale

Joker
Lake

KEELY'S CORNER
Rd

Kitty
Oil Field

gas
plant

88

IR

2

powerline

River

Pipeline

WMU
542

Lubicon
Lake

Lubicon
Lake

Lubicon

Loon
Oil Field

3

WMU
520

Pipeline

TWP Rd
850

See Map 48

See Map 50

Township

powerline

4

powerline

powerline

88

Whitefish
Fire
Lookout

5

SOUTH

HARMON

pipeline

6

Seal
Oil Field

VALLEY

Utikuma Lake
Oil Field

Pipeline

Peavine
Metis
Settlement

WMU
544

Utikoomak
Lake IR

River

Rd

Utikuma
River
Airfield

7

750

Utikuma
R.

See Map 35

49 **Red Earth Creek**

2.5km 0 5km Scale 1:250,000 (N)

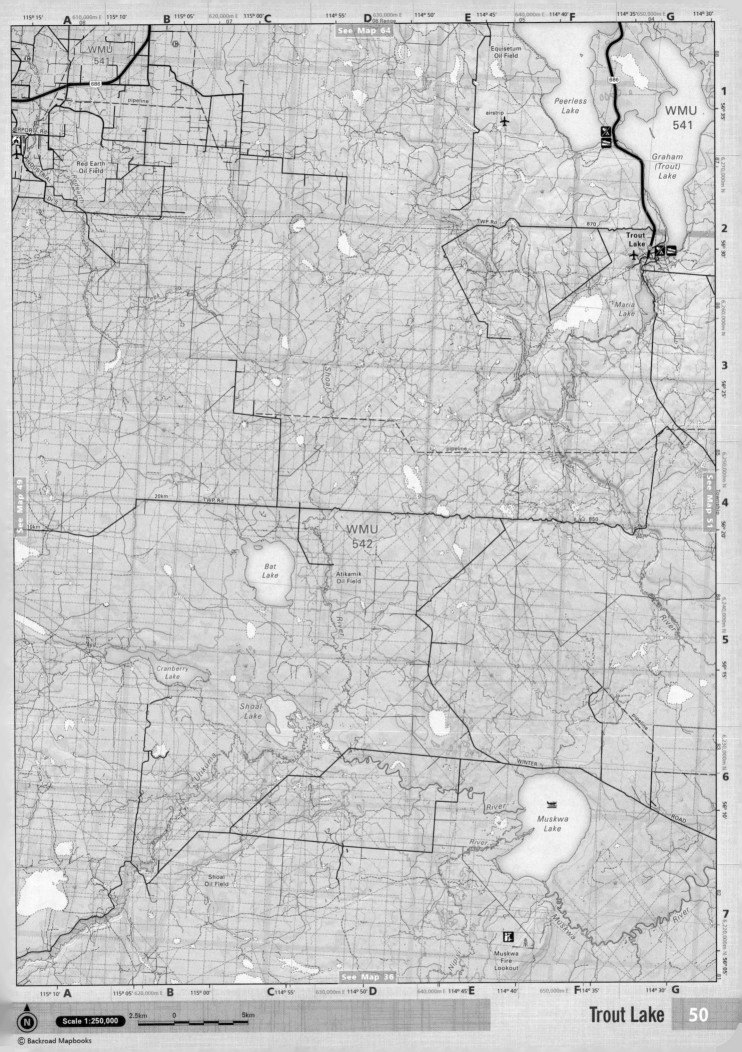

Scale 1:250,000

© Backroad Mapbooks

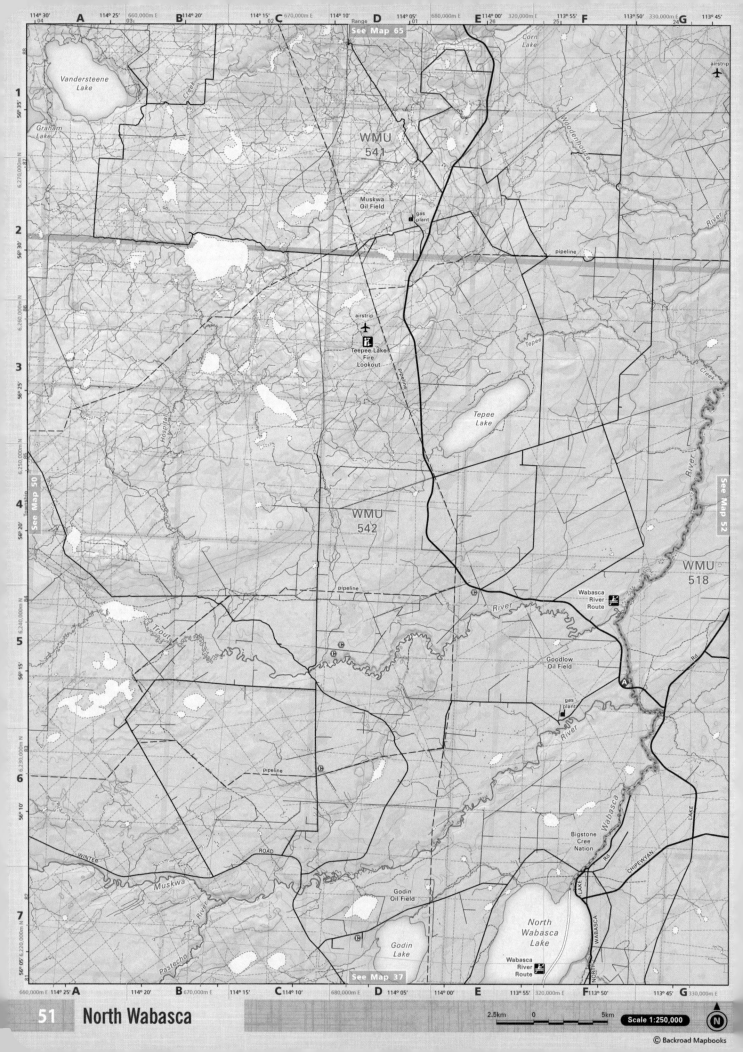

Vandersteene
Lake

Graham
Lake

WMU
541

Muskwa
Oil Field

gas
plant

airstrip

Teepee Lake
Fire
Lookout

Tepee

Tepee
Lake

WMU
542

pipeline

pipeline

River

Wabasca
River Route

WMU
518

Trout

Goodlow
Oil Field

gas
plant

River

pipeline

Bigstone
Cree
Nation

WINTER

Muskwa

ROAD

Godin
Oil Field

Godin
Lake

North
Wabasca
Lake

Wabasca
River Route

CHIPEWYAN

Pastecho
River

See Map 50

See Map 52

pipeline

Woodenhouse

Corn
Lake

airstrip

River

River

Creek

51 **North Wabasca**

2.5km   0   5km

Scale 1:250,000

© Backroad Mapbooks

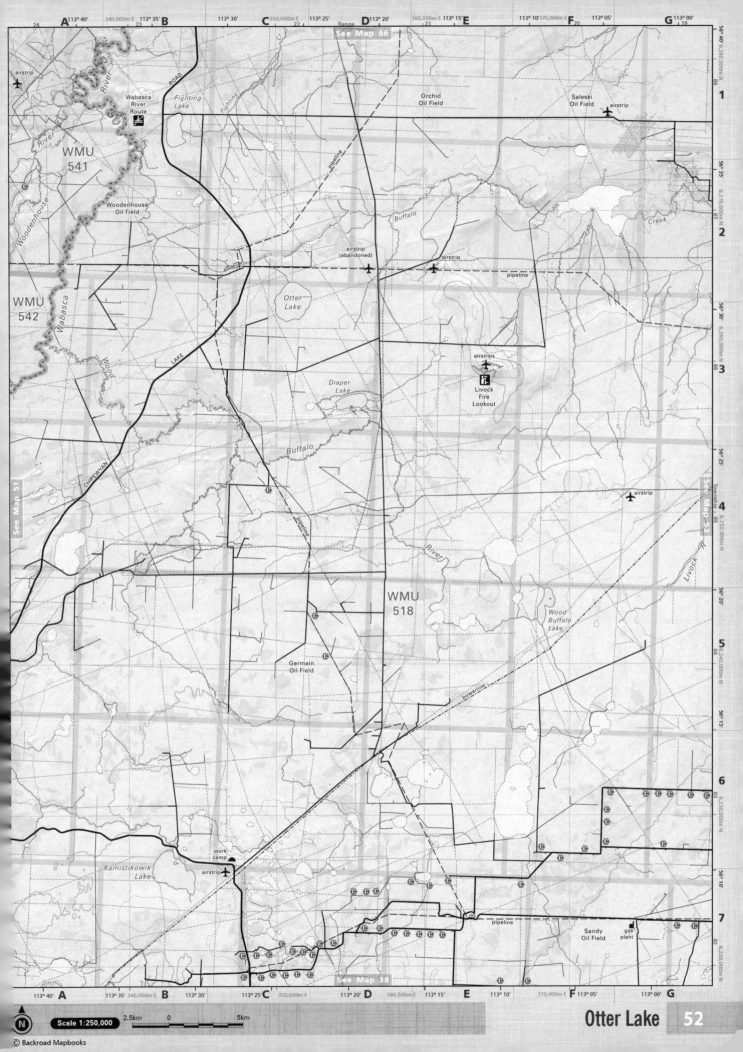

A 113° 40' 340,000m E 23 113° 35' B 113° 30' C 350,000m E 22 113° 25' D 113° 20' 360,000m E 21 113° 15' E 113° 10' 370,000m E F 20 113° 05' G 113° 00' 19

airstrip

Wabasca
River
Route

WMU
541

Fighting
Lake

Fighting

ROAD

Orchid
Oil Field

Saleski
Oil Field

airstrip

1

56° 40' 6,280,000m N 88

Woodenhouse

River

Woodenhouse
Oil Field

Buffalo

56° 35'

6,270,000m N 87

2

WMU
542

Wabasca

airstrip
(abandoned)

airstrip

pipeline

pipeline

56° 30'

6,260,000m N 86

3

Otter
Lake

airstrips

Livock
Fire
Lookout

Wood

LAKE

Diaper
Lake

56° 25'

6,250,000m N 85

See Map 51

CHIPEWYAN

Buffalo

River

airstrip

See Map 53

Township 86

4

WMU
518

Wood
Buffalo
Lake

Livock R

56° 20'

6,240,000m N 84

5

Germain
Oil Field

pipeline

powerline

56° 15'

6,230,000m N 83

6

Kamistikowik
Lake

work
camp

airstrip

56° 10'

6,220,000m N 82

pipeline

Sandy
Oil Field

gas
plant

7

See Map 38

A 113° 40' 113° 35' 340,000m E B 113° 30' C 113° 25' 350,000m E D 113° 20' 360,000m E 113° 15' E 113° 10' F 370,000m E 113° 05' G 113° 00'

6,210,000m N

N

© Backroad Mapbooks

Thickwood Towers
Snowmobile
Area

Hills

Thickwood

gas
plant

powerline

Buffalo

Saleski
Oil Field

Creek

Brûlé
Point

Athabasca
River
(DesNethe)
Trans Canada
Route

Brûlé
Rapids
Camp

River

Oil
Wells

gas
plant

River

Pointe
la Biche

Grand
Rapids
Wildland
Provincial
Park

Algar

River

Horse

Livock

River

Athabasca
River
(DesNethe)
Trans Canada
Route

Grand
Isl

Grand
Rapids

WMU
519

Algar
Lake

airstrip

Grande
Fire
Lookout

TWP Rd

850

WMU
518

Creek

pipeline

Creek

Deadman

powerline

Athabasca
River
(DesNethe)
Trans Canada
Route

House River
Indian Cemetery
IR

Granor
Oil Field

gas
plant

Pipeline

Loon

Athabasca

House

Borm

River

Quigley
Oil Field

Creek

2.5km   0   5km   Scale 1:250,000

© Backroad Mapbooks

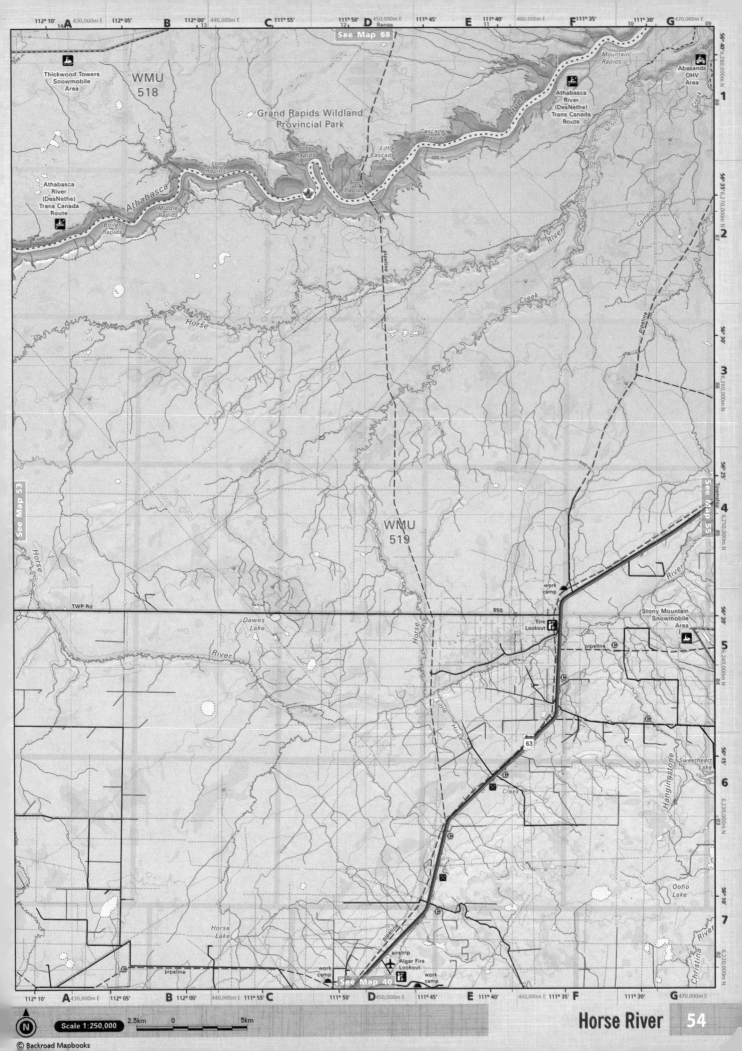

WMU
518

Grand Rapids Wildland
Provincial Park

Thickwood Towers
Snowmobile
Area

Athabasca
River
(DesNethe)
Trans Canada
Route

Boiler
Rapids

Middle
Rapids

Long
Rapids

Crooked
Rapids

Rock
Rapids

Little
Cascade
Rapids

Cascade
Rapids

Mountain
Rapids

Abasands
OHV
Area

Athabasca
River
(DesNethe)
Trans Canada
Route

Horse

Cameron

River

Creek

pipeline

Pipeline

See Map 53

See Map 55

Horse

Township

WMU
519

River

work
camp

TWP Rd

850

Dawes
Lake

Fire
Lookout

Horse

Little Horse

pipeline

Stony Mountain
Snowmobile
Area

Sweetheart
Lake

Hangingstone

63

Creek

Ooho
Lake

Horse
Lake

pipeline

Horse
Lake

pipeline

work
camp

airstrip
Algar Fire
Lookout

work
camp

Christina

River

See Map 40

© Backroad Mapbooks

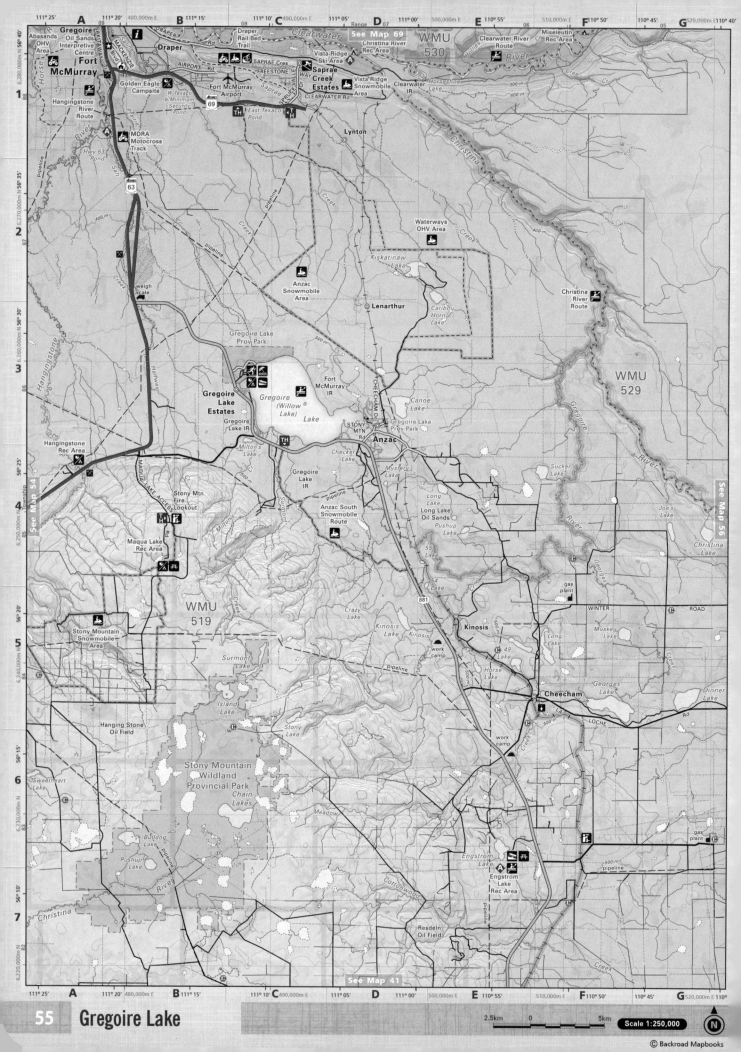

Scale 1:250,000

© Backroad Mapbooks

See Map 70
See Map 55
See Map 42

See Saskatchewan Mapbook

Whitemud Falls
Wildland
Provincial Park

Clearwater
River
Provincial Park

SASKATCHEWAN

ALBERTA

Saskatchewan

Campbell
Lake

airstrip

Gordon Lake
Fire
Lookout

Bunting
Bay

Little
Rocky
Point

Russenholt
Bay

Main
Point

Dorothy
Island

Irma
Island

Gordon

Nora
Lake

Kenee
Island

Cartwright Bay

Newcomen
Point

Lake

Gipsy

Creek

Edwin

Shortt
Lake

Gipsy Lake
Wildland
Provincial
Park

Mary
Lake

Merganser
Bay

Baker
Lake

Raft
Lake

WMU
529

Edna
Lake

Gipsy
Lake

Moose
Bay

Fire
Point

WMZ
73

Passed

Birch
Lake

Away

Creek

Christina River
Route

Gordon

WINTER

Rd

pipeline

Christina

Garson

Lake

Garson
Lake

956

LA

Christina
Crossing

LOCHE

Rd

Formby
Lake

Muskwa
Lake

North
Watchusk
Lake

Kimowin

River

Christina River
Route

River

pipeline

South
Watchusk
Lake

Kimowin
(Hook)
Lake

Kimowin River

Finlay
Lake

Newby

River

McAdam
Lake

ALBERTA

SASKATCHEWAN

British Columbia

WMU 7-46

WMU 7-33

WMU 525

WMU 526

Osborn

Doig River

Doig River IR

Cecil Lake Ecological Reserve

Goodlow

Betts Creek Oil Field

Clear Prairie Oil Field

Sweeney Oil Field

Bear Canyon Provincial Grazing Reserve

North Boundary Lake

German Lake

BRITISH COLUMBIA

ALBERTA

See Inset Map 71

See Map 43

See Map 58

See Northern BC Mapbook

2.5km 0 5km   Scale 1:250,000

© Backroad Mapbooks

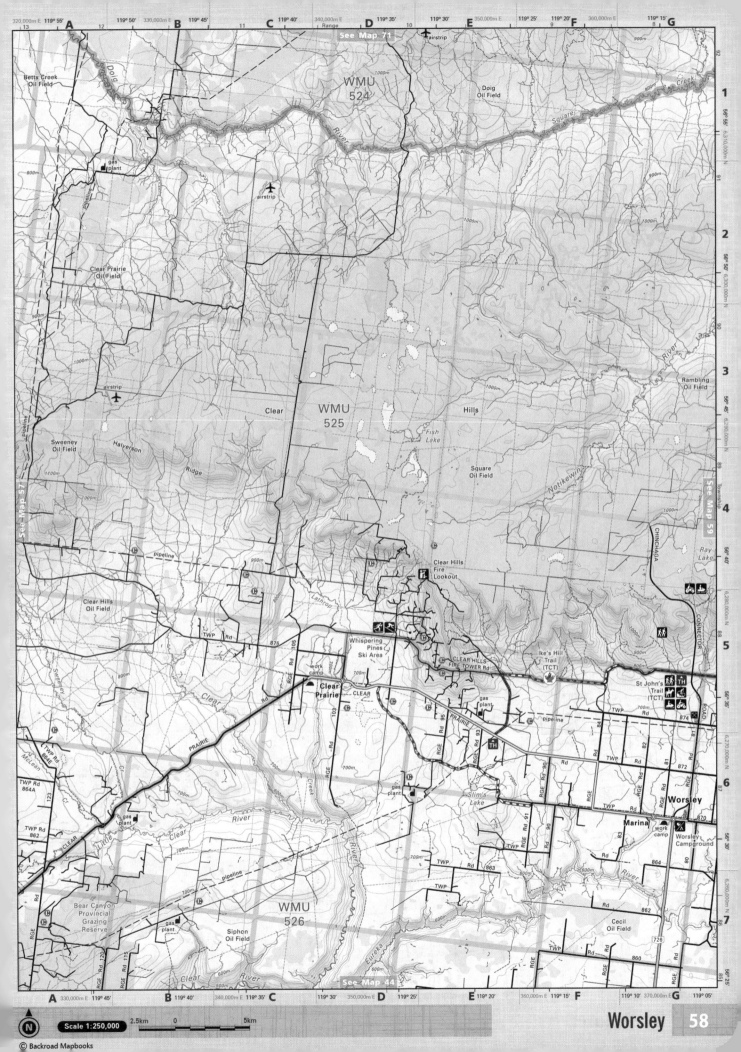

WMU
524

Betts Creek
Oil Field

gas
plant

Doig
Oil Field

Square

Creek

airstrip

Clear Prairie
Oil Field

airstrip

Rambling
Oil Field

Clear

WMU
525

Hills

See Map 57

See Map 59

Sweeney
Oil Field

Halverson

Fish
Lake

Ridge

Square
Oil Field

Notikewin

Ray
Lake

CHINCHAGA

pipeline

Clear Hills
Oil Field

Clear Hills
Fire Lookout

River

CONNECTOR

Lethrop

Whispering
Pines
Ski Area

CLEAR HILLS
FIRE TOWER Rd

Ike's Hill
Trail
(TCT)

St John's
Trail
(TCT)

TWP Rd

work
camp

Clear
Prairie

CLEAR

gas
plant

pipeline

ROAD

874

PRAIRIE

RGE
105

RGE
Rd

875

RGE Rd 103

RGE Rd 95

PRAIRIE

RGE Rd 93

TWP
Rd

TWP Rd
864A

gas
plant

TWP Rd
McLean

PRAIRIE

RGE Rd

RGE Rd 91

TWP Rd

Worsley

TWP Rd
862

gas
plant

CLEAR

Little

Clear

River

Creek

gas
plant

Slim's
Lake

work
camp

Marina

Worsley
Campground

River

864

870

RGE Rd 120

RGE Rd 115

Bear Canyon
Provincial
Grazing
Reserve

gas
plant

WMU
526

Clear

Siphon
Oil Field

River

Eureka

pipeline

TWP Rd

863

872

Cecil
Oil Field

862

726

860

See Map 44

N

Scale 1:250,000   2.5km   0   5km

Worsley 58

© Backroad Mapbooks

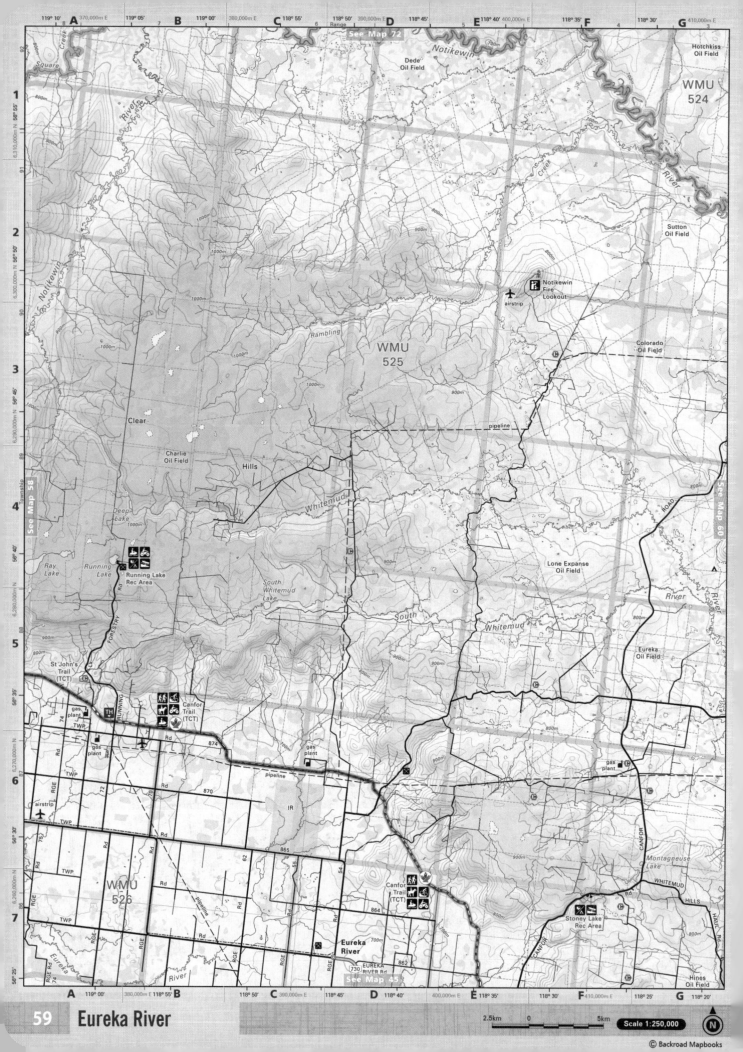

Scale 1:250,000

© Backroad Mapbooks

WMU
524

Hotchkiss
Oil Field

Notikewin

Buick
Oil Field

Stowe
Oil Field

Cub
Lakes

Pipeline

Manning
Oil Field

WMU
527

Stowe

Deadwood
Oil Field

airstrip

Manning

Plavin Homestead
Provincial Historic
Site (Undeveloped)

North
Star

CANFOR

Rosseau
Oil Field

Sulphur Lake
Rec Area

Sulphur
Lake
Sulphur Lake
OHV Area

WMU
525

Beaton
Oil Field

HAUL Rd

Silver

Creek

Whitemud

Lightning

WHITEMUD
HILLS

HAUL Rd

SULPHUR

Creek

800m

Beaton

260

Pipeline

Wagon

Dixonville
Oil Field

RGE

Rd

SULPHUR

Clear
Hills

Helen
Lake

WMU
526

Flood
Lake

Murdock
Lake

Bowesman
Lake

Jim

Buchanan

35

TWP Rd 882

LAKE

(TWP Rd 874)

689

Pluvius
Lake

Dixonville

Shady Lane
Campground
(private)

872

RGE Rd
233

River

870

N

Scale 1:250,000

2.5km   0   5km

© Backroad Mapbooks

Manning   **60**

WMU
528

Potoco
Oil Field

Manning & District
Ski Club

North Star
Oil Field

Buchanan
Creek
Oil Field

Peace
River
Route

WMU
527

WMU
520

Fairacres
Oil Field

Deadwood

Deadwood Fire
Lookout

Reinwood

Driftwood
Lake

Helen
Oil Field

Three Creeks
Prov. Grazing
Reserve

Cadotte Beach
OHV Trail

Cadotte
Oil Field

Hotchkiss

Notikewin

Manning

gas
plant

Little

Cadotte

See Map 47

2.5km   0   5km   Scale 1:250,000

© Backroad Mapbooks

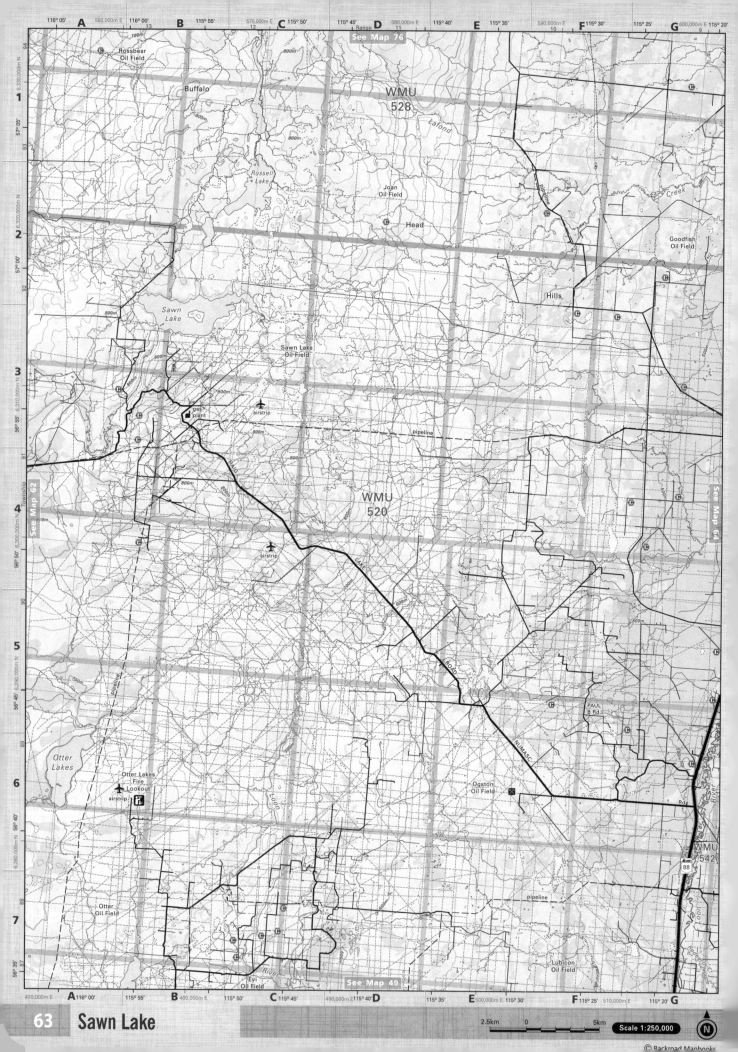

WMU
528

Rossbear
Oil Field

Buffalo

Russell
Lake

Lafond

Joan
Oil Field

Head

Goodfish
Oil Field

Creek

Hills

Sawn
Lake

Sawn Lake
Oil Field

gas
plant

airstrip

pipeline

See Map 62

Township 62

800m

WMU
520

airstrip

LAKE ROAD

NUMASC

PAUL
B Rd

See Map 64

Otter
Lakes

Otter Lakes
Fire
Lookout

airstrip

LOON

Ogston
Oil Field

River

Otter
Oil Field

Lubicon
Oil Field

Evi
Oil Field

WMU
542

88

See Map 49

pipeline

pipeline

63 Sawn Lake

2.5km   0   5km

Scale 1:250,000

N

© Backroad Mapbooks

WMU 528

WMU 541

WMU 520

WMU 542

Goodfish Oil Field

Redfish Oil Field

Kidney Oil Field

Kidney Lake

Trout Oil Field

Senex Oil Field

Goodfish Lake

Equisetum Lake

Long Lake

Round Lake

Peerless Lake

God's Lake

Peerless Lake

Equistum Oil Field

Birch Mountains

Bad Rapids

Panny Fire Lookout

Wabasca River Route

DISPATCH PANNY Rd

airstrip

airstrip

airstrip

gas plant

gas plant

gas plant

Red Earth Fire Lookout

Lafond Creek

Hunt Creek

Creek

Crooked Creek

Loon

Redearth Creek

Wabasca River

River

Pipeline

pipeline

pipeline

Pipeline

Pipeline

pipeline

88

686

990

TWP Rd

500m

500m

500m

500m

500m

500m

600m

600m

600m

700m

700m

700m

700m

700m

700m

700m

200m

115° 20'   115° 15'   610,000m E   115° 10'   115° 05'   620,000m E   115° 00'   Range   114° 55'   630,000m E   114° 50'   114° 45'   640,000m E   114° 40'   114° 35'   114° 30'

115° 15'   610,000m E   115° 10'   115° 05'   115° 00'   620,000m E   114° 55'   630,000m E   114° 50'   114° 45'   640,000m E   114° 40'   114° 35'   650,000m E   114° 30'

A   B   C   D   E   F   G

57° 10'   57° 05'   57° 00'   56° 55'   56° 50'   56° 45'   56° 40'

6,340,000m N   94   6,330,000m N   93   6,320,000m N   92   6,310,000m N   91   6,300,000m N   90   6,290,000m N   89   6,280,000m N   88

Township

Scale 1:250,000

WMU 531

Zig Zag Lake

Stone Lake

Birch

Osi Lake

Elizabeth Lake

Duck Lake

Odisque Lake

Sick Hill Lake

Mountains

800m

700m

Nikik Lake

Muskeg Lake

700m

Tawatchaw

Valley

700m

Liege Oil Field

Rabbit Lake

Spoon Lake

pipeline

Dunkirk

600m

Perfume Lake

600m

River

pipeline

Creek

Chipewyan Lake Fire Lookout

600m

gas plant

Chipewyan

Carrot Lake

Chipewyan Lake

airstrip

pipeline

Chipewyan Lake

Kipeecheechagum Lake

Rod Lake

Creek

Aguhway Lake

Mink Lake

Grew Lake

River

Clearwater Lake

Seaforth

Stomach Lake

pipeline

600m

WMU 518

Horse Lake

500m

500m

gas plant

River

Creek

Wabasca

LAKE

Scooter Lake

500m

500m

500m

Dead Calf Lake

Chipewyan

Slough Lake

500m

Island Lake

Wabasca River Route

WMU 541

gas plant

pipeline

River

Whistwow Lake

Fighting

500m

airstrip

Swan Lake

Blanchet Lake

MacKay

River

500m

500m

White Cow Lake

Baseline Lake

See Map 80

See Map 53

Athabasca Oil Sands

Birch

gas plant

Ells River Fire Lookout

Mountains

Ells River Route

Liege Oil Field

pipeline

Creek

AOSC

WMU 531

pipeline

River

Snipe

Rabbit Lake

Dunkirk

500m

Dover River

PARAMOUNT Rd

See Map 66

See Map 68

Township 66

WMU 518

WINTER ACCESS ROAD

500m

ROAD

River

500m

Mackay

River

500m

500m

Powerline Trail

transmission line

Thickwood Towers Snowmobile Area

A 112°55'   380,000m E   B 390,000m E   112°50'   C 112°40'   400,000m E   D 112°35'   E 410,000m E   112°25'   F 112°20' 420,000m E   G 112°15'

67   **Dunkirk River**

2.5km   0   5km   Scale 1:250,000   N

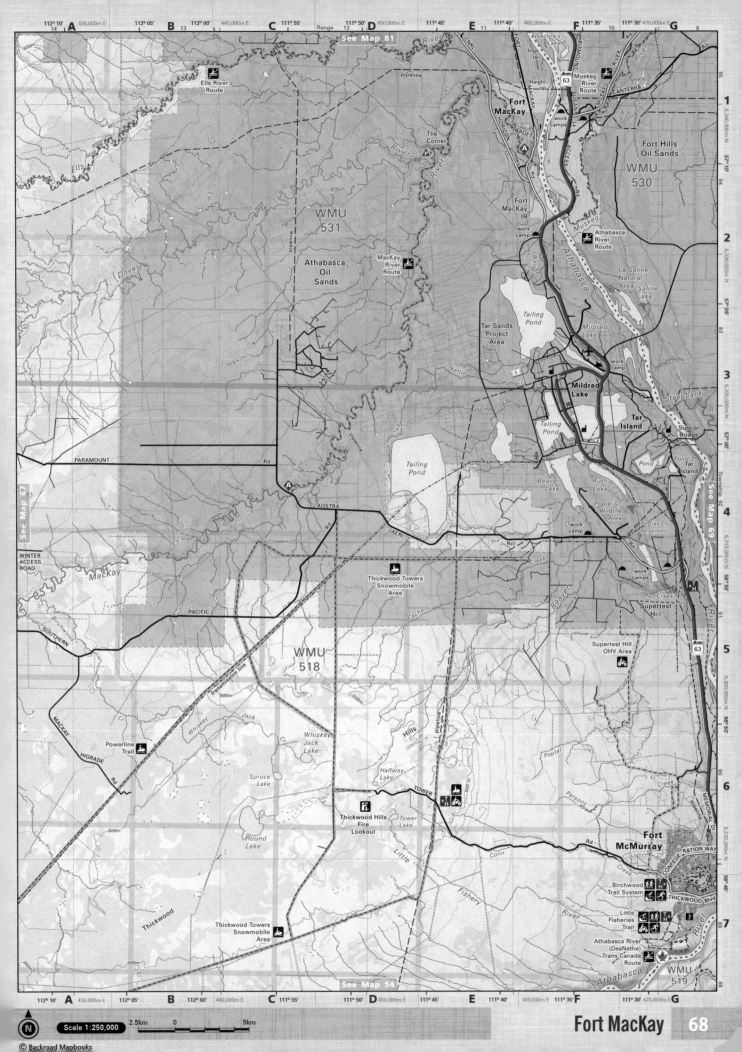

Fort MacKay **68**

Scale 1:250,000   2.5km   0   5km

© Backroad Mapbooks

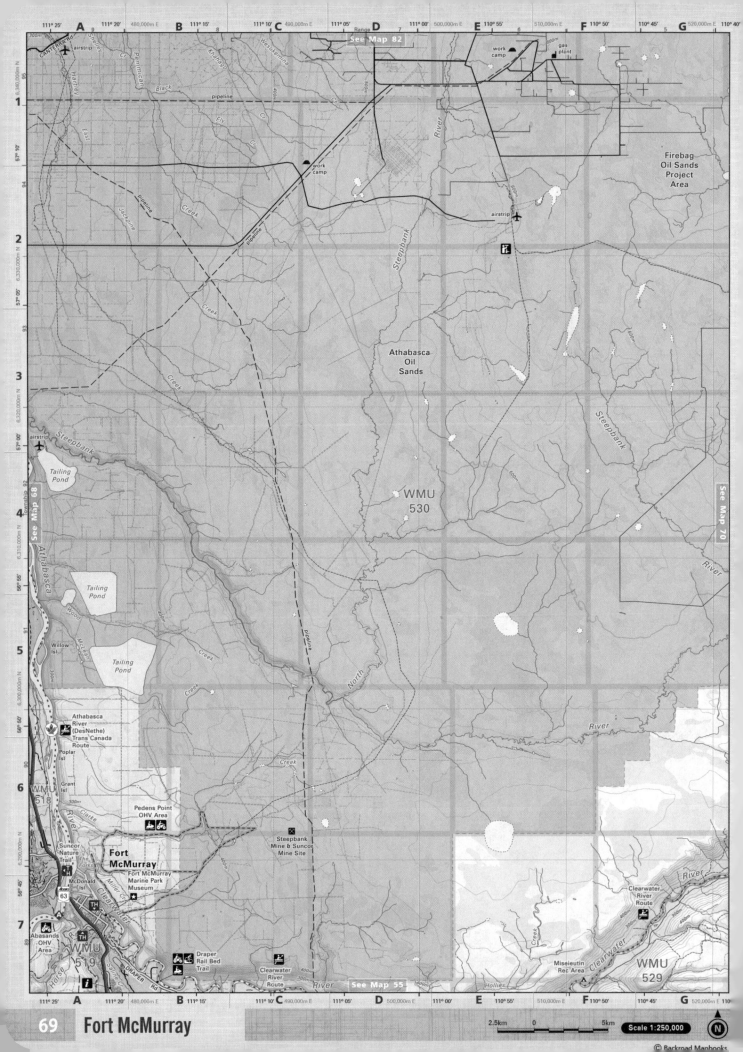

Firebag
Oil Sands
Project
Area

Athabasca
Oil
Sands

WMU
530

Tailing
Pond

Tailing
Pond

Willow Isl

Tailing
Pond

Athabasca
River
(DesNethe)
Trans Canada
Route

Poplar Isl

Grant Isl

WMU
518

Pedens Point
OHV Area

Steepbank
Mine & Suncor
Mine Site

Suncor
Nature
Trail

**Fort
McMurray**

Fort McMurray
Marine Park
Museum

McDonald Isl

63

Abasands
OHV
Area

WMU
519

Draper
Rail Bed
Trail

Clearwater
River
Route

Miseieutin
Rec Area

Clearwater
River
Route

WMU
529

work
camp

gas
plant

airstrip

work
camp

airstrip

2.5km   0   5km   Scale 1:250,000

© Backroad Mapbooks

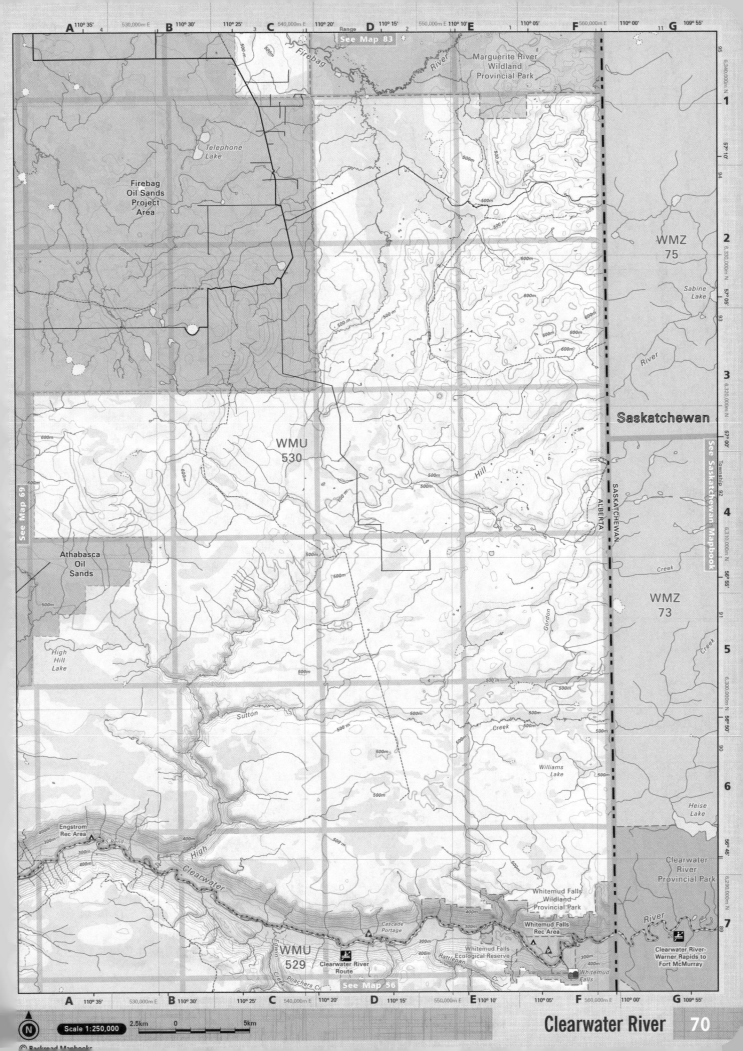

Firebag

Range

River

Marguerite River
Wildland
Provincial Park

Telephone
Lake

Firebag
Oil Sands
Project
Area

500 m

600m

500m

600m

600m

600m

**WMZ
75**

Sabine
Lake

River

Saskatchewan

**WMU
530**

600m

500m

600m

500m

Hill

500m

500m

ALBERTA

SASKATCHEWAN

Township 92

Range 11

**WMZ
73**

Creek

Athabasca
Oil Sands

500m

500m

Gordon

Creek

High
Hill
Lake

500m

500m

500 m

500m

500m

500m

Sutton

500m

Creek

500m

Williams
Lake

500m

Heise
Lake

500m

500 m

Engstrom
Rec Area

400m
300m
S Bend
300m
400m

High

Clearwater

400m

500m

Clearwater
River
Provincial Park

Erwin

Poachers Cr

Creek

**WMU
529**

Clearwater River
Route

Cascade
Portage

Rattlesnake

300m

400m

Whitemud Falls
Ecological Reserve

Whitemud Falls
Wildland
Provincial Park

300m

400m

400m

Whitemud Falls
Rec Area

Whitemud
Falls

River

Clearwater River-
Warner Rapids to
Fort McMurray

N

Scale 1:250,000   2.5km   0   5km

© Backroad Mapbooks

Clearwater River   **70**

A 110° 35' 530,000m E B 110° 30' C 540,000m E 110° 20' D 110° 15' 550,000m E E 110° 10' 110° 05' F 560,000m E 110° 00' G 109° 55'

Chinchaga Wildland Provincial Park

Scale 1:250,000

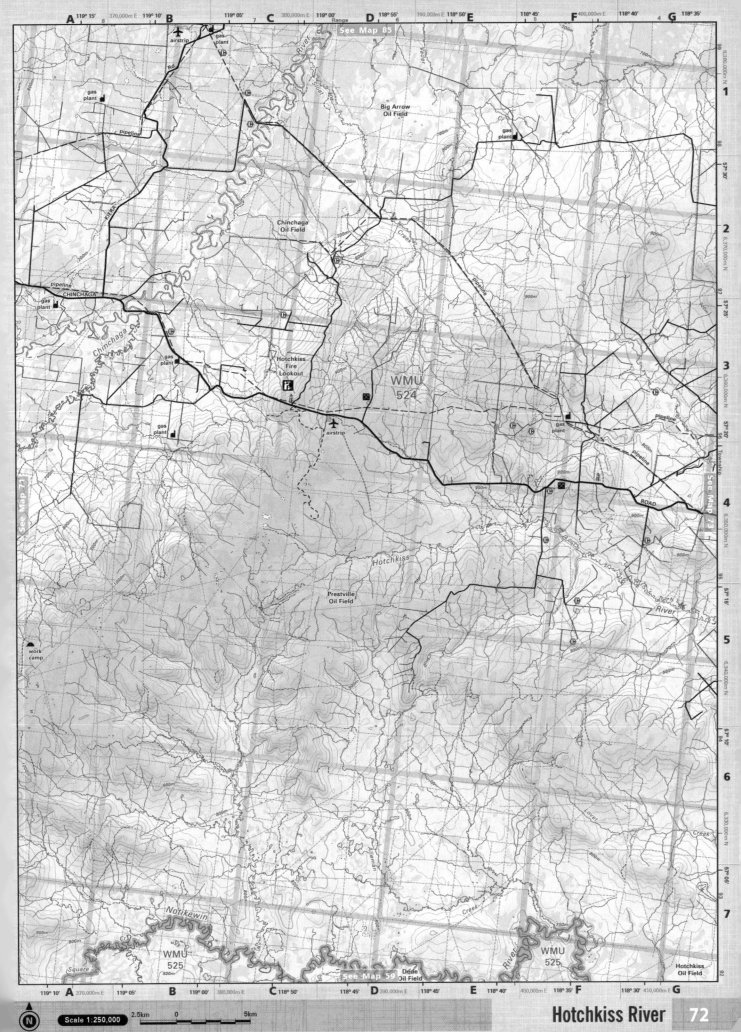

Big Arrow
Oil Field

gas plant

KIERA

pipeline
CHINCHAGA
gas plant

Chinchaga

Chinchaga
Oil Field

gas plant

Hotchkiss
Fire
Lookout

WMU
524

gas plant

gas plant

Pipeline

pipeline

airstrip

ROAD

Hotchkiss

Prestville
Oil Field

River

River

work camp

Lovel

Creek

Alleman

Creek

Creek

Notikewin

River

WMU
525

Square

WMU
525

Dede
Oil Field

Hotchkiss
Oil Field

See Map 71

See Map 73

See Map 59

119° 15'   119° 10'   119° 05'   119° 00'   118° 55'   118° 50'   118° 45'   118° 40'   118° 35'

A   B   C   D   E   F   G

119° 10'   119° 05'   119° 00'   118° 50'   118° 45'   118° 40'   118° 35'   118° 30'

370,000m E   380,000m E   390,000m E   400,000m E   410,000m E

N

Scale 1:250,000   2.5km   0   5km

© Backroad Mapbooks

Hotchkiss River   72

Naylor

Hills

Hawk

WMU
537

Cranberry
Oil Field

WMU
524

Kiya
Oil Field

gas
plants

gas
plant

GARIANNE

WMU
527

Hotchkiss

gas
plant

airstrip

gas
plant

pipeline

Chinchaga
Fire
Lookout

Battle River
Fire
Lookout

pipeline

TWP. Rd
940

RGE Rd
235

Hotchkiss
Oil Field

gas
plant

TWP Rd.
934

TWP Rd.
932

73 **Meikle River**

2.5km 0 5km

Scale 1:250,000

© Backroad Mapbooks

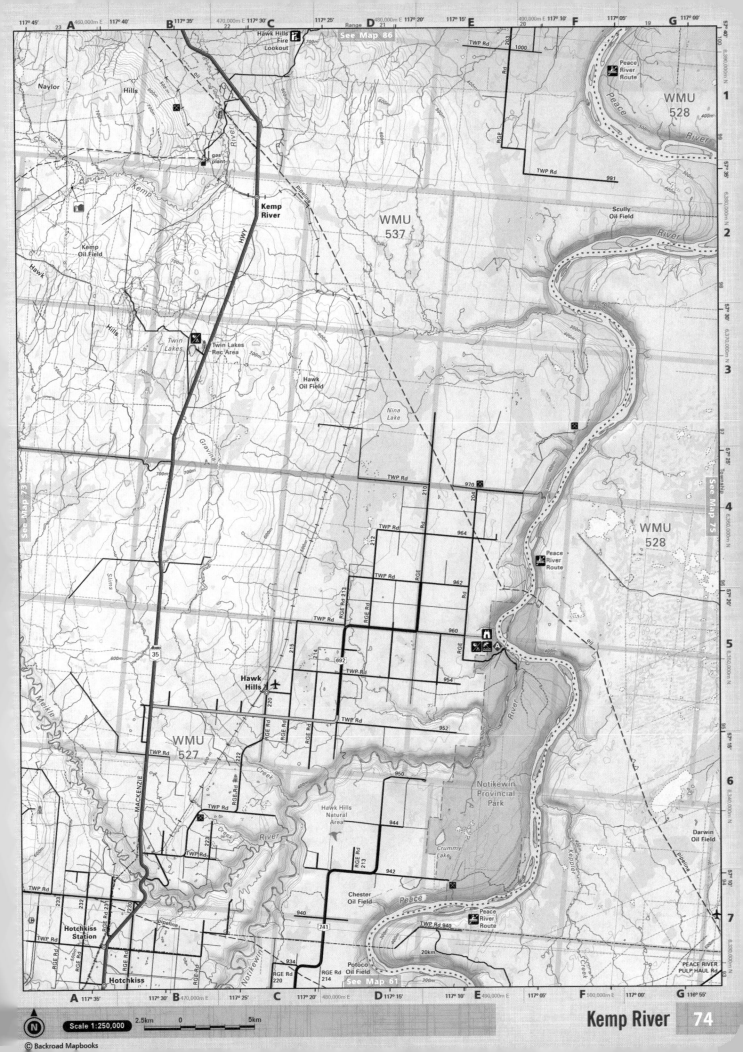

Scale 1:250,000

2.5km   0   5km

© Backroad Mapbooks

See Map 86

See Map 73

See Map 75

See Map 61

WMU 528

WMU 537

WMU 528

WMU 527

Naylor

Kemp River

Kemp Oil Field

Twin Lakes Rec Area

Twin Lakes

Hawk Oil Field

Nina Lake

Hawk Hills Fire Lookout

gas plant

Hawk Hills

Scully Oil Field

Peace River Route

Peace River Route

Peace River Route

Notikewin Provincial Park

Hawk Hills Natural Area

Crummy Lake

Chester Oil Field

Potoco Oil Field

Darwin Oil Field

Hotchkiss Station

Hotchkiss

Peace River Pulp Haul Rd

WMU
537

Peace
River
Route

Kahntah
Oil Field

Wolverine
Oil Field

WMU
528

Britts
Oil Field

See Map 74

See Map 76

Donaldson
Lake

Buffalo

River

Head
Hills

Buffalo

Darwin
Oil Field

gas
plant

pipeline

gas
plant

pipeline

pipeline

Bison
Lake

Bison
Lake

Bison Lake
Fire
Lookout

See Map 62

2.5km   0   5km

Scale 1:250,000

N

© Backroad Mapbooks

See Map 75

See Map 77

See Map 63

Wadlin Lake

Buffalo Head Hills
OHV Trails

Wabasca
River
Route

airstrip

Muddy

Buffalo

Wabasca

River

Burning
Sulphur
Natural
Area

River

Buffalo

Head

River

Talbot
Lake

airstrip

WMU
540

Buffalo Head Hills
OHV Trails

Hills

WMU
541

Rossbear

Creek

Rossbear
Lake

Talbot
Fire
Lookout

88

airstrip

airstrip

River

Wolverine

Russell

Talbot Lake
Oil Field

pipeline

Bison
Lake

BISON   LAKE   Rd

Rossbear
Oil Field

Creek

pipeline

N | Scale 1:250,000 | 2.5km | 0 | 5km

Talbot Lake 76

A 115° 20' 600,000m E   B 115° 15'   C 115° 10' 610,000m E   D 115° 05'   E 115° 00' 620,000m E   F 114° 55'   G 114° 50' 630,000m E   114° 45'   114° 40' 640,000m E   114° 35'

Wabasca

Owl

Mikkwa   River

airstrip

Senex   River

88

WMU
528

airstrip

See Map 76

Range
Township

Creek

WMU
540

Creek

pipeline

See Map 78

Wabasca

River

WMU
541

River

gas
plant

Wabasca
River
Route

pipeline

Panny
Oil Field

ROAD

Darling   Creek

PANNY

88

airstrip

Panny   pipeline

WMU
528

DISPATCH

Pipeline

Panny
Fire
Lookout

airstrip

2.5km   0   5km   Scale 1:250,000   N

Scale 1:250,000   2.5km 0   5km

© Backroad Mapbooks

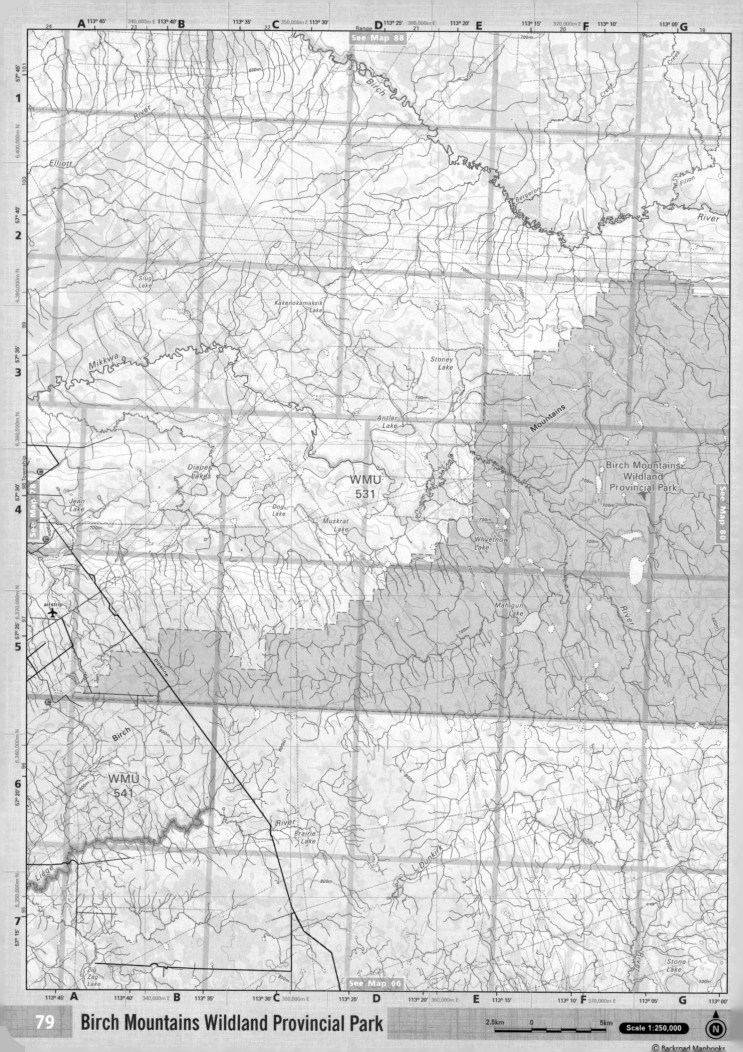

See Map 88

Birch

River

Bergeron

Elliott

Filion

River

Slug
Lake

Kakenokamaksik
Lake

Mikkwa

Stoney
Lake

Mountains

Birch Mountains
Wildland
Provincial Park

Antler
Lake

700m

Diaper
Lakes

WMU
531

See Map 78

Jean
Lake

Dog
Lake

Muskrat
Lake

Whyetnow
Lake

700m

See Map 80

airstrip

Mahigun
Lake

River

pipeline

Birch

800m

WMU
541

River

Prairie
Lake

Dunkirk

Liege

Zig
Zag
Lake

800m

Stone
Lake

See Map 66

2.5km 0 5km

Scale 1:250,000

N

© Backroad Mapbooks

See Map 79

See Map 81

Birch

River

Louise River

A-h Lake

McIvor R.

Michael Lake

Otasan Lake

Sand Lake

Tar Oil Field

Water-lily Lake

airstrip

Big Island

Big Island Lake

Mountains

Gardiner Lakes

gas plant

Birch Lakes

Birch Mountains Wildland Provincial Park

WMU 531

The Narrows

Namur R.

Fort MacKay First Nations

Ells

Legend Fire Lookout

Pelican Island

Ells Oil Field

Mikkwa R

Legend Lake

Namur Lake

River

Birch

Fort MacKay First Nations

airstrip

Ells River Route

pipeline

Creek

airstrip

Snipe

Creek

Chelsea

Athabasca Oil Sands

airstrip

pipeline

See Map 67

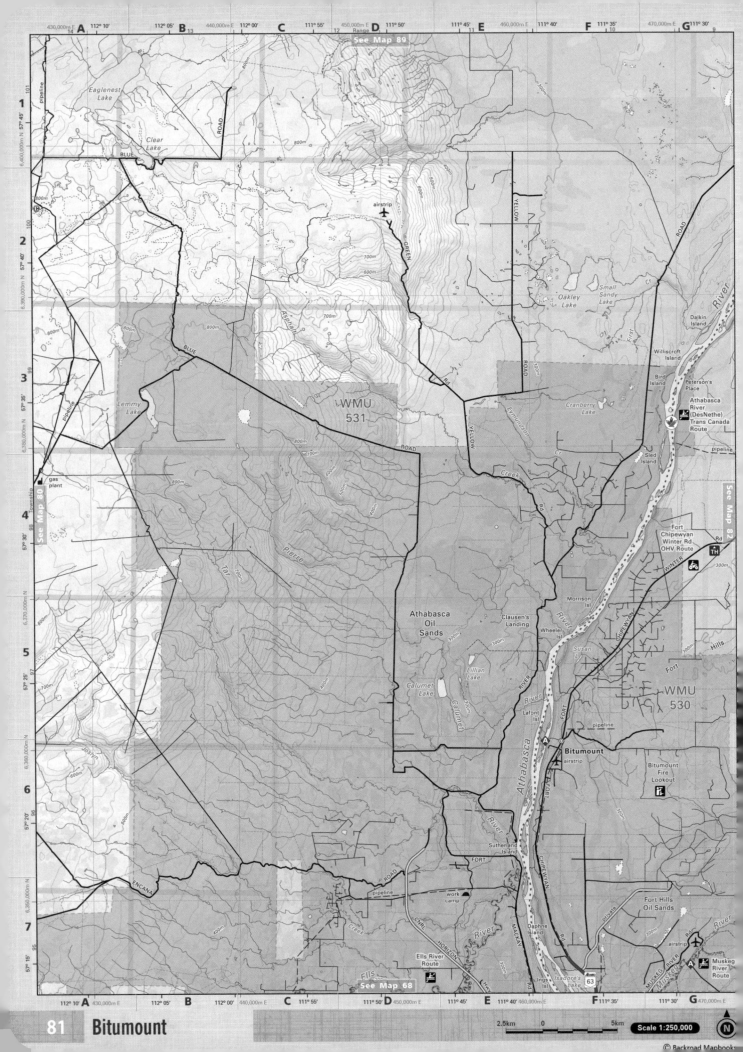

Eaglenest Lake

Clear Lake

BLUE

ROAD

airstrip

GREEN

YELLOW

Oakley Lake

Small Sandy Lake

First Cr

Dalkin Island

Williscroft Island

Bird Island

Peterson's Place

ASPHALT

BLUE

WMU 531

ROAD

Edmundson Cr

Cranberry Lake

YELLOW

Athabasca River (DesNethe) Trans Canada Route

pipeline

Sled Island

Lemmy Lake

Creek

Rd

See Map 82

pipeline

gas plant

Township

See Map 80

Tar

Pierre

800m

Creek

Fort Chipewyan Winter Rd OHV Route

TH

Athabasca Oil Sands

Clausen's Landing

Morrison Isl

Wheeler Isl

Susan

Fort

Hills

WMU 530

Lillian Lake

Calumet Lake

Calumet

River

Lafont Isl

pipeline

Athabasca

A

Bitumount

airstrip

Bitumount Fire Lookout

Joslyn

Sutherland Island

FORT

CHIPEWYAN

ENCANA

ROAD

pipeline

work camp

CNRL

HORIZON

Ells River Route

See Map 68

Ells

Creek

River

MACKAY

Daphne Island

Rd

private

Fort Hills Oil Sands

63

Isadore's Isl

Ings Isl

Muskeg River Route

MUSKEG RIVER

A

Muskeg River Route

2.5km   0   5km   Scale 1:250,000   N

© Backroad Mapbooks

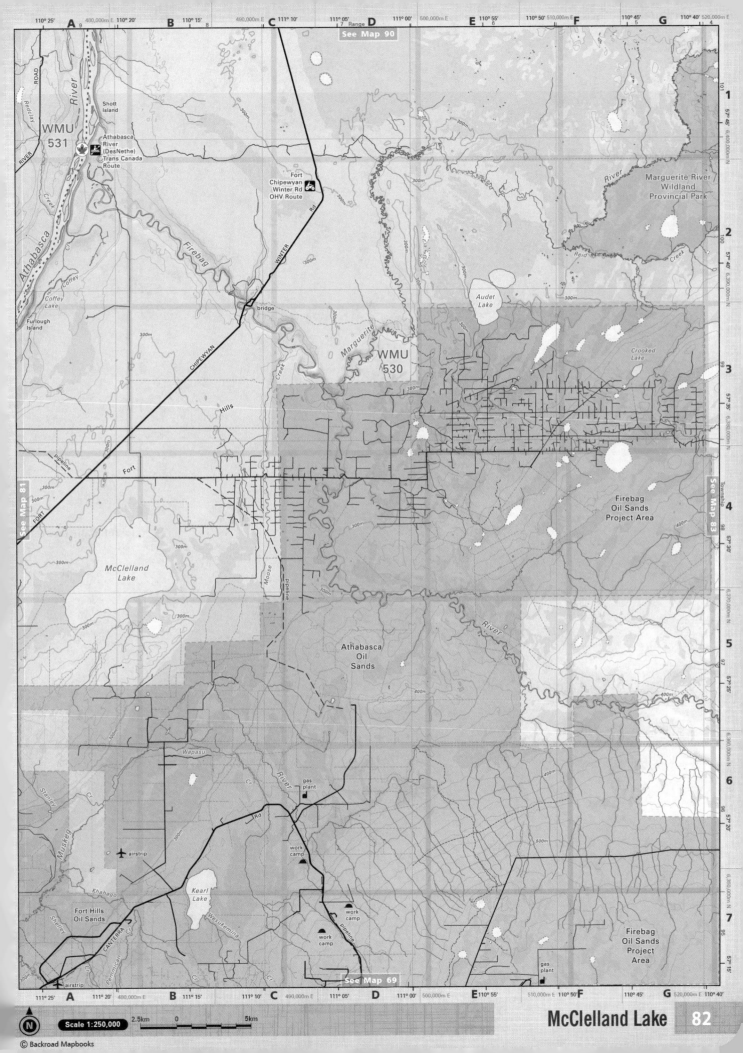

See Map 81
See Map 83
See Map 69

WMU
531

Athabasca
River

Red Clay

Shott Island

Athabasca
River
(DesNethe)
Trans Canada
Route

Fort
Chipewyan
Winter Rd
OHV Route

Firebag

Coffey Cr.

Coffey
Lake

Furlough
Island

bridge

WINTER

CHIPEWYAN

Rd

Marguerite

Creek

Hills

WMU
530

Marguerite River
Wildland
Provincial Park

River

Reid

Creek

Audet
Lake

Crooked
Lake

300m

pipeline

Fort

McClelland
Lake

Moose

pipeline

Firebag
Oil Sands
Project Area

Athabasca
Oil
Sands

River

400m

400m

Stanley Cr.

Muskeg

Wapasu

Cr.

River

gas
plant

Rd

400m

500m

airstrip

work
camp

Khahago

Kearl
Lake

Wesukemina

CANTERRA

Pemmican Cr.

Cr.

Fort Hills
Oil Sands

Shelley Cr.

airstrip

work
camp

pipeline

work
camp

gas
plant

Firebag
Oil Sands
Project
Area

N

Scale 1:250,000   2.5km   0   5km

© Backroad Mapbooks

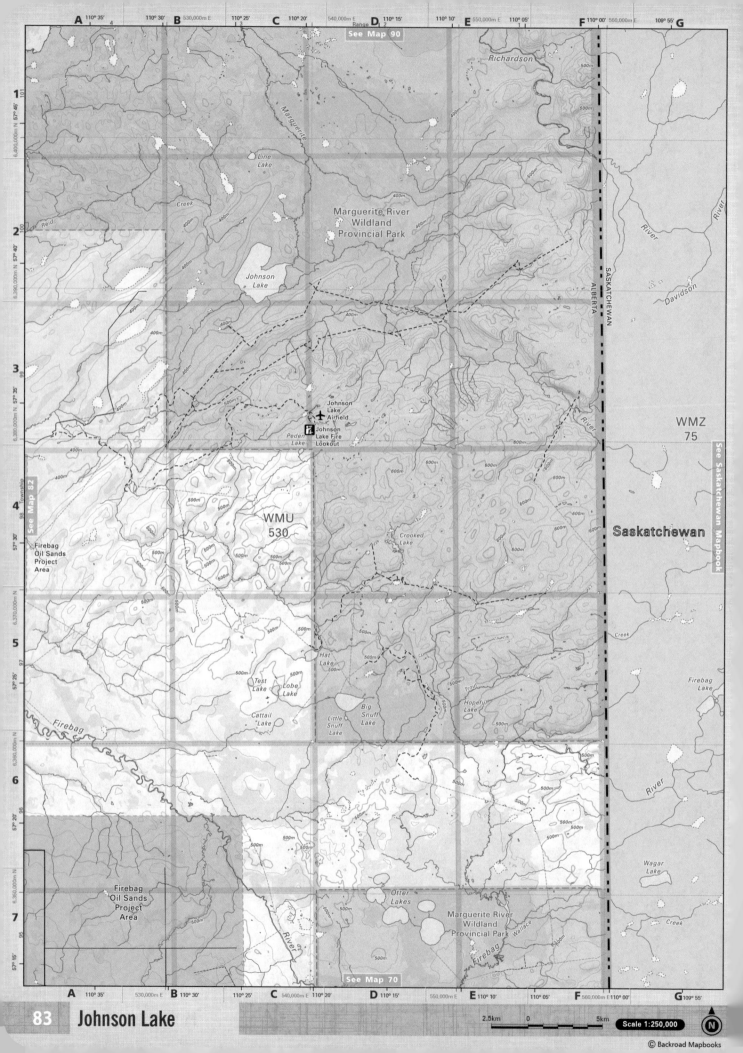

Richardson

Marguerite

Line
Lake

Reid

Creek

400m

400m

400m

Johnson
Lake

400m

Marguerite River
Wildland
Provincial Park

400m

500m

400m

Johnson
Lake
Airfield
Johnson
Lake Fire
Lookout

Peden
Lake

400m

400m

600m

600m

500m

600m

600m

WMZ
75

See Map 82

Firebag
Oil Sands
Project
Area

WMU
530

500m

500m

500m

500m

500m

500m

500m

Crooked
Lake

600m

600m

600m

600m

Saskatchewan

500m

500m

500m

Hat
Lake
500m

500m

Test
Lake

Lobe
Lake

Cattail
Lake

Little
Snuff
Lake

Big
Snuff
Lake

Trout

500m

Hopeful
Lake

500m

Firebag

Firebag

500m

500m

500m

500m

500m

River

500m

500m

500m

500m

500m

Firebag
Lake

Otter
Lakes

Marguerite River
Wildland
Provincial Park

Wallace

Firebag

Wagar
Lake

Creek

River

Creek

Davidson

River

River

ALBERTA

SASKATCHEWAN

See Saskatchewan Mapbook

See Map 70

83 | **Johnson Lake**

2.5km   0   5km   Scale 1:250,000   N

Township

Range

© Backroad Mapbooks

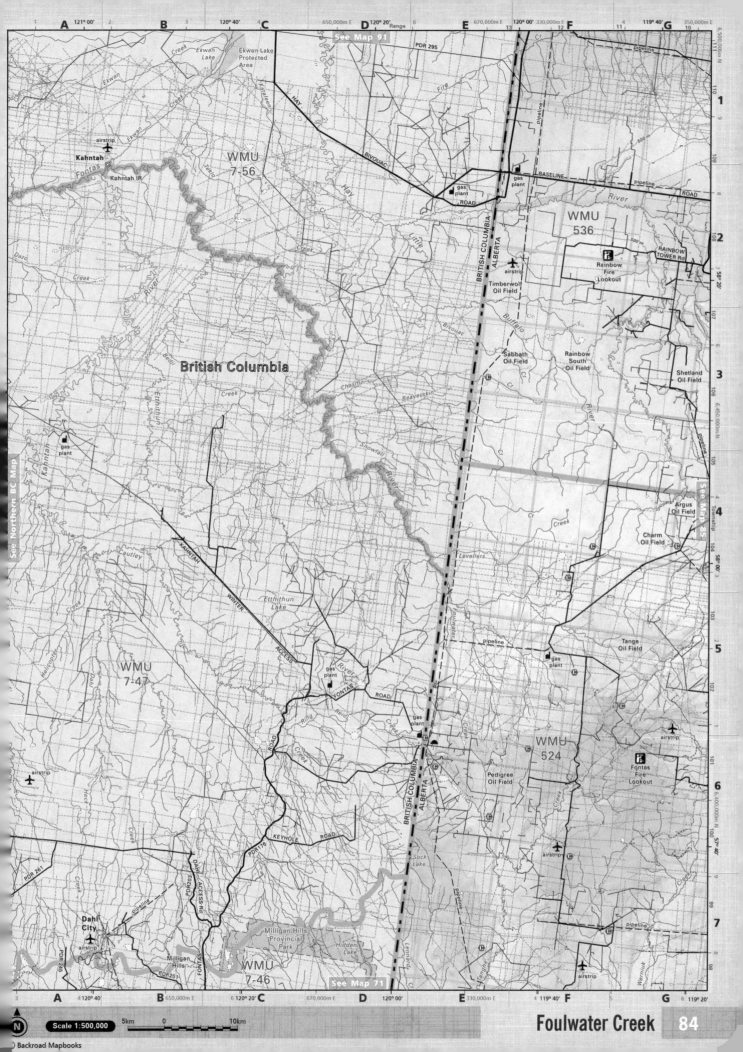

Scale 1:500,000

© Backroad Mapbook

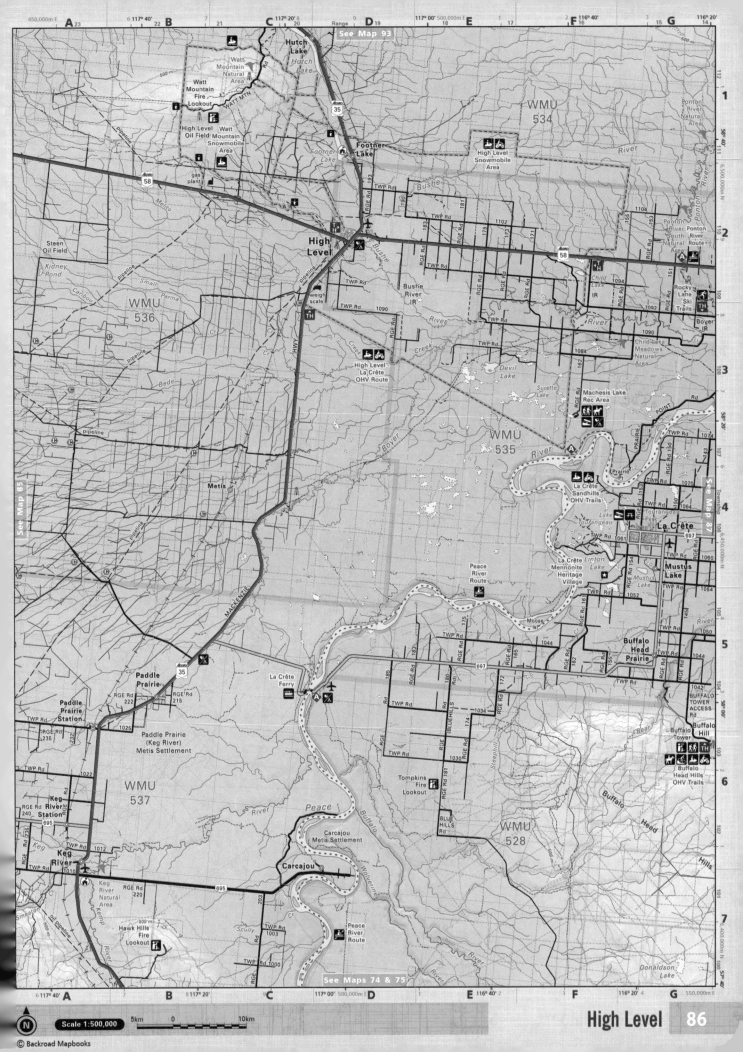

Scale 1:500,000   5km   0   10km

© Backroad Mapbooks

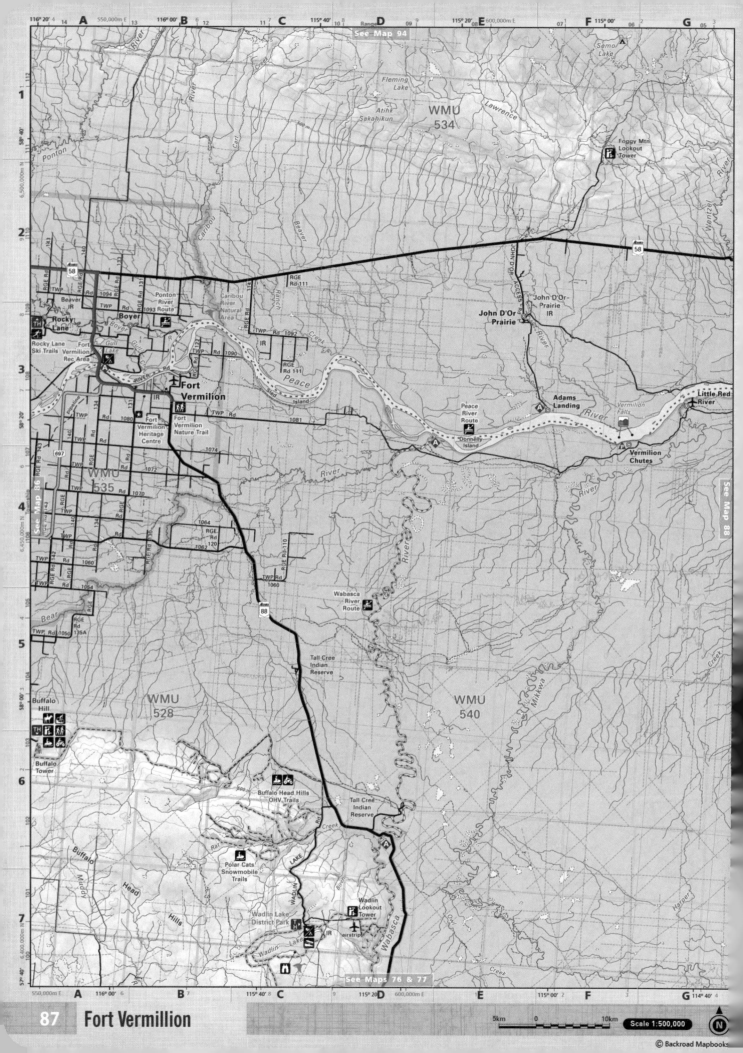

WMU
534

Foggy Mtn
Lookout
Tower

John D'Or
Prairie
IR

John D'Or
Prairie

Adams
Landing

Little Red
River

Vermilion
Falls

Peace
River
Route

Vermilion
Chutes

Beaver
IR

Rocky
Lane

Boyer

Ponton
River
Route

Caribou
River
Natural
Area

RGE
Rd 111

RGE
Rd 111

Rocky Lane
Ski Trails

Fort
Vermilion
Rec Area

Fort
Vermilion

Fort
Vermilion
Heritage
Centre

Fort
Vermilion
Nature Trail

WMU
535

Donnelly
Island

Wabasca
River
Route

Tall Cree
Indian
Reserve

WMU
528

WMU
540

Buffalo
Hill

Buffalo
Tower

Buffalo Head Hills
OHV Trails

Tall Cree
Indian
Reserve

Buffalo
Head
Hills

Polar Cats
Snowmobile
Trails

Wadlin
Lookout
Tower

Wadlin Lake
District Park

airstrip

5km   0   10km

Scale 1:500,000

© Backroad Mapbooks

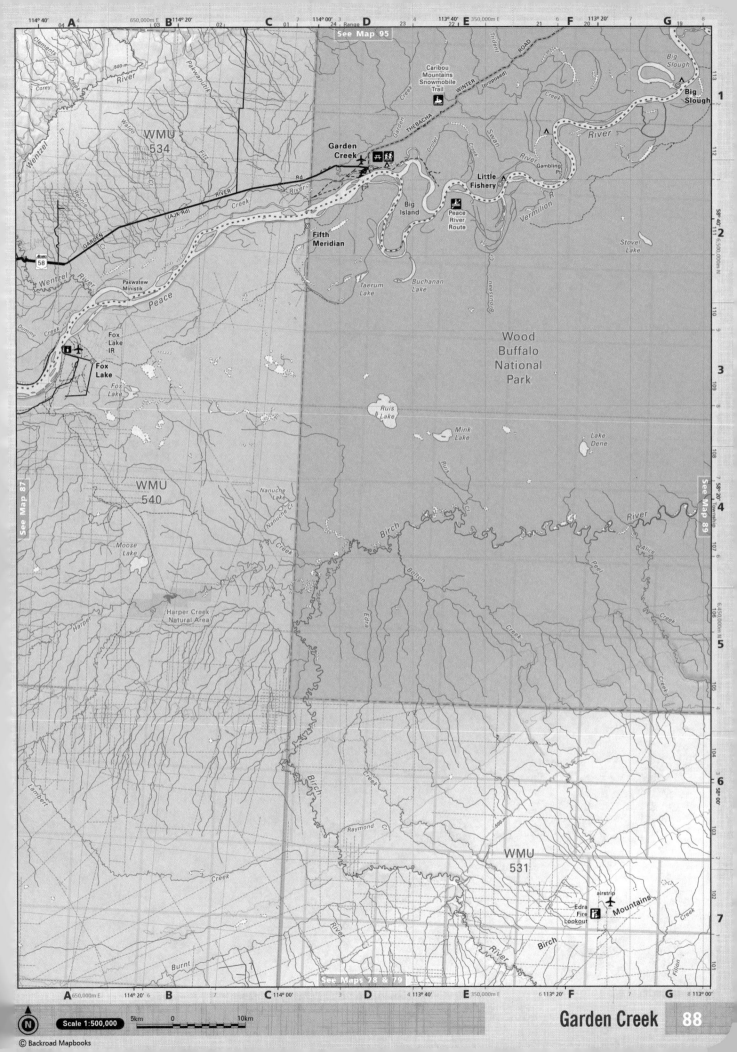

WMU 534

Garden Creek

Little Fishery

Fifth Meridian

Big Island

Peace River Route

Fox Lake IR

Fox Lake

Fox Lake

Wood Buffalo National Park

Caribou Mountains Snowmobile Trail

Gambling Pt

Big Slough

Big Slough

Stovel Lake

Ruis Lake

Mink Lake

Lake Dene

WMU 540

Nanuche Lake

Moose Lake

Harper Creek Natural Area

Birch River

WMU 531

Edra Fire Lookout

airstrip

Birch Mountains

See Map 87

See Map 89

See Maps 78 & 79

Scale 1:500,000   5km   0   10km

© Backroad Mapbooks

Garden Creek   88

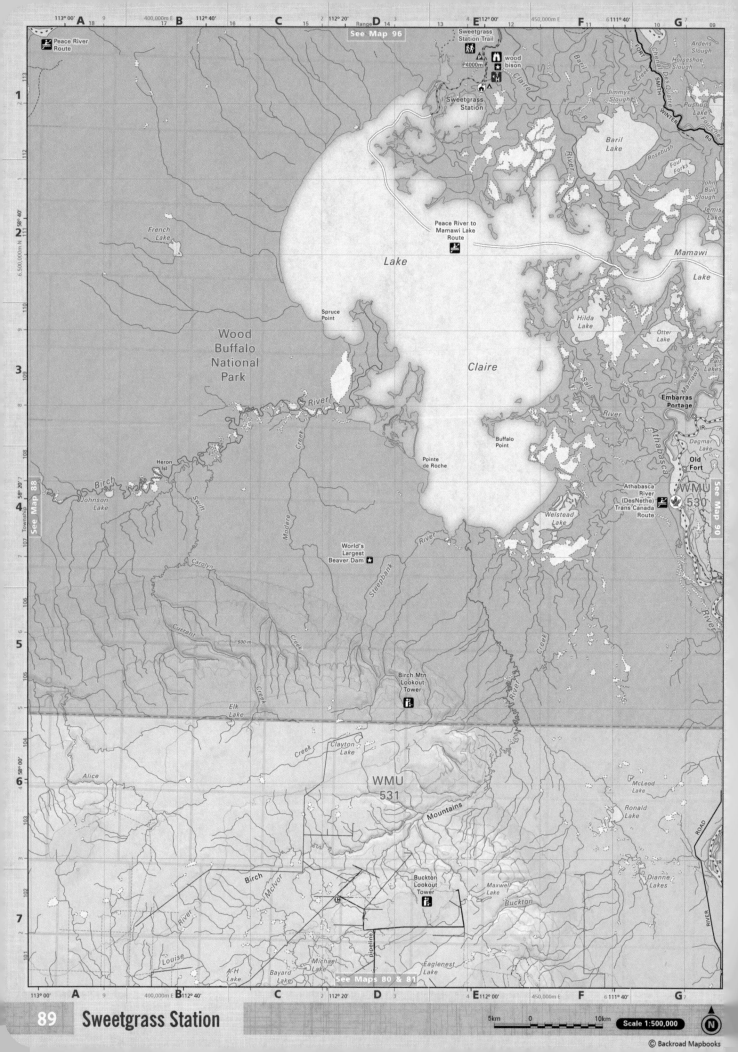

Scale 1:500,000

© Backroad Mapbooks

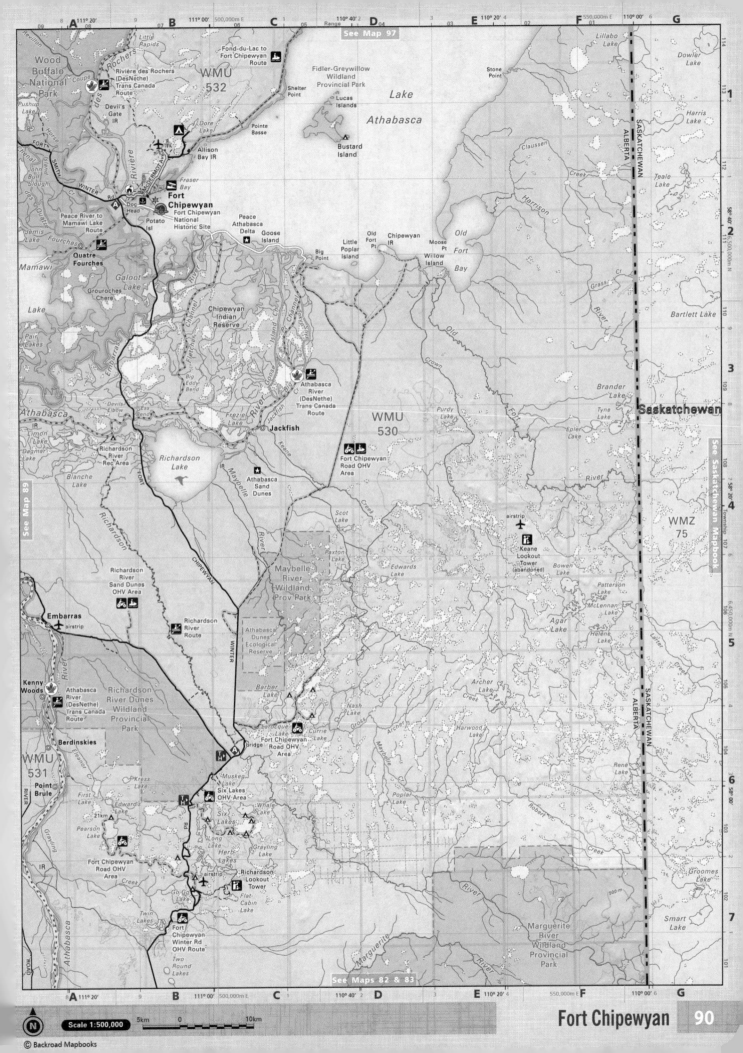

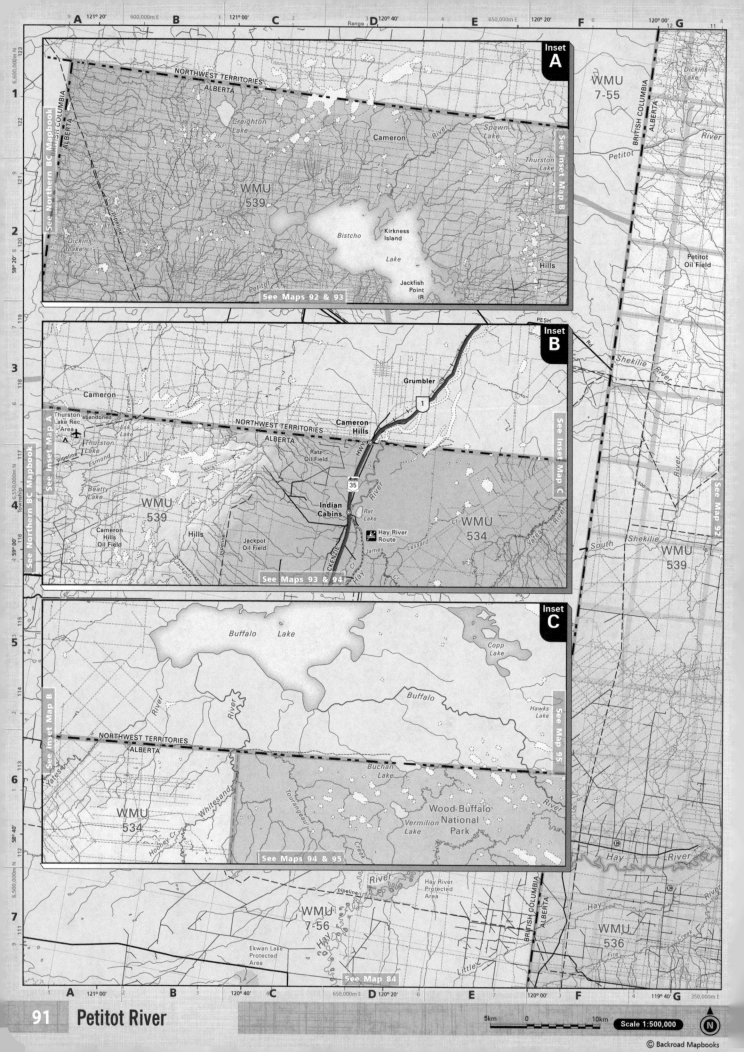

Inset **A**

See Inset Map B

Inset **B**

See Inset Map A

See Inset Map C

Inset **C**

See Inset Map B

See Map 95

See Map 92

NORTHWEST TERRITORIES
ALBERTA

Creighton Lake

Cameron

River

Spawn Lake

Thurston Lake

WMU
539

Bistcho

Kirkness
Island

Lake

Dickins Lake

Hills

Petitot

Jackfish
Point
IR

See Maps 92 & 93

WMU
7-55

Dickins Lake

BRITISH COLUMBIA
ALBERTA

Petitot

River

Petitot
Oil Field

PESH
Rd

Shekilie

River

Cameron

Creek

Thurston
Lake Rec
Area

abandoned

Grumbler

Cameron
Hills

NORTHWEST TERRITORIES
ALBERTA

Thurston Lake

Esk Lake

Esmond

Ratz
Oil Field

HWY

River

Beatty Lake

WMU
539

Hills

35

Indian
Cabins

Rat Lake

James

Lessard

Hay River
Route

WMU
534

Yates

River

Cr

South

Shekilie

WMU
539

Cameron
Hills
Oil Field

Jackpot
Oil Field

pipeline

Blackpot

Hay

Cr

MCKENZIE

See Maps 93 & 94

500 m

Buffalo   Lake

*Copp
Lake*

Buffalo

*Hawks
Lake*

River

River

NORTHWEST TERRITORIES
ALBERTA

*Buchan
Lake*

WMU
534

Yates

Whitesand

Tourangeau

Wood Buffalo
National
Park

*Vermilion
Lake*

Creek

Hooney Cr

See Maps 94 & 95

BRITISH COLUMBIA
ALBERTA

River

*Hay River
Protected
Area*

pipeline

WMU
7-56

Hay

River

Hay

River

River

WMU
536

Fire

Ekwan Lake
Protected
Area

Little

See Map 84

5km   0   10km

Scale 1:500,000

© Backroad Mapbooks

Kirkness Island

Bistcho Lake

Cameron

Hills

Jackfish Point IR

Bistcho Lake IR

gas plant
Bistcho Oil Field
airstrip

Petitot

River

airstrip

airstrip

Petitot Fire Lookout

Booths Hill

Donna

Wally Lake

airstrip

Amigo Oil Field

Elsa Lake

airstrip

Steen

Bistcho Lake OHV Route

pipeline

See Map 91

pipeline

Shekilie Oil Field

Peak Oil Field

Zama Oil Field

Larne River

See Map 93

500 m

Vardie

Zama SHEKILIE

WMU 539

gas plant

BEACH Rd

Zama City

Zama Pond

Adair Fire Lookout

Amber

Mirgo Oil Field

well disposal site

airstrip Zama Oil Field

ZAMA

Larne Oil Field

TH

Rd

well disposal site PLANT

PLANT Rd

gas plant

Omega River

Amber Oil Field

Virgo Oil Field

APACHE

Rd

Creek

Mega

airstrip

airstrip

APACHE RIVER

Dene Tha' IR

pipeline

Moody

Hay

Hay River Route

Hay

PLANT

Zama

Hay Lake

airstrip

Hay

River

Dene Tha' IR

Habay

River

River

airstrip

Lake

Chinchaga

Little Hay River

Hay-Zama Wildland Lakes Provincial Park

Dene Tha' IR

WMU 536

A

A

Nevis River

airstrip

abandoned

RGE Rd

Chateh

SOUTH ZAMA LAKE ACCESS

Assumption

Sousa Oil Field

gas plant

See Map 85

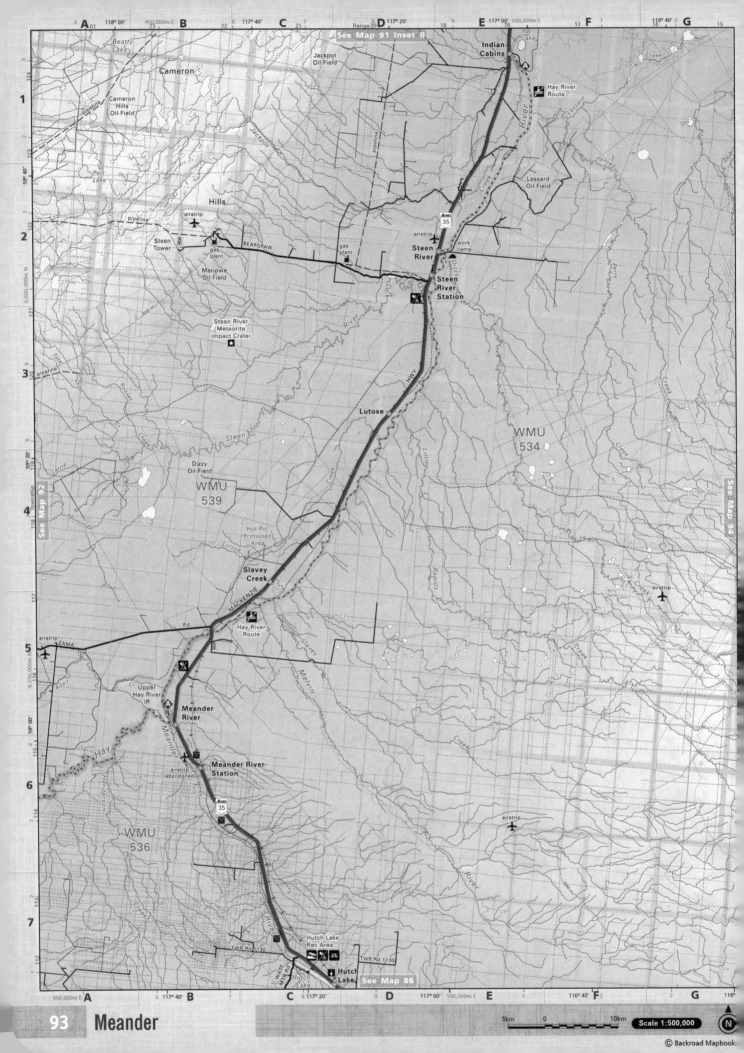

Beatty Lake

Cameron

See Map 91 Inset 8

Jackpot Oil Field

Indian Cabins

Rat Lake

Cameron Hills Oil Field

Pert Lake

Hills

airstrip

Steen Tower

gas plant

BEARSPAW

gas plant

Steen River

airstrip

work camp

35

Hay River Route

Lessard Oil Field

Marlowe Oil Field

Steen River Station

Steen River Meteorite Impact Crater

River

Rd

Lutose

HWY

WMU 534

Dizzy Oil Field

WMU 539

Creek

Rapids

Steen Creek

Hot Pol Protected Area

Lutose

Slavey Creek

MACKENZIE

Hay River Route

Rd

Slavey

Melvin

airstrip

ZAMA

airstrip

Adair

Cr Upper Hay River IR

Meander River

Meander

Creek

Hay

Henderson

Meander River Station

airstrip (abandoned)

35

WMU 536

River

airstrip

River

TWP Rd 1130

Hutch Lake Rec Area

TWP Rd 1130

WATT MTN Rd

Hutch Lake

Hutch Lake

See Map 86

See Map 92
See Map 94

5km 0 10km Scale 1:500,000 N

© Backroad Mapbook

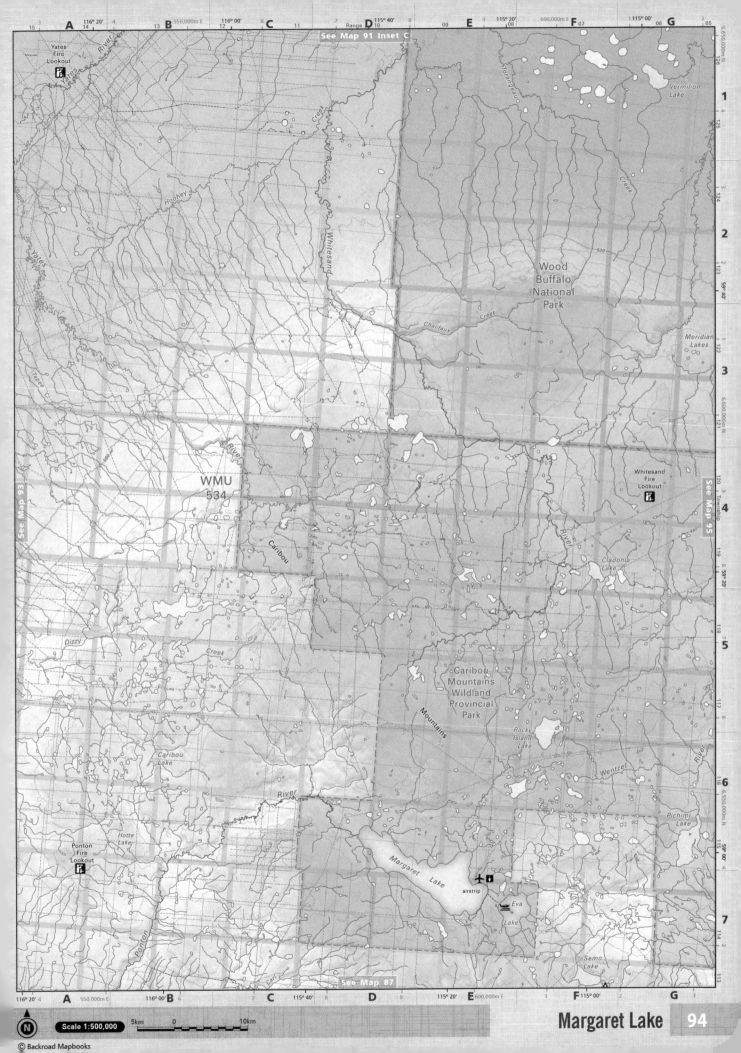

Yates Fire Lookout

Yates River

Hoosey Creek

Whitesand Creek

Tepee Cr.

Yates River

WMU 534

River

Caribou

Dizzy

Creek

Caribou Lake

River

Hotte Lake

Ponton Fire Lookout

Ponton

Carl

Chalifaux Creek

Creek

Torangeau

Wood Buffalo National Park

Vermilion Lake

Meridian Lakes

Whitesand Fire Lookout

River

Cladonia Lake

Caribou Mountains Wildland Provincial Park

Mountains

Rocky Island Lake

Wentzel River

Pichimi Lake

Margaret Lake

airstrip

Eva Lake

Semo Lake

See Map 93

See Map 95

See Map 87

N

Scale 1:500,000

5km   0   10km

© Backroad Mapbooks

Margaret Lake 94

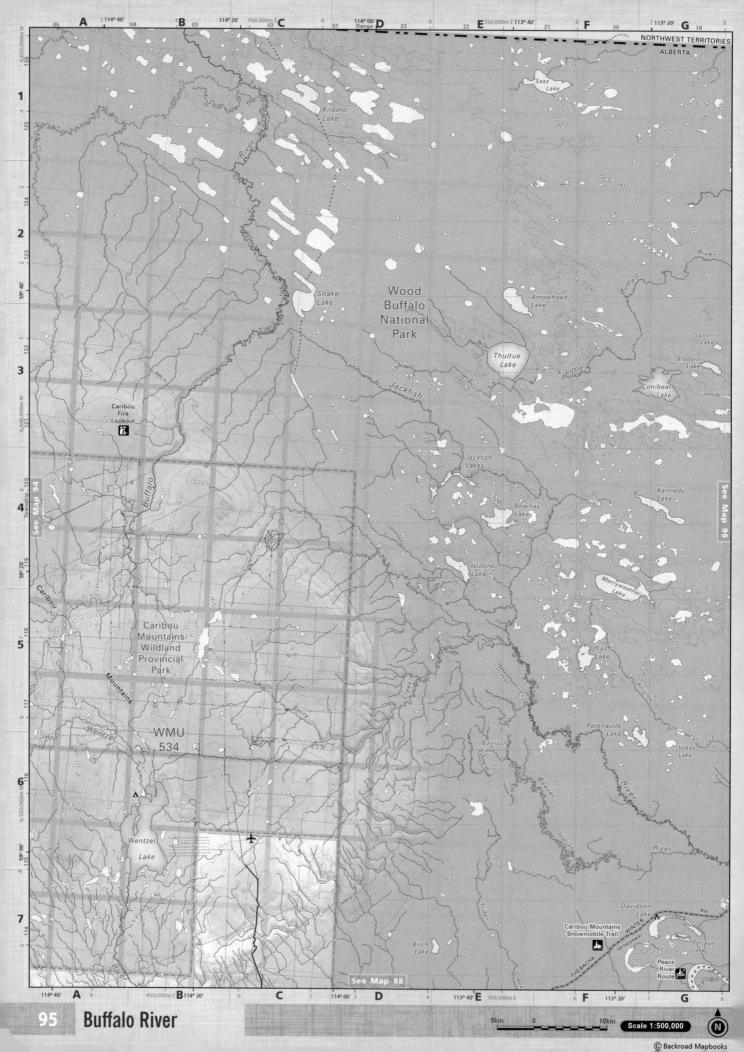

NORTHWEST TERRITORIES
ALBERTA

Sass Lake

Kilome Lake

River

Wood Buffalo National Park

Arrowhead Lake

Buffalo

Loon Lake

Snake Lake

Thultue Lake

Little

Brabant Lake

Conibear Lake

Jackfish

Caribou Fire Lookout

Jackfish Lakes

Kennedy Lake

See Map 94   See Map 96

Buffalo

Bowhay Lake

Merryweather Lake

Caribou Mountains Wildland Provincial Park

Isidore Lake

Caribou

Nash Lake

Mountains

WMU 534

Gravel Cr.

Knights

Wentzel

Berry

Patenaude Lake

Creek

Vokes Lake

Cr.

Burrisan Lake

Beaver

Wentzel Lake

Indian

River

River

Trident

Davidson Lake   Rd

Birch Lake

Caribou Mountains Snowmobile Trail

WINTER

THEBACHA

(proposed)

Portage Lake

Peace River Route

Creek

See Map 88

95 Buffalo River

5km   0   10km

Scale 1:500,000

N

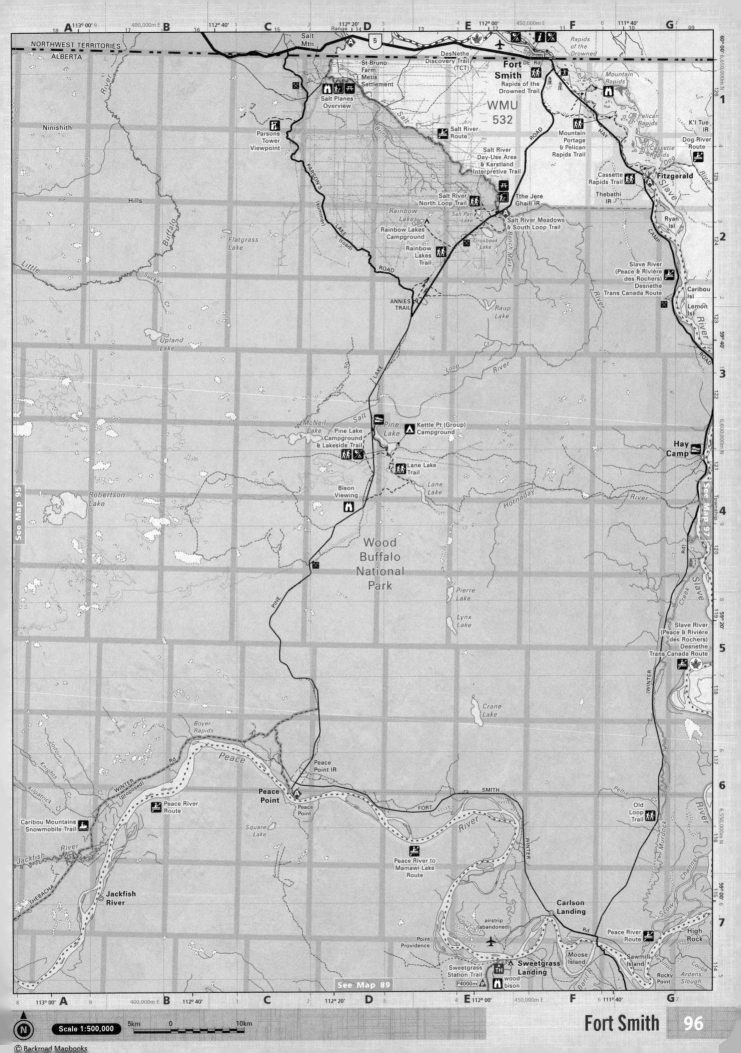

Scale 1:500,000

5km   0   10km

N

© Backroad Mapbooks

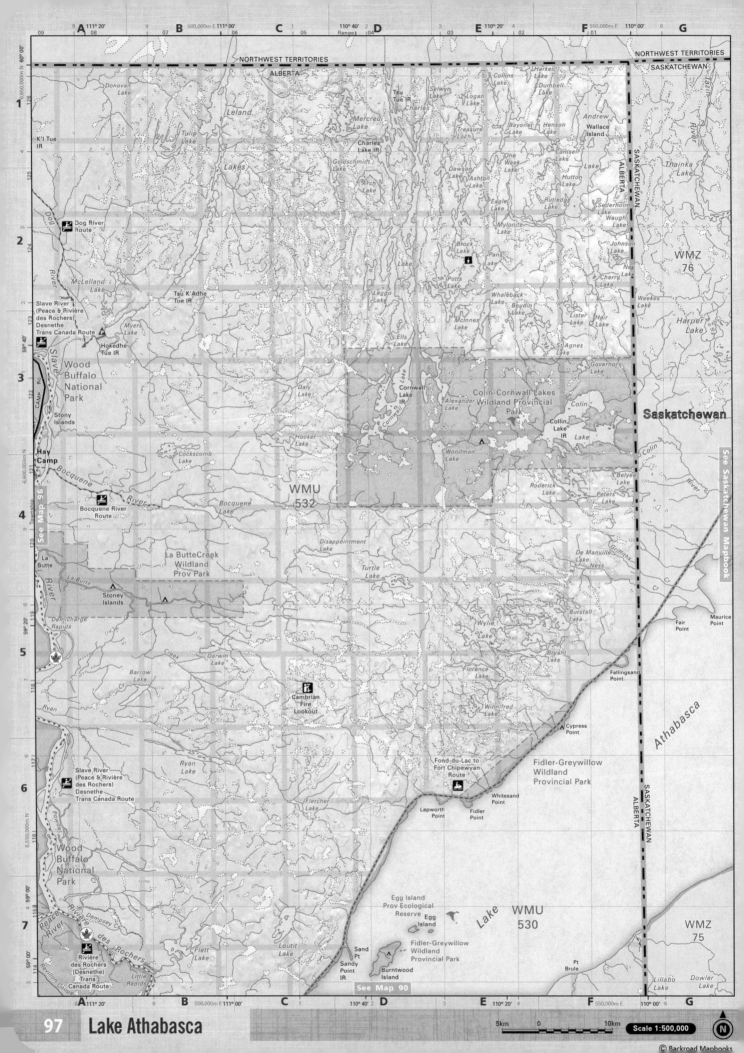

NORTHWEST TERRITORIES
ALBERTA

NORTHWEST TERRITORIES
SASKATCHEWAN

1

Donovan
Lake

K'I Tue
IR

Leland

Tulip
Lake

Lakes

Goldschmidt
Lake

Mercredi
Lake

Charles
Lake IR

Arch
Lake

Tsu
Tue IR

Charles

Selwyn
Lake

Logan
Lake

Treasure
Loch

Dawson
Lake

Ashton
Lake

Eagle
Lake

Harker
Lake

Dumbell
Lake

Collins
Lake

Bayonet
Lake

Henson
Lake

One
Week
Lake

Andrew
Wallace
Island

Camsel
Lake

Lake

Hutton
Lake

Rutledge
Lake

Thainka
Lake

Sederholm
Lake

Waugh
Lake

2

Dog River
Route

McLelland
Lake

Tsu K'Adhe
Tue IR

Myers
Lake

Lake

Leggo
Lake

Brock
Lake

Pans
Lake

Potts
Lake

Whaleback
Lake

Boudin
Lake

Johnson
Lake

Ney
Lake

Cherry
Lake

Lister
Lake

Hair
Lake

Weekes
Lake

WMZ
76

Harper
Lake

Slave River
(Peace & Rivière
des Rochers)
Desnethe
Trans Canada Route

Hokedhe
Tue IR

McInnes
Lake

Ells
Lake

St Agnes
Lake

Governor
Lake

3

Wood
Buffalo
National
Park

Stony
Islands

Hay
Camp

Bocquene
River

Cockscomb
Lake

Daly
Lake

Hooker
Lake

Cornwall
Lake IR

Cornwall

Lake

Alexander
Lake

Colin-Cornwall Lakes
Wildland Provincial
Park

Woodman
Lake

Colin

Collin
Lake
IR

Lake

Colin

Belyea
Lake

Roderick
Lake

Peters
Lake

Saskatchewan

See Saskatchewan Mapbook

4

Bocquene
River
Route

WMU
532

Bocquene
Lake

Disappointment
Lake

Turtle
Lake

De Manville
Lake
Ness

Griffiths
Cr

See Map 96

La Butte

La ButteCreek
Wildland
Prov Park

La Butte

Stoney
Islands

5

Demicharge
Rapids

Creek

Darwin
Lake

Barrow
Lake

Wylie
Lake

Florence
Lake

Bryant
Lake

Burstall
Lake

Fair
Point

Maurice
Point

Fallingsand
Point

6

Ryan

Slave River
(Peace & Rivière
des Rochers)
Desnethe
Trans Canada Route

Ryan
Lake

Cambrian
Fire
Lookout

Winnifred
Lake

Cypress
Point

Fond-du-Lac to
Fort Chipewyan
Route

Whitesand
Point

Fidler-Greywillow
Wildland
Provincial Park

7

Wood
Buffalo
National
Park

Peace
River

Rivière
des Rochers

Rivière
des Rochers
(Desnethe)
Trans
Canada Route

Little
Rapids

Flett
Lake

Fletcher
Lake

Loutit
Lake

Sand
Pt
Sandy
Point
IR

Lapworth
Point

Fidler
Point

Egg Island
Prov Ecological
Reserve

Egg
Island

Burntwood
Island

Fidler-Greywillow
Wildland
Provincial Park

Lake
WMU
530

Pt
Brule

Athabasca

ALBERTA
SASKATCHEWAN

WMZ
75

Lillabb
Lake

Dowler
Lake

See Map 90

5km · 0 · 10km
Scale 1:500,000
N

© Backroad Mapbooks

Service Directory

Find what you are looking for, from our trusted Service Directory Members.

▶ **Accommodations** ▶ **Tours & Guides** ▶ **Sales & Services**

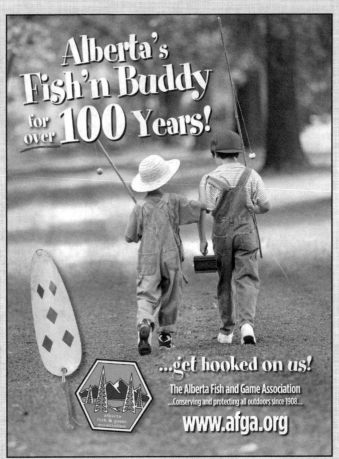

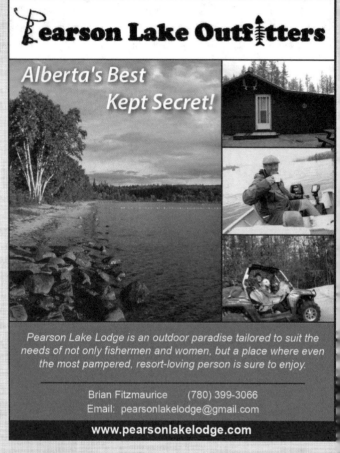
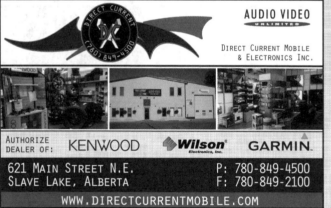

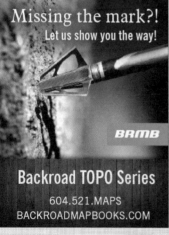

Trip Planning Notes

Adventures
Northern Alberta

The following is a how to navigate through the Adventures part of this guide. Each activity showcases countless different alternatives to help you plan your trip. We then link these adventures to the maps and surrounding area to help you discover more of the area and to better showcase all there is to experience.

▶ Adventure Summary

For each Adventure section we have provided a quick overview summary of that activity as it pertains to the region. This write-up will give you a feel for what the region has to offer as well as a better understanding of what the given area offers relative to that particular activity.

▶ Listing & Descriptions

Each Adventure section is made up of countless listings and descriptions of different activities. From a great fishing spot, recreation site or park to visit, to a great trail, natural attraction or area to explore. Each guidebook offers endless possibilities when it comes to planning your next adventure.

Sarah Point (Map 46/A5)
Sarah Point marks the northern tip of Malaspina Peninsula. It is a good spot for fishing because fish entering Desolation Sound must pass by the point. There are some wintering Chinook but the main fishery is from May and June for Chinook and late August to early September for Coho. Trolling around the point seems to work the best.

Thacker Regional Park (Map 15/F6)
Found in Hope, this 9 hectare park is home to a new spawning channel, built in 2001 for Coho, pink and chum salmon. The trail along the channel is partof the Trans Canada Trail and is very popular in fall when the salmon spawn. In summer, there is a popular swimming hole at the confluence of Sucker Creek and the Coquihalla River.

▶ Activities

Another great feature many of our listings have is the symbols that showcase the numerous activities that can be done on the trail or in the area. Most of the symbols are easy to decipher, but the Legend on Page VII provides a description for each symbol.

▶ Map references/navigating

Probably the most popular feature of each listing is the map reference that tells you where to find and explore these great adventures on our maps.

Cheam Peak (Map 5/A3)
Cheam is one of the most prominent peaks in the Fraser Valley. How far you have to ski depends on how high you can get a vehicle up the Chipmunk Creek Forest Service Road to the south. At the base of Cheam Peak is a lovely open meadow and the ascent, while stiff, isn't too difficult. Nearby Knight Peak is another popular ski destination.

Backroad
Adventures

With a small number of primary highways, and vast areas where few roads appear if any at all, northern Alberta can be a challenge to explore. Those willing to trek into the backcountry will find stretches of wilderness where people rarely set foot. Many of these spaces lie beyond any backroads, and will require a float plane, month-long canoe trip, extensive hiking excursion, or multi-day ATV trek to discover.

Closer to civilization you will find many historic settlements and sights to see. In fact, some of Alberta's oldest settlements appear in and around Fort McMurray in the east and Fort Vermillion, closer to the BC border, in the west.

The majority of the roads are in the southwest section of this mapbook, south of Peace River. This area has a number of interesting settlements and Backroad Attractions to explore. Heading north, Highway 63 connects Edmonton to the booming oil sands city of Fort McMurray. From there it is a short distance to Fort McKay. This is as far north as you can go – in summer. In winter, a road is built to Fort Chipewyan, and from there, to Fort Smith in the Northwest Territories. The winter road is usually open from mid-December to mid-March. Contact the Municipality of Wood Buffalo for more information before you go, at (780) 697-3600.

In Alberta, there are three primary user groups for unpaved backroads: forestry, oil and gas, and farming. Conditions on gravel roads can vary with the time of year, the weather, and the amount of traffic. Even the best gravel roads can become impassable to two-wheel (and sometimes four-wheel) drive vehicles during the spring or after a lot of rain. Generally, main haul logging roads are in good condition, while smaller secondary roads can become impassable due to lack of maintenance. Oil and gas exploration roads are similar to forestry roads, but they have a tendency to disappear at a moment's notice. Oil and gas exploration in the region continues unabated and new roads are constantly built, while old ones get deactivated or removed all together. Finally, there are roads developed for farming. These tend to be laid out in a logical grid pattern, allowing farmers to access their fields. While the roads are predictable, where they lead to is not. On occasion, rivers and lakes interrupt the roads' straight lines, making good destinations for backroad travellers.

Wherever you go, make sure you are equipped accordingly – Mother Nature can be fierce and unforgiving in northern Alberta.

Adam Ranch (Map 17/E2)

Adam Ranch is Canada's largest and most famous buffalo/bison ranch located in the heart of Alberta's Peace Country. The Adam Ranch sprawls across 7,284 hectares (18,000 acres) of pristine rivers, forests and grasslands, near Grande Prairie. Accommodation is arranged in the ranch bunkhouse, with wood stove, a bathroom with running water, and a TV. Recreational activities are steer-riding, hunting, boating, riding bucking horses and bulls, bull dogging, roping, and ladies barrel racing. Sleigh rides and dog team rides are available in snow season. Meals are provided. For general information call 780-814-5618 or Toll Free: 866-232-6283.

Amber Valley (Map 10/G3)

Let's be honest. Alberta's settlement history is very Eurocentric. Yes, there were large groups of Ukrainians and other non-English speaking Europeans, but they were almost all European. There were a few notable exceptions, though, and Amber Valley is one of the most notable. In 1911, a group of black settlers from Oklahoma made their way to Amber Valley, braving the harsh northern Alberta climate to build a community that was the largest community of Black people in the province until the 1930s. These days, about 100 people live in the area.

Athabasca Oil Sands (Maps 67–70, 80–83)

Suncor Energy and Syncrude Canada are the engines that drive Fort McMurray's–and to a lesser extent, Alberta's–economy. The Athabasca Oil Sands are the largest oil deposit in the world, with up to 2.5 trillion barrels of heavy oil. From May to September, you can take an "Experience the Energy" tour of one of these two mine sites and learn more about the process of extracting oil from sand.

Athabasca Riverfront (Map 10/C3)

The town of Athabasca is built on the site of Athabasca Landing, which was the terminus of the overland route from Edmonton to the Athabasca River. Established by the Hudson Bay Company in 1877, the landing became a trading post in 1884, and later, a boomtown known as "the Gateway to the north". Originally built as an alternate route from Fort Edmonton and Fort Assiniboine, the route soon became the main trade route to the north. Travellers and goods would be loaded onto watercraft, including steamboats, which would take passengers and freight. During the gold rush thousands of people descended on the landing. Prospectors would build their own boats to take down the Athabasca, then up the Peace River. It was a difficult journey, and only about 160 people actually reached Dawson. About 35 died on the way, and the rest turned back. Many chose to settle here as boat builders and the landing continued as one of the busiest inland ports in the province until the area was bypassed during the construction of the railway.

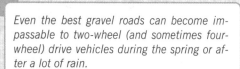

Even the best gravel roads can become impassable to two-wheel (and sometimes four-wheel) drive vehicles during the spring or after a lot of rain.

Athabasca Sand Dunes (Map 90)

Stretched out along Lake Athabasca and the Athabasca River is the world's largest area of active sand dunes north of 58 degrees. The dunes cross over into Saskatchewan, and are mostly difficult to access, as there is no road access to these dunes. They can get to 30 metres (98 feet) high, and stretch over 100 km (60 miles). While most sand dunes are associated with deserts, these most certainly are not. Instead, they are quite wet, bordering one of Canada's largest lakes, with a very shallow water table. In places, the dunes run right up against the boreal forest, creating a dramatic transition. South of the main dunes are series of more dunes along the Athabasca River, stretching as far as Fort Assiniboine. One of the most impressive is the dunes in the Athabasca Dunes Ecological Reserve, which can be accessed by ATV, then hiking in.

Beaverlodge Beaver (Map 16/B1)

Just west of Grande Prairie off Highway 43 you will find the little town of Beaverlodge. If you are on a road trip looking for wacky photo opportunities, you have come to the right place. Remind yourself once again that beavers are vegetarians as you approach this 5 metre (15 foot) tall behemoth that weighs over 1,350 kg (3,000 lbs). Sure, it's a tourist trap, but really, how much more Canadian can you get than a giant beaver?

Boreal Centre for Bird Conservation (Map 22/C2)

Found within the Lesser Slave Lake Bird Observatory, the Boreal Centre for Bird Conservation (BCBC) is the only educational and research facility in the world strategically located to study boreal birds on their breeding grounds. The centre offers 6,000 square feet of indoor and outdoor exhibits, interpretive programming, a gift shop, and office space. It also provides research space and computer work stations for staff, volunteers, and visiting researchers and educators. A research laboratory and accommodation at The Nest are available for researcher use. Visit www.borealbirdcentre.ca or call (780) 849-8240 for more information.

Centre of Alberta (Map 8/A6)

Ever wondered where the exact centre of Alberta is? Roy Chimiuk (worked 20 years as a surveyor) wanted to know as well and started a "Journey to the Centre of Alberta". Calculating Alberta's measurements vertically and horizontally, Roy was able to determine the exact location. Finding the exact location wasn't difficult, cutting a 5 km (3.1 mile) trail through rugged terrain and thick boreal forest was a gruelling task however. Today, the hike takes you along a beautifully maintained trail to an opening where artist Horst Lutz has created a stone statue of a grizzly cub sitting upon a cairn.

Fort Chipewyan (Map 90/B2)

Fort Chip is Alberta's oldest settlement, established as a trading post by Peter Pond of the North West Company in 1788. The fort was named after the Chipewyan people living in the area and is one of the most remote communities in the entire province. In summer, the only way to get there is by water, or more likely by air. In winter, a long, lonely winter road runs north from Fort McMurray and beyond. It is located on the western tip of Lake Athabasca, adjacent to Wood Buffalo National Park, approximately 223 km (139 miles) north of Fort McMurray.

Fort Dunvegen (Map 45/D7)

Nestled in the scenic Peace River Valley, Fort Dunvegan was established in 1805 by North West Company fur trader Archibald Norman McLeod, who named it after Dunvegan Castle in Scotland. A trio of buildings from the old Hudson's Bay trading post have been restored and features costumed interpreters who will take you through the Rectory of the Oblate missionary, the St. Charles Mission Church and the Factor's house. Dunvegan is an unincorporated community located 26 km south of the town of Fairview on the northern bank of the Peace River at the mouth of the Dunvegan Creek. While in the area, make sure to drive Alberta's longest vehicle suspension bridge where Highway 2 crosses the Peace River.

Fort McMurray Marine Park Museum (Map 68/A1)

The museum is a 1 hectare (4 acre) site located along the Clearwater River in Fort McMurray that is home to the last remaining shipyard in the entire province. Showcasing numerous ships, the Radium Scout, the Miskanaw Barge, the Dredge 250, the Kris, the McMurray, a Fuel Barge, and the Northern Alberta Railway Trains, visitors will find vessels that were an integral part of river transportation up and down the Clearwater and Athabasca Rivers. Passengers and freight were transferred at this very site destined for the north by the very ships found here today. For guided tours, admission costs and general inquiries contact visit www.fortmcmurrayhistory.com or call 780-791-7575.

Fort Vermilion Heritage Centre (Map 87/B3)

The first trading post along the Peace River was in Fort Vermilion back in 1788 when the earliest settlers arrived. After the bicentennial in 1988, it was deemed that all the history of the area should be commemorated, thus the Fort Vermilion Heritage Centre was constructed. The grand opening was in 1995 with visitors from all over Canada viewing the many displays and archives. Colourful furs, prehistoric bison bones, pictures and archives plus a log cabin built in 1923 are just some of the exhibits here. The centre blends together the past and the present so visitors can see and feel the diverse culture and history along the Peace River. Open from June thru September, this heritage centre provides free admission, however donations are greatly appreciated. Go to www.fortvermilionheritage.ca for information.

Kimiwan Birdwalk and Interpretive Centre (Map 33/F4)

The Kimiwan Birdwalk and Interpretive Centre is located south of Kimiwan Lake on the west side of McLennan, adjacent to Highway 2. A bird watchers paradise, there are gravel paths and raised wooden walkways to view over 200 species of birds spotted in the area. Along the lake, a variety of shorebird and waterfowl species dot the wetlands and the man-made ponds. In the interpretive centre, you will find a unique herbarium collection of local flora, a bird migration display and computer access to various unique birding files. Visit www.kimiwanbirdwalk.ca for more information.

Kleskun Hill (Map 17/C1)

Kleskun Hill sits 20 km northeast of Grand Prairie off Highway 43. This eroded remnant of a prehistoric river delta looks like a miniature of the massive badlands around Drumheller and protects one of the largest pieces of native grassland remaining in the Grande Prairie Region. Kles-Kun is believed to mean, "white mud" in one of the areas native languages and is believed to be an area where the very first settlers picked berries and hunted back in the 1800's.

If you plan to travel through remote areas it is imperative that you leave a detailed itinerary with friends or family.

Lac La Biche Mission National Historic Site (Map 12/A3)

Located 10 km west of the town of Lac La Biche, this National Historic Site is set on an isolated flat surrounded by fields at the south end of Lac La Biche. There are three main buildings, a rectory, a convent and a church on the site and all three are still in use by the local community. The Notre Dame des Victories/Lac La Biche Mission was established in 1853 by the Oblates. It was originally located near the Hudson's Bay company trading post but was moved to its present location in 1855. It became the hub of an important portage route that ran overland from St. Boniface to the mission and from the Athabasca-Mackenzie river system to Fort Good Hope.

La Crete Ferry (Map 86/C5)

Crossing the Peace River at Tompkins Landing (approximately 70 km south of High Level on Secondary Highway 697) on the ferry will take you through the integral part of the Pioneer Drive Loop through La Crete, Fort Vermilion and back down Highway 35 to High Level. The ferry is one of just two ferries still operating in the province of Alberta and runs 24 hours a day, 7 days a week. It can accommodate large trucks, semis and RV's but, from time to time, the ferry will not operate during periods of thick fog or dangerous water levels. In the winter, the ferry is replaced by an ice bridge as the river ice is thickened and the surface is maintained. Be aware that during freeze up (November – December) and melt down (April – May) the river is impassable. Check the La Crete Chamber of Commerce website at www.lacretechamber.com for ferry operation times and closures. Ferry wait times are 15 minutes round trip.

La Crete Mennonite Heritage Village (Map 86/G4)

Mennonite families were the first settlers here in 1936 and the Le Crete Mennonite Heritage Village depicts the buildings and lifestyle as more and more families migrated to this part of Northern Alberta. The museum village consists of 30 buildings spread over 4 hectares (10 acres) on the original homestead of Henry H. & Susanna Peters. The museum village displays the agricultural lifestyle of the early settlers and includes a shop, a school, flour mill, homes, barns and a saw mill. Open from June thru September from 10:00 AM to 4:00 PM weekdays, admission is free. Donations are appreciated.

Lesser Slave Lake Bird Observatory (Map 22/C1)

Approximately a 2 hour drive northwest of Edmonton on the east shoreline of Lesser Slave Lake, the Lesser Slave Lake Bird Observatory is found in the provincial park. Researchers have established that Lesser Slave Lake and nearby Marten Mountain towering at 1,020 metre (3,200 feet), acts as a natural barrier to migratory birds. These two barriers create a natural funnel along the shores of the lake for migrating birds. While in the area, be sure to check out the Boreal Centre for Bird Conservation, which is the only educational and research facility in the world strategically located to study boreal birds on their breeding grounds.

Peace Athabasca Delta (Map 90/B2)

Okay, so the only way here is by boat or plane. But this is truly one of Alberta's natural wonders; it's one of the largest freshwater deltas in the world, where two of Alberta's three largest rivers meet. In the spring and fall it sees hundreds of thousands of birds from all four major North American migrations.

Sexsmith Blacksmith Shop Museum (Map 31/A7)

While it isn't as old as Fort Chipewyan, Sexsmith is one of the oldest settlements in Northwestern Alberta. Explore that history in a unique way at this fully restored historic site, originally built in 1916. There are over 10,000 artefacts here, but more important, this is a working smithy, where you can watch the blacksmiths at work.

South Peace Centennial Museum (Map 16/B1)

Found just north of Beaverlodge, this charming pioneer village focuses on the agricultural history of this region, featuring hundreds of restored antique tractors, rare steam engines, stationary engines, horse drawn wagons, carriages and antique automobiles. Stroll through a working pioneer village, where you can watch interpreters make soap, butter or rope, card wool, render lard, separate milk the old fashioned way and even bake bread in a clay oven. Visit www.spcm.ca for more information.

Sweetgrass Station (Map 89/E1)

Found in extreme Northern Alberta within the Wood Buffalo National Park, this abandoned bison station was first used in 1957 to corral bison for disease testing and meat slaughter. Today, the remains are mainly historic buildings and corrals to explore in the expansive meadows and surrounding marshlands which are a haven for bird watchers and nature enthusiasts. The route to Sweetgrass Station from Sweetgrass Landing (on the south bank of Peace River) used to be a rough road used for bison management, but now there is a rough, difficult trail that sees more wild bison than humans these days. The 12 km (7.2 mile) trail can only be accessed by water, either by canoe or floatplane and can be difficult to track at times. Only experienced hikers with proper equipment should try this rugged hike. Tenting is permitted in the meadows, which is a good camp for visitors to explore the area from.

The Signing of Treaty No. 8 Historical Site (Map 20/D1)

Spurred by the discovery of gold in the Yukon in 1896, and growing agricultural settlement in the region, Treaty Number 8 was one of a series of treaties the federal government made with the First Nations of Canada. This treaty was first signed on 21 June 1899 at the western end of Lesser Slave Lake. The First Nations who signed were promised reserves, education, medicines, annual payments, farm equipment, stock, seed, and ammunition, along with the freedom to hunt, fish and trap and other rights. The Treaty Commission also traveled with a Scrip Commission which issued certificates called scrip to area Métis. These certificates entitled the bearer to either 240 acres of land or $240 towards the purchase of land. A blue highway sign signifying this important piece of Canadian history can be found on the north side of Highway 2, about 15 km east of High Prairie.

World's Largest Beaver Dam (Map 89/D4)

If you are looking to travel to a location only one other person appears to have ever visited, it could be the World's Largest Beaver Dam in Wood Buffalo National Park. The dam is roughly 850 metre (2,790 ft) long and can actually be seen on Google Earth. Located approximately 190 km from Fort McMurray, do not expect an easy trip. You will need to take a boat from Fort Chipewyan to the edge of Lac Clair. From there, it is a 16 km trek through thick foliage, muskeg and swamp. And oh yes, there are plenty of mosquitoes. Once you arrive, don't expect the welcome wagon, this beaver seems to really enjoy his solitude.

Fishing
Adventures

Northern Alberta is an angler's paradise. Alberta has very few fish bearing lakes, but many of them are found north of Edmonton. In fact, on these maps you will find 75% of all of Alberta's lakes (measured by surface area) and nearly half of all the fish-bearing lakes. That's the good news. The bad news is that many of these lakes have no road access. Some can be accessed by off-road vehicles, but dozens of Alberta's best fishing lakes can only be accessed by floatplane.

From big lakes (Alberta's five largest lakes are found on these maps) to small lakes, northern Alberta will certainly not disappoint. In fact, some of the smaller lakes in the Peace River Region rank among the best rainbow trout destinations in Canada. However, there are also many lakes in the area that do not contain fish, for a variety of reasons. Some are too shallow and are subject to winterkill. Some are too alkaloid for the fish to survive. Chances are, if a lake is not written up here, it does not hold fish, but you can always check with Alberta Sustainable Resources to confirm.

With all the attention lakes get in the north, anglers looking to fish moving water will be surprised by the breadth and variety the area has to offer. From small, mountain streams to large, slow moving rivers that resemble lakes, there is a stream to suit every wish. In most streams, the spring runoff begins to peak in mid-May and continues into June. It is best to wait until the end of May to begin fishing. In any event, the fishing regulations in place now prevent fishing in streams and rivers from November 1 until May 31 or June 15 depending on the area. This closure helps protect spawning fish and helps keep anglers off the ice, which is usually dangerously thin.

There are also many streams that do not hold game fish. As you move away from the mountains, the rivers are often slow moving and murky and hold little water in the summer. Oftentimes, these rivers have beaver dams, which prevent fish from spawning. In other streams, the water is either too warm, too shallow or does not hold enough oxygen to support game fish. You will sometimes find fish near the confluence of a larger stream; they usually are not native to the smaller stream, but just visiting.

Note that some of the lakes and rivers through this area have contamination warnings. These include Chrystina, Edith and Muskwa Lakes, as well as a variety of rivers in the Athabasca and Peace drainages. Check the regulations for specific information.

Fishing Adventures

Lake Fishing

Agar Lake (Map 90/F5)
North of the Marguerite River and east of the Richardson Dunes, there is a spray of lakes, scattered across the landscape. Some of these lakes are road accessible. Others, like Agar Lake, are only accessible by air. The lake is found very close to the Saskatchewan boundary. It is home to good populations of whitefish and pike.

Alexander Lake (Map 97/E3)
East of Wood Buffalo National Park and north of Lake Athabasca are hundreds of lakes that offer some great fishing for those willing to fly-in for it. Alexander Lake is one of those lakes, offering some great fishing for some reasonably large pike. This lake is open all year and has special retention limits here.

Albright Lake (Map 29/E4)
Albright Lake is found northwest of Beaverlodge and offers decent fishing for northern pike. Open year round, there are special limits for pike here.

Amisk Lake (Map 11/C5)
This long, narrow lake is located southwest of North Buck Lake. It holds northern pike to 4.5 kg (10 lbs), walleye to 2.5 kg (5 lbs) and plenty of small perch. You will also find lake whitefish and burbot. The lake is closed to angling in the spring and there is currently a zero retention limit on the pike and walleye.

Andrew Lake (Map 97/F1)
About as remote a lake as you can get in Alberta, Andrew Lake is located in the far northeastern corner of the province. Access here is by plane with most visitors taking advantage of the lodge on the lake. The biggest pike pulled out of these waters weighed 17 kg (37.5 lbs) and fish in the 13 kg/30 lb range are not unheard of. Lake trout also grow pretty big here, getting to 17.5 kg (38 lbs). Anglers will also find whitefish and yellow perch but should check the regulations as there is a bait ban and special retention limits here.

Antoine Lake (Map 12/A3)
Located 10 km east of the town of Lac La Biche, this mid-sized lake is easily accessed from Highways 55 or 663. It holds good sized northern pike and yellow perch.

Arch Lake (Map 97/D2)
One of the literally hundreds of lakes that are north of Lake Athabasca, Arch Lake offers great fishing for those willing to go through the trouble to fly-in. The lake is home to some large northern pike (over 60 cm/23 inches) and yellow perch. The lake is open year round and only 3 pike over 63 cm (25 in) may be kept.

Archer Lake (Map 90/E5)
This fly-in lake is located just outside of Wood Buffalo National Park. It holds northern pike, yellow perch and whitefish. There are special restrictions on this lake including no fishing during the spring and generous limits.

Ashton Lake (Map 97/E2)
A fly-in lake located just outside of Wood Buffalo National Park, Ashton holds plenty of big trout, northern pike, yellow perch as well as good numbers of lake whitefish. The lake is open year round; check the regulations for retention limits.

Atlantic Richfield Dam (Map 7/E2) 🎣
Located 23 km north of Swan Hills off Highway 33, the holding ponds for this dam contain stocked rainbow trout. The trout are catchable as they are about 18 cm (7 in) in size when they are stocked.

Baptiste Lake (Map 10/A3)
There are a number of summer cottages as well as a recreation area with campsite and boat launch around this mid-size lake, west of Athabasca. The fishing pressure is heavy, but it can still produce some big northern pike, up to 9 kg (20 lbs). It also holds walleye, yellow perch, lake whitefish and burbot. Check the regulations for the spring closed season and special retention limits.

Barbara Lake (Map 13/F6)
Located northwest of La Corey off Range Road 62, this mid-sized lake is home to northern pike; currently you can keep three over 63 cm (25 in).

Barber Lake (Map 90/C5)
A remote lake found on the boundary of the Maybelle River Wildland Park. The river is accessible by air and by ATV. The lake holds northern pike, walleye and whitefish.

Barrow Lake (Map 97/B5)
This fly-in fishing lake is part of the Ryan Creek system that drains into the Slave River. The lake is reported to offer excellent fishing for walleye and northern pike. The latter can get up to 11.5 kg (25 lbs). Whitefish and cisco are also present but no cisco may be retained. Check the regulations for the spring closed season and other retention limits.

Base Lake (Map 40/D6)
Base Lake is located west of Highway 63, smack dab in the middle of nowhere. Access to this lake is limited. It holds northern pike to 2 kg (5 lbs), walleye, as well as plenty of yellow perch and lake whitefish. Check the regulations for spring closures and special retention limits.

Bayonet Lake (Map 97/E1)
A fly-in lake located in the far northeastern corner of the province, Bayonet is open all year for northern pike, lake trout, yellow perch and lake whitefish. Check the regulations for special retention limits.

Behan Lake (Map 26/F4)
This remote fishing lake is found west of Secondary Highway 881. It is home to good numbers of yellow perch, as well as northern pike to 72 cm (28 in). Access to this lake is best left to the winter; however, it may be possible to access the lake after a long period of dry weather. The lake is subject to winterkill.

Berry Lake (Map 36/E2)
There is no road access to Berry Lake, but when it is dry enough the lake can be accessed by ATV. However, it is much more common to visit this one in winter on a snowmobile. The lake is home to northern pike and yellow perch. Check the regulations for retention limits.

Beaver Lake (Map 12/C3)
Located near Lac La Biche, this lake is a popular fishing destination. The lake has two basins, both with an average depth of between 6 and 9 m (18–30 ft). A very shallow section that can only be passed by boats with a very shallow hull separates the two sections. There are a number of islands, some of which barely poke out of the water (and in high water, don't), so caution is advised. The lake holds northern pike, walleye, yellow perch, lake whitefish and burbot. Watch for special retention limits.

Big Chief Lake (Map 26/E4)
Located just north of the tiny settlement of Philomena, the lake holds good numbers of northern pike and yellow perch. Watch for the spring closure and special retention limits here.

Bistcho Lake (Map 92/E1–98 Inset A)
Bistcho Lake, in the far northwest corner of Alberta, is one of Alberta's biggest lakes. It covers 413 sq. km (159.5 sq. miles). Like most big lakes, it produces big fish, with northern pike up to 14 kg (30 lbs) and lake whitefish and walleye to 4 kg (8 lbs). Walleye have been stocked in large number in the past. Access is fly-in in summer (there is a rough, sometimes impassable ATV route, too) or by snowmobile in winter. The lake is 85 km north of Zama City. There is a private lodge (Tapawingo Lodge) on the lake. Check the regulations for several special restrictions here.

Blackett Lake (Map 12/F3)
Located in Lakeland Provincial Park, Blackett Lake holds northern pike, walleye, yellow perch, lake whitefish and burbot. There are lots of pike but they are small and good-sized walleye here. The lake is accessed by a 10 km long multi-use trail. In winter, most people get to the lake by ATV.

Blanche Lake (Map 90/A4)
The winter road (which can be ridden by ATVs in the summer) runs to within about 5 km of Blanche Lake. Unfortunately, the lake is on the other side of the Richardson River, which could prove problematic to get across. Most people fly-in to the lake, where you will find northern pike to 4.5 kg (10 lbs), walleye to 2.5 kg (5 lbs) and lots of perch. Watch for spring closures and special retention limits.

Blue Lake (Map 20/B6) 🎣
This hard to access lake is found south of High Prairie at the end of a road that you don't want to be on if it's been raining. The lake has good ice fishing (and the road is usually easier to navigate in winter), even although it can be prone to winterkill. Anglers should find feisty rainbow trout that get up to 2 kg (4 lbs). The trout are stocked on a regular basis. Anglers will also find some northern pike, yellow perch and lake whitefish. Watch for spring closures.

Bocquene Lake (Map 97/B4)
This long, narrow lake can be accessed by canoeing across the Slave River from Hay Camp, then upstream on the Bocquene River to the lake during spring when the water is high enough. Most people fly-in instead. The lake has northern pike, walleye, lake trout, yellow perch and lake whitefish. Watch for special retention limits.

Bolloque Lake (Map 9/G6)
Found south of Secondary Highway 663, to the southwest of Athabasca, Bolloque Lake is home to both pike and perch. See the regulations for special limits and seasonal closures.

Bowen Lake (Map 90/F5)
One of about a billion lakes scattered throughout the mixed boreal forest/sand dunes south of Lake Athabasca, Bowen Lake is one of the biggest of the group. It is home to northern pike, yellow perch and lake whitefish. The lake is fly-in only.

Boyle Fishing Pond (Map 11/A5)
This small pond is found 5 km south of Boyle along Secondary Highway 831. It is stocked annually with rainbow trout.

Brander Lake (Map 90/G3)
Located very near the Saskatchewan boundary, Brander Lake is one of the many small, fly-in lakes scattered south of Lake Athabasca. The shallow lake holds some pretty large pike.

Brintnell Lake (Map 36/E4)
Found east of Nipisi Lake, you are best to wait until the muskeg freezes in winter to access this one...the cutlines leading into this area tend to be quite marshy in summer. Anglers will find northern pike to 4.5 kg (10 lbs), as well as perch and lake whitefish. Watch for spring closures and special retention limits.

Bryant Lake (Map 97/F5)
This fly-in lake is located a few kilometres north of Cypress Point on Lake Athabasca. It has good fishing for big northern pike and lake trout, as well as scrappy yellow perch and lake whitefish. This lake is open year round but watch for special retention limits.

Buffalo Bay (Map 34/E6)
While officially a part of Lesser Slave Lake, Buffalo Bay is really its own lake, joined to the main lake by a wide channel. The fishing here is different than in the main lake, too. Most notably the catches are smaller. However, with northern pike to 7 kg (15 lbs), walleye to 4.5 kg (10 lbs), lake whitefish to 2.5 kg (5 lbs) yellow perch to 0.5 kg (1 lb), these fish are nothing to sneeze at. Check the regulations under Lesser Slave Lake for special restrictions.

Burnt Lake (Map 11/F4)
Burnt Lake offers average fishing for northern pike, walleye and yellow perch. The lake is found east of Boyle to the north of Secondary Highway 663.

Burnt Lakes (Map 78/F6)
These two lakes are located smack dab in the middle of nowhere. Access into the lakes is by air only. They hold northern pike to 4.5 kg (10 lbs) and lake whitefish to 3 kg (6 lbs). Check the regulations for spring closures and special retention limits.

Burstall Lake (Map 97/F5)
A fly-in lake located north of Lake Athabasca, Burstall Lake is home to some big northern pike and lake trout. Anglers will also find yellow perch and lake whitefish. This lake is open year round but watch for special retention limits.

Cadotte Lake (Map 48/D2)
Located along the south side Secondary Highway 986 near the Woodland Cree First Nation and Little Buffalo Lake Settlement, this fair size lake is home to northern pike. Watch for spring closures and special retention limits on the pike.

Calder Lake (Map 36/E3)
There is no road access to Calder Lake. ATVers might be able to access the lake in the fall along cutlines that cut through the marshy area. Most anglers who make the trip to this lake do so in winter. Like most of the lakes in the area, it contains northern pike and yellow perch. Watch for spring closures and special retention limits.

Calling Lake (Map 24/C4)
This big lake is a popular fishing lake complete with a provincial park campsite and boat launch on its southern shore. The lake is home to some nice size fish including northern pike to 7 kg (15 lbs), walleye to 3 kg (7 lbs) and lake whitefish and burbot that can reach 2.5 kg (6 lbs). There are also plenty of big perch here that can top 1 kg (2 lbs). Check the regulations for the open season and retention limits.

Caribou Lake (Map 94/B6)
This fly-in lake is located northeast of High Level. It holds walleye to 1 kg (2.5 lbs), northern pike to 3 kg (6.5 lbs), lake trout and good numbers of lake whitefish and burbot. This lake is open year round but watch for special retention limits.

Cecil Thompson Park [Junction] Pond (Map 47/C4)
Also known as Junction Pond, this stocked pond is found at the rest area at the junction of Highway 2 and Secondary Highway 688, 7 km east of Peace River. It was once the home of Cecil Thompson, an early pioneer. Today, visitors will find an aerated fishpond in the park that is stocked annually with rainbow trout. While it is open for fishing in winter, it can be dangerous, as the aerator causes thin ice and open water.

Chain Lakes (Map 10/B1–24/B7)
The lower Chain Lake is stocked annually with large numbers of rainbow trout that can grow to 2.5 kg (4 lbs). The middle lake holds northern pike. Most of the action centres on the lower lake due to the easier access and recreation area with campsite and boat launch. There is an electric motor only restriction on the lakes along with spring closures and limits on the pike.

Charles Lake (Map 97/D2)
This fly-in only lake is located north of the Colin Cornwall Lakes Wildland Park, just south of the Northwest Territories. It is a long, narrow lake, about 40 km long and up to 35 metres (115 feet) deep. The cold water is home to big northern pike and lake trout. You will also find yellow perch and lake whitefish here. Check the regulations for retention limits.

> Alberta's five largest lakes are found on these maps. They are, in ascending order, Utikuma Lake, Bistcho Lake, Lesser Slave Lake, Lake Claire and Lake Athabasca (which is partially in Saskatchewan).

Charron Lake (Map 11/D2)
Charron Lake is a larger, rather shallow lake that is subject to winterkill. It holds northern pike and yellow perch. Watch for spring closures and special retention limits.

Cherry Lake (Map 97/F2)
This lake is one of the hundreds of small to mid-size lakes found north of Lake Athabasca. It is very near the Saskatchewan boundary and holds northern pike, yellow perch, lake trout and lake whitefish. Check the regulations on retention limits.

Christina Lake (Map 41/D7–F7)
This long narrow lake is found just east of Secondary Highway 881. There is a lodge at the west end of the lake where boats can be rented. The lake holds big northern pike to 12 kg (25 lbs), big walleye to 5 kg (11 lbs), as well as yellow perch and lake whitefish. Ice fishing is popular. Check the regulations for spring closures and other restrictions.

Chrystina [Windy] Lake (Map 7/F2)
Chrystina Lake is stocked regularly with brook trout, which can get up to 2.5 kg (5 lbs). The lake is found north of Swan Lake on a road that can be rough when it gets wet. Despite this, the lake is a popular year round fishing destination complete with a recreation area with campsite and boat launch. As the alternate name implies, it can get windy here.

Chump Lake (Map 11/C4)
Located just north of Caslan, this lake has a wonderfully descriptive name, which may describe what people feel like after getting stumped here. Fortunately, the fishing is not bad for walleye, pike and perch. Chump Lake is one of only a few lakes in the area with a limit of three pike. Walleye are catch and release only.

Claude Lake (Map 12/C3)
Located northeast of the town of Lac La Biche, alongside Secondary Highway 668, Claude Lake has northern pike, walleye and yellow perch. Walleye are catch and release only.

Clyde Lake (Map 26/F3–27/A4)

Found just off the northwest corner of the Cold Lake Air Weapons Range and about 10 km west of Highway 881, this lake is home to northern pike and yellow perch. The lake is closed to angling in the spring.

Cockscomb Lake (Map 97/B4)

It may be possible to make your way to Cockscomb Lake (stop sniggering) from the Bocquen River via a creek. Possible, that is, but not practical. Most people who fish here come in by plane. The lake has decent sized northern pike along with lots of perch and lake whitefish. Watch for retention limits.

Cold Lake (Map 14/E6)

Cold Lake is one of the largest lakes in Alberta covering more than 540 sq. km (210 sq. miles), part of which is found in Saskatchewan. The lake is over 104 metres (400 ft) deep and covers more than 540 sq. km (210 sq. miles). It holds the widest variety of fish species (22, including lake trout, northern pike, walleye, yellow perch and lake whitefish) of any lake in the province. The standard saying in angling circles is "big lake, big fish" and Cold Lake certainly doesn't disappoint. The local Cree even have a legend of a monster fish—kinosoo—who haunted these waters, eating unwary paddlers. The fishery collapsed in the 1940s, but stocking and stricter regulations have allowed the lake to make a remarkable comeback. The largest lake trout hauled out of these waters (the largest ever caught in the province) weighed in at 23.6 kg (52 lbs), walleye can get up to 6 kg (14 lbs) and northern pike can get to 14 kg (30 lbs).

Colin Lake (Map 97/F3)

Considered to be one of the best northern pike lakes in Alberta, Colin Lake is a fly-in lake that is managed by an operator out of Fort McMurray. This means the fish get big here, really big. Northern pike average 9–14 kg (20–30 lbs) and come pretty readily to those able to make it in. Although less abundant, there are also trophy lake trout roaming the lake that occasionally top the 9 kg (20 lb) mark. Also look for yellow perch and lake whitefish. Check for special retention limits.

Collins Lake (Map 97/E1)

Not to be confused with nearby Colin Lake, this lake is located well north of Lake Athabasca, on the boundary between Alberta and the Northwest Territories. It has good fishing for fairly good size lake trout and northern pike along with smaller yellow perch and lake whitefish. Check for special retention limits.

Corner Lake (Map 14/B5)

The small lake holds northern pike and yellow perch.

Cornwall Lake (Map 97/D3)

While the fishing here isn't as good as nearby Colin Lake, this fly-in lake still produces northern pike up to 18 kg (40 lbs). The lake also holds lake trout, yellow perch and lake whitefish. Check the retention limits.

Corrigall [Round] Lake (Map 25/C5)

Located west of the settlement of Wandering River, this medium-size lake is quite shallow and subject to winterkill. It holds northern pike and good numbers of yellow perch. Check the regulations for spring closures and retention limits.

Cow Lake (Map 26/E5)

Found along a road (or series of roads) that you probably wouldn't want to try and drive when wet, this smaller lake holds good numbers of northern pike, yellow perch and burbot. Watch for spring closures and retention limits.

Cowper Lake (Map 42/C3)

To get to Cowper Lake, you will need an ATV or a snowmobile to follow the rough track north from the Alberta Pacific Road. The lake is one of the biggest in the area west of Secondary Highway 881. Despite the difficult access is still rather popular. Anglers will find northern pike over 60 cm (23.5 in) long yellow perch. Note the special regulations including the fishing closure in the spring.

Cranberry Lake (Map 50/B5)

Cranberry Lake contains northern pike and yellow perch. There is no road access to the lake, but it can be accessed in winter or extended dry spells along cutlines. Watch for spring closures and retention limits.

Crooked Lake (Map 4/G5–5/A6)

Found west of Fox Creek, this Crooked Lake suffers from winterkill. Recent reports are the yellow perch are small (in the 15 cm/6 in range) and best caught through the ice. During open water season, a 4wd vehicle and small boat are recommended. Anglers will find some northern pike as well. Watch for spring closures.

Crooked Lake (Map 10/A1)

This Crooked Lake is a medium size lake found northwest of Athabasca that holds some pike and lots of perch. The fish can be decent size here, with the odd northern pike reaching 4.5 kg (10 lbs) yellow perch reaching 1 kg (2 lbs).

Cross [Steele] Lake (Map 9/F4)

There is a popular provincial park on the shores of Cross Lake that offers camping facilities and a boat launch. The lake holds pike and perch. Watch for spring closures and special retention limits.

Cummings Lake (Map 45/F5)

Cummings Lake, located just outside of Fairview, has recently begun (2012) to be restocked with rainbow trout. There was a stocking program here in the past for rainbow and brown trout but it was suspended due to a yellow perch problem. Aerators have been installed to ensure the lake is oxygenated throughout the winter. There is a recreation area with campsite and boat launch on the lake.

Cutbank Lake (Map 16/E1)

Located just north of Saskatoon Lake, this lake is less than half an hour's drive from Grande Prairie. There are a lot of shrimp in the lake to help fatten up the brook trout in the lake. The brookies have not been stocked for several years. The good news is the fish grow fast, but the bad news is they have so much food they are very difficult to catch. The lake suffers from heavy weed growth and fishing is at its worst in summer.

Cutbank Lake (Map 29/G2)

Found north of Jackfish Lake, this out of the way lake is home to northern pike and some burbot.

Darwin Lake (Map 97/B5)

This fly-in lake is south of La Butte Creek Wildland Park. The lake holds some decent size northern pike and lots of yellow perch and lake whitefish.

Deep Lake (Map 16/E1)

Deep Lake is found north of Saskatoon Lake and west of Bear Lake northwest of Grande Prairie. Although smaller than these more popular lakes, Deep Lake does hold northern pike to 3 kg (6 lbs) and feisty yellow perch. This lake is closed to angling in the spring.

Dickson Lake (Map 29/E4)

While northern pike are the biggest catch in Dickson Lake, a lot of people chase after the lake's arctic grayling. Grayling are smaller, but notorious for the fight they provide. Check for spring closures and special retention limits.

Disappointment Lake (Map 97/C4)

This lake is aptly named. It does not hold many fish, and the northern pike, yellow perch and lake whitefish it does are usually small.

Eaglenest Lake (Map 81/D1–89/D7)

A fly-in lake in the middle of nowhere, Eaglenest holds some decent size northern pike and lots of yellow perch and lake whitefish. Watch for spring closures and special retention limits.

East Dollar Lake (Map 19/B2)

Outdoor Canada has named East Dollar Lake one of the twenty best rainbow trout destinations in Canada, which is pretty high acclaim for such a small lake. The pothole lake (small, round and deep) is part of a series of lakes (known collectively as the Dollar Lakes) and holds rainbow trout to 4.5 kg (10 lbs) and brown trout to 1.5 kg (3 lbs). Both are supplemented with stocking. While ice fishing is possible, the lake is aerated, which can lead to dangerous ice conditions. There is an electric motor only restriction on the lake.

East Texaco Trout Pond (Map 55/C1)

This small pond is located about 10 km east of Fort McMurray along the Airport Road (Highway 69). It is one of the better lakes in the area, with the odd stocked rainbow trout getting over 30 cm (12 in). It is best to visit this pond early in the year before the weeds take over in June.

Economy Lake (Map 17/E6)

Home to a campground maintained by Canfor, this lake is found 35 km south of Highway 43 on the Forestry Trunk Road (Secondary Highway 734). Anglers will find walleye and yellow perch here.

Edith Lake (Map 7/E2)

They tried stocking Edith Lake with artic grayling in the mid-1980s, but they didn't seem to take. You might still find one or two, but you will more likely hook a brook trout. The brookies are stocked annually and can get up to 2.5 kg (5 lbs). Yellow perch can also be found here.

Edwards Lake (Map 27/B1)

Edwards Lake is one of a bunch of good fishing lakes found along the Conklin Road near Goodwin Lake. The smaller lake holds pike and whitefish. Yellow perch and burbot are also present but watch for spring closures here.

Elinor Lake (Map 12/E4)

Located just outside the boundaries of Lakeland Provincial Park, the lake is accessed from the south, through Elinor Lake Recreation Area. The lake offers good fishing for walleye (catch and release only), northern pike and yellow perch. The lake holds lesser populations of burbot and lake whitefish.

Engstrom Lake (Map 55/E6)

There is a recreation area with campsite on Engstrom Lake, which is stocked with rainbow trout to help offset winterkill. The annual stocking program is done several times each year from May to September with catchable trout. It is reported to be one of the better trout lakes in the Fort McMurray area with the odd trout reported over 35 cm (14 in). Only small motor boats that can be launched by hand are allowed on the lake. Note the motor restriction.

Equisetum Lake (Map 64/G7)

Located just north of Peerless Lake, this mid-size lake has good fishing for northern pike to 7 kg (15 lbs), walleye to 4 kg (8 lbs), lake whitefish to 2.5 kg (5 lbs) and yellow perch to 1 kg (2 lbs). Burbot can also be found. The lake is just south of the highway, but the road in can be treacherous when wet. Watch for spring closures and special retention limits.

Eva Lake (Map 94/E7)

This fly-in lake is located in the Caribou Mountains in Wood Buffalo National Park. The lake holds good numbers of arctic grayling, pike and lake whitefish. A National Park Fishing License is needed to fish here.

Fairview College Reservoir (Map 45/F5)

This small, stocked reservoir is located on the college campus in Fairview. It holds plenty of small rainbow trout that are stocked annually and are catchable when released.

Fawcett Lake (Map 23/D3–F3)

Fawcett Lake is a bigger lake located north of Smith. There is access to both the east and west ends of the lake, but most use the recreation area at the west end, complete with boat launch. The lake is known for having plenty of walleye to 3 kg (6 lbs) but check for special retention limits. The lake also holds the odd northern pike (to 9 kg/20 lbs), yellow perch, lake whitefish and burbot. Check the regulations before heading out.

Figure Eight Lake (Map 46/D3)

Figure Eight Lake is located 25 km west of Peace River off Secondary Highway 737. This is one of the best rainbow trout lakes in Alberta, with trout growing to 2 kg (4 lbs) in size. These trout are stocked with catchable size fish to help the fishery. The lake also contains brown trout. There is a recreation area offering a campsite and launch for electric motor only boats.

Fleming Lake (Map 87/D1)

Fleming Lake is a fly-in or snowmobile accessible lake found north of Highway 58. The lake is home to good numbers of pike and grayling. Check the regulations for special retention limits.

Florence Lake (Map 97/E5)

This fly-in lake is just north of Lake Athabasca. There are a few lake trout and northern pike, along with good numbers of yellow perch and lake whitefish. There are special retention limits here.

Footner Lake (Map 86/D1)

This lake is located just north of the small community of Footner along Highway 35. Small numbers of catchable rainbow trout are stocked here on a regular basis.

Fork Lake (Map 12/F7)

Fork Lake is found south of the lonely Highway 55 some 95 km west of Cold Lake. It holds northern pike, yellow perch, lake whitefish and burbot.

Fox Creek Pond (Map 5/D6)

Found in the community of Fox Creek, this small pond gets stocked each spring with 500 rainbow trout. The size of the stocked fish varies but they are sometimes catchable at time of release.

Freeman Lake (Map 7/C3)

Getting to this lake can be a bit confusing on the maze of backroads west of Swan Hills. Once you get there, the fishing is pretty good for northern pike to 3.5 kg (7 lbs) and smaller perch and grayling. There is a zero retention limit on grayling and other special restrictions here. Campers will find a recreation area campsite on the lake.

Frenchman Lake (Map 12/G7)

Frenchman Lake is found off Highway 55, just outside Lakeland Provincial Park. The medium sized lake is one of the rare lakes where you can actually keep up to three walleye over 50 cm (21 in). The lake also holds northern pike, yellow perch, lake whitefish and burbot.

Gardiner Lakes (Map 80/C2)

Located on the edge of Birch Mountain Wildland Park, these bigger lakes hold plenty of walleye to 3 kg (6 lbs), northern pike to 4.5 kg (10 lbs) and lots of smaller yellow perch, lake whitefish and burbot. There is a bait ban in effect and spring closures.

Garson Lake (Map 56/F5)

Located alongside the La Loche Winter Road and crossing into Saskatchewan, this is a great ice fishing lake. In summer, it is fly-in only. The lake has lots of northern pike, yellow perch and whitefish. Check the regulations for spring closures and retention limits.

Ghost Lake (Map 9/G2–10/A2)

Ghost Lake is a small lake found northwest of Athabasca. It is quite shallow and subject to winterkill, but still offers northern pike and yellow perch. There is a campground with boat launch on the east side of the lake, but note the 12 km/hr. speed limit for boats on the lake. Watch for spring closures and special retention limits here.

Gift Lake (Map 35/A2)

Located just west of Utikumasis Lake, Gift Lake contains northern pike, walleye, yellow perch and lake whitefish. In addition to getting permission to fish here, watch for spring closures and special retention limits.

Gilroy Lakes (Map 7/B3)

These small lakes are accessed via cutlines from the backroads west of Swan Hills. The main lake contains northern pike.

Gipsy Lake (Map 56/D4)

Located north of the La Loche Winter Road, Gypsy Lake is home to some trophy-size northern pike, as well as yellow perch, lake whitefish and burbot. It can be accessed by snowmobile in winter or by floatplane in summer. Most take advantage of the lodge on the lake. Check the regulations for special retention limits.

Giroux Lake (Map 5/C3)

Found northwest of Fox Creek, Giroux Lake is home to good numbers of average sized northern pike. There is a second lake (Upper Giroux) that offers similar fishing to the first. To get to the lake, head northwest on Highway 43 for about 33 km. Watch for a road that heads east to near the lakes, although you will have to hike the last few hundred metres. Carrying a small boat to the lakes would help improve your chances.

God's Lake (Map 64/G7)

Located just east of Peerless Lake, God's Lake has good number of walleye to 2.5 kg (5 lbs), yellow perch, lake whitefish and burbot, but the fish of choice here is the northern pike. The aggressive fish can grow to over 9 kg (20 lbs) and measure in at more than a metre. This is despite the fairly good road access into the lake.

Goodfish Lake (Map 64/E7)

Access into this smaller lake found just northwest of Peerless Lake can be difficult when the road is wet. When it is not wet, the lake has good fishing for northern pike, walleye, yellow perch, lake whitefish and burbot. Watch for spring closures and special retention limits, especially the zero retention of walleye.

Goodwin Lake (Map 26/E2)

Goodwin Lake is one of the largest of a series of good fishing lakes found on the Conklin Road, which leaves Secondary Highway 881, loops past these lakes, then rejoins the highway. Like most lakes in the area, Goodwin is home to pike and perch. Check the regulations for closures.

Goose Lake (Map 18/E6)

Goose Lake is located south of Highway 34 near Sturgeon Lake. There is no road access to the lake, which holds northern pike and lots of perch. Check the regulations for spring closures.

Goosegrass Lake (Map 65/A6)

Located just off the Trout Mountain Road, this smaller lake holds decent size northern pike and lots of small yellow perch. The pike have been known to reach to 4.5 kg (10 lbs). Check the regulations for special restrictions here and closures.

Gordon Lake (Map 56/C3)

This larger lake is located north of the La Loche Winter Road, but you will still have to fly-in. As a result, the lake holds plenty of yellow perch and big northern pike. There are spring closures and special retention limits here.

Graham [Trout] Lake (Map 50/G1)

Trout Lake is actually a settlement at the south end of Graham Lake, but the water body itself is called both. Whatever you call it, you likely will not forget fishing here, especially if you pull one of the monster lake trout that lurk in the lake's depths. They can grow to a whopping 16 kg (35 lbs) but none can be retained. There are also walleye (to 5 kg/12 lbs) and northern pike (to 10.5 kg/25 lbs), lake whitefish to 3 kg (6 lbs), yellow perch to 0.5 kg (1 lb) and burbot in the lake. There is camping and a boat launch onto the lake. Watch for spring closures and special retention limits.

Gregoire Lake (Map 55/C3)

Gregoire Lake is one of the most popular fishing lakes in the Fort McMurray area. It offers lots of northern pike and walleye, although the walleye limit is zero. The pike are usually small, but there are reports of some big northern pike to 7 kg (15 lbs). Yellow perch, lake whitefish and burbot are also found here. There is a boat launch at the provincial park, which is found on the more sheltered western side of the lake. Ice fishing is also popular here. Check the regulations for closures and other restrictions.

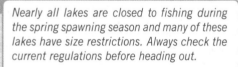

Nearly all lakes are closed to fishing during the spring spawning season and many of these lakes have size restrictions. Always check the current regulations before heading out.

Grist Lake (Map 28/B3)

Located just south of Winefred Lake, Grist Lake is home to pike and lake trout to 7 kg (15 lbs). There are also some good size lake whitefish. There are spring closures here.

Grovedale Fish Pond (Map 16/G4)

Also known as Highway 40 Pond, Grovedale is located just off Highway 40, about 20 km south of Grande Prairie. The recreation area makes a nice picnic spot with a chance for the kids to catch a few fish. Every year the small pond is stocked with a thousand catchable rainbow trout.

Haig Lake (Map 62/G5)

Access is better than many other lakes in this book, but you will still need a 4wd vehicle when it is wet. Regardless, this does not deter too many anglers searching for the walleye here. You will also find northern pike to 4.5 kg (10 lbs), lake whitefish to 2.5 kg (5 lbs), yellow perch and burbot. Check the regulations for closures.

Heart Lake (Map 26/G7)

Heart Lake is a larger lake located east of Imperial Mills and Secondary Highway 881. Here you will find good fishing for big fish. Northern pike regularly top 4.5 kg (10 lbs), walleye up to 4 kg (8 lbs), lake whitefish to 3 kg (6 lbs) and even big yellow perch are reported. Burbot can also be found. The boat launch is in good condition, but there is a day-use fee to us it. Check the regulations for special restrictions.

Heart River Reservoir (Map 34/A4)

Found north of High Prairie along Range Road 175, there is a small recreation area at the dam that provides camping and access to the man-made lake. Anglers will find northern pike, walleye and yellow perch here. If you prefer, white sucker also roam the lake.

Helena Lake (Map 12/F4)

One of the bigger lakes in Lakeland Provincial Park, Helena Lake holds northern pike to 2 kg (4.5 lbs), walleye to 1.5 kg (3.5 lbs), yellow perch, lake whitefish and burbot.

High Level Pond (Map 86/D2)

Every so often this small pond in High Level gets stocked with 500 catchable rainbow trout. It makes for a nice little fishery, especially for younger kids.

Highway 63 Trout Pond (Map 55/A1)

This stocked trout pond is found on the west side of Highway 63 near the Motocross Park south of Fort McMurray. Similar to the other trout ponds, it is stocked with catchable size rainbow each spring. There are also lots of small yellow perch here.

Hilda Lake (Map 14/C6)

Located west of Ethel Lake off Secondary Highway 897, Hilda Lake holds northern pike to 2 kg (4.5 lbs), walleye to 1.5 kg (3.5 lbs), yellow perch, lake whitefish and burbot.

Hooker Lake (Map 97/C3)

Hooker Lake (it's a fishing reference…really) has plenty of good size pike. Which can be, you know, hooked. Access is limited.

Hope Lake (Map 11/B5)

This small lake is found west of North Buck Lake and features a popular park complete with a campsite and boat launch. The lake holds northern pike, walleye, yellow perch and burbot. There is a rustic boat launch on the lake. Check the regulations for special restrictions.

Horse Lake (Map 11/E2)

This small lake is found just west of Lac La Biche, the lake off Secondary Highway 858. The lake offers fair northern pike fishing. See the regulations for closures and retention limits.

Horseshoe Lake (Map 9/F6)

This tiny, horseshoe-shaped lake is found just north of Long Island Lake and just south of Spruce Island Lake. It offers a unique fishery for the area, with periodically stocked brook trout being the fish of choice. Northern pike can also be found here.

Hutch Lake (Map 86/C1–93/C7)

Hutch Lake is found about 15 minutes north of High Level on Highway 35. The lake is home to northern pike, walleye and yellow perch. A rustic campsite and boat launch are also found on the lake. There are spring closures here.

Iosegun Lake (Map 5/D5)

Located 11 km north of Fox Creek, Iosegun Lake is famed for its walleye fishing. It is considered one of the best walleye lakes in Alberta but none can be retained without a special permit. The lake also holds good populations of northern pike, lake whitefish, burbot and to a lesser degree yellow perch. There is a recreation area on the lake complete with a campsite, picnic area and boat launch. See the regulations for all the special restrictions here.

Ironwood Lake (Map 12/F5)

Located near the southern boundary of Lakeland Provincial Recreation Area, this medium sized lake is a popular fishing destination. Home to northern pike, walleye, yellow perch, lake whitefish and burbot, the lake is also known for its great canoeing. There is a 20 site campground on the shores of the lake but the boat launch is unusable during low water. Watch for spring closures and special retention limits.

Island Lake (Map 10/A2)

Located northwest of Athabasca, this medium-size lake is home to unusually large lake whitefish. There are also good numbers of northern pike and yellow perch lurking around the bays and islands of the lake. Most of the development is on the western shore of the lake, but the park on the southern shore is the place visitors come to camp and launch a boat.

Island Lake (Map 66/F7)

Not to be confused with any of the other Island Lakes in Alberta (and there are a bunch of them), this Island Lake is a fly-in lake northwest of Fort McMurray. It is home to good numbers of potentially trophy class northern pike and walleye as well as some yellow perch. Because of its remoteness, the fishing is almost always good.

Jackfish Lake (Map 10/E3)

This Jackfish Lake, found east of Athabasca, holds yellow perch. There is a campground and boat launch on the medium size lake.

Jackfish Lake (Map 30/A3)
As you might gather from the name, Jackfish Lake (located due north of Hythe, past Spring Lake) is home to northern pike. There are lots of feisty, but small, yellow perch in this lake. The lake is closed to angling in the spring.

Jackson Lake (Map 12/F3)
Located in Lakeland Provincial Park, this mid-sized lake holds northern pike, walleye, yellow perch, lake whitefish and burbot. Most haul in a canoe, but note the 3.2 km portage.

Jane Lake (Map 7/G1)
Jane Lake is a small lake found tucked in the hills east of the Deer Mountain Lookout. It is occasionally stocked with rainbow trout, but it doesn't see much pressure, as there is no road access. It can be accessed by ATV along cutlines from the Deer Mountain area.

Jenkins Lake (Map 10/A1)
This long, narrow lake is one of a group of good fishing lakes northwest of Athabasca near Highway 2. It holds northern pike, walleye, yellow perch, lake whitefish and burbot. Check the regulations for spring closures and special retention limits.

Jessie Lake (Map 8/B1)
Jesse Lake is about 16 km from the nearest road and is accessed by ATV or snowmobile. The lake is occasionally stocked with rainbow trout, which provide good action in the spring and fall.

Joker Lake (Map 49/A2)
Joker Lake is located to the north of Secondary Highway 986, about 13 km east of Little Buffalo. There is good road access to the lake, which holds smaller northern pike as well as lots of yellow perch. It is subject to winterkill; see the regulations for pike retention limits.

Kakut Lake (Map 31/D4)
Reports are mixed on Kakut Lake. Some say there are no fish in the lake; others say it holds good numbers of northern pike. There is a small campsite on the lake.

Kakut Lake Pond (Map 31/D4)
This long, narrow pond holds rainbow trout that have been stocked in the past. There are also yellow perch found here. The pond is one of the few lakes in the area that allows for good shore fishing. Fly anglers, in particular, appreciate the casting space. Ice fishing is not recommended as an aerator keeps the ice thin, while the annual June Fishing Derby attests to the good trout fishing here.

Kimowin [Hook] Lake (Map 56/F6)
This lake, located near the Saskatchewan boundary, is accessible by floatplane and ardent ATVers in summer or by snowmobile from the La Loche Winter Road. The lake has small northern pike and big yellow perch. Watch for special restrictions.

Kinnaird Lake (Map 12/F3)
Kinnaird Lake can be reached by ATV trail or canoe from Jackson Lake. It holds the usual Lakeland combination of northern pike, walleye, yellow perch, lake whitefish and burbot. The pike are small (barely legal), but the perch are quite large. Ice fishing is also popular here.

Kinosiu Lake (Map 11/F4)
Found in the Lac la Biche area hot bed of fishing lakes, this long narrow lake features a goitre at its northwestern tip. The lake holds northern pike and yellow perch.

Kirby Lake (Map 27/G2)
Kirby Lake is another fly-in access lake. If you can't afford the flight in (especially considering the fishing is good, but unremarkable, for northern pike, yellow perch and lake whitefish), it is best wait until winter, when it can get into the lake with a snowmobile. Check the regulations for restrictions.

Krause Lake (Map 7/D3)
South of Swan Hills off Highway 32, this lake is home to good numbers of pike and perch. There is a recreation area, complete with campsite, on the popular lake.

La Crete Pond (Map 86/G4)
Found in the community of La Crete this small pond gets stocked with 1,500 catchable rainbow trout every year. These trout can be fun to catch until they are fished out.

Lac La Biche (Map 12/B2)
The name Lac La Biche literally translates to Red Deer Lake. This big lake has a number of access points, including Sir Winston Churchill Park, a public launch in the town and a number of resorts around the lake. Here you will find northern pike to 5.5 kg (12 lbs), walleye, yellow perch, lake whitefish and burbot. While the area is a popular fishing destination, the lake itself is not due in part to the wind. The walleye stocks are recovering, but it is still catch and release only for these prized sportfish.

Lac La Biche Trout Pond (Map 12/B3)
This small trout pond is found in the town of Lac La Biche and holds stocked rainbow trout. Although it is a former sewage lagoon, don't hold that against it because fishing can be good.

Lake Athabasca (Map 90/B2–97/G5)
This big lake (Alberta's largest, if you include the section that spills over into Saskatchewan) is home to some big lake trout and northern pike. In fact, it was in the Saskatchewan portion of the lake that the world's biggest lake trout was caught. It weighed in at 46 kg (102 lbs). Lunkers in the 13.5 kg (30 lb) range are caught occasionally; usually in September when the big fish congregate in prime spawning areas. The lake also holds the Canadian record for biggest northern pike, at 19 kg (42 lbs). About half that size is more common. You will also find walleye, goldeye, yellow perch, lake whitefish and burbot. Check the regulations before heading out for restrictions.

Lake Claire (Map 89/E3)
Found in Wood Buffalo National Park, Lake Claire is actually the biggest lake entirely in Alberta, covering 1,436 sq. km (554 sq. miles). A National Park Fishing License is needed to sample this big, shallow lake. However, the lake is only 2 metres (6.5 ft) deep so anglers should stick to top water presentations when looking for the northern pike, walleye and lake whitefish that roam the lake.

Larocque Lake (Map 90/C5)
Located well north of Fort McMurray on the Chipewyan Winter Road, this lake is found at the end of a long, roughly 100 km, ATV ride through the dunes. The lake holds yellow perch and lake whitefish. Most people don't come to fish this lake specifically, but it makes a good alternative when the other lakes in the area (like Barber Lake) are slow. There are special restrictions here.

Lawrence Lake (Map 9/G1–23/G7)
This mid-size lake is found just off Highway 2. There is a recreation area campground and boat launch tucked between the highway and the lake, which holds northern pike and yellow perch. Check the regulations for closures and other restrictions.

Legend Lake (Map 80/A5)
This fly-in lake is found at the south end of Birch Mountains Wildland Provincial Park. The remote lake holds northern pike and lake whitefish. Watch for spring closures.

Leggo Lake (Map 97/D2)
One of a series of long narrow lakes found in the far northeast corner of the province, Leggo Lake holds good size lake trout and northern pike. However, there are more yellow perch and lake whitefish to be found.

Lesser Slave Lake (Maps 20–22, 34–36)
Lesser Slave Lake contains a number of sportfish, including arctic grayling and yellow perch and northern pike that have been known to tip the scales in the 7.5 kg (15 lb) range. But the lake is better known for its walleye fishery. It is considered the best walleye lake in Alberta (some would say in Canada) and it has become the destination of choice for anglers seeking the prized sport fish that can get to 4 kg (8 lbs). Fishing is good from March through to fall and ice fishing is possible. In the early season, Shaw's Point at the west end of the lake is a popular hotspot. In summer, the fish are distributed fairly evenly around the lake, usually at a depth of 3–5 metre (9–15 ft). The lake is heavily regulated so make sure to check the regulations before heading out.

Lily Lake (Map 22/D1)
Access to this small lake is by foot from the Marten Mountain Lookout in Lesser Slave Lake Provincial Park. Those that make the trek in the spring or fall will find the fishing can be fast and furious for occasionally stocked brook trout.

Limon Lake (Map 90/A3)
This fly-in lake is located just south of the Athabasca River. It is one of a few lakes in the area with good size walleye, as well as northern pike and yellow perch. Watch for spring closures.

Fishing Adventures

Logan Lake (Map 27/A6)
Logan Lake is found north of Heart Lake. It has a number of islands in it and holds northern pike to an impressive 9 kg (20 lb) weight, as well as walleye yellow perch. Check the regulations for spring closures.

Long Lake (Map 2/F5)
Long Lake is found at the end of a series of backroads west of Highway 40 and east of the Kakwa Tower. Actually, the lake is not accessed by road but ardent anglers can follow the hydro right of way north from the road for about 500 metres to the lake. The lake holds rainbow trout and arctic grayling. It is possible to carry a canoe or float tube to the lake but no motors are allowed.

Long Lake (Map 11/A7)
This long, narrow lake is found just off Secondary Highway 831. There is a nice campground and a boat launch at Long Lake Provincial Park. The lake holds northern pike to 4.5 kg (10 lbs), walleye to half that, yellow perch. Ice fishing is also popular here.

Long Lake (Map 18/E6)
There is no road access to this remote lake found southwest of Valleyview. There are cutlines, but they run through very marshy areas, making access in summer very difficult. The lake is usually fished in winter and accessed by snowmobile. It holds pike and perch.

Long Lake (Map 64/G7)
There's a whole whack of Long Lakes in Alberta. This one is found just north of Peerless Lake. It is home to northern pike to 7 kg (15 lbs) and walleye to 2.5 kg (5 lbs). There are also lots of yellow perch.

Loon Lake (Map 49/F1)
Loon Lake is a big lake east of Red Earth Creek. It holds big northern pike and walleye, along with smaller yellow perch.

Loutit Lake (Map 97/C7)
This fly-in lake, just north of Lake Athabasca, holds good numbers of walleye, as well as northern pike. Yellow perch and lake whitefish can also be found.

Machesis Lake (Map 86/F3)
One of the most popular lakes in the High Level area, Machesis Lake is also one of the few lakes in the area with a campsite on its shores. There is also a boat launch and a pair of docks for visitors to use. The lake holds stocked rainbow to 1.5 kg (3 lbs) and a few brook trout.

Margaret Lake (Map 94/E7)
Located in the Caribou Mountains, just inside the southwest corner of Wood Buffalo National Park, this remote, fly-in fishing lake is home to some large lake trout. There are rumours of fish as big as 27 kg (60 lbs) being pulled from this lake, although the standard catch is much closer to 5 kg (10 lbs). The lake is also home to northern pike to 11 kg (25 lbs), whitefish to 2.5 kg (5 lbs), arctic grayling and burbot. There is a private lodge on the lake. Watch for special retention limits.

Marie Lake (Map 14/D5)
Located 5 km northeast of English Bay on Cold Lake, Marie Lake holds northern pike to 2.5 kg (5.5 lbs), walleye to 2.3 kg (5 lbs), yellow perch, lake whitefish and burbot.

Marigold Lake (Map 7/B3)
Access to Marigold Lake is limited, but you can get to it along ATV trails. It can be accessed directly from Swan Hills along these trails or you can drive to the staging area (about 20 km from Swan Hills) along rough 4wd roads. From the staging area, it is a 3 km trek to the lake. The lake is stocked with brook trout, which provide good action in the spring and fall.

Marten Lakes (Map 36/F6)
The three Marten Lakes are actually the headwaters for different water systems. Marten River flows west to join Lesser Slave Lake, while the Willow River flows northeast towards Secondary Highway 754. All three lakes hold northern pike, yellow perch and lake whitefish.

May Lake (Map 14/C4)
May Lake is located 16 km northeast of Cold Lake's English Bay. The remote lake holds walleye to 2.3 kg (5 lbs), catch and release only. The lake also holds good sized northern pike, as well as yellow perch, lake whitefish and burbot.

McGuffin Lake (Map 12/F3)
McGuffin Lake is found in Lakeland Provincial Park and is accessed by a 4 km trail from the Shaw Lake Road staging area. It holds the typical mix of warm water fish: northern pike, walleye, yellow perch, lake whitefish and burbot.

McLelland Lake (Map 97/A2)
Located north and east of Hay Camp on the Slave River, this lake can only be accessed by floatplane. The cold, clear water of the lake holds good size lake trout, northern pike and walleye. Lesser game fish like yellow perch and lake whitefish can also be hooked here.

McMillan Lake (Map 36/G4)
This winter access only lake is located via 15 km of cutlines north of Secondary Highway 754. It holds northern pike, yellow perch, lake whitefish and burbot. The lake is subject to winterkill.

McMullen Lake (Map 37/D4)
While this lake is only 1 km from Secondary Highway 754, it's a rather marshy kilometre over muskeg. It is usually left until winter to fish for northern pike to 4 kg (8 lbs), yellow perch, lake whitefish and burbot.

Meekwap Lake (Map 5/F3)
Roads come close but you will still have to hike into this lake, which is about 40 km northeast of Fox Creek along a series of backroads that can be rough in wet weather. The lake holds smaller northern pike and yellow perch. Watch for spring closures.

Mercredi Lake (Map 97/D1)
Located in the far northeast corner of the province, this lake has lots of lake trout and lake whitefish and plenty of northern pike and yellow perch. It is, like all the lakes north of Lake Athabasca, fly-in only.

Minimum Security Trout Pond (Map 55/B1)
Another contestant in the best named place to fish contest, this pond was once stocked with rainbow trout. It is found east of Fort McMurray on Highway 63 and still holds the odd trout.

Some of the lakes and rivers through this area have contamination warnings. These include Chrystina, Edith and Muskwa Lakes, as well as a variety of rivers in the Athabasca and Peace drainages.

Mink Lake (Map 35/D1)
Mink Lake holds some pretty big perch (to 1 kg/2 lbs) and some northern pike. Most of the people who fish this lake, which is found north of the much bigger Utikuma Lake and Secondary Highway 750, do so in winter.

Missawawi Lake (Map 11/G4)
Also known as Big Egg Lake, this large, shallow lake is found 10 km southwest of Lac La Biche. It has wide fluctuations in water levels, so much so that in the late 1940s, farmers were driving tractors across Venice Narrows. At that time, the water got so low, the fish died off from the lake. While there is still good fishing for northern pike and yellow perch, the water levels are in decline again and a severe winterkill is a possibility.

Mistehea Lake (Map 37/B2)
Mistehea Lake is found well off the highway and is surrounded by many, many hectares of muskeg. Access into the area is only possible in winter, via the Doucette Lookout Road and a series of cutlines. Look for pike and perch here.

Mitsue Lake (Map 22/E4)
While Mitsue Lake is not small, it pales in comparison to nearby Lesser Slave Lake. The fish are also smaller, but the northern pike do get to about 4.5 kg (10 lbs). The lake also holds yellow perch.

Moonshine Lake (Map 44/E7)
Moonshine Lake is found about one hour north of Grande Prairie making it a popular destination during the summer. There is a large campground, along with a separate day-use area complete with boat launch offered through the provin-

cial park. The lake can suffer from algae growth in hot weather, but the fishing for the stocked rainbow trout is good during the shoulder seasons. Starting in 2012, brook trout are now being stocked, while northern pike can also be found here. There is an electric motor only restriction and ice fishing is not recommended as the aeration system can create dangerously thin ice.

Moore Lake (Map 14/B6)
Moore Lake is 25 km northwest of Ardmore. The lake holds the classic mix of northern pike, walleye, yellow perch, lake whitefish and burbot.

Muskoseepi Pond (Map 17/A2)
Located in Muskoseepi Park in Grande Prairie, this pond is stocked annually with several hundred rainbow. The pond is prone to winterkill so do not expect to catch any monsters.

Muskwa Lake (Map 50/F6)
A winter road works its way northwest from Secondary Highway 754 to the north end of this lake. In summer, the only access is by floatplane. The lake is home to good numbers of northern pike, walleye, yellow perch and lake whitefish. Watch for spring closures and special retention limits.

Musreau Lake (Map 3/A3)
Musreau Lake is a popular fishing lake south of Grande Prairie. There is a recreation area campsite at the lake's north end, which is often full during the summer. The spring fed lake holds rainbow trout to 1.5 kg (3 lbs) that are best caught in the spring and fall. The road into the lake from Highway 40 can be difficult in wet weather, but it doesn't seem to deter the anglers.

Myers Lake (Map 97/A3)
Myers Lake is one of the most westerly lakes in the spray of lakes found in the northeastern corner of the province. It has plenty of good size northern pike and walleye. The lake also holds yellow perch and lake whitefish.

Namur Lake (Map 80/B3)
Namur Lake defines the southeast corner of the Birch Mountain Wildland Park. It is a remote fly-in fishing lake with lots of big fish: lake trout to 16 kg (35 lbs) and northern pike to 9 kg (20 lbs). Even the lake whitefish grow to a good size. The lake also has arctic grayling, yellow perch and burbot. There is a bait ban in effect and spring closures.

Narrow Lake (Map 9/G5)
This long and, yes, narrow lake is found west of Athabasca, not far from Secondary Highway 663. It holds northern pike, walleye and yellow perch.

Nipisi Lake (Map 36/C4)
Located east of Highway 88, roads come close but access in the summer remains difficult. Most visitors to the lake come in the winter, where they can ice fish for northern pike to 9 kg (20 lbs) or lake whitefish to 2 kg (4 lbs). Anglers will also find yellow perch and burbot.

North Buck Lake (Map 11/C4)
North Buck is a very popular fishing lake, due in no small part to its ability to produce northern pike to 9 kg (20 lbs) fairly regularly. It also has walleye, yellow perch, lake whitefish and burbot. There is a recreation area on the southeast end offering camping and a boat launch.

North Leland Lake (Map 97/B1)
This fly-in lake, located just this side of the Northwest Territories, is open for fishing all year round and is one of the few lakes to offer fly-in ice fishing. The resort based lake has crystal clear water allowing you to see quite deep. The lake holds some big lake trout, northern pike, walleye and lake whitefish along with plenty of yellow perch.

North Wabasca Lake (Map 37/E2-51/E7)
This big lake offers good fishing for big northern pike and walleye, to 7 kg (15 lbs) and 4.5 kg (10 lbs) respectively. The lake also has good fishing for yellow perch and lake whitefish. There is good road access to the southern part of the lake and a recreation area offering camping and a boat launch is found further up the east side. This lake is heavily regulated.

Nose Lake (Map 1/F2)
It is about a 3 km hike into Nose Lake from the Nose Mountain Road. There is a campsite at the lake itself for folks who want to bring a tent and spend the night. The lake holds brook and bull trout and whitefish.

Ole's Lake (Map 43/G1)
This small lake is located 8 km east of the BC border, north of Highway 64. It holds stocked rainbow, which can grow to 1.5 kg (3 lbs). Although there is a campsite, you will need to hand launch your boat if you want to get out on the water.

One Week Lake (Map 97/E1)
This fly-in lake offers lots of small northern pike, yellow perch and whitefish. It is a remote lake found in the northeast corner of the province near the bigger Andrew Lake.

Orloff Lake (Map 24/B3)
This backcountry lake can be accessed by ATV in summer or the winter road when the muskeg freezes up. The lake holds good numbers of northern pike, walleye, yellow perch, lake whitefish and burbot.

Parker Lake (Map 22/E6)
Accessed by a series of trails and cutlines south of Highway 2, an ATV is highly recommended to find this small lake. Fishing is fairly steady in the spring and fall for rainbow and brook trout. Both the rainbow and brookies are stocked every so often.

Pastecho Lake (Map 37/A2)
Located well off anything resembling a road, this lake is located west of Mistehae Lake and is accessed via cutlines north of the Douchette Lookout. Considering the muskegs in the area, the lake sees most of its visitors in winter. It contains northern pike, yellow perch and lake whitefish. Watch for spring closures.

Peace Ponds (Map 46/G4)
There is a pair of walk-in fishing ponds found a short walk into the wilderness park, west of Peace River. There are two ponds; one is stocked with catchable rainbow trout each year. The other holds arctic grayling.

Pearson Lake (Map 90/A6)
Pearson Lake can be accessed by a long ATV/snowmobile ride along the Fort Chipewyan Winter Road. It holds northern pike, walleye, yellow perch, lake whitefish and burbot. Check the regulations for spring closures.

Peerless Lake (Map 50/F1-64/G7)
This big lake is a popular fishing destination. It is famous for its huge lake trout, which occasionally get up to 12.5 kg (30 lbs). The lake also holds northern pike and walleye that can reach 4.5 kg (10 lbs), as well as yellow perch and lake whitefish. But most anglers who make the trip to Peerless are looking for those big lakers. Try big silver and blue or plain silver spoons that resemble the whitefish and tulibee the lakers feed on. There is a steep, difficult to access boat launch at the south end of the lake where camping is also possible. Check the regulations before heading out.

Piché Lake (Map 26/F7)
This medium-size lake is located a few hundred metres off Secondary Highway 881 north of Imperial Mills. However, the easiest way to access the lake is by boat up the Piché River from Heart Lake. It has northern pike, yellow perch, walleye, lake whitefish and burbot.

Pichimi Lake (Map 94/G6)
This fly-in lake is located in the Caribou Mountains, just inside Wood Buffalo National Park. The lake has great fishing for northern pike to 14 kg (30 lbs), lake trout to 18 (40 lbs) and lake whitefish to 2.5 kg (5 lbs). Arctic grayling and burbot also roam the lake. A National Park Fishing License is needed to fish here.

Pinehurst Lake (Map 12/G5-13/A5)
One of the big lakes in Lakeland Recreation Area, Pinehurst offers good fishing for good sized northern pike and walleye. You will also find yellow perch and lake whitefish. There is a boat launch at the campsite. Watch for spring closures and special retention limits.

Pine Point Borrow Pit (Map 5/C5)
There are fish in this small speck of a pond found north of Fox Creek, just off Highway 43. Not many fish, but some, as there are a few hundred rainbow trout stocked here annually. The pond doesn't see a lot of pressure for its proximity to Fox Creek and to the highway.

Potts Lake (Map 97/E2)
Potts Lake is a fly-in lake (there is a six-person cabin that can be rented from Mikisew Sport Fishing). The lake is rumoured to produce well for northern pike and lake trout that can tip the scales at 16 kg (35 lbs). Anglers can also find yellow perch and lake whitefish.

Fishing Adventures

Powder Lake (Map 11/E3)
Powder Lake is located north of North Buck Lake off the east side of Secondary Highway 855. Powder Lake holds northern pike and yellow perch. Watch for spring closures.

Preston Lake (Map 29/D6)
This Preston Lake is west of Hythe and may hold average size northern pike. We say may, because the Beaverlodge River has become so dammed by beavers that the fish are not able to spawn and the fishery is suffering.

Primrose Lake (Map 14/F3)
Only a small piece of this large Saskatchewan Lake falls on the Alberta side of the border. Further this stretch of the lake is surrounded by the Cold Lake DND making access a rather precarious option.

Rainbow Lake (Map 85/A3)
Rainbow Lake is a long, narrow lake found south of the town of Rainbow Lake. It is well known, at least locally, for having good numbers of northern pike, which can get to 9 kg (20 lbs). It is also home to a fair number of walleye to 2 kg (4 lbs), lake whitefish and burbot. There is a recreation area campsite on the lake.

Rainbow Lake Pond (Map 85/A1)
This small pond is located about 2 km east of the town of Rainbow Lake. It is stocked annually with rainbow trout, but is prone to winterkill. Don't expect the fish to get too big.

Raspberry Lake (Map 5/E6)
Located west of Iosegun Lake, Raspberry Lake can only be accessed by foot, ATV or snowmobile. It holds northern pike and yellow perch. Check the regulations for spring closures.

Rich Lake (Map 12/F6)
Rich Lake is found just south of Lakeland. It is home to good numbers of pike and perch.

Richardson Lake (Map 90/B4)
Richardson Lake is a fairly big lake, although it pales in comparison to the nearby Lake Athabasca. The lake is accessed along the winter road or by floatplane. It holds lots of walleye, as well as northern pike and yellow perch.

Roche Lake (Map 8/B3)
Roche Lake is about 11 km from the nearest road (which is best driven with a 4wd). Most people who fish here come by ATV or snowmobile. The lake holds northern pike and yellow perch.

Rock Island Lake (Map 24/C1)
Tanasiuk Recreation Area is on the shores of this lake, offering camping and boat launching facilities. The lake has northern pike to 7 kg (15 lbs) and walleye to 2.5 kg (5 lbs). Anglers will also find yellow perch, lake whitefish and burbot.

Roderick Lake (Map 97/F4)
Located just south of Colin Cornwall Wildland Park, Roderick Lake holds northern pike, yellow perch and lake whitefish. It is fly-in access only.

Round Lake (Map 64/G6)
Found just north of Peerless Lake, Round Lake is found at the end of a poor road. It holds northern pike, walleye, yellow perch, lake whitefish and burbot. There are reports of decent sized walleye in this lake.

Running Lake (Map 58/A6)
This tiny lake is found northeast of Worsley. The road in is not in very good shape, especially in wet weather. This does not seem to deter a steady stream of visitors to the recreation area that offers a boat launch and campground. The lake holds stocked rainbow and brook trout. Rainbow are stocked even numbered years, while brookies are stocked odd numbered years.

Russell Lake (Map 63/B2)
Offering northern pike, yellow perch and lake whitefish, there is no road access to this lake, found well west of Highway 88. Access is by air or by really determined canoeists portaging in from Sawn Lake, although this latter route would require bushwhacking through the muskeg.

Ruth Lake (Map 68/G4)
A man-made lake north of Fort McMurray, Ruth Lake is subject to winterkill like most other lakes in the area. There are infrequent reports of small yellow perch and the odd northern pike. Being so close to town, the lake was fished heavily after the perch were stocked several years back.

Ryan Lake (Map 97/B6)
Ryan Lake is a fly-in fishing lake, where you will find good fishing for walleye, northern pike, yellow perch and lake whitefish. Mikisew Sport Fishing has a cabin on the lake.

Rycroft Reservoir (Map 31/C2)
Also known as Nardam Lake, this small lake is stocked annually with rainbow trout, although it is subject to winterkill. It is located 1.5 km west of Rycroft.

Sand Lake (Map 80/G1)
The northernmost of a series of lakes that run along the east side of Birch Mountains Wildland Park, Sand Lake is fly-in only. The lake has northern pike to 4.5 kg (10 lbs), as well as yellow perch and lake whitefish.

Sander Lake (Map 37/C2)
Accessed from a rugged road west of North Wabasca Lake, there is a creek stringing Beaver, McLeod and Sander Lakes together. The feasibility of driving the entire road is questionable in summer, but ATV's and snowmobiles should have no trouble getting to Sander. The lake holds northern pike, walleye, yellow perch and lake whitefish.

Sandhill Lake (Map 11/D3)
Sandhill Lake rests on the east side of Secondary Highway 855 northeast of Boyle. The mid-size lake is home to fair numbers of pike and perch.

Sawn Lake (Map 63/A2)
There are rough roads that come fairly close to Sawn Lake, but the last little way into the lake is often pretty wet. Most people leave this lake until winter. It holds some big northern pike; with fish over 9 kg (20 lbs) possible. Anglers will also find some walleye and yellow perch. Check the regulations for special restrictions.

Seibert Lake (Map 13/A3)
One of a trio of big lakes in Lakeland area, you will find some big fish here. Currently, you are allowed to keep one northern pike over 100 cm (42 in) and walleye over 50 cm (21 in). The lake also holds yellow perch, lake whitefish and burbot. There is a bait ban in effect. There is a boat launch at the campsite on the eastern shores of the lake.

Semo Lake (Map 94/F7)
There are rumours that it is possible to take an ATV in to Semo Lake from a rough road north of Highway 58 east of Fort Vermillion. The last stretch follows cutlines. However, people who are heading to this lake are more likely doing so by floatplane. The lake holds lake trout, northern pike and lake whitefish.

Sexsmith Pond (Map 31/A7)
This small pond, found in Heritage Park in Sexsmith, was stocked in the past with rainbow trout. The pond is aerated to help trout survive over winter.

Skeleton Lake (Map 11/B5)
Found 6 km east of Boyle, Skeleton Lake holds smaller northern pike, walleye, yellow perch, lake whitefish and burbot can be caught here. There is a private campsite on the lake. Check the regulations for spring closures.

Smoke Lake (Map 5/C6)
Smoke Lake is one of the definitive walleye fishing lakes in Alberta. While they only reach 2.5 kg (5 lbs) here, they are plentiful and seem to like being caught. The lake also holds northern pike to 9 kg (20 lbs), whitefish to 3.5 kg (7 lbs) yellow perch to 1 kg (2 lbs). The lake is west of Fox Creek on a good gravel road and features a recreation area with campsite and boat launch. Ice fishing is popular here.

Snipe Lake (Map 19/F4)
Snipe Lake is a big lake found east of Valleyview. The lake is stocked with walleye and also holds northern pike to 9 kg (20 lbs), lake whitefish to 2.5 kg (5 lbs), yellow perch to 0.5 kg (1 lb) and some burbot. Check the regulations for spring closures.

South Leland Lake (Map 97/B2)
Not as well documented as the more popular lake to the north, South Leland Lake is another good fly-in lake near the Northwest Territories. Similar to most lakes in the area, expect big fish with some fast action. Lake trout, northern pike and walleye are the main species, but lake whitefish can also be found here.

South Wabasca Lake (Map 37/F2–38/A3)
If you do not have a boat to access this bigger lake then you likely will not have much luck. However, there is a road that follows the northeast shore of this lake for a ways. The lake holds northern pike, walleye, yellow perch, lake whitefish and burbot. Check the regulations for special restrictions.

Spawn Lake (Map 98 Inset A)
There are few places in Alberta as remote as this. Found north of the already tough to access Bistcho Lake, Spawn Lake is found right on the boundary between Alberta and the Northwest Territories. The only way in to the lake is via floatplane. For your effort, you will be rewarded with good fishing for northern pike, walleye, lake whitefish and burbot.

Spencer Lake (Map 13/A3)
Spencer Lake is not usually fished in the summer, as there is poor access, except via an ATV trail along the Air Weapons Boundary Trail. However, it is a popular ice fishing destination. From the south, the lake can be accessed by snowmobile across Seibert Lake. The lake holds good numbers of northern pike, walleye, yellow perch and lake whitefish.

Spring Lake (Map 30/A4)
Spring Lake is a popular recreational lake north of Hythe. It holds stocked rainbow, which can grow big (to 3.5 kg/8 lbs), as well as stocked brook trout. There is a campsite on the lake and an electric motor only restriction.

Square Lake (Map 12/C1)
Square Lake isn't really square; it is more a kind of a trapezoid shape. Regardless, the lake has good fishing for northern pike and yellow perch. It is found north of Lac La Biche, near Tweedle.

Many of the lakes across the prairies are too shallow or too alkaloid to support fish.

St. Agnes Lake (Map 97/F3)
This remote fly-in lake is located north of Colin-Cornwall Lakes Wildland Park. It has 'okay' fishing for lake trout, northern pike, yellow perch and lake whitefish.

Stoney Lake (Map 55/C7)
Stoney Lake is also known as Montaganeusse Lake since it was created by damming the Montaganeusse River. It is stocked annually with trout (odd numbered years with rainbow trout, even numbered years with brook trout) that provide steady fishing in the spring and fall. There is a campsite, boat launch and nice beach at the lake.

Sturgeon Lake (Map 18/E4)
There are two provincial parks on the shores of Sturgeon Lake, both of which offer boat launches. The lake is a good size and holds some good size fish, including northern pike to 14 km (30 pounds), walleye to 2.5 kg (5 pounds), lake whitefish to 2 kg (4 pounds), yellow perch to 1 kg (2 pounds) and burbot. The lake suffers from an algae bloom in summer, which forces the walleye to hang out at shallower depths than in clearer lakes. Ice fishing is also popular here. Check the regulations for special regulations.

Sulphur Lake (Map 60/A4)
This small lake is quite popular despite the fact it is fairly remote and the road in is questionable when wet. There is a camping area and a boat launch onto the lake, which holds rainbow trout (stocked in even numbered years) to 1.5 kg (3 lbs) as well as brook trout (stocked in odd numbered years). The lake is open to ice fishing, but there is an aeration system on the lake, which can be dangerous in winter.

Swan Lake (Map 18/C4)
Swan Lake can suffer from heavy algae blooms in summer, which hampers fishing quality. As a result, fishing is best in spring and fall for the large number of rainbow trout that are stocked every year. Anglers will find northern pike as well. There is a campsite and a steep boat launch at the recreational area. Check the regulations for special restrictions.

Swartz Lake (Map 7/B3)
This small lake is found in the hills west of Swan Hills, but there is no road access to it. You will have to hike or more likely ATV or snowmobile in to the lake. There are reports of fair numbers of northern pike in the lake.

Talbot Lake (Map 76/D4)
Talbot Lake is typically accessed by ATV along cutlines from near the Senex Creek Rest Area on Highway 88. It is about 20 km from Highway 88 to the lake, which is rarely fished. Those who do make the journey will find plenty of hungry northern pike and good numbers of yellow perch.

Tamarack Lake (Map 7/A3)
Tamarack Lake is another in a series of a half dozen popular fishing lakes found west of Swan Hills that does not have road access. It is about 13 km to the lake along cutlines and ATV/snowmobile trails. The lake is stocked with rainbow trout.

Tea Lakes (Map 8/A2)
Two small lakes are located east of Chrystina Lake and south of the Salteaux River. Access to the lakes is by ATV or snowmobile, usually from Chrystina Lake. They are occasionally stocked with rainbow trout.

Thurston Lake (Map 99 Inset B)
Another remote access lake northeast of Bistcho Lake, Thurston Lake is even closer to the Northwest Territories and is also a fly-in lake. But what it lakes for in size, it makes up for in size of fish. In 1999, a northern pike came out of this lake that was an (unconfirmed) 129 cm (50 inches) long, a full foot longer than the then-record sized fish. Needless to say, the lake grew in popularity as a fly-in destination. In addition to pike, the lake holds walleye, lake whitefish and burbot.

Touchwood Lake (Map 12/G3–13/A3)
Located in the northern portion of Lakeland Recreation Area, Touchwood Lake is a well-known walleye lake and is catch and release only to protect this great fishery. Other fish you can keep include northern pike (one over 63 cm/25 in), yellow perch, lake whitefish and burbot. There is a boat launch at the campground on the northern shores of the lake.

Tucker Lake (Map 13/G6–14/A6)
Located west of English Bay on Cold Lake, this medium sized lake holds northern pike, yellow perch and lake whitefish.

Twin Lakes (Map 56/A1)
Located 65 km north of Manning on Highway 35, there are 49 campsites and a hand launch at this popular recreation area. The east lake is very popular with anglers year round for stocked rainbow trout.

Two Lakes (Map 1/D4)
The two lakes that make up Two Lakes are located 128 km southwest of Grande Prairie on a rather rough backroad. While high clearance 2wd vehicles can make the trek, most people recommend a 4wd, especially in wet weather. With three separate camping areas and a boat launch, fishing pressure can be heavy. To counteract this pressure, the North Lake is stocked annually with thousands of rainbow (you will also find brook trout), while the South Lake is stocked every couple of years with cutthroat. It also contains rainbow trout. Ice fishing is possible here.

Uflyfish Ponds (Map 22/F4)
For something a little different, try the Uflyfish Ponds, located southeast of Lesser Slave Lake, near Mitsue Lake. Yes, these are private ponds, and yes, you have to pay to fish there, but who can argue with the chance to catch two rainbow up to 4.5 kg (10 lbs)…you don't even need a fishing license, because the ponds are private.

Utikuma Lake (Map 35/D2–36/A2)
Located north of Lesser Slave Lake, Utikuma Lake is another large lake that holds fairly large fish in its depths. How large? Well, the northern pike get up to 4.5 kg (10 lbs), walleye get to 2 kg (4 lbs) and lake whitefish get to 2.5 kg (5 lbs). You are probably not going to break any Alberta catch records here, but a 4.5 kg pike is nothing to laugh at. And you might land some burbot as well.

Utikumasis Lake (Map 35/C2)
Located just west of Utikuma Lake, this lake is much smaller, but for some reason, produces much larger northern pike, up to three times as large. While it doesn't happen every day, it is possible to pull a 13.5 kg (30 lb) pike from these waters. Walleye, yellow perch, lake whitefish and burbot are also found in this lake. Check the regulations for special restrictions.

Wadlin Lake (Map 87/C7)

Fishing in Wadlin Lake is good, although not spectacular. You are allowed to keep one walleye (over 50 cm/18 inches), several whitefish or a few burbot. The lake also holds northern pike and yellow perch, but these must be released if caught. There is a regional campground with a boat launch on the lake.

Wappau Lake (Map 26/F1)

This long, narrow lake holds pike and perch. Access is relatively easy, but it is quite a ways from civilization on a backroad that can be difficult to navigate when it is wet. Watch for spring closures.

Weaver Lake (Map 37/D2)

It may be possible to canoe (or at least line a canoe) up the outflow creek, but not likely. As a result, the lake is best accessed in the winter. It holds northern pike and yellow perch. There are spring closures here.

Weberville Pond (Map 47/B2)

This small pond in Weberville, which is north of the town of Peace River, is stocked annually with a thousand catchable rainbow trout.

Wentzel Lake (Map 95/B6)

A fly-in fishing lake in in Caribou Mountains Wildland Park, Wentzel Lake is known for its amazing walleye fishing. Sure, there's lake trout, northern pike, lake whitefish and burbot but the fishing for walleye is rumoured to be phenomenal when they congregate around the river mouths during spawning time in spring.

West Texaco Trout Pond (Map 55/B1)

This trout pond is stocked annually with rainbow trout and produces mostly small trout. It is located south of Fort McMurray near the start of Airport Road (Highway 69), close to the Golden Eagle Campsite.

Winagami Lake (Map 33/G5)

There is a breakwater at the boat launch on this big lake, which provides a great place to shore fish from. Most anglers bring a boat to search the lake for decent size northern pike and walleye. There are also yellow perch, lake whitefish and burbot. Watch for spring closures.

Winefred Lake (Map 28/B2–42/B7)

Known to produce trophy sized northern pike and walleye, Winefred Lake is feed by three streams providing ample food and good spawning areas to maintain a consistent fishery. With over 640 sq. km (400 sq. miles), several islands and drop-offs there is no shortage of space to fish. Anglers will also find artic grayling, lake whitefish and burbot. There are spring closures here as well as a resort on the lake.

Winnifred Lake (Map 97/E5)

Not to be confused with Winefred Lake south of Fort McMurray, this fly-in lake promises lots, but is rumoured to deliver poorly. It has average size northern pike and lake whitefish. The lake is shallow, which helps keep the fish stunted.

Wolf Lake (Map 13/E4)

Like most lakes in the area, the walleye limit in Wolf Lake is zero. You will also find northern pike, although most fall under the 63 cm (25 in) minimum length requirement, and yellow perch. It is open season on perch (up to 0.5 kg/1 lb), with a 15 fish maximum catch limit currently. There is good road access into the lake and a recreation area provides a place to camp and launch a boat from.

Woodman Lake (Map 97/E4)

Woodman Lake is a fly-in lake located north of Lake Athabasca. It has good fishing for northern pike to 7 kg (15 lbs) as well as lake whitefish.

Wylie Lake (Map 97/E5)

This fly-in lake is found north of Lake Athabasca. It is home to lake trout to 19 kg (42 lbs), northern pike to 16 km (35 lbs) and lake whitefish.

Zama Pond (Map 92/E5)

Found in the amusingly named "Zama City" (population less than 100), this trout pond is stocked with rainbow trout every other year and is subject to winter kill.

River & Stream Fishing

Adams Creek (Map 21/F4)

Adams Creek flows west from Grizzly Ridge Wildland Park and into Swan River. Access to most of the creek is difficult, but Highway 33 crosses it just before it flows into the Swan River. The creek contains small arctic grayling to 0.5 kg (1 lb).

Akuinu River (Map 8/D3–G1)

The Akuinu River is a major tributary of the Salteaux. Access to the river is poor, but if you can get to it, the river produces well for those feisty arctic grayling.

Algar River (Map 53/F5–G1)

The Algar flows into the Athabasca 70 km upstream from Fort McMurray near the series of rapids that help make up part of Grand Rapids Wildland Park. Access to the river is difficult without a plane or possibly a jetboat. It holds arctic grayling, northern pike, walleye and Rocky Mountain whitefish.

Amisk River (Map 11/C5–12/A4)

A number of roads that branch from Secondary Highways 663 and 855 provide good access to this small river. Anglers will find pike and walleye in its upper reaches.

Ante Creek (Map 4/D2)

This Simonette River tributary is found at the end of a maze of backroads north of Fox Creek. The creek holds quite a few generally small arctic grayling.

Assineau River (Map 21/G2–22/A4)

Flowing north out of the Grizzly Ridge Wildland Park and into Lesser Slave Lake, access is limited in the middle and upper reaches. The lower section has the best access, as it is crossed by Highway 2, paralleled by the road into Assineau and bridged a couple of times before flowing into the lake. The creek contains arctic grayling to 1 kg (2 lbs) that are generally much smaller.

Athabasca River (Maps 8–11, 23–25, 39, 53, 54, 67–70, 80–83)

The Athabasca flows 1,538 km (938 mile) north and east, draining a large portion of Alberta as it makes its way to Lake Athabasca, in the northeastern corner of the province. It is the second largest drainage system in Alberta. It is home to the only species of native rainbow trout east of the Rocky Mountains. In addition to the famed Athabasca Rainbow Trout, the river holds arctic grayling, brook trout, bull trout, burbot, flathead chub, goldeye, lake chub, lake whitefish, longnose dace, longnose sucker, mountain whitefish, northern pike, pygmy whitefish, slimy sculpin, spoonhead sculpin, spottail shiner, trout, walleye, white sucker, yellow perch...basically if it swims in a river, you will probably find it somewhere along the Athabasca. Most people fishing the Athabasca in this region go looking for a monster pike (up to 9 kg/20 lbs), walleye (to 5.5 kg/12 lbs), grayling or mountain whitefish. Be sure to check the regulations before heading out.

Beaver Ranch Creek (Map 87/C3)

This creek flows south into the Peace River, between Fort Vermilion and John D'Or Prairie. Highway 58 crosses the creek, which is where most people access it (although some undoubtedly access it by riverboat from the Peace). The creek holds pike to 4.5 kg (10 lbs), walleye to 2 kg (4 lb) and grayling to 0.5 kg (1 lb).

Beaverlodge River (Map 16/B3–29/D6)

The Beaverlodge River is home to northern pike and arctic grayling. It is neither fast nor deep and has a number of beaver dams that create nice holes. The river flows from the BC border into the Redwillow River just above that stream's confluence with the much bigger Wapiti River. There is an ongoing attempt to rehabilitate the waters of the Beaverlodge. Once a major grayling habitat, the fish have dwindled due to oil and gas development and forestry near the headwaters. New trees are being planted to stabilize the banks and remove a large percentage of the sediments that flow into the river.

Big Mountain Creek (Map 17/A6–B4)

This Wapiti River tributary is crossed by a number of roads, including Highway 40. The Big Mountain Creek Recreation Site is also found along its banks. The creek contains arctic grayling.

Birch River (Map 80/B2–89/C3)

The Birch River can only be accessed by plane or by some truly psychotic paddlers wishing to paddle into the Athabasca Delta, across Lake Claire, then up the Birch. Not likely, although we'd love to hear from you if you do try it. The river drains the Birch Mountains into Lake Claire in Wood Buffalo and holds northern pike as well as arctic grayling. A National Park License is needed in that section of the river.

Boulder Creek (Map 21/F7)
Highway 33 crosses Boulder Creek just before it flows into the Swan River. It is the best access to the creek, which offers small arctic grayling.

Boyer River (Map 86/D4–87/B3)
Easily accessed from a variety of roads south of Highway 58, the Boyer winds its way north and east parallel to the Peace, before finally flowing into the Peace about 2 km downstream (and across the river from) Fort Vermilion. The creek holds northern pike to 4.5 kg (10 lbs), walleye to 2 kg (4 lbs) and grayling to 0.5 kg (1 lb).

Buffalo River (Map 76/A2–86/D6)
The Buffalo is a hard-to-access river that flows into the Peace a few kilometres upstream from Tompkins Landing Ferry. It can be accessed from the Peace or from cutlines south of La Crete. The river holds good numbers of northern pike to 4.5 kg (10 lbs), walleye to 2 kg (4 lbs) and arctic grayling to 0.5 kg (1 lb).

Bull Creek (Map 2/D3)
One of a number of creeks that feed into the Cutbank River, Bull Creek offers fishing much like the Cutbank, with bull trout to 1 kg (2 lbs) and whitefish and grayling.

Cadotte River (Map 48/D2–61/E6)
The Cadotte River flows out of Cadotte Lake and north into the Peace River. It contains some pike, but the fishing is reported to be rather slow.

Calling River (Map 24/D4–G6)
The Calling River flows east out of Calling Lake and is crossed by a couple roads before flowing into the Athabasca River. It holds some big fish, with rumours of northern pike to 9 kg (20 lbs), walleye to 4.5 kg (10 lbs) and goldeye to 1 kg (2 lbs).

Caribou River (Map 87/B2)
This small, meandering river is crossed by Highway 58 north of Fort Vermilion. The river is a Peace River tributary and holds the typical mix of Peace River fish including arctic grayling, northern pike and walleye.

Chicken Creek (Map 1/G6)
This is a Kakwa tributary, which contains bull trout and arctic grayling. It is catch and release only.

Chinchaga River (Map 71/D1–92/F6)
The Chinchaga is a long, lonely river that can only be accessed from a handful of locations. The main access points are where Highway 58 crosses the river on the way to Rainbow Lake. Here you will find northern pike to 4.5 kg (10 lbs), walleye to 2 kg (4 lbs) and arctic grayling to 0.5 kg (1 lb). Check the regulations for bait bans and other restrictions.

Christina River (Map 40/F1–55/D1)
The Christina is a major tributary of the Clearwater River, flowing across a broad, mostly inaccessible landscape southeast of Fort McMurray. There are a couple places where the river can be accessed in the Conklin area. It holds northern pike, walleye, arctic grayling and burbot. Check the regulations before heading out.

Clarke Creek (Map 69/A7)
This fairly remote stream joins the Athabasca near Fort McMurray. It is a good grayling stream.

Clear River (Map 44/A3–58/E7)
While the Clear River is crossed by Highway 64 west of Cleardale, the fishing here is terrible. Better fishing is to be had just upstream from the river's confluence with the Peace. Of course, there is no road access here, so the river sees few visitors. Those who do make the effort will find northern pike, walleye and grayling.

Clearwater River (Map 55/D1; 69/A7–70/G7)
The Clearwater is one of the main rivers in Northeastern Alberta, but can only be accessed upstream of Fort McMurray, either by jetboat or floatplane. The river holds arctic grayling, northern pike, walleye, whitefish and burbot. Check the regulations before heading out.

Cornwall Creek (Map 18/B3)
This small Simonette River tributary offers good fishing near its confluence with the Simonette for grayling, walleye and bull trout.

Coutts River (Map 8/A3–F1)
The Coutts River is a good grayling river with no road access. However, ATV riders could (and do) string together a series of cutlines to access the river.

Crooked Creek (Map 64/D6–F7)
Crooked Creek is crossed by Secondary Highway 686 northeast of Red Earth Creek. Part of the Loon River system, the creek has good size grayling.

Cutbank River (Map 4/G3–6/B1)
The Cutbank River is a major tributary of the Smoky. While there is no one road that follows the river, there are many places where roads come close to the river or cut across it, providing good access. Even Highway 40 crosses the river. The river contains arctic grayling to 0.5 kg (1 lb) in its upper reaches and whitefish to 1.5 kg (3 lbs) in the lower river. The river also holds some good size northern pike, walleye and bull trout.

Daniel Creek (Map 1/G7–5/A6)
Daniel Creek is a catch-and-release only creek that sees few visitors due to its remote location. It is a Kakwa tributary and as such has good numbers of bull trout and arctic grayling.

Deep Valley Creek (Map 3/E7–4/C3)
Deep Valley Creek winds its way the landscape between the Washkahegan and Simonette River for many kilometres before finally making up its mind and flowing into the Simonette. The Shell Simonette Road crosses the creek, as do several smaller roads that fall off the main trunk. The creek holds arctic grayling, Rocky Mountain whitefish and bull trout. Check the regulations for bait bans and other restrictions.

Dover River (Map 68/C5–F4)
The Dover flows into the MacKay River upstream of Fort MacKay and can only be accessed by jetboat. It holds pike and walleye.

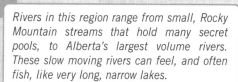

Rivers in this region range from small, Rocky Mountain streams that hold many secret pools, to Alberta's largest volume rivers. These slow moving rivers can feel, and often fish, like very long, narrow lakes.

Driftpile River (Map 21/A6–C2)
Highway 2 crosses the Driftpile near the end of its meandering trek across the landscape south of Lesser Slave Lake. From here, roads head up and downstream for at least a few kilometres, providing good access. You will find northern pike to 4.5 kg (10 lbs) and arctic grayling to 1 kg (2 lbs). Access to the upper reaches is much more difficult.

Driftwood River (Map 23/A1–B4)
While two main roads provide good access to the Driftwood, the fishing is more productive in the lower reaches. Some mighty fine pike (to 4.5 kg/10 lbs) have been pulled out of this meandering stream.

East Prairie River (Map 20/F6–34/C6)
The East Prairie River meanders north from the Swan Hills, eventually crossing Highway 2 west of Slave Lake. Like most rivers that flow into Slave Lake, pike and walleye inhabit the lower sections of the river. Check the guides for regulations below Highway 2. The pike and walleye become less plentiful as you travel upstream, where you will start to find arctic grayling. Unfortunately, access to the upper reaches is difficult.

Economy Creek (Map 17/F4)
Flowing east out of Economy Lake, underneath the Forestry Trunk Road (Highway 734) and then north to its confluence with the Simonette River, you would think this is a big creek. It is not. It does, however, offer pike and walleye in its lower reaches and grayling in its upper reaches.

Ells River (Map 81/B3–F3)
The Ells River can be accessed along a road north of Fort MacKay. This road can be treacherous when wet. The river holds arctic grayling, northern pike, walleye, yellow perch, whitefish and burbot. Check the regulations for bait bans and other restrictions.

Fishing Adventures

Fawcett River (Map 23/C3)
Fawcett River drains Fawcett Lake into the Lesser Slave River. It is road accessible right where it flows out of the lake and right before it flows into the river. You will find arctic grayling, northern pike and walleye in the river.

Firebag River (Map 83/A1–F4)
The Firebag River can be accessed by ATV along the Fort Chipewyan Winter Road north of Fort McMurray. Closer to the mouth of the Athabasca, jetboats are the mode of access. The river holds pike and walleye.

Florence Creek (Map 22/F7)
Florence Creek is a tributary of Parker Creek. Like Parker Creek, it contains arctic grayling.

Freeman Creek (Map 7/D4)
Freeman Creek drains Freeman Lake into the Freeman River. It is crossed by a number of backroads in its upper reaches, while the last few kilometres parallel Highway 32. It contains rainbow trout and arctic grayling.

Freeman River (Map 6/F3–8/B7)
The Freeman River flows east from the Swan Hills to join up with the Athabasca River near Fort Assiniboine. There are many points of access to the river, both in the upper and lower reaches. Popular access points include the Freeman River Recreation Area, near the Highway 32 crossing and at the Secondary Highway 658 crossing. You will find rainbow trout to 0.5 kg (1 lb) and arctic grayling to 1 kg (2 lbs) in both the upper and lower reaches of the river. As you get close to the Athabasca, you will find the occasional northern pike or walleye.

Goose River (Map 6/D2–19/B6)
The Goose River flows west from the Swan Hills and eventually drains into the Little Smoky south of Valleyview. There are long sections of this river that are mostly inaccessible, but there are a couple of good access points, most notably where Secondary Highway 745 crosses it. The river contains northern pike to 4.5 kg (10 lbs), walleye and bull trout to 2.5 kg (5 lbs), whitefish to 1 kg (2 lbs) and arctic grayling to 0.5 kg (1 lb). Check the regulations for bait bans and other restrictions.

Grayling Creek (Map 1/F1)
As the name would lead you to believe, this creek has arctic grayling in it. It also has bull trout and whitefish. Access to the creek is along cutlines from the Nose Mountain Road.

Gregoire River (Map 55/D4–F3)
Secondary Highway 881 crosses the Gregoire River where it flows out of Gregoire Lake and again a few kilometres further south. The river holds pike and grayling.

Grouard Channel (Map 34/E7)
This short, broad channel connects Buffalo Bay to Lesser Slave Lake. It is closed March 1 to June 15 while the walleye spawn. When it is open, the channel contains big fish including northern pike to 7.5 kg (15 lbs), walleye to 4.5 kg (10 lbs), whitefish to 2.5 kg (5 lbs) yellow perch to 0.5 kg (1 lb). This section can be fished with a boat or from the bridge over the channel.

Gunderson Creek (Map 1/E3)
Gunderson Creek flows through Two Lakes Recreation Area and into Nose Creek. An old backroad crosses it near its confluence with Nose Creek, where you will find bull trout, arctic grayling and whitefish. The middle stretch of the river can be reached by trail and the upper section can be accessed at the Two Lakes Recreation Area.

Hangingstone River (Map 54/G6–69/A7)
The Hangingstone is a popular grayling river found just south of Fort McMurray. It holds arctic grayling to 1 kg (2 lbs) and northern pike to 2.5 kg (6 lbs) and best accessed off Highway 63. Check the regulations for closures.

Harper Creek (Map 18/B3)
This small Simonette River tributary offers good fishing near its confluence with the Simonette for grayling, walleye and bull trout.

Harper Creek (Map 88/B5)
Harper Creek is a remote creek found near the southwest corner of Wood Buffalo National Park. Access into this area is difficult and the creek sees little pressure for its arctic grayling and northern pike.

Hay River (Map 91/F7–73/E1, Map 99 Inset B)
The Hay River's headwaters are in Alberta, but the river flows into BC for a fair distance before crossing back into Alberta to flow into Zama Lake. It is possible to access the river at Habay, just outside the Hay-Zama Wildland Park, but the easiest place to access the river is at Meander River, as well as a few crossings further north. The river holds big fish with northern pike reaching 7 kg (15 lbs) and walleye rumoured to 4.5 kg (10 lbs). Also present are arctic grayling and burbot. See the regulations for restrictions.

Heart River (Map 47/C4–E7)
There is good fishing in the Heart River, just up from its confluence with the Peace. Here you can find northern pike to 3.5 kg (8 lbs), walleye to 4 kg (9 lbs), goldeye to 1 kg (2 lbs), rainbow trout to 2.5 kg (5 lbs) and bull trout.

High Hill River (Map 70/E7–F5)
The High Hill River flows into the Clearwater about 75 km upstream from Fort McMurray. The only way to access the river is by jetboat heading up or by canoe heading down. The river is reportedly a fairly good grayling stream.

Horse River (Map 54/C7–63/A7)
The Horse River flows into the Athabasca at Fort McMurray. It holds arctic grayling to 1 kg (2 lbs). There are angling trails along the east side of the river.

Hotchkiss River (Map 61/B2–61/A4)
The Hotchkiss flows east into the Notikewin and is best accessed by Highway 35 north of Manning. Alternatively the Chinchaga Forest Road provides fair access (when it is not wet). The river offers northern pike to 4.5 kg (10 lbs), walleye to 2.5 kg (5 lbs) and arctic grayling to 0.5 kg (1 lb).

House River (Map 39/E1–40/B3; 53/E7)
The House River runs parallel to the Athabasca for a fairly long way before finally joining the big river near Grand Rapids. The easiest place to access the river is where Highway 63 crosses it south of Cross Lake Provincial Park. The river holds pike and walleye near the mouth as well as arctic grayling further upstream. Check the regulations for closures.

Inverness River (Map 21/B7–E6)
The Inverness River flows east from the Swan Hills into the Swan River. It contains northern pike to 1 kg (2 lbs) and arctic grayling to 0.5 kg (1 lb). There are a number of backroads that cross the river west of Highway 33.

Island Creek (Map 21/F5)
Island Creek is another tributary of the Swan River that has its headwaters in the Grizzly Ridge Wildland Park. Highway 33 and a rough backroad cross the small creek that contains small arctic grayling.

Jackfish River (Map 41/D6)
This is a short river that drains Christina Lake into Christina River. There are a number of places to access the river, including the Secondary Highway 881 bridge. The river holds arctic grayling, northern pike and walleye. Check the regulations for closures.

Kakwa River (Map 1/A7–3/C2)
The Kakwa flows northeast from the Kakwa Wildland and into the Smoky River. It is a fairly large river with many tributaries. The best access is from Highway 40 south of Grande Prairie. From here to the Smoky, the river contains bull trout to 2.5 kg (5 lbs), rainbow to 1.5 kg (3 lbs) and whitefish to 1 kg (2 lbs). You may find an arctic grayling or two, but they tend to stick to the upper reaches of the river.

Keane Creek (Map 90/D4)
Another remote stream that cannot be accessed by road, Keane Creek is instead accessed by a 180 km ATV trip along the Fort Chipewyan Winter Road. The creek holds arctic grayling, northern pike, walleye and yellow perch.

Keg River (Map 85/F6–86/D6)
The Keg River flows east of the Chinchaga and into the Peace. It is surprisingly easy to access, as there are a number of roads that cross it, including Highway 35. It holds northern pike to 4.5 kg (10 lbs) and walleye to 2 kg (4 lbs). Farther upstream near the headwater, you will also find arctic grayling.

Kemp River (Map 59/G1–86/A7)
The Kemp flows north, parallel to Highway 35 near Keg River the community for a few kilometres allowing for fairly easy access to the lower reaches. The Kemp holds a fair number of small grayling.

La Biche River (Map 11/G1–25/B7)
The La Biche River drains the lake of the same name (or, if you prefer, the Lac of the same name) into the Athabasca. There are a couple easy points of access, including where Highway 63 crosses it. The river holds northern pike to 4.5 kg (10 lbs), walleye to about half that, as well as as well as arctic grayling, brook, bull and rainbow trout, goldeye, whitefish and yellow perch.

Lafond Creek (Map 64/D4)
Highway 88 crosses Lafond Creek just before it flows into Loon River. This is the main access point for anglers looking for northern pike, walleye and goldeye.

Lambert Creek (Map 88/B6)
This remote river may or may not be accessible by ATV from Fort Vermillion by ATV along the winter road, but we haven't heard of anyone willing to make the nearly 100 km ride. Chances are the creek is rarely, if ever fished, other than by folks from Fox Lake and by people willing to fly in and land at the Lambert Creek Tower Airport, which despite the name, is not very close to the creek at all. If you go, expect feisty grayling.

Latornell River (Map 3/E4–18/A5)
The Latornell River is paralleled by the Forestry Trunk Road for a few kilometres near Misery Mountain. Beyond that, access is limited. You will find arctic grayling in the upper reaches of the river and walleye near the Simonette River.

Lawrence River (Map 87/E1–F3)
Like most of the rivers that flow south into the Peace in the John D'Or Prairie area, this river holds fairly large pike and walleye, as well as the odd grayling further upstream.

Lesser Slave River (Map 22/D3–23/D5)
This river drains Lesser Slave Lake into the Athabasca River. The closer you fish to the lake, the bigger the fish are. In fact you may find northern pike to 9 kg (20 lbs) and walleye to 3.5 kg (8 lbs). The river also contains arctic grayling, which can get to 1 kg (2 lbs). There is good fishing near the confluence with the Athabasca as well.

Lick Creek (Map 1/C6)
Lick Creek flows into the Torrens River 155 km south of Grande Prairie near Two Lakes Road. This remote mountain stream has rainbow and cutthroat trout, as well as a rainbow-cutthroat hybrid.

Northern Pike are found throughout Alberta, except in the foothills and mountains, and have been known to weigh up to 22 kg (50 lbs). The popular sportfish inhabits slow streams and shallow, weedy clear water lakes and marshes.

Lignite Creek (Map 17/D5)
This tributary of the Smoky is accessible from the east along cutlines from the Economy Lake Area. It is about 10 km to the creek from the east. From the west, it is possible to get within a couple kilometres of the creek from backroads in the Smoky Flats area. The creek offers bull trout, whitefish and arctic grayling.

Little Clear River (Map 58/E7)
This small volume river is found near the BC Boundary off the Clear Prairie Road. It holds a fair number of arctic grayling.

Little Smoky River (Maps 5, 19, 32, 33)
Despite the name, the Little Smoky is a pretty big river. It flows from south of our maps to join the Smoky west of Falher. The Little Smoky is an amazing fishing river, with grayling and bull trout being the prime catches here. It contains bull trout to 4.5 kg (10 lbs), whitefish to 1.5 kg (3 lbs) and arctic grayling to 1 kg (2 lbs). During late summer to the middle of October, fishing can be fast and furious. The river is heavily regulated; check the regulations before heading out.

Loon River (Map 49/C1–64/E4)
Highway 88 parallels the Loon River for nearly 80 km, providing good access to the river. Anglers can expect to find northern pike up to 4.5 kg (10 lbs), walleye to 2.5 kg (5 lbs), goldeye to 1 kg (2 lbs), arctic grayling to 0.5 kg (1 lb) and burbot. Check the regulations before heading out.

Lynx Creek (Map 1/E6)
This heavily regulated creek has a short open season for cutthroat. Check the regulations for exact dates and note the bait ban.

MacKay River (Map 68/C7–F4)
The MacKay flows into the Athabasca at Fort MacKay, but only has a few road accessible sections. The river holds has northern pike to 4.5 kg (10 lbs), walleye and arctic grayling.

Marguerite River (Map 83/B2–F2)
This river is jetboat accessible only and requires running up the Firebag River from the Athabasca. The Marguerite holds arctic graylings and Rocky Mountain whitefish.

Marten Creek (Map 36/C7–E6)
Also referred to as Marten River, the lower reaches of this stream are easily accessible where Highway 88 crosses it. Another popular access point is at the Marten River Campground in Lesser Slave Lake Provincial Park. Access is progressively more difficult as you make your way upstream. The river holds average size grayling.

May River (Map 26/E1–41/A6)
The May River is found northwest of Conklin, but access to the river is poor, especially in wet weather. The river holds pike and grayling.

McLean Creek (Map 58/D7)
McLean Creek holds good numbers of arctic grayling. It is accessed along the Clear Prairie Tower Road.

Meander River (Map 93/B5–C7)
The Meander River parallels Highway 35 north of Hutch Lake, but the best access is just north of the Meander River settlement. It holds some very big walleye to 4.5 kg (10 lbs), as well as northern pike to 7 kg (15 lbs).

Meikle River (Map 74/D3–74/C3)
Highway 35 crosses the Meikle just north of Manning. This is the main access point for anglers looking for the Northern Alberta special of arctic grayling, northern pike and walleye.

Mikkwa River (Map 78/D2–87/G3)
There is no road access to this remote river and access to its headwaters might involve a flight in. The lower reaches, however, can be accessed where it flows into the Peace. Similar to most Peace tributaries, the Mikkwa boasts of larger than average pike and walleye, as well as arctic grayling further upstream. Check the regulations for restrictions.

Moosehorn River (Map 7/A2–E1)
The Moosehorn River flows east from its headwaters and into the Swan River north of Swan Hills. There are a number of good access points to the river, especially in the lower half. It contains arctic grayling to 0.5 kg (1 lb).

Morse River (Map 7/D3–G6)
The Morse River sees fairly heavy fishing pressure for rainbow trout and arctic graylings to 0.5 kg (1 lb), due in no small part to easy access. The river flows east from Morse Lake and is crossed by Highway 32, then paralleled by Highway 33 to near its confluence with the Freeman River.

Muskeg River (Map 68/G4–83/B3)
The Muskeg flows into the Athabasca just upstream of Fort MacKay. Road access is limited by the gate at the Muskeg River Mine. The river offers arctic grayling, northern pike and walleye.

Muskwa River (Map 50/F7–51/G5)
This long, remote river is mostly inaccessible, save for near where it flows into the Wabasca River. Even here, access is not easy. In winter, access is easier, along a winter road. The river holds northern pike, walleye, yellow perch and burbot. Check the regulations for restrictions.

Narraway River (Map 1/C4–15/C7)
The Narraway River is a major tributary of the Wapiti that starts in BC. It is a fairly remote river, with one road and a couple trails providing access. The river holds bull trout to 2.5 kg (5 lbs), whitefish to 1 kg (2 lbs) and arctic grayling to 0.5 kg (1 lb).

Nipisi River (Map 36/C4–50/E7)
The Nipisi River drains Nipisi Lake, making its slow, meandering way north into Muskwa Lake. Nowhere along its course is there road access to the river, so few people fish much past where it flows out of the lake. The river contains northern pike to 4.5 kg (10 lbs) and arctic grayling to 0.5 kg (1 lb). Anglers will also find walleye and burbot. Check the regulations for restrictions.

Fishing Adventures

North Cutbank River (Map 1/F3)

The North Cutbank River is a short river that drains Nose Lake into the Cutbank. There is no road access to the river so anglers will have to bushwhack in. The river holds brook and bull trout and grayling.

Nose Creek (Map 1/E3–15/F5)

Nose Creek flows north from the mountains east of Two Lakes. The creek (which is bigger than some rivers), has many tributaries and offers good fishing for arctic grayling and whitefish in the upper reaches. Near it's confluence with the Kakwa, you can also find northern pike and walleye.

Notikewin River (Map 58/G5–61/C3)

The upper reaches of the Notikewin are mostly inaccessible, but the lower reaches are quite easy to access in and around the town of Manning and northeast to Notikewin River Provincial Park. Like most Peace tributaries, it holds a mix of northern pike to 4.5 kg (10 lbs), walleye to 2.5 kg (5 lbs) and arctic grayling to 0.5 kg (1 lb).

Otauwau River (Map 22/D6–G3)

While the upper reaches of this river are mostly inaccessible, the lower stretch is accessed and/or crossed by a number of roads, including Highway 2, before it flows into the Lesser Slave River. The river offers arctic grayling.

Otter River (Map 48/D1–63/A6)

The Otter River is a tributary of the Cadotte River that can be accessed of the Bison Lake Road. It is home to pike and grayling.

Parker Creek (Map 22/E6–G7)

This stream drains Parker Lake into the Salteaux River. The creek has good fishing for grayling.

Peace River (Maps 43–47, 61–62, 74–75, 86–88, 95–97)

The mighty Peace River, which begins in the mountains of British Columbia, is Alberta's largest river. It also has the highest volume of flow. The river flows northeast across the province, through the town of Peace River and empties into the Slave River. Main tributaries include the Wapiti, Smoky, Little Smoky and Wabasca Rivers. As you might expect, there are a lot of fish in the river, including northern pike to 4.5 kg (10 lbs), walleye to 3.5 kg (8 lbs), as well as arctic grayling, bull trout, rainbow trout, goldeye and whitefish. Due to the size and difficulty of shore access in many areas, drift fishing is a popular alternative. Consult the regulations before heading out.

Pembina River (Map 9/A3–C7)

While the majority of this river is covered by the Central Alberta Backroad Mapbook, the Pembina winds its way onto these maps for a few dozen kilometres before flowing into the Athabasca. There are a couple of bridges in this section that provide easy access to the river. The lower stretches of the river are home to some big rainbow and bull trout (to 9 kg/20 lbs) and walleye (to 4.5 kg/10 lbs) as well as some goods size goldeye (to 1.5 kg/3 lbs). Arctic grayling and whitefish are also present. Check the regulations before heading out.

Petitot River (Map 91/G1–92/C1)

This is one of the most remote rivers in Alberta, draining Thurston Lake (east of our maps in BC) into Bistcho Lake. There is a fly-in lodge on Bistcho Lake, but there are also cutlines that can be followed on an ATV north of Zama City. Anglers will find northern pike, walleye, arctic grayling and burbot. Check the regulations for special restrictions.

Piché River (Map 26/D7–F7)

Piché River joins Heart Lake with Piché Lake. At this point, the river is more like a lake and even offers a similar fishery. Northern pike, walleye and yellow perch and all roam the waters. See the regulations for closures.

Pine Creek (Map 10/E5–11/D1)

There are a number of places to access this creek as it flows north and east across the country east of the town of Athabasca. The creek eventually flows into the La Biche River at the south end of the wildland park. Anglers will find pike and walleye, with the better fishing coming closer to the confluence of the two streams.

Pinto Creek (Map 16/A4–C7)

Backroads cross Pinto Creek every dozen kilometres or so allowing for good access to the lower half of the creek. However, the best fishing is near the confluence with the Wapiti. It contains bull trout to 2 kg (4 lbs), whitefish and grayling.

Ponton River (Map 87/A3–94/C6)

The Ponton is a small river that flows from the untracked wilderness north of Fort Vermilion and into the Boyer, which then flows into the Peace. There are a couple of places to access the river, including the Highway 58 bridge. It holds the usual mix of northern pike to 4.5 kg (10 lbs), walleye to 2.5 kg (5 lbs) and arctic grayling to 1 kg (2 lbs).

Poplar Creek (Map 68/G6)

Poplar Creek is accessed from a bridge on Highway 63, 25 km north of Fort McMurray. The creek holds arctic grayling, northern pike, walleye and whitefish. It may also hold yellow perch, which is pretty unusual for a creek.

Pouce Coupé River (Maps 30/B2–43/F3)

A tributary of the mighty Peace, the Pouce Coupé creates a dramatic gorge when it re-enters Alberta east of Dawson Creek. Access in this area is challenging, although a couple Range Roads due cross the river north of Highway 49. Anglers can expect to find pike and walleye, as well as rainbow and bull trout.

Puskwaskau River (Map 18/D2–31/G6)

Flowing from Puskwaskau Lake to the Smoky River, this meandering river offers pike and walleye.

Redearth Creek (Map 50/B3–63/G7)

Redearth Creek contains some sizable pike, up to 7 kg (15 lbs), as well as walleye to 2.5 kg (5 lbs) and arctic grayling to 0.5 kg (1 lb). It is accessed along backroads east and north of Red Earth Creek, the settlement.

Redrock Creek (Map 2/B5)

Redrock Creek is found west of the Kakwa Fire Tower. It holds bull trout, whitefish and grayling. It is a tributary of the Kakwa, so it is catch and release only.

Redwillow River (Map 15/C3–16/C3)

The Redwillow River flows east from the BC Rockies into Alberta, where it joins the Wapiti River. Several roads lead to and cross the river south of Beaverlodge. It contains northern pike to 4.5 kg (10 lbs) and walleye to 2.5 kg (5 lbs) in its lower reaches and arctic grayling to 0.5 kg (1 lb) in the upper sections. You will also find bull trout and whitefish throughout the river.

Richardson River (Map 83/G1–90/A4)

This lonely river drains a series of unnamed lakes on the east side of the Athabasca, passing through some of the most dramatic sand dune scenery in the Athabasca area. The river is accessed via a 130 km ATV trek through the sandhills along the winter road. Anglers will find arctic grayling, northern pike, walleye, goldeye, whitefish and burbot.

Rivière des Rochers (Map 90/B2–97/A7)

Linking the Peace/Slave confluence with Fort Chipewyan, this big river does hold fish, but darned if you will be able to find any in its silty depths. Fishing is poor for arctic grayling, northern pike, goldeye and whitefish.

Saline Creek (Map 55/C2–69/A7)

This creek flows into the Hangingstone just before that river flows into the Clearwater. Like the Hangingstone, it is known for its arctic grayling fishing. The creek also holds some pike.

Salteaux River (Map 8/A2–23/A4)

The upper reaches of the Salteaux are fairly inaccessible expect by ATV. The mid-point is reached by backroads south of Highway 2, while the upper reaches are crossed by Highway 2 itself. The river provides good grayling fishing.

Saprae Creek (Map 55/C1)

Saprae Creek flows into the Clearwater upstream of Fort McMurray. Despite the fairly good road access, it remains a fairly good grayling stream.

Sawridge Creek (Map 22/B4)

Sawridge Creek flows north out of the Grizzly Ridge Wildland Park, through the town of Slave Lake and into the Lesser Slave River. Access to the river is very good through the town. This is too bad, because there are no grayling in the river through that section. Instead, you will have to go farther upstream to find these fish.

Shelter Creek (Map 1/F4)

A tributary of Nose Creek, access to Shelter Creek is along cutlines and trails off of Nose Mountain Road. The creek holds good numbers of grayling, whitefish and bull trout.

Simonette River (Map 3/C7–17/F3)

The Simonette is a major tributary of the Smoky. The confluence is just east of the Simonette River Recreation Area, which is the prime access point for the lower reaches of the river. You will find northern pike to 3.5 kg (8 lbs) and walleye to 2 kg (4 lbs) in this section. As you move farther upstream, you will find bull trout to 4.5 kg (10 lbs), whitefish to 1.5 kg (3 lbs) and arctic grayling to 1 kg (2 lbs). See the regulations for special restrictions.

Fishing Adventures

Slave River (Map 96/F1–97/A7)
By sheer volume of water moved, this is Alberta's biggest river, a combination of the Athabasca (or rather, the Riviére des Rochers, which drains Lake Athabasca) and the Peace. It is also one of the most turbulent and finding fish is nearly impossible for all the silt in the water. Fishing is poor for arctic grayling, northern pike, goldeye and whitefish.

Smoky River (Maps 3, 17, 31, 32, 46, 47)
The Smoky is a major tributary of the Peace River and is a big river in its own right, draining much of the area south and west of the town of Peace River. There are many places to access the river. Near its confluence with the Peace, the Smoky holds northern pike and walleye to 4.5 kg (10 lbs) and goldeye. As you move farther upstream, you will find bull trout (to 4.5 kg/10 lbs), whitefish to 1.5 kg (3 lbs) and arctic grayling to 1 kg (2 lbs). Check the regulations for restrictions.

South Heart River (Map 34/E6–G1; 48/F6)
The South Heart River is a long, rambling river that flows across a mostly inaccessible area north of Winigami Lake. However, there are a few roads and many cutlines that cross this upper stretch of river. Past Winigami Lake, the river flows south then east into Buffalo Bay. This section of the river is much more accessible and it is in this section that you will find northern pike to 4.5 kg (10 lbs) and walleye to 2.5 kg (5 lbs). See the regulations for closures, bait restrictions and retention limits.

Spirit River (Map 30/E2–32/A1)
Another tributary of the Peace River, Spirit River is better known by the townsite of the same name. As a Peace tributary anglers can look for northern pike, walleye, rainbow and bull trout.

Steepbank River (Map 68/G5–69/C6)
The Steepbank is found on the wrong side of the Athabasca. There is no road access to the river, but it is easy to access by boat. The river holds arctic grayling, northern pike, walleye and yellow perch.

Stetson Creek (Map 1/D5)
Crossed by a 4wd road that continues past Two Lakes Recreation Area, this creek contains rainbow and grayling. Although not common, both fish can reach 0.5 kg (1 lb) in size.

Stoney Creek (Map 21/F6)
This short creek flows down from the Grizzly Ridge Wildland Park and into the Swan River. Most anglers access the creek from Highway 33 in search of grayling to 0.5 kg (1 lb).

Strawberry Creek (Map 21/D3)
Strawberry Creek flows into Lesser Slave Lake at Giroux Bay. Highway 2 crosses and then parallels the creek for a few kilometres if travelling west. This section of the creek is the easiest to access in the lower reaches where pike and perch are found. Anglers will also find walleye, grayling and burbot. Check the regulations for closures and bait bans.

Swan River (Map 7/B2–21/F1)
The Swan River is a major tributary of Lesser Slave Lake that runs north from Swan Hills to the big lake. Highway 33 provides good access for most of the river's meandering course. The lower reaches have pike and walleye, while the faster moving upper reaches hold grayling that can be a bit bigger than those in the rivers tributaries.

Sweeney Creek (Map 58/D7)
Found in the Clear Hills area, this creek is home to fair numbers of arctic grayling.

Torrens River (Map 1/A6–C4)
The Torrens River is a tributary of the Narraway. It is home to plenty of rainbow and bull trout and whitefish. Below the falls you will also find arctic grayling. See the regulations for bait bans and closures.

Utikuma River (Map 35/F2–50/F6)
There is good access to most of the Utikuma River as it is crossed by Highway 88 south of Red Earth Creek and paralleled by a backroad. The river contains arctic grayling, northern pike and walleye.

Valley Creek (Map 1/E3)
A small tributary of Nose Creek, Valley Creek is home to grayling, whitefish and bull trout.

Wabasca River (Map 37–38, 51–52, 63–66, 76–79)
The Wabasca is a long, lonely river that is only accessible in a few places. You will find big northern pike and walleye (to 7 kg/15 lbs and 4.5 kg/10 lbs respec-

tively) and good numbers of arctic grayling, yellow perch, whitefish and burbot. The easiest place to access it is along Secondary Highway 264, which crosses the river a couple times, or Highway 88, which also crosses it a couple times. See the regulations for closures.

Wandering River (Map 25/D6–26/A2)
The Wandering River and Pine Creek meet northwest of Lac La Biche to become the La Biche River. Both hold pike and walleye.

Wapiti River (Map 15/A7–17/E3)
The Wapiti flows from its headwaters in BC (about 56 km west of the BC/Alberta boundary) and into Alberta, flowing just south of Grande Prairie and finally joining the Smoky River east of the city. There are many good places to access the river, the easiest being the Highway 40 bridge south of Grande Prairie. You will find big northern pike, walleye and bull trout in the river. Further upstream some good size arctic grayling and mountain whitefish can be lured. Check the regulations before heading out.

Waskahigan River (Map 4/B7–5/A2)
There are a few roads that cross the Waskahigan River's upper reaches, but for the most part, the river is inaccessible until just before its confluence with the Little Smoky. Here the river is crossed by Highway 43 and is home to a recreation area. (The site is to be moved when the highway is twinned in 2004). The river holds pike and walleye in its lower reaches, while the upper river holds arctic grayling and whitefish to 0.5 kg (1 lb). There is an advisory not to eat whitefish caught here.

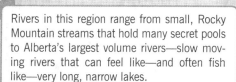

Rivers in this region range from small, Rocky Mountain streams that hold many secret pools to Alberta's largest volume rivers—slow moving rivers that can feel like—and often fish like—very long, narrow lakes.

Wentzel River (Map 88/A2–94/G6)
The Wentzel flows south into the Peace. The long, lonely road to Garden Creek crosses the river, but should not be attempted in wet weather. Even in dry weather, a 4wd is recommended. It holds the typical Peace tributary mix of big pike, small walleye and even smaller arctic grayling.

West Prairie River (Map 20/C5–34/B7)
This long, rambling river flows through High Prairie before joining the South Heart River. Highway 2 and Secondary Highway 749 provide good access to the lower reaches, which hold pike and walleye. The upper reaches, which are much less accessible, hold grayling. See the regulations for closures.

Whitemud River (Map 46/G1–47/C1; 61/C7)
Not to be confused with the stream that flows through Edmonton, this Whitemud is a tributary of the Peace River. It is crossed by Secondary Highway 743 a couple times as well as Highway 35 (near Dixonville) further west. The river is home to pike and walleye.

Winefred River (Map 42/A2–B7)
The Winefred River drains Winefred Lake into the Christina River. Access is limited to near the mouth of the river and one further upstream. These roads can be pretty bad in wet weather. As you might expect, there are grayling, pike and walleye.

Wolf Creek (Map 2/B4)
This relatively short creek is a tributary of the Cutbank River. Look for grayling.

Wolverine River (Map 76/A3–86/D7)
The Wolverine flows into the Peace upstream from Tompkins Landing Ferry. There is no road access to the river and access is by boat only. Jetboats can come upstream from Fort Vermilion. Canoeists might want to try putting in near Carcajou, canoeing across the river, then taking out at either the road north of Carcajou or at Tompkins Landing. The Wolverine holds northern pike, walleye and goldeye.

Hunting
Adventures

Hunting has long been a popular activity for thousands of Alberta residents and visitors to the province. While there are trophy hunters who come to Northern Alberta to hunt, there are also plenty of sustenance hunters, too. Every year, these people head out in pursuit of waterfowl, deer, moose, bear and other quarry. Northern Alberta features nearly all the game species that you will find in the province.

With habitat and terrain ranging from mountains to forested uplands and prairies, you will find everything from bighorn sheep to moose and ptarmigan in this region. The exception is introduced game birds (grey partridge and ring-necked pheasants), which are rarely found in the north.

Generally, hunting in Alberta is divided into two categories, each with its own special rules, regulations and techniques. Big game species include ungulates like deer and moose and predators like bear and wolves, while game birds include birds like grouse and pheasant. Waterfowl, such as duck and geese, are also game birds, but require a Federal Migratory Game Bird Hunting Permit in addition to a Game Bird License and a Wildlife Certificate. Traditionally, hunting seasons are in fall of each year, but there are select seasons in spring and winter as well. Season dates and bag limits vary from year to year and sometimes change without warning. As always, it is the responsibility of the hunter to keep up to date on changes to regulations, dates and bag limits. After all, hunting is a highly regulated activity and it is your responsibility to know the rules and regulations before heading out. The regulations are available on line at www.albertaregulations.ca.

All hunters in Alberta need a valid Wildlife Identification Number before they can buy a hunting license. Hunters must also have a valid Wildlife Certificate, plus the applicable license for the species and seasons hunted. In addition, there are a variety of specialized forms of hunting practiced by enthusiasts across Alberta. These include bow hunting, muzzle-loaded firearms, crossbow hunting and falconry. Each of these has its own set of rules and regulations and permits. For instance, bow hunters may hunt during the general seasons as well as archery-only seasons, but require a special bow hunting permit. As of 2008, hunters are able to purchase or renew their Wildlife Identification Number and purchase draw applications online. First-time hunters need to either complete the Alberta Conservation and Hunter Education Course or pass the Alberta Hunter Competency Exam.

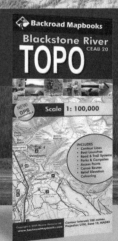

Big Game Species

Bear

There are two species of bear found in Alberta: black bear and grizzly bear. Of the two, grizzly bear are the least common and are closed to hunting throughout the province. Black bear, however, are hunted in Alberta in both spring and fall. Actually, calling them black bear can be misleading as the bear's long fur ranges from a deep black to a light blonde. Cinnamon and blond-coloured black bears are often mistaken for grizzlies, although they are much smaller, ranging from 100 to 200 kg (220 to 440 lbs) for an adult boar and from 45 to 140 kg (100 to 310 lbs) for sows. Black bear also lack the pronounced shoulder hump and dish-shaped face of a grizzly.

Black bear are omnivorous and opportunistic and will eat leaves, berries, roots, fish, mice, young deer, ants, grubs, honey, carrion and garbage. They are common in the open forest of the foothills and mountains of western Alberta. Logging and road building in the area has improved bear habitat and as a result, populations are on the rise, with an estimated 36,000 animals in the province.

Baiting is permitted in a number of Wildlife Management Units (WMUs), but is only allowed from two weeks preceding open season to the end of the season. These bait sites are not allowed within 1.6 km (1 mile) of occupied dwellings (unless it is your own), provincial parks, forest recreation sites and some industrial sites. Owners of bait sites must post their name, WIN, big game guide outfitter-guide permit number, as well as signs around the bait site to warn other people that a bait site is in the area. Check with local fish and wildlife offices for specific details.

> *White-tailed deer are the most common cloven-hoofed animal in Alberta. They are named after their notable white tail.*

Elk

Elk are one of the most distinguished and distinguishable members of the deer family, especially the bulls, with their large, sweeping antlers and dark brown heads. Elk are also known as wapiti are much larger than the other members of the deer family in Alberta, with bulls weighing up to 450 kg (1,000 lbs) and cows to 270 kg (600 lbs). The elk antler has a large single beam with up to six tines projecting from it. Bulls challenge each other for possession of cows and the elk is the only member of the deer family in Alberta that collects a harem.

Elk are found in areas of woodland mixed with grassland such as around the edges of forests and in mountain meadows. They forage on forbs and grasses in the summer and aspen bark and twigs in the winter when food is scarce. These animals are found mainly in the foothills and mountains. They migrate from high summer ranges to winter ranges in lower mountain valleys and foothills. There are an estimated 26,000 elk in Alberta. As a result, elk are less commonly hunted but also tend to see more pressure from hunters. Like most ungulates, elk are more found in the transitional zones in the southern part of this book.

Moose

Moose are one of the most prized animals to hunt in Alberta. They are the largest member of the deer family and the largest ungulate in North America. Because of their size, they have few predators. Moose are quite distinctive looking (some would say downright ugly). They have long legs, a large, drooping snout and a flap of skin in the shape of a bell under their throats. The have broad hooves and are usually dark brown to black. Male moose have large, broad antlers that are extremely prized among hunters. A full sized bull moose can stand 2.75 metres (9.25 feet) tall.

Moose are found across the province with about their population estimated to be around 115,000. Typically, moose have preferred to live in muskegs, brushy meadows and groves of aspen or coniferous trees, especially where there are nearby lakes, ponds or streams. They prefer the transition zones between prairie and wooded areas. Moose cannot see very well, but they have an acute sense of smell and hearing. When frightened, they will trot away with long smooth strides; threading their way through bush and trees that you wouldn't think they'd be able to navigate.

In Northern Alberta, populations have been shifting. Northeastern Alberta, typically a moose stronghold, has seen populations crash, while populations are on the rise in the parklands and prairies. The Peace Region is notorious for its good moose hunting, but the lower boreal forests from Manning south should not be ruled out.

Mule Deer

Mule deer take their name from a distinctive feature, in this case, their large mule-like ears. In addition to the big ears, mule deer can be identified by their thin, black-tipped tail and their large antlers that divide into two equal tines. Like whitetails, mulies are greyish brown in winter and reddish-brown in summer. They are slightly larger with bucks averaging about 100 kg (220 lbs) and does about 70 kg (155 lbs).

Mule deer have an excellent sense of smell, sight and hearing, but mulies are often much more curious and will stop even when fleeing to have one last look. This often makes them an easier species to bag. Mule deer are scattered throughout the province, but are concentrated in the south and west side of the province, especially around the mountains. They like to hang out in mixed-wood forests, hilly areas and the edges of coniferous forests. Current estimates of the population are around 133,000, which is about half the population of white-tailed deer.

White-Tailed Deer

White-tailed deer are the most common cloven-hoofed animal in Alberta. They are named after their notable white tail. When the deer run, their tails are held erect, exposing the white underside, hence the name "white-tail." White-tails have no rump patch and are usually a greyish brown in winter and a reddish brown in summer. Bucks average 90 kg (200 lbs), while does average about 60 kg (130 lbs). Their antlers have un-branched tines extending up from single beams.

White-tails possess excellent senses of sight, smell and hearing and bound away gracefully when frightened. They are often found along the transition areas of forests or in open brush feeding on buds, twigs, saplings and evergreen needles in the winter and on grass, fruit and leaves in the summer. They are frequently found in wooded river flats or in aspen groves. Their range is expanding westward into the foothills and they are becoming more common in the boreal forests of the north, too where they browse on forbs, chokecherry, Saskatoon and other shrubs. In addition to food, brushy patches also provide good cover.

The provincial population of white-tailed deer is estimated to be over 230,000. The best hunting times are usually in the early morning and late evening, but deer can be bagged at any time of the day, especially around the November rut. Depending on location, hunting seasons can start as early as August and end as late as November. Better success is usually found in transition areas between wooded uplands and farmlands.

Game Birds

Ducks

There are, broadly speaking, two types of ducks, Dabbling and diving. Dabbling ducks are typically found in fresh, shallow marshes and rivers rather than large lakes and bays. They are good divers, but usually feed by dabbling or tipping, rather than diving underwater, thus the name. The speculum or coloured wing patch is generally iridescent and bright and often a telltale field mark. Dabbling Ducks include blacks, mallards and green winged teals are most commonly found in the many open wetlands and lakes. Any ducks feeding on land will likely be a dabbling duck, as these birds are sure-footed and can walk and run well on land. They eat vegetables and are just as likely to be found in a farmer's field as they are in a marsh.

Diving ducks also get their name from their feeding habits as well, diving deep below the surface of the water to find food. They feed on fish and aquatic plants. Diving ducks include canvasbacks, redheads, ring-necked ducks and greater and lesser scaup. Since their wings are smaller in proportion to the size and weight of their bodies, they have a more rapid wing beat than dabbling ducks.

Diving ducks are sometimes found in small marshes (especially ring necks), but are more frequently found in larger lakes. They favour deeper open water areas where there is a good growth of underwater vegetation. The classic set-up for hunting divers includes a boat, a dog and lots of decoys. The boat is needed to transport gear, set out decoys, retrieve birds and just get onto the water and away from the launch. A boat blind can be invaluable; while a dog will certainly help retrieve birds in much less time than it would take you to drag the boat out from under cover, get the bird and return the boat to cover.

Ducks will more readily land if the area is already "safe", so having decoys out will certainly help. In fact, the more the better! Good camouflage is essential, as ducks are very skittish. Some duck hunters even go so far as to paint their gun. Non-Canadians have a shorter season than Canadian residents and canvasback and redhead have special numbers restrictions.

Geese

There are four species of geese hunted in Alberta: snow geese, Canada geese, white-fronted geese and Ross' geese. Canadian geese are one of the most popular waterfowl and the most common species of goose in the province. In the early season, they can be found in agricultural areas, especially where there are lakes and wetlands nearby. They are not common in areas where there are a lot of trees and little water or food, as in the Whitecourt area.

Hunting geese in a field is like similar to hunting dabbling ducks. Find an area, put out decoys and get under cover, either with camouflage gear or with netting. Geese like to land near where other geese are feeding, so set your decoys up so that you lead the birds to where you want them. The more decoys you use, the more likely geese are to land, as they find security in numbers. Feeding geese tend to make lots of noise, especially when they see competition approaching, so a goose call usually helps. Hunters, who are not used to hunting goose, especially duck hunters; often use too light a load and fire from too far away. While geese are big birds, they have a relatively small vital zone and it can be hard to get a clean shot. And their huge wingspan makes them look deceptively slow. The birds should be within 50 metres (50 yards) of you before firing.

Grouse

Not known for being the most cunning bird on the block, grouse are still a popular bird to hunt. What they lack in brains they make up for in colouring. You can nearly step on one of these birds before they take off in a chaotic explosion of feathers. On a still autumn morning, whilst sneaking through the forest watching and listening for the slightest hint of movement, this burst of activity can get the heart racing and the hands shaking. Once in the air, grouse are quick and often fly a random pattern through the forest, making them hard to hit. In fact, that's grouse hunting in a nutshell: go walk through the woods until you flush a grouse and then try and shoot it down in the two second (at most) window you have. More often than not, grouse hunters will walk for hours without success.

Grouse like to hang out in dense young forest or along transition zones near the edge or streams. Because they are often found in the thick brush, they are often hard to flush and the thick woods will often block your shot. There are four game species of grouse found in Alberta. Ruffed grouse have a ruff of black features about their neck and are usually about 43 cm (17 inches) long. They like sprouse and blue grouse are distributed evenly across the province, although blue grouse populations are smaller. Blue grouse are usually a slate gray colour (and not, as you might expect, blue) with a solid black tail and are usually about 53 cm (21 in) long. Spruce grouse are smaller, only 38 cm (15 in) long and usually mottled grey, brown and black with a noticeable red patch under their eye. Sharp-tailed grouse are about the same size as ruffed grouse, but look more like a spruce grouse. However when flushed, spruce grouse usually fly a short distance and hide in the trees, while sharp-tailed grouse tend to fly a much longer distance. Sharp-tailed grouse are usually found in greater numbers farther north (WMUs 360, 523, 544).

Currently, the bag limit is ten apiece for ruffed grouse and spruce grouse and five each for sharp-tailed grouse and blue grouse. The season can run from mid-September to the end of November, depending on which WMU you are hunting in. Check the regulations for exact dates. Note that sage grouse are listed as an endangered species and it is illegal to hunt them in Alberta.

Willow Ptarmigan

Willow Ptarmigan are not big birds, averaging about 40 cm (16 inches) long. The willow ptarmigan has a black tail, which distinguishes it from the white-tailed ptarmigan whose tails are, as you might guess, white. However, in summer willow ptarmigan have more white on their wings than white-tailed ptarmigan. Also during summer, the cocks are distinguished from the hens by their reddish-brown heads, backs and breasts. In winter, both sexes are entirely white except for their black tails, eyes and bills.

The only breeding population of willow ptarmigan found in Alberta occurs in the mountains of northern Jasper National Park and Willmore Wilderness Park. A second population of willow ptarmigan can be found in Northern Alberta in the winter. The ptarmigan spend the summer in the alpine zone or just below timberline. In winter they move to lower valleys. When a cock arrives at the breeding ground,

he establishes a territory from which he excludes all other males. He displays his plumage and makes a variety of boom and hoot sounds to attract a mate. The hen will stay within the territory the male has established and incubates 7 to 10 eggs in a nest, usually hidden under a bush. Eggs hatch in about 22 days and the young remain with the hen, feeding on insects and plants. Adults eat leaves, berries and seeds, but only few insects. As fall approaches, willow ptarmigan flock together in preparation for migration to wintering areas.

The hunting season is only open in early winter before the birds fly south. As a result the best hunting is in the far north in the valleys.

Wildlife Management Unit Highlights

WMU 349 Swan Hills
This unit sits in the Parkland region of Alberta and has a three point boundary as the towns of Swan Hills, Whitecourt and Fox Creek provide natural barriers for good big game hunting for moose, elk, white-tailed and mule deer and black bear. Good places to try are around Meekwap, Iosegun and Giroux lakes or along the Freeman River in the northern sector.

WMU 350 Saulteaux River
Sitting on the southern shores of Lesser Slave Lake, this unit is bordered by Highway 2 south of the small city of Slave Lake and Highway 33 running north/south on the western boundary. Grizzly Ridge Wildland Provincial Park is a good place to try your luck hunting white-tailed and mule deer, moose and black bear. Other hotspots reported are north of Windfall and Long End lakes and on either side of the Saulteaux River.

WMU 351 Goose River North
This part of Northern Alberta is characterised by long ridges, rolling foothills and streams carved out in valley bottoms. White-tailed and mule deer pick their way through meadows of dwarf birch and willows while ungulates like moose, deer and elk roam the stands of lodgepole pine and black spruce. Watch for black bear as they are opportunistic omnivores and will eat berries, fish, small rodents and insects.

The prairies of the Peace Region offer some of Alberta's finest waterfowl hunting. Like duck, geese are found anywhere wetlands and agrarian landscapes collide.

WMU 353 Deep Valley
Bordered by the Forestry Trunk Road to the west, Highway 43 to the north and east and the Smokey River to the south, this management unit has several very productive areas for big game hunting. Look for moderate populations of white-tailed and mule deer, moose and elk, as well as lower populations of black bear around the regions of Crooked Lake and the Deep Valley River.

WMU 354 Simonette
Similar to its neighbour to the north, this unit features moose, elk, white-tailed and mule deer, plus diminishing black bear population the further southeast you travel. Good places to try are between the Simonette and Latornell Rivers, where big game of all shapes and sizes stop for refreshing drinks in the clear rivers and streams.

WMU 355 Redrock Creek / WMU 356 Cutbank
These zones represent the transitional area where the Mountain Region meets the Foothills; a mountainous rocky tundra changing into heavy stands of lodgepole pine, spruce and aspen. Within this management unit, there are hundreds of lakes, rivers and streams teeming with big game and game bird hunting opportunities. Moose, elk and deer mingle with the omnivorous black bear in this region; as do several species of waterfowl.

WMU 357 Beaverlodge

With the province of BC on its western border and the major city of Grande Prairie found travelling east along Highway 43 through Beaverlodge and Wembley, this wildlife management unit hosts a number of different big game and waterfowl species. This being said, populations are low in this region due to urbanization, but you will still find moose, elk, deer and black bear in this part of Alberta. Goose hunting has been reported to be quite good the further from the cities you travel. Be sure to check boundaries and regulations regarding hunting in this region.

WMU 358 Saddle Hills / WMU 359 Blueberry

This region represents the last of the rolling foothills and long ridges and gives way to the northern Boreal region of Northern Alberta with its vast expanses of coniferous and deciduous forests and thousand of kilometres of wetland. Here you will find a variety of big game and game birds, especially waterfowl that make the thousands of lakes and marshlands their home.

WMU 360 Snipe Lake

As the Smokey River winds its way along the western border of this management unit, you will find high populations of whitetails and mulies inhabiting areas of grassland meadows with dwarf birch and willows trees lining valley bottom streambeds. Further east will take you to Snipe Lake and some of the best goose and duck hunting in Northern Alberta. Be aware of the East Prairie Metis Settlement on the extreme eastern borders of this unit.

WMU 445 Narraway

Arguably the smallest management unit in this region of the province, it packs a punch as far as big game hunting goes. There are good populations of moose, elk and black bear. Good spots to try are between the BC border and the Narraway River or anywhere within or north of the Kakwa Wildland Provincial Park.

WMU 503 Lac La Biche

This small management unit surrounds the shores of Lac La Biche, providing freshwater for practically every big game and waterfowl species in the whole area. Ungulates such as moose, elk and deer share this habitat with carnivorous predators like cougar and to lesser extents black bear. With all the wetlands here, various species of goose and duck can be found in and around any of the numerous lakes. Also look for the gray partridge milling about the flat agricultural regions here.

WMU 506 Tawatinaw

This unit has several towns stretching from its northern boundary near Athabasca down the western border through the towns of Meanook, Perryvale, Tawatinaw and Nestow. Moose, elk and deer are the main targets in this region, but there are also healthy populations of black bear and cougar. Good duck and goose hunting can be found in the extreme north along the shores of Flat Lake.

WMU 509 Calling Lake / WMU 510 Baptiste Lake

These two management units share the same type of landscape in the Foothills region of Alberta. Generally, foothills are regarded as a transitional relief form combining some of the elements of a lower-elevation, flat landscape with those of mountainous topography. From the Athabasca River in the western sector winding east through countless lakes, streams and rivers to Cross Lake Provincial Park, you will find excellent white-tailed and mule deer hunting. Moose and elk love the marshlands as do several species of duck and goose. Look for gray partridge and ruffed grouse in the flatlands to the south.

WMU 511 Pelican Mountains

If you are looking for excellent duck hunting, look no further than this unit. In particular, Calling Lake is a waterfowl haven. Big game roam these parts too with large pockets of white-tailed and mule deer picking their way through stands of pine, birch and aspen. The area between the Otter Orloff Wildland and the Lesser Slave Lake Provincial Park has been known to draw healthy numbers of moose and black bear as well.

WMU 512 Crow Lake

This management unit is split down the middle by Highway 63 with Crow Lake Provincial Park to the east and the Athabasca River to the west. Big game in this region includes moose, white-tailed and mule deer, black bear and game birds like spruce and ruffed grouse and gray partridge.

WMU 514 Marie Lake

This small unit sits between the Cold Lake Air Weapons Range to the north, the province of Saskatchewan to its east, and countless little rivers, creeks and streams dotting the landscape to the west and south. Within these boundaries you will find moderate populations of white-tailed deer, moose and black bear along with gray partridge and ruffed grouse.

WMU 515 Heart Lake

Buffalo, Rattail, Little Beaver and Logan lakes are the main focal points in this management unit. They all make for excellent duck hunting as waterfowl by the thousands flock to this region. Big game in this area includes moose, deer and black bear roaming the heavily forested areas of white and black spruce. Be aware of your boundaries as hunting is strictly forbidden with the Cold Lake Air Weapons Range along the eastern border.

WMU 516 Pelican Lake

This unit is a sort of transitional zone between the foothills to the south and the boreal forests of the north. Bordered by Secondary Highway 813 to the west and Athabasca River in the east, you will find moderate to high populations of whitetails and mulies and moose hanging around the wetland region. The carnivorous cougar and omnivorous black bear also call this part of Alberta home.

WMU 517 Winefred Lake

Bordered by Saskatchewan to the east and the Cold Lake Air Weapons Range to the south, all areas west and north have great big game hunting. High populations of white-tailed deer and moose have been reported in this region along with black bear and the elusive cougar. Be careful hunting in cougar country as these great felines move through the forests with grace and ease. Game bird hunters will find this unit teeming with spruce and ruffed grouse as well as several species of duck and goose.

WMU 518 Thickwood Hills / WMU 519 Algar Lake

The Athabasca River flows through the centre of this management unit and on either side – east or west – you will find some of the best big game hunting in this part of the province. This region is characterized by vast expanses of mixed wood forests of coniferous spruce, pine and larch and deciduous poplar and birch broken up by countless lakes, swamps and rivers. Look for high populations of ungulates like the white-tailed deer, the majestic and elusive moose, omnivores like the black bear and the most cunning and dangerous predator in this region; the cougar.

WMU 520 Cadotte Lakes-Otter Lake

Sitting pretty much in the dead centre of Northern Alberta's wildlife management units, this region is home to moderate to high populations of white-tailed and mule deer, moose and black bear. Good places to try your luck include the areas around the Otter Lakes, Jackpine and Codette Rivers and south of Lubicon Lake. There are several Indian reserves in this unit so be sure you are aware of your hunting boundaries.

WMU 521 Puskwaskau / WMU 522 Birch Hills

These two units combine the best of the boreal forest region and the foothills of Northern Alberta. Bordered to the west by the Smokey River, this unit provides hunters with excellent white-tailed and mule deer hunting. Check the areas around Sturgeon Lake and all areas around the birch hills region in the northern sector. Moderate populations of moose and black bear also inhabit this region; as does game birds and waterfowl such as grouse, geese and ducks.

WMU 523 Kimiwan-Winagami Lakes

Set amongst the diminishing rolling vistas and long ridges of the foothills, you will find this landscape slowing turning to thick stands of aspen, pine and spruce combined with wetlands and deep clear lakes as you head north. A plethora of big game call this region home as large ungulates such as white-tailed and mule deer, moose and elk wander through this central-north region of Alberta. Look for various species of game birds like grouse and to a lesser extent the gray partridge.

WMU 524 Chinchaga River / WMU 525 Clear Hills

These units run parallel with the British Columbia border to the west and the Chinchaga River in the northeast. A healthy population of white-tailed and mule deer roam these parts (more mulies the further south you go) along with the majestic and elusive moose picking its way through the heavily forested stands of black spruce, pine and larch. There are also wetlands and swamps in the southern region of this unit that attract waterfowl with various species of duck and goose inhabiting the hundreds of lakes and river here.

WMU 526 Upper Peace River

Highway 64 runs directly west-east (or east-west) through the centre of this wildlife management unit, providing easy access to the hunting in the vicinity. This area has a lot of urbanization within it, so make sure you are within the hunting limits. This being said, there are still areas with populations of deer, moose, black bear and game birds such as spruce and ruffed grouse.

WMU 527 Whitemud-Hotchkiss Rivers / WMU 528 Buffalo Head Hills

The Peace River winds its way along the western boundary of this management unit, providing quality hunting for big game and game birds. Moving westward, you will find hundreds of lakes, streams, creeks and rivers; the perfect areas for hunting. Moose along with white-tailed and mule deer inhabit this region of dense coniferous and deciduous forests. This part of Alberta is also known for high populations of grouse and waterfowl.

WMU 529 Gordon Lake

Backed by Saskatchewan to the east, this management unit offers several big lakes that provide excellent sources of fresh water for big game animals. Look for moose, deer and black bear around North and South Watchusk Lakes, Christina River and Gordon Lake, which is located within Gypsy Lake Wildland Provincial Park. Game bird hunters will find excellent grouse hunting amongst stands of mature spruce, cedar or fir that allow bird to find refuge from the weather and predators.

WMU 530 Delta

This wildlife management unit starts at Lake Athabasca; the northernmost point. It runs along the Saskatchewan border south through the Marguerite River Wildland Park and past the Firebag Oil Sands Project Area (watch your boundaries) before hitting its southern point at the Clearwater River. Within this region of Alberta you will find good predator hunting with moderate to high numbers of black bear and cougar. Ungulates such as white-tailed deer and the majestic moose also call this area home.

WMU 531 Birch Mountains

Situated south of the Wood Buffalo National Park, the main feature in this region is the moose, black bear and cougar hunting in the vicinity of Namur Lake and the Birch Mountains Wildland Provincial Park. Other places to try are along the Birch River and the numerous tiny lakes north of the park.

WMU 532 Chipewyan

Bordered by the Northwest Territories and the province of Saskatchewan, this unit is the biggest in Northern Alberta. However, with Wood Buffalo National Park occupying over 80% of the area (no hunting allowed), big game are segregated to the northeast corner of this wildlife management unit. Moose, white-tailed deer, black bear and cougar can be found in low to moderate populations within this zone. Also look for high populations of willow ptarmigan.

WMU 534 Caribou Mountains

This wildlife management unit is the second biggest in Northern Alberta, with the Caribou Mountains Wildland Provincial Park occupying a third of the region. Located on the eastern side of the Mackenzie Highway (Hwy 35), there are literally thousands of lakes and rivers which provide an abundance of freshwater for a variety of big game. Caribou, moose, white-tailed and mule deer and black bear all call this region of Alberta home. Also look for pockets of willow ptarmigan picking their way through the Precambrian rock and the Canadian Shield forests. Be aware of your boundaries as a portion of Wood Buffalo Provincial Park sits in the northwest corner.

WMU 535 High Level-la Crete

This small management unit contains three Indian reserves in the northern sector so be careful of your boundaries here. As the Peace River flows through this unit, you will find high populations of black bear along with moderate amounts of whitetails and mulies. Moose have been reported to inhabit the region around Devil and Surette Lakes.

WMU 536 Rainbow Lake

Highway 58 takes you from the furthest boundary in the east at High Level west through countless rivers, streams, creeks and the ever present expanses of coniferous forests to the town of Rainbow Lake. To the north of the highway you will find the Hay-Zama Wildland Lakes Provincial Park and a good variety of waterfowl. The area also reports very good hunting for big game with high populations of whitetails and mulies, plus moderate amounts of moose and black bear.

WMU 537 Naylor / Hawk Hills

As the Paddle Prairie Metis Settlement takes up a large chunk of this management unit in the northeast, hunting is limited to a small corridor in the northwest and anywhere south of the Keg River. White-tailed and mule deer are the predominant species to hunt here, but moderate populations of moose and black bear inhabit this region as well. Both spruce and ruffed grouse call this unit home as well; look for them in the deciduous forests where shrubbery of rose, willow and alder grow.

WMU 539 Bistcho Lake

Located in the extreme northwest corner of the province, this cold, desolate management unit borders the Northwest Territories and British Columbia. Many of the regions here are accessible only by air; meaning that there is truly some big game in this region. The predominant species here are caribou, moose and black bear, but this unit is also home to moderate populations of willow ptarmigan. As this region is vast and unforgiving, it's best to hunt with a certified outfitter for your best opportunity to bag that trophy animal.

WMU 540 - Mikkwa River / WMU 541 Panny River

The meandering Peace River provides a natural boundary in the north of this management unit. Travelling south you will find moderate populations of moose, caribou and black bear. Look to the wetlands and marsh areas for moose and caribou, while black bear prefer the river regions for their steady diet of fish. Try your luck along the banks of the numerous rivers and creeks south of Moose Lake. If game bird hunting is your preference, populations of willow ptarmigan reside in sparse pine and birch forests, thickets with willow and alder trees, tundra and mountain slopes.

Hunting is a highly regulated activity and it is your responsibility to know the rules and regulations before heading out. The regulations are available online at www.albertaregulations.ca.

WMU 542 Muskwa Lake

Between Peerless Lake which sits in the northeast corner of this wildlife management unit and Muskwa Lake in the dead centre, this area (along with the countless rivers, streams and creeks) provides food and water for various big game, waterfowl and game birds. Look for whitetails, moose and black bear to the east as well around the North Wabasca Lake region.

WMU 544 Utikuma Lake

This wildlife management unit supports a healthy variety of big game, waterfowl and game birds as the region slowly transitions from the southern foothills and deep valley streams to boreal forests and heavily forested areas of both coniferous and deciduous stands. White-tailed and mule deer dominate this area, with huge pockets around the massive Lesser Slave Lake in the south and the smaller Utikuma Lake to the north. Be aware of your boundaries in this unit as the Peavine and Gift Lake Metis Settlements occupy a large chunk of land in the northwest region.

WMU 651 Lakeland Provincial Park
No hunting

WMU 726 Air Weapons Ranges
No hunting

WMU 841 Lakeland Provincial Recreation Area
No hunting

WMU 926 Greene Valley
No hunting

Paddling
Adventures

Northern Alberta is big country, full of big lakes and some big rivers. This is not a place of two-hour whitewater runs, but of weeklong paddles without seeing any sign of civilization. There are small lakes and small rivers, too, but they can be problematic to explore. In most cases, the small rivers are tough to paddle without bringing along a chainsaw. On the other hand, some of the smaller lakes suffer from algae bloom that creates a less than appealing scum on the water later in the summer.

As with most areas across the country, as long as you can access it, chances are you can paddle it. But there are good lakes for paddling and there are bad ones. A lot of the small, shallow lakes can get scummy in the summer, so you might want to avoid these later in the summer. On the other hand, a lot of the big lakes can get windy and should be avoided by people with open canoes. These big lakes do make fine multi-day trips, but finding a good place to camp is often a concern in the thick boreal forest.

With the exception of a few rivers along the BC boundary, there is little whitewater to speak of. However, where one type of paddling ends, another begins, and northern Alberta is home to a handful of great multi-day (or multi-week) paddling trips. There are four big rivers in this area: the Peace, Athabasca, Clearwater and Rivière des Rochers/Slave River are some of the most storied rivers in Canada. Outside of the big rivers, there are very few other rivers that can be paddled. This is because many of the rivers and streams in this area do not move a lot of water and are often dammed by beavers or choked with willows or fallen trees.

For river routes, we have included the put-in and take-out locations, the length of each run as well as general comments. To grade the rivers, we have used a modified version of the International River Classification System. The Grade of a route describes the overall difficulty of a river, while specific features are given the designation Class. We would also like to remind river paddlers that conditions are always subject to change and advanced scouting is essential. The information in this book is only intended to give you general information on the particular river you are interested in. You should always obtain more details from a local merchant or expert before heading out on your adventure. Regardless of your route, always remember to be safe and be aware of weather conditions and water temperature.

Paddling Adventures

Lake Paddling

Beaver Lake (Map 12/C4)
Beaver Lake offers great sport fishing, beautiful landscapes and excellent bird watching. There is a paved road to the campground gate on the northwest side of the lake. Old Canoe Island Natural Area is directly across from the Beaver Lake Recreation Area and offers a number of inlets and islands to explore.

Christina Lake (Map 41/D7–F7)
Named in honour of Christine Gordon, the first while woman to live permanently in the Fort McMurray area, this long, narrow lake makes a great destination for a weekend trip. There is good road access, at the west end of the lake, but no road access to the east end of the 20 km (12 mile) long lake. The lake offers great fishing for northern pike and walleye.

Chrystina Lake (Map 10/F2)
This small lake is found north of Swan Hills on roads that are good in dry weather, but impassable (at least in a 2wd vehicle) in wet weather. As with most lakes with a provincial park campsite (there are six campsites here), canoeing is a popular pastime. The lake is also known as windy lake so beware of afternoon blowups.

Cold Lake (Map 14/F6)
Cold Lake is Alberta's seventh largest lake, and as a big lake, is prone to getting windy. The lake is usually accessed from the Cold Lake Marina or from the provincial park. There is some good sheltered padding in and around the provincial park. The rest of the lake could be circumnavigated over the course of a number of days, but most people don't bother doing extended trips here as the wind can blow paddlers off the lake for days at a time.

Crow Lake (Map 39/G5–40/A4)
Crow Lake is located about 20 minutes south of Mariana Lake on the east side of Highway 63 when coming from Fort McMurray. The area around the lake is protected by a park and an ecological reserve and there are stands of old growth spruce around the lake that are over 150 years old. A recent fire and the twinning of Highway 63 along the western boundary of the park are moving the park campground to the north shore of Crow Lake. It will be a rustic campground with 30 campsites and vault toilets. Power boats are not allowed on the lake, making it a great destination for paddlers.

Engstrom Lake (Map 55/E6)
This smaller lake is found about half an hour south of Fort McMurray off Secondary Highway 881. The sheltered lake is fairly quiet, with a number of nooks and crannies for paddlers to explore. The campground here has been closed to public use but day users are still welcome.

> Northern Alberta is big country, full of big lakes and some big rivers. This is not a place of two-hour whitewater runs, but of week-long paddles without seeing any sign of civilization.

Figure Eight Lake (Map 46/D3)
This small lake is one of the best fishing lakes in Alberta for rainbow trout. Because of its small size and no gas engine restriction, paddling is popular, if only as a means to an end. But you do not have to bring a rod to enjoy a quick paddle around the lake. There are 20 non-serviced forested campsites at this recreation area.

Footner Lake (Map 86/D1)
This small, only 1 km by 4 km, lake is located approximately 10 km north of High Level. The lake makes a great destination for a morning or afternoon paddle. As there is an airport right beside the lake, watch for float planes while canoeing.

Gregoire Lake (Map 55/C3)
There is a provincial park on the western shores of this lake, which is the biggest lake in the Fort McMurray area. This is important, because the park is where most people put-in (although there is good road access around much of the lake). It is also important because paddlers will find this area fairly

sheltered. Like most big lakes, Gregoire is prone to wind, but the prevalent winds are from the west. The lake can be circumnavigated and there are a lot of bays to explore. There is good fishing here, too. The boat sees heavy use from powerboats, but it is big enough to share.

Hay-Zama Lake (Map 92/B7–D6)
These two connected lakes are located at the centre of the Hay-Zama Wildland Park. This protected area is a unique wetland habitat with numerous birds including bald eagles and great horned owls to look for. There are also approximately 500 Wood Bison in the park. The shore and shape of this lake can change due to water levels. Visitors should also be wary of the wind as the big lake can large waves. Check the weather before heading out.

Heart River Reservoir (Map 34/B6)
The recreation area at Heart River Dam has been ill-kept over the years, but it is still possible to launch a canoe in the holding ponds behind the dams and spend a few hours paddling about. The prime draw to the area is fishing and there are 4 non-serviced campsites here as well.

Hutch Lake (Map 86/C1–93/C7)
Located 30 km north of the town of High Level, this man-made is the result of a dam at its' north end. The lake, shaped like a bent cigar, is long and narrow and winds can whip up waves. Be sure to check the weather before setting out. Access to the lake is from the recreation area campsite at the north end of the lake, which is accessible from Highway 35.

Iosegun Lake (Map 5/D5)
Some canoeists will find Iosegun Lake a little large and exposed to winds for their sensibilities. Others will appreciate the fact that it takes more than an hour to circumnavigate the lake. Still others will bring a rod in the hopes of landing one of the big walleye or pike that inhabit the lake. The lake is open to powerboats, so keep an eye out for inconsiderate boaters. There are 52 non-serviced campsites and, although there is a hand pump for water, those planning to stay overnight should bring their own water or a water purifier.

Island Lake (Map 10/A2)
This pretty, medium-sized lake is a collection of bays, islands and arms that make it perfect for exploring with a canoe. There are many cottages around the shores of the lake and there are many access points along the western shores of the lake. The fishing here is quite good for northern pike, perch and large lake whitefish.

Krause Lake (Map 7/D3)
There is a group use campsite on the shores of Krause Lake, a small lake that should take very little time to circumnavigate in a canoe. More often than not, paddlers on this lake come armed with a fishing rod and are chasing after either the pike or perch that inhabit the lake.

Lac Cardinal (Map 46/E4)
This big lake, found just north of Fairview, is a popular recreation destination despite holding no fish. Queen Elizabeth Provincial Park provides the main access point for paddlers. The lake can be a busy place throughout the summer and is subject to strong winds.

Lakeland Canoe Routes (Map 12/F2)
Lakeland Provincial Park is an anomaly in Alberta since it lends itself to canoe tripping. There are dozens of lakes here, many of them separated by only a narrow strip of land. Although they bill themselves as Alberta's only Backcountry Canoe Circuit, there are in fact so many interconnected lakes up here that it's hard to cover them in only one route. Instead, you can string together these lakes in a variety of ways. There are free canoe carts to use at all but the shortest of portages and a number of backcountry campsites have been developed to accommodate the 2,000 or so paddlers who do this circuit every year. Despite the seemingly high number, it is easy to find a campsite to call your own.

The route starts with a 3.2 km portage from the Jackson Lake Staging Area to the shallow north arm of the lake. Here options lead south to Blackett, west through McGuffin or east past Touchwood. Each offers its own character along with a bit of creek paddling and portages.

If venturing to Blackett Lake, there a beaver dam that you will have to portage 750 metres around on the creek from Kinnaird to Blackett. The route to McGuffin Lake leads past a trio of small lakes, strung together by a creek and easy portage into McGuffin. Getting to Touchwood Lake requires a relatively long 1.7 km portage, followed by a relatively short paddle, followed by an even longer 2.2 km portage. From here, it is possible to portage 2 km over to Seibert Lake, or paddle to the Touchwood Lake Campground at the north end of the lake.

Paddling Adventures

Lake Tourangeau (Map 86/G4)
Located 2.5 km west of La Crete, this smaller lake has a day-use picnic site and boat launch. The lake also offers good fishing.

Lesser Slave Lake (Map 20–22, 34–36)
While you would not want to be caught out on this huge lake in just a canoe when the wind blows up, it is the closest thing to sea kayaking that Alberta has to offer (at least this close to Edmonton). In fact kayak touring is becoming a popular pursuit on the big lake. It is also possible to boot about in a canoe, as long as you stay near shore. The usual launching spots are around one of the two provincial parks on the shores of the lake.

Machesis Lake (Map 86/F3)
Machesis Lake is a tiny lake 51 km southeast of High Level. The lake is a popular destination with anglers and it holds good numbers of rainbow and brook trout. Paddlers share the lake with power boaters. There are 19 non-serviced campsites at the recreation area on the lake.

Maqua Lake (Map 55/B4)
Maqua Lake is located southwest of Gregoire Lake, off Highway 63. Maqua is a small lake that has been set aside for paddling, as powerboats are not allowed here. The lake holds no fish, but it is a nice lake to paddle around. There are 15 group campsites for those wishing to spend the night with family and friends.

Mariana Lake (Map 40/B2)
Mariana Lake is easily accessed from Highway 63, 100 km south of Fort McMurray. The lake is long and narrow and is a nice, safe place to paddle.

Moonshine Lake (Map 44/E7)
Moonshine Lake is the liquid heart of Moonshine Lake Provincial Park. It is not a large lake, but canoeists can enjoy a leisurely paddle on a sheltered lake. Most paddlers, however, bring a fishing rod in search of the stocked rainbow trout. There is camping and a boat launch at the lake.

Musreau Lake (Map 3/A3)
This is a deep, cold, relatively large lake, located south of Grande Prairie. There is a recreation area on the lake, which provides canoe rentals in case you do not bring your own, along with 69 non-serviced campsites. Although there is a hand pump for water, those planning to stay overnight should bring their own water or a water purifier.

Ole's Lake (Map 43/G1)
Located near the BC boundary, this small lake is best known for holding good numbers of stocked rainbow. There is no boat launch, which means that if you want to get out onto the water to paddle, your only option is to hand launch. There are 16 non-serviced campsites and, although there is a hand pump for water, those planning to stay overnight should bring their own water or a water purifier.

Pinehurst Lake (Map 12/G5–13/A5)
One of the biggest lakes in the Lakeland Recreation Area, Pinehurst is a great place to go kayaking. While not part of the lake circuit, there is a small lake a short canoe carry to the south of the lake, which can be explored. The lake is open to powerboats and offers good fishing.

Poplar Creek Reservoir (Map 68/G6)
The Poplar Creek Reservoir is located 25 km north of Fort McMurray, just off Highway 63. The small, narrow lake is a nice, safe place to paddle and there are a lot of birds and river otters. At the north end are cattails, which are fun to paddle through. Note that there is a weir at the southeast end of the lake which should be avoided. There is a 100 metre portage from the parking area to the put-in location.

Rainbow Lake (Map 85/A3)
Located 45 km south of the town of Rainbow Lake, this long, narrow lake is perfect for canoeing since it is fairly sheltered from the wind. About the only thing that isn't perfect is the fact the lake is open to powerboats. Still, the remote lake does not see a whole lot of use and there's plenty of room for all who come. The lake has good fishing for walleye and northern pike. There is a 19 site campground and a number of tent only sites along the lakeshore. A 4wd vehicle is necessary to get you through the muddy sections after heavy rains.

Saskatoon Lake (Map 16/E1)
Saskatoon Lake is a bird watching paradise with large numbers of grassland, forest and shore birds. In contrast to most of the lakes in the region, there are no fish

to note in these waters. This means that anyone canoeing this lake is canoeing it for the sheer pleasure of it or as a means of getting a better look at the birds.

Six Lakes/Richardson Backcountry Area (Map 90/C6)
You wouldn't expect to find endless sandy beaches in the middle of the Boreal forest, but that's exactly what you will find in the Six Lakes area. However, the only way in to the area is by float plane or with ATVs along the Fort Chipewyan Winter Road, but once you get here, there are dozens of lakes that offer great paddling. Options include: Herb Lake, Keith Lake, Jackson Lake, Six Lakes, Barber Lake and Larocque Lake, but there are countless others to discover. Most of the lakes have designated campsites with fire pits, picnic tables and outhouses that are maintained by Alberta Sustainable Resource Development. Nearby are two wildland parks and one ecological reserve that can be accessed by foot only if you are looking for an even more remote adventure.

Smoke Lake (Map 5/C6)
Found west of Fox Creek along good gravel roads, this lake is home to a popular recreation area. It is also a great fishing lake and together with Iosegun Lake offers some of the best walleye fishing in the province. The lake is a comfortable size, not so big as to be completely exposed to the wind and not so small as to be circumnavigated in an hour. Watch out for powerboats. There are 47 non-serviced campsites and although there is a hand pump for water, those planning to stay overnight should bring their own water or a water purifier.

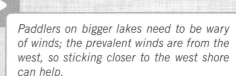

Paddlers on bigger lakes need to be wary of winds; the prevalent winds are from the west, so sticking closer to the west shore can help.

Stoney Lake (Map 59/C7)
Stoney Lake Recreation Area, located northwest of Peace River off the Canfor Road, offers secluded canoeing and fishing. The campground at the recreation area is user maintained and offers rustic camping.

Sturgeon Lake (Map 18/E4)
Sturgeon Lake can get a bit reedy and green in the summer with algae blooms, but it is a good fishing lake. The island at the west end of the lake is home to both bald eagles and great horned owls to look for. There are two provincial parks on the lake—one on the north shore, one on the south—from which to access the large, open lake. Watch out for powerboats as well as high winds.

Two Lakes (Map 1/D4)
The two lakes that make up the popular Two Lakes Recreation Area are both good canoeing lakes. Most people who make the long, sometimes rough trip from Grande Prairie also bring their fishing gear. Non anglers can look for shore birds and wildlife since the area is a summer and winter elk range and both grizzly and black bear wander the shore in the spring and summer looking for fish and berries in the fall. There are also osprey and loon nests in the area. For those wishing to camp, there are three camping areas, open from May 1st to October 13th. Gunderson Meadows has 32 non-serviced sites, Moberly Flats has 30 non-serviced sites and Pine Hollow has 24 non-serviced sites. Bring your own water or a water purifier. Boat launches allow for easy access.

Wadlin Lake (Map 87/C7)
Located south of Fort Vermillion, Wadlin Lake is one of the larger lakes in the Fort Vermillion area. There is a campground with boat launch in the northeastern corner of the lake.

Winagami Lake (Map 33/F4–G5)
Located southeast of McLennan, Winagami Lake is surrounded by the Winagami Wildland Provincial Park. This large lake has a campground with 15 non-serviced and 35 power sites. However, it should be noted that power boats are permitted on this lake so paddlers are well advised to head out earlier in the day to avoid the chop.

Winefred Lake (Map 28/B2–42/B7)
This big lake is south of the town of Conklin and is accessed from the south by a backroad. There is a large fishing lodge on the lake.

River & Stream Paddling

Athabasca River
(Maps 8–11, 23–25, 39, 53, 54, 67–70, 80–83, 89–90)
The Athabasca is one of the country's great rivers, flowing out of Jasper National Park and crossing the province in a north easterly direction, making its way to Wood Buffalo National Park. While much of the route outside of Jasper features little more than a few riffles here and there, the middle section of the river has a slew of nasty rapids, including the infamous Grand Rapids. A trip from Jasper to Fort Chipewyan would take the better part of two months to do taking paddlers over a 1,538 km (938 mile) long route that winds its way through mountains, prairies, forests and muskeg. The river through this area of Northern Alberta can be broken up into three distinct areas:

Athabasca River – Vega to Athabasca (Map 8/F7–10/D4)
There are a few rapids on this short section of the Athabasca, nothing more serious than a Class II/III. The put-in point is at Vega Crossing in the Vega/Timeau OHV Area. Take-out is in the town of Athabasca. This 138 km (84 mile) section is very slow moving and more importantly, campsites are few and far between. The only reason most people run this section of river is as part of a tip-to-tail trip. For a shorter run, it is possible to put-in (or take-out) at the Highway 2 Bridge near Hondo or at Smith, which is a few kilometres downstream.

Athabasca River –Athabasca to Fort McMurray (Map 10/D4–69/A7)
There are 15 named rapids on this section of the Athabasca and plenty of others, ranging from easy Class II rapids to a whole series of boat crunchers, including a major Class VI+. This 384 km (234 mile) section of the river begins in the town of Athabasca and usually takes a week and a half to do, mostly because of the time spent portaging. Grand Rapids itself has claimed the lives of many, many people and should not be underestimated. Closed boats are essential. People looking for a shorter run on this river will find take-out points at the 40 km (24 mile) mark, the 77 km (47 mile) mark and the 170 km (104 mile) mark. After this, you are committed through the rapids on to Fort McMurray and your take-out point. Mark Lund's new Guide for Alberta Paddlers is essential reading for anyone attempting this section.

Athabasca River – Fort McMurray to Fort Chipewyan (Map 69/A7–90/B2)
This 300 km (180 mile) paddle should take a week or ten days to do, depending on the speed of paddle as you travel from Fort McMurray to Fort Chipewyan. There are no rapids of note, but the trip is through a vast, roadless wilderness and travellers must be self-sufficient. As the only way back from Fort Chipewyan is by air, many people only paddle to Fort MacKay, a 40 km (24 mile) paddle since there is good access to here or rather to Bitumount, a few kilometres downstream. The most difficult section will be finding a navigable channel through the Athabasca Delta since each spring the river reforms, usually in another channel. Do not attempt to paddle across Athabasca Lake directly, as the big lake is prone to high winds.

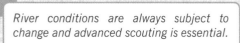

River conditions are always subject to change and advanced scouting is essential.

Bear River (Map 16/F1–17/C3)
This slow moving stream flows through Grande Prairie and down to the Wapiti River. Access to the river outside of town is limited and most people just paddle or float within the city limits on hot summer days. Paddlers can even work their up the stream to the Grande Prairie Reservoir.

Beaverlodge River (Map 16/B3–29/D6)
The Beaverlodge River can be paddled, but by all reports, it is not much fun. Part of the problem is a number of beaver dams along the river create a series of annoying portages. These are about the most difficult part of the entire trip, as the river is neither deep nor fast. It runs from the BC border south to the Redwillow River just above that stream's confluence with the much bigger Wapiti River west of Grande Prairie. There is an ongoing attempt to rehabilitate the waters of the Beaverlodge. New trees are being planted to stabilize the banks and remove a large percentage of the sediments that flow into the river and have affected the arctic grayling that reside here.

Bocquene River (Map 97/A4)
This narrow, meandering river can be paddled upstream from its confluence with the Slave to Bocquene Lake. The river is best paddled in spring, when the water levels are higher; however, finding the overgrown mouth of the river can be difficult. While it is not a long river, it will take the better part of the day to paddle, as there are a number of beaver dams and other barriers to navigate. The lake offers some good fishing for those able to cross the Slave from Hay Camp and paddle all the way up the creek. The trip offers great variety, from mixed forest, to the granite cliffs of the Canadian Shield and then open jack pine forest where some great campsites can be found.

Chinchaga River (Map 85/G6–F1)
This long, meandering river has rarely been run and information is scarce. Low water limits the time it can be paddled (think early spring) and lack of information tends to keep people away from this wilderness river. The water level is monitored by Alberta Environment so if planning a trip, check to see if the river can be run. At high levels, you can drift down the river at 5–7 kph (3–4 mph) while at low levels, there is not much point even attempting it as flow drops to a trickle.There are two sections that can be paddled. From a bridge over the Chinchaga, just north of Keg River to the Highway 58 Bridge is a long Class II/III wilderness paddle that will take upwards of a week to do. There is a little park at the Highway 58 Bridge where people like to float downstream for a kilometre or so and then hike back up to the bridge.

Christina River (Map 41/A6–89/D7)
The Christina is a long, remote river that drains into the Clearwater River about 18 km (11 miles) upstream from Fort McMurray. This is a river that you need to catch at the right water level. Too high and the river is very pushy, which can be dangerous on a river with so many tight curves. Too low and the river becomes a rock sieve, ready to munch your canoe. You can run the whole river or just do the first, shorter section if time is a factor.

Christina River –Jackfish River Bridge to Janvier (Map 41/C6–G3)
This shorter section starts with a put-in at the Jackfish River Bridge. The Jackfish River flows into the Christina a few kilometres upstream. There is a bridge on Secondary Highway 881 north of Conklin. From here to Janvier, expect to spend the better part of the day (six to eight hours) paddling a mix of flatwater and Class II rapids. The lower section of the river (from Chard) is a very easy float trip. You will have to ask for permission from the Chipewyan Prairie Band to take-out at Janvier, so an option for shy folks would be to take-out near Chard.

Christina River –Janvier to Fort McMurray (Map 41/G3–69/A7)
From Janvier or Chard to Fort McMurray is mostly an easy float, but with a fairly long section of Class II and Class III rapids, mostly around corners (and there are a lot of corners) as you descend into the Clearwater River Valley. Give yourself 4–7 days do this 209 km (130 mile) section to Fort McMurray. The best time to run it is in late spring when the water level is high but not too high. As this is wilderness, expect to see lots of wildlife as you explore the area.

Clearwater River (Map 69/G7–70/G7)
The Clearwater River is 295 km (180 miles) long, running southwest from its headwaters at Broach Lake in Saskatchewan. Most of this route falls east of these maps. It is floatplane access to Lloyd Lake, where most people canoeing the entire river start the trip; floatplane access is also available at Careen Lake, Lac La Loche and at Whitemud Falls. For paddlers without the budget for a floatplane, Highway 955 crosses the river at Warner Rapids. The upper portion of the river features many Class IV rapids and there are up to 14 portages. The Alberta section of the river is easier, although there are still seven sets of rapids between Whitemud Falls to the Cascade Rapids. For those not wishing to make the full trip, it is also possible to have a guide take you up-river in a jet boat.

Dog River (Map 96/G2–97/A3)
The Dog River is accessed by paddling across the Slave River from Fort Fitzgerald and then upstream. After about 30 km (18 miles), a winter road allowance crosses the river. From here, it is possible to carry your boat over a kilometre to a series of remote lakes, including Myers &McLelland.

Ells River (Maps 67, 68, 80, 81)

Linking Gardiner Lake with the Athabasca River, this is a rarely travelled canoe route owing to the fact that access to Gardiner Lake is fly-in only. The Namur Lake Lodge is found on Gardiner Lake and paddlers may want to spend their first night at the lodge before heading down the Ells River. There are very few signs of civilization between the lodge and the take-out at Bitumount and paddlers need to be self sufficient.

Hangingstone River (Map 55/A1–69/A7)

Whitewater kayakers in Fort McMurray are mostly out of luck when it comes to challenging runs. There's a nice stretch of whitewater on the Athabasca, but access is difficult. However, during spring the Hangingstone River gives whitewater paddlers a short, challenging run that descends into the Athabasca River Valley. The put-in is a short hike from Highway 63 a few kilometres south of the Highway 69 junction (watch for unmarked trails heading to the river from the highway where the two are at their closest point). The take-out is found at the Lions Park next to Highway 63.

> *Regardless of your route, always remember to be safe and be aware of weather conditions and water temperature. Always wear your PFD (personal floatation device) and ensure it is fitted properly.*

Hay River (Map 92/D6–93/E1)

The Hay River is an oddity in Northern Alberta. Unlike all the other rivers that cross the northern third of the province, the Hay is actually within striking distance of a road for much of its distance. Highway 35 meets up with the Hay at Meander River and follows the river valley across into the Northwest Territories. It would be a marshy slog to the road in places, but it could be done. Most people choose to do the river in one 420 km (263 mile) paddle that will take the better part of two weeks or more to paddle. The Alberta portion of the river, from Habay to Indian Cabins, is 238 km (149 miles) long. A good overnight location is Adair Creek, which is about 31 km (19 mi) from the access point found east of Habay. Other details are few and far between, but there is a series of rapids at km 117 (mile 73), about 40 km before the Hay joins with the Meander, to be wary of. Further upstream there are a number of rapids and a couple major waterfalls (Alexandra & Louise), but these are found mostly in the Northwest Territories.

Jackfish River (Map 41/D6)

The Jackfish River drains Christina Lake into the Christina River. Most people paddle the river from the lake to the Secondary Highway 881 Bridge, although it is possible to continue onto the Christina River for a multi-day trip. The river is narrow and shallow, but there are some fun little rapids.

Kakwa River (Map 1/G6–3/C2)

The most common put-in is at Porcupine Flats, which involves an hour hike down to the river. The trip is 160 km (100 miles) from Porcupine Flats to the McLeod Flats Campground on the Smoky River (Map 17/B7), which is the most common take-out. An alternative is to take-out at the Highway 40 Bridge (Map 6/B5). The rapids through this section range from Grade II to Grade IV. Many rafting companies who run the river make this trip 3 days but it can be done in 2 days or even 1 when there are high flows. On a three day trip, camp stops are normally at Little Kakwa Falls the first night and at the confluence with the Smoky River on the second night.

La Biche River (Map 11/D1–25/B7)

The La Biche starts out easy enough at it's put-in at the Highway 63 Bridge. As it begins to drop into the Athabasca River Valley, it begins to pick up speed and difficulty and should be left to intermediate paddlers. There is a rough road to the confluence. Be sure you can get there with your vehicle, because your next real take-out is about ten days away, on the other side of some of the nastiest whitewater in Northern Alberta.

Little Smoky River (Maps 5, 19, 32, 33)

The first road access to the Little Smoky (in this book) is just west of Smoke Lake off the Bigstone Road. The river flows generally north, crossing Highway 43 at Little Smoky (another possible put-in/take-out), Secondary Highway 665, Secondary Highway 669, Highway 49 and Secondary Highway 744 before flowing into the Big Smoky just below the Highway 49 Bridge. The river is mostly an easy Grade 1 paddle and provides good fishing.

MacKay River (Map 67/B7–68/F2)

The MacKay is a Grade II river with a few Class III rapids in high water. Access is 62 km northwest of Fort McMurray on Tower Road, where it crosses the MacKay. The take-out is found just outside of the town of Fort MacKay at the bridge. The 80 km (50 mile) run can be done in one long (10 hour) day, but better done in two half days. It is about 4.5 hours from the put-in to the "corner", 2 hours from the "corner" to the confluence of the Dover and another 3.5 hours from the Dover to the take-out. The "corner" is a narrow, sharp bend where the water forces your boat to the outside wall and through a hole. It is followed by a rock garden and another sharp bend. There is a portage but if you miss it, due to the high banks and swift flowing water, you will have to run it. Like most of the smaller volume rivers in the north, paddling is best done during spring run-off, say from April to June. In low water, the river is highly technical, as you must navigate through a field of exposed boulders and rocks. Although there are a number of good campsites along the river, once on this remote wilderness river there are few options to get off as walking out through dense bush and muskeg is not feasible.

Muskeg River (Map 81/G7)

The Muskeg offers a relatively shorter run of about 19 km (11.6 miles). The put-in is found about 75 km north of Fort McMurray. Head east on a paved road for a couple kilometres, then turn east again and put-in at the bridge over the river, near the Muskeg River Mine gate. From here, it is a three to five hour paddle down to the Highway 63 Bridge. The run is marked by lots of tight corners and banks choked with willows. There is one ledge that can be run or portaged around, but the portage is unmarked. Below that are a few broken ledges that can be run or lined. The best time to paddle is May and June or after a heavy (but not too) rain. The river is difficult in low water as there is not enough water to float a boat and in high water it can be tricky because it is too pushy. While you're only about a kilometre from the road, bailing would be tough as the bush is very thick.

Narraway River (Map 1/C4–15/C7)

The Narraway is a river that is rarely run by itself. It is either run as the end of the Torrens River or the start of the Wapiti River. It is possible to put-in from a road off Two Lakes Road and take-out at the Boundary Road Bridge for a good day-trip, but few people run the Narraway for its own sake. If you want to see the whole river, it takes about three days from the put-in at Torrens Chutes to the take-out at Wapiti Garden or a nine-hour paddle from Boundary Road to the Wapiti Garden, seven of which are on the Wapiti River.

Peace River (Maps 43–47, 61–62, 74–75, 86–88, 95–97)

The mighty Peace flows east from the Northern Rockies in British Columbia and across Northern Alberta to the Athabasca Peace Delta. It is an easy, slow moving river with the exception of the Vermillion Chutes and is considered one of the province's great canoe touring rivers.

Peace River – BC to Dunvegan (Map 43/F3–45/D7)

It is 170 km (75 miles) from the Cherry Point put-in, just east of the BC boundary, to Dunvegan. There are a few alternate take-out spots (Cotillion Park and Many Islands, just to name two) that can be used to shorten the route. The river rolls along through a lush valley, with many gravel bars and some islands along the way. The river does braid and you may find yourself having to portage or line when the water in one channel gets too shallow. This and riverboats are your only concerns on this easy Grade I river. You can float from put-in to take-out in three days, but if you hustle, you can do it in two. The Peace is a dam-controlled river; keep in mind that the water levels can fluctuate rapidly when choosing a campsite.

Peace River –Dunvegan to Peace River (Map 45/D7–47/B4)

For people looking for a longer float, this 100 km (60 mile) section from Dunvegan to Peace River will add another two days' paddle to the previous trip or it can be done on its own. As before, there are a number of alternate put-ins or take-outs. This section is very similar to the previous section, a Grade I trip on a dam-controlled river with lots of channels to choose from. The occasional riverboat can make things exciting.

Paddling Adventures

Peace River –Peace River to Fort Vermillion (Map 47/B4–87/A3)
The 430 km (262 mile) section of the river from Peace River to Fort Vermillion has no rapids of note. There are a few places where the river can be accessed to make this a shorter route (any highway crossing, Notikewin River Provincial Park, etc.). It will take about ten days to paddle this run.

Peace River –Fort Vermillion to Peace Point (Map 87/A3–96/C6)
The 307 km (185 mile) section of the Peace River from Fort Vermillion to Peace Point will take about a week to do. The Grade II paddle starts at the boat launch in Fort Vermillion. An alternate take-outs/put-in is at Adam's Landing at km 74. Further along you will pass the community of Fox Lake at km 102, but there is no road access. While the river is fairly easy, it is extremely remote and planning is essential. The Vermillion Chutes are found at km 78 and are extremely difficult at high water levels (Class V). At lower water levels they are only rated Class III. Anyone attempting to run the chutes must be aware of the mandatory portage around the Vermillion Falls, a 4–5 metre (13–16 ft) drop, just to the east. Past here, the river regains its former composure and becomes an easy float north to the take-out. However, the relatively easy Boyer Rapids at km 288 can pose a problem for some.

Peace River –Peace Point to Fort Fitzgerald (Map 96/C6–96/G1)
The final 224 km (136 mile) stretch of the trip starts at Peace Point on the Peace River and ends at Fort Fitzgerald on the Slave River. The confluence of the two rivers is at exactly halfway on the run. The majority of the river is a Grade II float, although once you hit the Slave, the river is much bigger and much faster. There are a few rapids to note including three Class III rapids before the take-out at Fort Fitzgerald. Beyond Fort Fitzgerald there are four Class VI+ rapids that are not navigable, so paddler's take-out here. An alternate take-out is at the Hay Camp, at km 191. A popular side trip is the hike from Sweetgrass Landing to Sweetgrass Station, an old bison station in the heart of the Peace-Athabasca Delta. Past Fort Smith in the Northwest Territories you can resume your journey. It should take about a week to follow the Class I paddle to Fort Resolution on Great Slave Lake.

Peace River to Mamawi Lake Route (Map 96/C6–90/B2)
This is an uncommon route that starts at Peace Point on the Peace River and traverses south to Fort Chipewyan. There is a 4 km (2.4 mile) portage from the Peace to Sweetgrass Creek, which continues south to drain into the east end of Lake Claire. From the lake, you need to navigate through to Mamawi Lake and eventually over to Fort Chipewyan on Lake Athabasca. The lakes are big and shallow and are known to become quite rough. Trippers will also need to wind their way through the maze of channels at the east end of Mamawi Lake. It is easy to get lost in those channels.

Ponton River (Map 86/G2–87/A3)
This short, windy river offers a very easy paddle through a valley filled with wildlife. There are a few sections that offer a moderate (but ungraded) challenge, but the majority of the trip is a flatwater float. The river can be accessed at a variety of bridge crossings northwest of Fort Vermillion. The farthest north you can put-in is from the end of a road just north of Highway 58. Head north, then east, to the dead end. A trail heads into the bush to the south. From here, it is a couple hours to the Highway 58 Bridge, a couple hours more to the Rocky Lane Bridge and the better part of a day to the Peace River, where you have to paddle about 2 km upstream to Fort Vermillion. On a windy day, paddling upstream can be extremely tough.

Redwillow River (Map 15/F3–16/A3)
The Redwillow is a low volume river. In summer, there is not enough water to float a boat down. In spring and early summer, this is a Grade I trip that should take about five hours to make it down to the Redwillow Park off Secondary Highway 722. An alternate put-in/take-out is found just shy of the halfway point, north of Elmworth.

Richardson River (Map 90/C6–B2)
The Richardson River is a long, lonely river found north of Fort McMurray. The river drains out of Marguerite River Wildland Provincial Park but most paddlers pick up the route where the Fort Chipewyan Winter Road crosses the river near the Richardson River Dunes Wildland Park. The river has been only rarely run and information is scarce on the actual difficulty of the paddle. Take-out at Fort Chipewyan.

Rivière des Rochers to Slave River Route (Map 90/B2–96/G1)
This river drains Lake Athabasca north to its confluence with the Peace River, where the two merge to become the Slave River. The paddle starts on Lake Athabasca, at Fort Chipewyan and ends at Fort Fitzgerald, on the Slave River. The only real challenge on this section is the weirs, one at Revillon Coupé and another at Little Rapids. Continuing north on the Slave, you will find four Class III rapids, the first at the confluence with the Peace, then at Primrose, Demicharge and Stony Islands. It will take about four days to paddle the 163 km (100 mile) route. An alternate take-out is at the Hay Camp, at km 100. Do not proceed past Fort Fitzgerald, as beyond this point is a series of unrunable Class VI+ rapids.

Salt River (Map 96/E2–D1)
One of the most difficult rivers in the area to run, the Salt River is not filled with rapids, but rather, is rarely filled with enough water to float a boat. It is usually only navigable for a couple of weeks in early spring. The put-in is where the Pine Lake Road crosses the river and the take-out is the Highway 5 Bridge. The area is a prime bird watching location.

Simonette River (Map 3/E6–17/F3)
The local kayak club uses this river as an introduction to moving water, putting in where the Forestry Trunk Road crosses the river. It is possible to put-in south and east of this point, where a trio of roads cross the river east of the Forestry Trunk Road (Map 3/E6 is the farthest south) and paddle to the Forestry Trunk Bridge east of Grand Prairie. It is a fairly easy trip through a mostly untracked stretch of land.

Slave River (Map 96/F1–97/A7)
The Slave River is one of the best whitewater kayak areas in Western Canada. Located near Fort Smith, there are a number of different runs that can take from an hour to a full day. These runs include Cassette Rapids, Pelican Falls, Mountain Portage and Rapids of the Drowned. Depending on your skill level, you can select a section of the river offering you from Class I to Class V, from technical creek style drops to big water playboating to easy beginner wave trains. The Fort Smith Paddling Club can help you select the best runs for your abilities.

Smoky River (Maps 3, 17, 31, 32, 46, 47)
The Smoky River is one of the major rivers in north central Alberta, draining much of the South Peace region into the Peace River. It is a big river with many places to access it from.

Smoky River – Latornell Flats to McLeod Flats (Map 3/D3–17/B7)
The section of the Smoky from Latornell Flats to McLeod Flats Campground features lots of whitewater. While most of these rapids are only Grade II or II+, watch out for the Chute, a Grade IV+ rapid with 2 metre high (6 foot) standing waves. This set of rapids is unavoidable, or at least, only avoided by an extremely difficult portage around the entire canyon (we have not found anybody yet who has actually made the portage, so we cannot confirm if it can be done). Note: accessing the put-in can be rather difficult since the last 8 km or so of the road is 4wd accessible only.

Smoky River –McLeod Flats to Highway 43 (Map 17/B7–17/F2)
The river moves fairly quickly until its confluence with the Wapiti River, when it slows down. There are some Grade II rapids along this section of the Smoky River, all of which are avoidable. This leg of the trip from McLeod Flats to the Highway 43 Bridge is 61 km (38 miles) long and should take the better part of two days. Along the way you will pass an island with a cabin owned by the Grande Prairie River Rats.

Smoky River –Forestry Trunk to Highway 43 (Map 17/F3–F2)
A short, easy trip from the Forestry Trunk Road (on the Simonette River) to the take-out on the Highway 43 Bridge combines parts of the Simonette and Smoky River into a four hour paddle through some scenic territory east of Grande Prairie. There are no rapids, although there are a few rocks that poke up in low water. The trip is 23 km (14 miles) long, most of that on the Smoky.

Smoky River –Highway 43 to Highway 49 (Map 17/F2–32/E3)
This section of the Smoky, between the Highway 43 Bridge and the Highway 49 Bridge, is remote, but easy to paddle, with only a few riffles and the occasional gravel bar to worry about. It should take two or three days to paddle the 122 km (76 miles) between the two highway bridges.

Smoky River –Highway 49 to Peace River (Map 32/E3–47/B4)

If you thought the Smoky had lost all its fight, think again. There are numerous places where the river narrows and the ride gets just a little more exciting on this section between the Highway 49 Bridge and the take-out in Peace River town. The rapids north of the Highway 49 Bridge maybe Grade II, but they are still enough to capsize a canoe if you are not careful. There are a couple of take-out options through this area, including the Shaftsbury Ferry south of town or the park just downstream from the bridge in town.

Torrens River (Map 1/C4)

It is a bit of a hike to the put-in below Torrens Chutes, but this is one of the few true whitewater rivers on our maps. The exciting run is about 10 km (6.2 miles) from the put-in to the confluence with the Narraway River and just a bit longer to the take-out on the Narraway. It is possible to continue along the Narraway to the Wapiti, a trip of about three days.

Trans Canada Trail: The Water Route
(Maps 10–11, 23–25, 39, 53–54, 67–70, 80–83, 89–90, 96–97)

The Trans Canada Trail is twice divided as it makes its way through Alberta. In Calgary, a second, northern route leaves the main trail and heads north, then east. In the town of Athabasca, where the historic Athabasca Landing Route hits the river, the route divides again. This time, the main northern route continues in a north easterly direction, while a water route heads off to the northwest, following the Athabasca River to Lake Athabasca. From here, the route continues on the Rivière des Rochers and then the Slave River, into the Northwest Territories. Both the Athabasca and the Slave have difficult rapids and only experienced paddlers should attempt to run these sections of rivers. There are a few shorter sections that can be run without hitting any major rapids, but access points are few and far between en route to Fort McMurray, Fort MacKay or Fort Chipewyan. Once into the Northwest Territories, the route continues 2,329 km (1,447 miles) to Tuktoyaktuk on the Arctic Ocean.

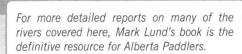

For more detailed reports on many of the rivers covered here, Mark Lund's book is the definitive resource for Alberta Paddlers.

Wabasca River (Maps 51–52, 63–66, 76–79, 87)

The Wabasca River weaves its drunken way across north-central Alberta, flowing from North Wabasca Lake. Despite all odds, it finally heads in a generally northwest direction, where it flows into the Peace River just downstream of Fort Vermillion. From here, paddlers can head downstream or upstream on the Peace; it should take about two days to make it to Fort Vermillion. The whole river can be paddled in approximately 8 days but it can take double the time depending on water levels. The river is rated as a Class I-III and some of the larger rapids may require either lining or portaging. When the water is low, large exposed rocks will cause issues and inexperienced paddlers should avoid this river in those conditions.

Wabasca River – North Wabasca Lake to Loon River (Map 37/F1–77/B6)

The 237 km (148 mile) Grade II paddle from the recreation site on North Wabasca Lake to the Loon River has a couple access points along its way, but it mostly meanders its way through a large, roadless swatch of forest and muskeg. There are a number of difficult rapids along the way that also have a profound effect on the time it takes to run the river depending on the water level. At high water, this section could take four days; at low water, double that. The rapids, which can be run at high water, become obstacles in low water, which you may have to line around. There is a bridge over the river near Goosegrass Lake, but a more common take-out is just past the Loon River, where Highway 88 comes very close to the river. Here you will find another bridge over the river on an exploration road.

Wabasca River –Loon River to Tall Cree Bridge (Map 77/B6–87/D6)

Highway 88 generally follows the river through the section from Loon River to the Tall Cree Bridge, but only crosses the river once between the put-in and take-out. Elsewhere, the road is close, but is quite difficult to access due to brush and the muskeg. This 111 km (69 mile) section of the river can be done in two or three days. The first half has no rapids worth mentioning, while the last half has some Class III rapids, passing through a canyon-like valley. Like the upper reaches, the rapids are worse in low water when the boulders start to poke out of the water.

Wabasca River –Tall Cree Bridge to Peace River (Map 87/D6–D3)

The easiest section of the river is north of the Tall Cree Bridge and it can be paddled in 2 to 3 days. It is 105 km (66 miles) from the Tall Cree Bridge to the confluence of the Wabasca and Peace Rivers. From there, your options are to continue down the Peace, or more likely, make arrangements with a jet boater in Fort Vermillion to pick you up. The river here is slow moving, meandering its way northward. It's less than 50 km/30 miles from the bridge to the Peace as the crow flies, but you will have traveled twice that by the time you hit the confluence. There are few rapids, but again, watch out for rocks at low water levels.

Wandering River (Map 25/D5–B7)

Highway 63 crosses the Wandering River just south of Lyle Lake. You could put-in at the lake, but most put-in at the bridge, on the south side of the river. The top part of this run has tight corners, a number of beaver dams and some Class II rapids to negotiate. After that, it is basically an easy float to where the highway crosses the river again. This section should take a couple hours. From here, it is possible to float downstream to the La Biche River and then on to the Athabasca. There is rough 4wd access to this point; make sure you can know your take-out, because there are not many options once you hit the Athabasca.

Wapiti River (Map 15/A7–17/E3)

The Wapiti is a major tributary of the Smoky River, which in turn is a major tributary of the Peace. The Wapiti flows from the mountains south of Grand Prairie, first through the foothills, then into the boreal forest. There are some easy rapids, especially in the upper sections, but many sections of the river are quite remote.

Wapiti River – Upper Wapiti (Map 1/C1–16/A4)

The first section of the Wapiti is a nine hour trip that is best done over two days. The put-in is 1.5 hours southwest of Grande Prairie off Two Lakes Road. Watch for PTI's Two Lakes Trailer Camp; turn left here and follow the road down to a bridge over the Narraway River. From the bridge it is a short, steep climb down to the river. If you start late in the day, there is a great campsite along the east bank of the river, about 300 metres (1,200 ft) from the bridge. There are no other spots to camp until you hit the Wapiti, about two hours paddle from the bridge. It is another seven hours from where the Narraway flows into the Wapiti to the take-out at Wapiti Gardens. Access to the take-out is south and east of Hinton Trail on a flat with many cabins. The first section of the trip is along the Narraway River, which is a small, scenic and swift river. It is rated Grade II, with lots of rapids and some rocks to dodge. This river is very remote and there is no road access between the put-in and take-out.

Wapiti River –Wapiti Gardens to Highway 40 (Map 16/A4–16/G3)

From Wapiti Gardens, there are some Grade II rapids along this section of the river, but the majority of this run is Grade I. The biggest rapid (Class II) is located near the start of the trip, on the outside of the first left bend with a gravel bar. The rapid can be avoided by sticking close to the gravel bar. It is 16 km (10 miles) to the Redwillow Creek Confluence, another 16 km to Pipestone Creek and another 26 km (16 miles) to the take-out at the Highway 40 Bridge. While this section of the river is easily accessible and fairly close to Grande Prairie, it is still very wild. Give yourself two days to do this section of river and lookout for riverboats.

Wapiti River – Highway 40 to Highway 43 (Map 16/G3–17/F2)

It is 26 km (16 miles) from the Highway 40 Bridge to the Smoky River and another 20 km (12 miles) to the take-out at Highway 43 Bridge, making a 46 km (28 mile) total trip. This will take you the better part of two days, with no access points after the Weyerhaeuser railway bridge (at about 13 km/8 miles). There are no rapids to speak of on the Wapiti River. Chances of seeing wildlife through this section are good. There is also a trapper's cabin perched above the river at the Bear Creek confluence (north side of river), with great views over the river and valley. The Smoky River is much faster than the Wapiti and it should only take about three hours to paddle the stretch from the confluence to the take-out.

Park
Adventures

Parks and recreation areas are great ways to discover the beauty and splendour of Alberta. In fact, many of the most spectacular areas in Alberta are found in the wide variety of parks and protected areas in the province. These sites range from roadside camping facilities to remote backcountry parks with no roads, no facilities, and, if you're lucky, a few developed trails. As you travel north in Alberta, there are fewer population centres and the parks become much more remote—access is often an issue.

Although there is only one national park in this region, it is Canada's largest. Established to protect the bison that gave this park its name, Wood Buffalo National Park is not easily accessed due to its location. More common are provincial parks, which protect provincially significant natural, historical and cultural features. Some parks are more recreation oriented, with hundreds of campsites, RV hook-ups, playgrounds, stores and showers, trails and boating. Others are more conservation oriented, with fewer facilities.

For the naturalist, there are a variety of natural areas, ecological reserves and wildland parks to explore. Some are very fragile, with little recreational use. Others are more accessible and used for hiking, skiing, berry picking and wildlife watching. The public are welcome to visit, as long as they respect the sensitive areas these sites protect.

Another popular park type area in Alberta is the provincial recreation area. These are usually small campsites and day-use areas, with a strong emphasis on recreation. Virtually anything you can do in the outdoors is enjoyed in and around any given recreation area.

Adding to the mix are a range of county, regional or municipal parks that are usually frequented by highway travellers or locals looking for a place to get away for a day or night. These range from beautiful campgrounds to places to pitch a tent near town. Some of these sites charge fees, while others are free.

For the typical camper, the season runs from the Victoria Day (May) long weekend to the Labour Day (September) long weekend. Some of the parks and recreation areas also have limited camping during the winter months. Camping fees vary, based on services provided.

Regardless of your interest, we have provided a detailed list of the various parks and recreation areas below. The symbols beside our listings will help you pick a destination that suits your wishes. Make sure you check www.albertaparks.ca to check on park status or upcoming events while you are planning your trip.

Park Adventures

Baptiste Lake Beach and Campground (Map 10/A3)

This popular recreation lake is found 16 km west of the town of Athabasca. There are 12 unserviced sites here, as well as a day use area with picnic shelter (a nominal fee is charged), a boat launch, beach and playground.

Bear Lake Regional Park (Map 16/F1)

There is a small beach and a boat launch at this 10 site campground northeast of Grande Prairie. Bear Lake is relatively large, but very shallow, merely 2 metres (6 ft) deep at its deepest and there are no fish in the lake. It is a popular place to kite board and there is a picnic shelter and tables in a grassy area by the lake as well.

Beaver Lake Recreation Area (Map 12/C3)

This pristine lake, 6 km east of Lac La Biche, offers exceptional sport fishing, exhilarating landscapes and excellent bird watching opportunities. The south arm of the lake is dotted with small islands where you may occasionally spot nesting bald eagles, while boat rentals and fishing charters are also available. In addition to 92 reservable campsites (67 of which have electrical hook-ups) and 10 group sites, there is a playground, washrooms with showers, a boat launch, fish cleaning station and a tackle shop.

Big Mountain Creek Recreation Area (Map 17/A5)

Located 40 km south of Grande Prairie on Highway 40, this group use site is located on Big Mountain Creek and has 25 sites with fish cleaning stations and pit toilets. In the summer, the groups that stay here tend to be anglers and there is off-site ATVing available. In the winter, this is a popular snowmobile staging area. Reservations can be made by calling 780-532-8010.

Many of the most spectacular areas in Alberta are found in the wide variety of parks and protected areas in the province.

Birch Mountains Wildland Park (Map 79/A580/G2)

This park with no on-site facilities is home to one of Canada's only free-roaming wood bison herds outside of Wood Buffalo National Park. The lakes in the parks support good fishing year-round, but access to this area is difficult, as there are no roads; the only (easy) way in is by floatplane. There is a commercial lodge on Namur Lake.

Bison Flats Recreation Area (Map 3/D5)

There is no road access to this recreation area on the banks of the Smoky River. Instead, campers will have to walk down a short ways to the site. If you have a 4wd, you can drive to within about 2 km of the site. There are seven tenting units and the fishing in the Smoky River is worth the walk. As you might expect, anglers are the prime users of the site.

Brownvale Campground (Map 46/D6)

There are 10 campsites at this municipal campground found 1.5 km west and 5 km north of Brownvale and Highway 2. Camping is free at the 19 sites and there are trails to explore. Group camping and picnic areas are also available, along with a beach and boat launch. The lake is stocked with rainbow trout.

Calling Lake Provincial Park (Map 24/D5)

Calling Lake is a popular provincial park found 55 km north of Athabasca. There is an 81 reservable-unit campground here with power, as well as a day use area, playground, boat launch, fish cleaning stations and 5 group camping areas. The big draw here is the lake and watersports. The lake is known for its walleye and also sports northern pike, perch, whitefish and burbot. The big, round lake is prone to chop that are sometimes big enough to chase the powerboats off, let alone the canoeists. Birding is also an activity here. Reservations are available.

Caribou Mountains Wildland Park (Maps 94, 95)

This park extends the protected area around Wood Buffalo National Park to the west. It is best known as a wildlife refuge with a few bird species that usually do not live this far south, as well as a substantial woodland caribou herd. There is no road access and few visitors make it into the 5,910 square km park.

Chain Lakes [Lower] Recreation Area (Map 10/B1)

Located on the southernmost of the Chain Lakes (thus the name), this site is all about the water activity. There are 20 rustic non-reservable campsites, which are mostly used by anglers, a boat launch and a fish cleaning station. There is an electric motor only restriction on the lake.

Camp Carter (Map 45/A3)

This municipal campground is located on the banks of the Peace River, about 25 km west of Hines Creek on Secondary Highway 685. There is space for 20 vehicle units, which are large enough for RVs, and a boat launch on the Peace River, along with a picnic shelter, trails and a children's playground. For more information call 780-685-3925.

Cecil Thompson Park (Map 47/C4)

Found 7 km east of Peace River off Highway 2, this small park offers 6 free campsites, a day use area with pit toilets, fishing and a playground.

Chinchaga Wildland Park (Map 71)

Located about 140 km west of Manning off a 4wd road, this remote wilderness park was set aside as habitat for a number of species, including Trumpeter Swan, Grizzly Bear and Woodland Caribou. The Chinchaga River, which marks the northern boundary of the park, can be paddled during high water levels (although there is little information about this route). Halverson Ridge could make a good hiking destination.

Christina River Remote Public Land Recreation Area (Map 55/D1)

This small, 2 unit campsite is located 25 km upstream from Fort McMurray along the Clearwater River. It is water accessible only, although snowmobilers do visit the area in winter.

Chrystina Lake Recreation Area (Map 7/F2)

The road into Chrystina Lake is paved most of the way, but the last few kilometres are in shockingly bad shape, at least in wet weather. A 4wd vehicle is recommended. There are no facilities.

Clear River Regional Park (Map 44/B1)

The Cleardale Agricultural Society maintains a campsite on the Clear River west of the town itself. Home to a nice has a kitchen shelter highway travellers can also stop to picnic or try their luck fishing on the river.

Cold Lake Provincial Park (Map 14/F4–F7)

Made up of several parcels around Cold Lake, only the northern part of the lake and park are in this book. The North Shore has some fine beaches and the Martineau Valley is a good wildlife viewing area.

Colin-Cornwall Lakes Wildland Park (Map 97/E3)

Located in the far northeastern corner of the province, this park is about 340 km north of Fort McMurray by air, which is the only way to access the park. The park contains large lakes, sand plains and dunes, as well as mixed boreal forest. Because of all the lakes, the park is home to a number of bird species, including the provincially rare Mew Gull and Semipalmated Plover.

Cotillion Park (Map 44/A3)

Found a fair distance north of Highway 49, this municipal park has 12 campsites, including serviced sites for RVs, a large day use area with picnic shelter, a group use BBQ area, washrooms with showers and a boat launch on the Peace River. It a scenic park that provides one of the few access points to the mighty Peace River in the area. There is abundant wildlife in the area, trails and horse corrals for equestrian riders and hoodoos to view.

Park Adventures

Crane Lake East & Bodina County Parks (Map 14/B6)

Found 30 km west and north of Cold Lake, there are 29 non-powered camp-sites at the eastern site and 47 powered sites and three cabins at the Bodina County Park. The sites were once recreation areas, but have been divested to the Municipal District of Bonnyville. There are shower facilities, a store, fish cleaning facilities, firewood for sale, a camp kitchen, a hand pump, hiking trails, a boat launch and a beach where you can take the kids swimming. For information, or to reserve a space, call 780-826-7165 for Bodina or 780-573-9940 for the East Park.

Cross Lake Provincial Park (Map 9/F4)

Located about an hour north of Westlock on Highway 44, this popular park has comprehensive facilities and activities available andis visited year round. One of the prime pursuits here is fishing as well as other water sports including windsurfing and waterskiing. But the park also has a series of trails that can be explored on foot in summer or on skis in winter. There is also good bird watching here, with nesting bald eagles and osprey around the edge of the lake. There are 130 reservable sites with power in the campground and a day use area. Amenities include cook shelters, fish cleaning stations, a boat launch, a pier, interpretive viewpoint, horseshoe pitch, washrooms with showers and playground. Reservations are available.

Crow Lake Provincial Park (Map 39/G4–40/A4)

The campground at Crow Lake has been closed for several years due to dam-age sustained in the House River Forest Fire and there is no word on when or if it will be reopened. Together with the nearby ecological reserve, this park protects the lake and surrounding uplands. The lake is a great canoeing destination since no powerboats are allowed.

Cummings Lake Recreation Area (Map 45/F5)

Cummings Lake is found 2 km north of Fairview and offers a variety of ac-tivities and amenities. Campers will find 28 well-spaced campsites complete with electrical hook-ups set in the forest near the edge of the lake. There is also a group campsite, boat launch and dock on the lake as well as a large day use area, with threeball diamonds, horse shoe pitch, playground and a picnic shelter. Anglers will find the lake is now mainly a perch lake, while trail enthusiasts will find 11 km of trails that connect to the town and golf course. Adding to the mix are over 75 species of birds that have been identified here.

Demmit Regional Park (Map 29/E4)

This site is located just east of the BC border along Highway 2. The campground has 20 unserviced sites and is perhaps a little too close to the busy highway for its own good. Amenities include pit toilets and a cook structure with wood stove.

Dunvegan Provincial Park (Map 45/D7)

Built near the site of the old Fort Dunvegan, which is one of the oldest fur trading and missionary sites in Alberta,the historical significance and the natural beauty of the lovely Peace River Valley help make this park a popular destination. There are 65 reservable campsites with power and a large day use area. The site also features Alberta's only suspension bridge.Other amenities include a playground, horseshoe pit, cook shelters and modern washrooms. The boat launch is across the bridge on the other side of the river. Under the highway bridge and down a short access road is Maples Park, a rather pretty day use only site with a picnic area and playground that sees a fraction of the visitors as Dunvegan.

Dunvegan West Wildland Park (Maps 31, 43–45)

Designed to protect some interesting landscapes as well as wildlife habitat, this park is spread out on unconnected parcels along the Peace River Valley. This is one of the most diverse and ecologically productive valleys in Canada and it shows. There are no facilities in the park and access is limited.

Economy Lake Campground (Map 17/E6)

Located 35 km south of Highway 43 on the Forestry Trunk Road (Second-ary Highway 734), this former forestry recreation area is now operated and maintained by Canfor. There are nine campsites that are oriented in groups of three, making this a good place for small groups. The site is quite rustic and offers little more than an outhouse, picnic tables and fire rings. Fishing is a very popular activity in the lake for walleye and perch.

Edith Lake Day use Area (Map 7/E2)

This former recreation site near Swan Hills is still marked on many maps as having camping. It does not, although the site is still open for day use. The prime users at the site are picnickers and anglers looking for brook trout. The site is found just off Highway 33 and offers a covered picnic shelter for groups to use and a small dock.

Engstrom Lake Recreation Area (Map 55/E7)

Found 80 km south of Fort McMurray, the campground has been closed to the public, but the day use area and boat launch are still available on the eastern shore of Engstrom Lake. The lake offers good fishing for rainbow trout all year round. Note the motor restriction.

Engstrom Recreation Area (Map 70/A6)

This small site along the Clearwater River is only accessible by jet boat or canoe during the summer and snowmobile in the winter. There is a small campground, but no other facilities.

Ethel Lake County Park (Map 14/D6)

This small municipally managed campground, with12 unserviced sites, pro-vides access to Ethel Lake. Found 10 km north of Cold Lake, visitors will also find horseshoe pits, a swimming area and boat launch as well as a camp kitchen. Reservations are recommended by calling 780-594-2267.

Falher Municipal Campground (Map 33/C3)

Best described as an RV corral set on the edge of town, there are a couple of trees to break the wind and a small pond. Recreation opportunities are lim-ited, as is the scenic values of the site. There are 30 sites, 18 of which have power, washrooms with showers and a playground in the campground. The day use area has a picnic shelter.

Fawcett Lake [West] Recreation Area (Map 23/C3)

This recreation area is located 18 km north of Smith. There are 58 reservable campsites as well as a group use area. Amenities include fish cleaning sta-tions, a pier, boat launch, grocery store and pit toilets. There is a nice beach for swimming and fishing is quite popular for lake whitefish, northern pike, perch and walleye. In winter, snowmobilers use the boat launch area to ac-cess the lake.Reservations can be made by calling (780) 829-2211.

Fidler-Greywillow Wildland Park (Map 90/D1–97/F6)

This park protects two islands and a portion of the north shore of Lake Athabasca north of Fort Chipewyan. Access to the park is by floatplane or boat only in summer. In the winter, it is possible to visit the park along the winter road that runs by here. There are boat accessible tenting sites com-plete with pit toilets on Bustard Island and at Cypress Point.

Figure Eight Lake Recreation Area (Map 46/D3)

Figure Eight Lake is located 25 km west of Peace River; the signs to the lake can be confusing, but stick with it, you should get there…eventually. The lake wasn't a lake until 1969, when volunteers from Brownvale drained the slough, cleared it and brought in sand. Today it is a popular fishing lake, which is stocked with rainbow trout. There are 20 non-reservable rustic campsites and a handlaunch for non-motorized vessels. In winter the trails are open to cross-country skiing. Amenities include fish cleaning stations, cooking shelter, pit toilets and a pier.

Fort Assiniboine Sandhills Wildland Park (Map 8/E7)

Protecting a portion of the Athabasca River Sandhills, the park features a num-ber of hiking/biking trails and random camping is allowed along the trails.Eques-trian facilities, a few staging areas, hitching rails and pit toilets are also found here. There are a number of viewpoints out over the Athabasca River Valley from various points along the trail. The park contains 436 recorded species of plants, twenty of which are considered rare in Alberta, as well as many different species of birds and animals. Snowmobiles are allowed on the connecting trail through the park, which links Fort Assiniboine with the Vega/Timeu Riding Area.

Fort Vermilion Recreation Area (Map 87/A3) ✂ 🐟

Located 10 km west of Fort Vermilion, this recreation area sports a rustic 10unit non-reservable campsite that offers free camping. The site is found along the Peace River, which offers good fishing for about a dozen different fish species, including bull trout and walleye. Amenities include cook shelters and pit toilets.

Forfar Recreation Park (Map 9/G5) ✂ 🏕 🏊 🚤 ⛵ 🛶 🐟 ☎

Forfar Recreation Park is the jewel in the crown of the County of Athabasca parks. The name Forfar was given to the local school in the early 1900s. The school is gone, but the name remains. The park has a campground with 72 unserviced sites, as well as a group camping area with cookhouse and woodstove, two beaches, ATV compound, playground, a boat launch and pier, all set in a pretty forested area on the shores of Long Lake. There is a nominal day use fee. Reservations can be made by phoning 780-675-5253 during the camping season.

Freeman River Recreation Area (Map 7/D5) ✂ 🏕 🚤 🐟

This is a gorgeous, verdant site tucked into the crook created by the Freeman River and Highway 32. There are 10 non-reservable, non-serviced, well-spaced units set in a mature pine forest and the river is accessed through the day use area. The campground is available year round and has fish cleaning stations and pit toilets. A rough angler's trails run up and downstream. The highway is close to the campsite, but thankfully it is usually not very busy in the evenings. Snowmobilers use this site as a staging area in the winter.

George Lake Campground (Map 45/E3) ✂ 🏕 🚤 🛶 🚻

Found off Highway 64 near Hines Creek, this is a popular community campsite is the site of an annual music festival. In summer boating is popular, but anglers will be disappointed that the lake is barren. There is a dock and the campground was the site of the Dumont Brothers Trading Post and therefore named after one of the brothers named George. The surrounding area is a prime wildlife viewing area for birders.

Ghost Lake Campground (Map 10/A1) ✂ 🏕 🏊 🛶 🐟

This small, 5 unit campground with pier and fish cleaning stations is located in the trees along the shoreline of the small Ghost Lake, which is easily accessed off Highway 2. There is a nominal fee for using the boat launch.

Gipsy Lake Wildland Park (Map 56/D4)
🏕 🛶 🥾 🚣 🛷 🚵 🐟 🎣 🚻

This remote wildland park is broken into three parcels, protecting a series of big lakes south of Fort McMurray. The biggest lake is Gordon Lake, but the most popular is Gipsy, which is home to a fly-in fishing and hunting lodge. The lodge also offers snowmobiling, cross-country skiing, hiking and canoeing.

Grand Rapids Wildland Park (Map 53/D6–54/F1)
🏕 🛶 🚣 🥾 🚤 🚵 🐟 🎣 🚻

This long, narrow wildland park lies upstream from Fort McMurray and protects Rapids Reach of the Athabasca River. This section of the river is very scenic, but paddlers will find it extremely challenging. Grand Rapids itself has claimed many lives. There is good fishing through the area and there is even a commercial lodge in the park. Access is by boat, float plane, snowmobile or ATV. Backcountry camping is permitted in the park and there are some strategically located pit toilets.

Greene Valley Provincial Park (Map 47/C5) 🥾 🐟 🚻

Access into Greene Valley is found 2 km south of Peace River, the town. The day use only park is a popular destination for hikinglocated in the Heart River Valley. The Heart River is a major tributary to the Peace River and this park is a wildlife corridor that serves as a winter range for moose and mule deer. There are pit toilets on site.

Gregoire Lake Provincial Park (Map 55/C3)
✂ 🏕 🚤 🏊 🛶 🚣 🥾 🛷 🚵 🐟 ☎

This big campground is found 29 km southeast of Fort McMurray on Secondary Highway 881. It has 140 reservable sites, 60 of which have electrical hook-ups.Amenities include washrooms with showers, fish cleaning stations, a boat launch, grocery store, horseshoe pitch, playground, lifejacket loaner station and picnic shelter. There are about 10 km of trails in the park, but the heart of the park is the lake and fishing, swimming, boating, windsurfing, waterskiingand canoeing are the most popular activities. In winter, snowmobilers use the boat launch area to access the lake and there is ice fishing. Reservations are available.

Grizzly Ridge Wildland Park (Map 21/G5–22/B4)
⛺ 🥾 🚣 🚵 🛶 🐟 🎣 🚻

This wildland gets its name from the Swan Hills Grizzly, which reside in (or at least wander through) the area. There is random camping permitted around the Grizzly Lookout Tower, but nowhere else in the area. Those that make it in will find good fishing for grayling in the various creeks. ATV riding and hunting are also permitted in the park.

Grovedale Fish Pond Recreation Area (Map 16/G5) 🏕 🐟

This small day use recreation area is located just off Highway 40, about 20 km south of Grande Prairie. There are 14 day use sites that see most of their use from anglers, as the small pond is stocked with rainbow trout.

Hangingstone Recreation Area (Map 55/A4) ✂ 🥾 🚻

This small park is located just off Highway 63. It is used mainly as a road stop for people travelling to Fort McMurray, although birders fancy this location as well. There are 56 non-reservable, rustic sites in the campground, along with pit toilets and a playground. There are also a few short hiking trails in the area.

Harman Valley Municipal Campground (Map 47/G5)
✂ 🏕 🥾 🚣 🎿 🚻

Located northeast of the town of Nampa, this municipal campground is well maintained, with several campsites, a kitchen shelter, horseshoe pit, playground and ball diamond, gazebo and short hiking trails.

Hay-Zama Lakes Wildland Park (Map 92/B7) ⛺ 🏊 🚵 🎣 🚻

Access to this remote wildland park is limited. There are a series of lakes, flood plains and deltas, making this an internationally significant wetland that sees hundreds of thousands of birds migrate through here in fall. Over 100,000 ducks and nearly 30,000 geese stop here annually. As a general rule, only hardcore birders visit this park, as the majority of the park is either lake or wetland. It is also home to a herd of re-introduced wood bison.

Heart River Dam Recreation Area (Map 34/B6)
✂ 🏕 🚤 🛶 🚣 🥾 🐟 🚻

The Heart River Dam Recreation Area is a utilitarian site that could be (and probably was) so much more. The setting is okay—just off the dam's holding pond against a stand of aspen. The problem is the small, non-reservable 4 unit site is self-maintained and it can be in a desperate state. Please help keep the site clean. The area itself is a popular bird watching area, while anglers and canoeists often explore the lake. There's a hand launch, pit toilets and fish cleaning station.

Hilliard's Bay Provincial Park (Map 34/F7)
✂ 🏕 🚤 🏊 🛶 🚣 🥾 🚵 🐟 ☎ 🚻

On the northwestern shores of Lesser Slave Lake, Hilliard's Bay is a large park with lots of space for campers. There are 174 reservable sites, 139 with electrical hook-ups and 35 without, and a group use site. Amenities include washrooms with showers, fish cleaning stations, a horseshoe pitch, playground and picnic shelter. There is a boat launch and a beach, as well as a 2.2 km trail along the shoreline that connects the camping area to the launch and day use area. In addition to a variety of water sports, there are a variety of trails to explore including a section of the Trans Canada Trail and the Boreal Forest Trail. In winter, the park is host to a couple groomed ski trails and ice fishing. Reservations are available.

Hilltop Lake Municipal Campground (Map 30/F5) ✂

There is space for nine vehicle units at this small municipal campground that is quite similar to forestry recreation area. The site lies next to Secondary Highway 724 and the small lake.

Hommy Grande Regional Park (Map 30/A7) ✂ 🏕 🐟

The park is found on Highway 43, northwest of Beaverlodge and provides good access to the Beaverlodge River, which holds pike and grayling. There are 23 powered campsites, a group use area with a picnic shelter, playgrounds, a ball diamond and pit toilets here.

Hope Lake County Park (Map 11/B4)

Located 20 km northeast of Boyle off Highway 63, this quiet, family-friendly campground is a popular destination with locals. There are 60 campsites, a group area that can accommodate 13 units, a sandy beach, swimming area, play area, ATV parking, boat launch and a small day use area available for a small fee. There is a 12 km/hr speed limit for boats on the lake and if you don't have your own boat, you can rent one. Reservations can be made in season by calling 780-689-7911.

Hubert Lake Wildland Park (Map 8/G5–12/B6)

This wildland is a mix of small lakes, wetlands and sand dunes. It is an important nesting area for blue herons and sandhill cranes, while a small herd of caribou wander in out of the wild land. There are no facilities.

Hutch Lake Recreation Area (Map 93/C7)

Off Highway 35 north of High Level, there is a rustic camping area on the west side of the lake with 13 well-spaced, unservicedsites, pit toilets, boat launch and day use area. Fishing is the main activity here, although it is possible to paddle around the lake.

Iosegun Lake Recreation Area (Map 5/D5)

Iosegun Lake is fabled in song and story as one of the top fishing lakes in Alberta for walleye. It is also a good place to find whitefish and pike. The popular recreation area has 52 campsites, pit toilets, cook shelters, fish cleaning stations, a picnic area, a boat launch, loading ramp, and a group-use area with a picnic shelter. Not everyone here comes for the fishing, though, and the lake sports a nice beach. Boating and canoeing are also popular. In winter, there is cross-country skiing and the parking lot is used as a staging area for snowmobiling in the area.

> Reservations for most provincial parks and recreation areas are available by calling 1-877-537-2757 or visiting www.reserve.albertaparks.ca.

Island Lake Campground (Map 10/A2)

This pretty lake is found 20 km northwest of the town of Athabasca on Highway 2. The campground is on the east side of the lake. The lake has many islands and bays, making it a great place for canoeing. There are 11 campsites here and a group campsite, fish cleaning and bird watching stations, a dock, as well as a boat launch for small boats. Call 780-675-2273 to make group camping reservations.

Jackfish Lake County Park (Map 10/E3)

Located northeast of the town of Athabasca, this popular county park features a campground, beach with swimming area, boat launch and pier. There are 35 unserviced sites at the campsite, playground and group area with picnic shelter. Call 780-675-2273 or 780-213-0038 for group site reservations and general inquiries.

Kakut Lake Park (Map 31/D4)

Maintained by the Kakut Lake Resort Association, this large, open community campground has been around since about 1961. Camping has been free for most of that time, but there is now a nominal charge for use. There is water on-sitealong with a camp kitchen, ball diamonds and playground. The lake is stocked with rainbow trout.

Kakwa River Recreation Area (Map 3/B5)

Located on the banks of the Kakwa River just off Highway 40, this 14 unit, user maintained campground is popular with anglers. There are pit toilets and fish cleaning stations. It also sees use from folks travelling up Highway 40 towards Alaska. Hiking and horseback riding are other popular activities here.

Kakwa Wildland Provincial Park (Map 1/B7)

Capturing the last of the Rocky Mountains in Alberta before they cross the boundary into BC, this is an exciting but underutilized area. Access is limited to one road from Grande Prairie to the north or by trail from Willmore Wilderness Park or BC. The road to Kakwa is maintained to Two Lakes Recreation Area. Beyond the lakes, the road becomes a little rough and even four-wheel drive vehicles will have trouble in bad weather. In fact, the road is often used as a trail by hikers, bikers, ATVers and horseback riders in summer and snowmobilers and skiers in winter. Once in the park, you will find a number of informal trails totaling about 60 km. You can camp almost anywhere you want to, but the only established site is at Dead Horse Meadows Recreation Area. To lessen the impact of random camping, there are 1 kilometre no-camp zones surrounding the Dead Horse Meadows and the Kakwa Day use Area. Backcountry camping does require a permit.

Klondike Ferry County Park (Map 8/F7)

Located 8 km west of Vega on Secondary Highway 661, the Klondike Ferry is one of the last operating ferries in Alberta. Along with 10 campsites, pit toilets and group camping area, there is a sheltered picnic area and trails to explore this historic area. The ferry takes you across the Athabasca River and into the Sandhills Wildland Park where many hiking and bicycling trails are found.

Krause Lake Recreation Area (Map 7/D3)

This is a group campground, great for weddings or family gatherings, near the Swan Hills airport and the local golf course. It serves as a staging area for snowmobilers in winter and ATV's in the summer and fall.

La Biche River Wildland Park (Map 11/B1–25/D6)

Protecting an area of undisturbed boreal forest, this area is home to black bear, lynx, wolverine, caribou, moose and beaver. There are no facilities at the park, but there are unmaintained trails and backcountry campsites for hikers, horseback riders and in the winter, snowshoers. The park is found northwest of Lac La Biche off Highway 63. There is good fishing in the La Biche River for arctic grayling, brook, bull and rainbow trout, pike and walleye to name a few. Hunting and OHV riding are permitted in the park, please follow the regulations.

La Butte Creek Wildland Park (Map 97/A5)

Abutting Wood Buffalo National Park, this remote park sees few visitors due to the boat access. Getting up La Butte Creek in a boat is near impossible so it is best to land on the upstream side of the creek. The park is open to backcountry hiking and camping, but there are many wetlands in the park, making navigation difficult.

La Glace Park (Map 30/D6)

This small park is located near the settlement of La Glace. It is a popular rest area for highway travellers and has 4 unserviced campsites, a playground and ball diamonds.

Lac Cardinal Recreation Area (Map 46/F4)

Located right next to Queen Elizabeth Provincial Park, this municipally owned area has a number of picnic tables and 16 or so first come first serve campsites. People typically crowd into the open grassy area wherever they find space. There is a playground, camp kitchen and pit toilets. Usually, it is not that busy, but on summer weekends and during the rodeo it can get pretty crowded. There is a beach on Lac Cardinal and the campground is located on the same grounds as the Pioneer Village.

Lakeland Provincial Park (Map 12/F4)

Nearly 600 sq. km (230 sq. miles) of rugged backcountry make up this park. This is a park where you can enjoy several days of travel in solitude, taking in the scenery and wildlife foot or cycle. Four lakes within park boundary (Kinnaird, Jackson, Dabbs and Blackett) provide backcountry canoe route oppor-

tunities complete with several island campsites and secluded sand beaches. Winter provides cross-country skiing, snowshoeing and ice fishing opportunities. Traditional camping can be found just east of the park along several lakes in the Lakeland Recreation Area. There is OHV staging in the park as well, with access to Mile 10, Dabbs Lake, Blackett Lake and Helena Lake Trails.

Lakeland Recreation Area (Map 12/G2–F5)

The rolling hills, boreal mixed wood and old-growth forests of this area provide a perfect setting for camping, mountain biking, hiking and canoeing. Four different lakes in the recreation area provide four campgrounds for different interests: Pinehurst Lake, where there are 63 camping units, is a favourite spot for anglers; Ironwood, home to 20 camping units, is an excellent canoeing lake; the campground at Touchwood is rustic but with 98 sites it is the largest of the four and has a playground; and finally Seibert Lake, where there are 43 camping units, is an ideal setting for bird watching and photography. Due to low lake levels, there is no boat launch at Ironwood, though hand launching a boat is possible. OHV and snowmobiling are permitted in the area. Winter activities include ice fishing.

Lawrence Lake Recreation Area (Map 23/G7)

There are 13 unserviced campsites at this recreation area 50 km northwest of Athabasca on Highway 2. Visitors will also find a day use area, pit toilets, fish cleaning stations, cook shelters and a boat launch. It makes a nice stop over for highway travellers looking to do some pike fishing or canoeing.

Leddy Lake Regional Park (Map 47/A2)

While it would never be mistaken for a provincial park, the 34 sites at Leddy Lake are spacious and well separated from each other and 6 even have power. The site is very rustic, but pretty enough, in its own way. There is a boat launch and an open day use area on the waterfront as well as playground for the kids. Nearby Lake St. Germaine is also protected in this park reserve.

Lesser Slave Lake Provincial Park (Map 22/D2–36/C7)

At 1,160 square km Lesser Slave Lake is Alberta's third largest lake and this 7,617 hectare park at the lake's east end is Alberta's third largest provincial park. From the Town of Slave Lake, the first point of interest in the park is Devonshire Beach, a 7 km long white sand beach that is reverting back to a natural state. Past the beach is a picnic site and popular shore-fishing area. The next stop of note as you travel north along Highway 88 is the Lesser Slave Lake Bird Observatory (visit www.lslbo.org for information). Finally, at the north end of the park is the 112 site Marten River Campground, 72 of which have power and there is a deluxe cabin that will sleep up to 10 people. Most of the sites are private and all are nice. Amenities include washrooms with showers, a playground, fish cleaning stations, picnic shelters, amphitheatre, horseshoe pits and wheelchair accessibility. Stitching these areas together is the Freighter Lakeshore Trail, a 20 km trail along the lakeshore. Other activities include interpretive programs, ice fishing, snowmobiling, biking and various water sports like windsurfing and waterskiing. Reservations are available.

Lesser Slave Lake Wildland Area (Map 35/A7–36/B7)

This wildland area protects important fish spawning and rearing habitat, as well as important winter range for moose. The area is also used by nesting bald eagles and osprey. Access into the area is by boat or via the Trans Canada Trail, which passes through the park. There are no facilities within the park.

Little Smoky River Recreation Area (Map 33/C7)

Lying on the north side of Highway 49 between Valleyview and Falher this is a rustic site. There are a few trails that lead to the river, but not much else. Across the river is a ski area. Currently the park is closed; please check the Alberta Parks website for current information.

Long Lake Provincial Park (Map 11/B7)

As the name suggest, this park surrounds a lake that is narrow and long– some 13 kilometres with an average width of about 500 metres. There are plenty of things to do for the whole family making it a popular option with the Edmonton crowd as it is only an hour and a half from the city. Child-friendly

beaches and hiking are accessible from the 226 site, 145 of which have power and 6 walk-in tenting, campground. There are a bounty of amenities in this park including a concession stand, playground, grocery store, laundry facilities, washrooms with showers, change rooms, cook shelters, golf course, boat and hand launches, horseshoe pitch, fish cleaning stations, cook and picnic shelters and wheelchair accessibility. Windsurfing and waterskiing are popular in the summer, but the park also makes a nice get-away in winter, when ice fishing and snowmobiling is allowed on the lake itself. Downhill skiing is available just adjacent to the park. Reservations are available.

Machesis Lake Recreation Area (Map 86/F3)

Machesis Lake is found 30 km southeast of High Level via a maze of backroads south of Highway 58. There are 19 unserviced sites in the campground, with fish cleaning stations, pit toilets, a boat launch and a pair of docks for visitors to use.

Many Islands Campsite (Map 44/F2)

This municipal campground is located on the banks of the Peace River south of Highway 64. In addition to the 24 scenic riverside campsites, the rustic campground offers a boat launch, picnic shelter and playground. There are also trails to explore in the area. Bird watchers can also enjoy annual bird migrations from this location.

Maqua Lake Recreation Area (Map 55/B4)

Located south of Fort McMurray, this site has a small day use area that provides access to Maqua Lake. There is also a reservable group camping area with pit toilets that can accommodate a party with up to 15 units. The small lake holds no fish and powerboats are prohibited thus canoeing and swimming are the two most popular activities here. In winter, there are undeveloped snowmobile trails in the area. Reservations are available.

Marguerite River Wildland Park (Map 83/F1–90/F7)

This large wildland park is located along the Saskatchewan boundary 100 km northeast of Fort McMurray. It protects a portion of the Athabasca Dunes. While it is open to backcountry camping, hiking and hunting, few people ever visit as access if fly-in only.

Maybelle River Wildland Park (Map 90/C5)

This park completely surrounds the Athabasca Dunes Ecological Reserve (which is the heart of Alberta's largest active sand dune complex). The park itself protects a series of sand dunes, plains and kames around the reserve. There is no road access so most come by ATV or on foot.

McLeod Flats Campground (Map 17/B7)

Formerly known as Smoky Flats, Canfor has taken over and renamed this camping area after a former employee. Of the 19 campsites, 14 are grouped in pairs of two. This is a popular area for fishing in the Smoky River or just relaxing. There's even a beach volleyball area. This is also a geocaching location as well.

Miseieutin Public Land Recreation Area (Map 69/F7)

There are four campsites at the small recreation area on the Clearwater River. The site can only be accessed by water. There are some hiking trails in the area.

Moonshine Lake Provincial Park (Map 44/E7)

This park is found between Spirit River and the BC border. There are 110 campsites, 50 of which have electrical hook-ups, in addition to a small beach and dock at the northern end of the lake. Amenities include washrooms with flush toilets and showers, change rooms, fish cleaning stations and a picnic shelter. At the southern end of the lake, a large day use area, including a launch (for electric motor-powered boats only), a group campground, playground, ball diamonds, horseshoe pitches and a series of hiking/biking/skiing trails, is available for day visitors. Watersports are also popular including windsurfing and waterskiing. In the winter there is a skating rink and winter camping. Reservations are available.

Muskoseepi Park (Map 17/A2)

Bear River runs through the heart of Grande Prairie and so does this long, thin park as it stretches along the ravine. A trail follows the creek, offering a view of wildlife in the city. The park features a fishing pond, dog park, lawn bowling facilities, amphitheatre, mini golf, skate board and spray parks and cultural information centre. Crystal Lake, located in the northeast section of the city, also offers excellent bird watching opportunities.

Musreau Lake Recreation Area (Map 9/A3)

The word Musreau means young moose. It also means something noisy or devil-like. The lake probably took its name from the latter, as pockets of gas bubble to the surface from the bottom of the lake. In the winter, the pressure from the gas builds, causing the ice to fracture with a loud crack. Musreau Lake is located 80 km south of Grande Prairie on Highway 40. There are 69 unserviced sites in the campground here, as well as a large day use area with a picnic shelter, pit toilets and fish cleaning stations. The recreation area provides canoe rentals and a boat launch, while fishing, hiking and ATVing are popular activities in the area.

North Buck Lake Recreation Area (Map 11/D4)

Nestled in a scenic sandhill region, North Buck Lake offers 125 non-reservable campsites, 30 of which have power. Operated by the Buffalo Lake Metis Settlement, amenities include cook shelters, fish cleaning stations, a pier, boat launch and playground. Home to deer, elk and moose, the area is also a great place for bird watching. Anglers will find good fishing, while paddlers can explore the quieter coves of the lake to avoid the wind surfers and water-skiers that frequent the lake.Reservations are available.

North Wabasca Recreation Area (Map 37/F1)

Located well north of Slave Lake, off Secondary Highway 754, this popular fishing lake has 35 campsites in a small recreation area on its eastern shores with pit toilets and picnic tables. The lake is best known for its fishing, but the site features a beautiful sandy beach that is popular with families. In winter, the boat launch is used as a snowmobile staging area.

Nose Lake Recreation Area (Map 1/F2)

Nose Lake is located 130 km south of Grande Prairie. The sheer distance of industrial road travel is daunting enough but the actual lake is a 3 km walk from the road. The travel involved explains why this site sees little use. Many people bring a canoe or kayak or just a belly boat to float and fish the lake.

Notikewin Provincial Park (Map 74/E6)

Located on the shores of the Peace River at its confluence with the Notikewin River, this park offers 19 campsites with fish cleaning stations and pit toilets. There is also a sandy beach on the river and hand launching a canoe in either river is possible. A short trail leads to a viewpoint over the river valley. Birding is also popular here.

O'Brien Provincial Park (Map 16/G3)

Back when it opened, there was camping on the banks of the Wapiti River, but two floods in two years forced the campgrounds to close. Now, O'Brien Provincial Park is a day use only park located 10 km south of Grande Prairie on Highway 40 with fire pits and pit toilets. In summer activities include fishing, paddling and mountain biking. It is also a popular winter destination to ski or snowshoe next to the river.

Ole's Lake Recreation Area (Map 43/G1)

This small lake is located 8 km from the British Columbia boundary. There are 16 unserviced sites in the campground with pit toilets, a playground and hand launch. Most of the activity here (besides camping) is water related including swimming, paddling and fishing, but wildlife viewing opportunities also exist.

Otter-Orloff Lakes Wildland Park (Map 24/B2)

The nearest road to this wildland park lies a few kilometres to the north, meaning access is by foot. There are animal trails and random backcountry camping in the park, which is home to a colony of great blue heron. Because of the hike-in access and the many marshy areas, the park is infrequently visited.

Peace River Wildland Park (Maps 31–32, 45–47)

This wildland park stretches out along the Peace River and Smoky River Valleys to help protect the prime wildlife habitat in the area. There are no facilities onsite and access into the park is limited, but backcountry hiking and camping along with ATVing and hunting are permitted. Wildlife like deer, elk, black bear and wolf are common in the area.

Pines Recreation Area (Map 5/C5)

North of Fox Creek on Highway 43, thisreservable, group use campsite can accommodate 20 units. It is a rustic site with pit toilets and a picnic shelter. Reservations are available.

Pipestone Creek Municipal Park (Map 16/E3)

Forget Drumheller and Dinosaur Provincial Park. Where Pipestone Creek flows into the Wapiti River is the site of Canada's largestPachyrhinosaurus dinosaur fossil site. Indigenous peoples used to camp here as far back as the 1800s and now the district of Grande Prairie maintains a large park here. There are 99 unserviced sites and a group camping area. Day use visitors often come here to swim in the creek. Currently there is a small museum and a dinosaur themed playground.

Poacher's Landing Recreation Area (Map 10/G1)

Tucked into a bend in the Athabasca River, this recreation area has a 6 unit campsite with pit toilets and a picnic shelter. There are a number of trails in the area that are open to hikers and horseback riders, while the Poacher's Landing Recreation Society also maintains some trails in the area that are open to members only. There is a corral, ATV and snowmobile loading ramp and hitching rails for the horses.

Pratt's Landing (Map 45/A5)

Found off Secondary Highway 682, west of Fairview, there is a small (free) campsite and boat launch on to the Peace at Pratt's Landing. Visitors will also find a picnic shelter and abundant wildlife in the area. Alberta's only lighthouse helps boaters find the campground at night. Birding is popular here, especially during the spring and fall migrations.

Queen Elizabeth Provincial Park (Map 46/F4)

Queen Elizabeth Park is found on Lake Cardinal, or, more properly, Lac Cardinal. The campground has 82 sites, 44 of which have power, spread across seven separate camping areas. Amenities include a boat launch, cook shelters, a horseshoe pitch and playground. There is a large day use area next to the large, sandy beach anda reservable group use site that can accommodate 20 units. In addition to birdwatching, water sports are popular, including paddling, sailing, windsurfing, waterskiingand boating, but there are no fish in the lake. During winter, the trails are open to skiers and snowshoers. Some of the sites and trails are wheelchair accessible. Nearby are the Lac Cardinal Pioneer Village, the rodeo grounds and a municipal park with another dozen or so campsites. Group site reservations are available.

Rainbow Lake Recreation Area (Map 85/A3)

Rainbow Lake is a long, thin lake 45 km south of the town that shares its name. The lake has 16 user maintained campsites that are most often visited during fishing season. Amenities include fish cleaning stations, pit toilets and a pier.

Red Willow Park (Map 16/A3)

This site, on the shores of the Red Willow River, is located 19 km southwest of Beaverlodge on Secondary Highway 722. This park is day use only with 5 sites for a family picnic, a ball diamond and a playground. Although swimming in the river is popular, the river can be fast and people have been swept away.

Richardson River Dunes Wildland Park (Map 90/A5–B6)

Located across the Athabasca River from the southeast corner of Wood Buffalo National Park, this park protects a portion of the largest sand dune complex in Canada. The area is seldom visited, due to the difficult access that requires crossing the river (usually by boat). Visitors can backcountry camp, hike and hunt here.

Running Lake Recreation Area (Map 59/B4)
There are 17 unserviced sites at the Running Lake campsite, a popular fishing lake north of Worsley. Amenities include fish cleaning stations, pit toilets and a pier. In winter, visitors can also find informal snowmobile trails in the area.

Saskatoon Island Provincial Park (Map 16/E2)
Saskatoon Island is found 22 km west of Grande Prairie. This scenic area was once an island, but is now a land bridge between Saskatoon and Little Lake. The park has 108 reservable sites, 55 of which have power, separated into three areas. Some of the campsites are sheltered in the aspen forest, while others are more open. Amenities include cook shelters, fish cleaning stations, washrooms with flush toilets and showers, a horseshoe pitch, playground and wheelchair accessibility. The park also offers a group use camping area that can accommodate 25 units, a large day use area with a ball diamond and concession stand, a volleyball court, a series of hiking/ski trails and a birdviewing platform by Little Lake. A big draw to the park is the annual swan migration in fall. This is also a popular area with berry pickers during Saskatoon berry season. Reservations are available.

Shuttler Flats Recreation Area (Map 15/G6)
This rustic group use site, with pit toilets, is available to individuals when not booked by a group. Indeed, it is often used by folks who cannot make it to Two Lakes when the road is in bad shape. Most of the groups in the area are either fishing in Nose Creek or ATVing the area trails (ATVs are not allowed on-site). In winter, snowmobiling is popular in the area. Call 780-538-5350 for information and to make group reservations.

> For the typical camper, the season runs from the Victoria Day (May) long weekend to the Labour Day (September) long weekend. Some of the parks and recreation areas also have limited camping during the winter months.

Simonette River Recreation Area (Map 17/F3)
Located 10 km south of Highway 43 on the Forestry Trunk Road (Hwy 734), there are 25 rustic sites with pit toilets in the campground on the banks of the Simonette. This is a popular destination with anglers looking for arctic grayling and bull trout.

Sir Winston Churchill Provincial Park (Map 12/B2)
Located on an island in Lac La Biche, this park is a birder's paradise. More than 230 bird species have been spotted in this park, including Caspian terns and a colony of double-crested cormorants. A bird viewing telescope was installed in 2002. There are 72 powered sites in the campground, which is nestled in an old-growth mixed wood forest. Amenities include washrooms with showers, fish cleaning stations, cook shelters, a boat launch, amphitheatre, picnic shelter and playground. There are also 15 group campsites, 8 of which are powered, and 34 picnic sites. Activities include environmental education and interpretive programs, fishing, sailing, water skiing, wind surfing and, in winter, cross-country skiing and snowshoeing.

Smoke Lake Recreation Area (Map 5/C6)
Smoke Lake is a great fishing lake. It, along with Iosegun Lake to the north, defines fishing in the Fox Creek area. It is a great place to find walleye, but it also holds pike, perch and whitefish. In addition to fishing, this is a popular destination for water sports (canoeing, boating and waterskiing). So it is no surprise that this is a large recreation area, with 47 sites in the campground, pit toilets, a boat launch, fish cleaning stations and a loading ramp for snowmobiles. In the winter visitors ice fish and cross-country ski here as well.

Smoky River Recreation Area (Map 17/F2)
On Highway 43 west of Grande Prairie, this rustic site is mainly used as an access point to the Smoky River.

Spring Lake Recreation Area (Map 30/A4)
Another non-government recreation area, Spring Lake was built in 1974 by Proctor and Gamble as a year round recreation area. In summer, camping, swimming and hiking are the main pursuits and there are 30 sites in the rustic campground. The beach has a roped off swimming area and there is a dock at the day use area for anglers. In winter, there is a downhill ski area and 26 km (15.6 miles) of groomed cross-country ski trails.

Stoney Lake Recreation Area (Map 59/F7)
Stoney Lake is stocked with trout and that is the big draw to this lake. There is a beach at the campsite, where you can swim from or maybe just paddle around the lake in a canoe. There are 15 rustic sites at this lovely backcountry wilderness site with pit toilets and a boat launch.

Stony Mountain Wildland Park (Map 55/B6)
This large, remote wildland park is located south of Fort McMurray. The easiest access to the park is to hike in from Maqua Lake. Backcountry camping, ATV riding and hunting are all permitted in this park.

Strong Creek Park (Map 47/A5)
There are 18 rustic campsites at this park, which is located just south of the town of Peace River, where Strong Creek flows into the Peace River. Visitors will find some short hiking trails in the area, as well as picnic shelters, pit toilets, a playground, ball diamond and a historical site.

Sulphur Lake Recreation Area (Map 60/A5)
Located on a small lake 56 km northwest of Dixonville, this recreation site has a 16 unit rustic campground with pit toilets. A pier, fish cleaning station-sand boat launch help anglers, while hiking, biking, paddling and swimming are other popular summer activities. During winter, there are informal snowmobile trails in the area and ice fishing opportunities.

Swan Lake Recreation Area (Map 18/C4)
Swan Lake is found west of Valleyview, off Highway 43. The rustic campground has 24 unserviced sites with fish cleaning stations and pit toilets for amenities. There is also a large day use site with 10 picnic tables, a pier and a steep boat launch (for electric motors only) on the lake. The lake contains stocked rainbow trout and is a fine place to go for a short canoe trip. Both ATV and snowmobile riding opportunities are found off site.

Tanasiuk Recreation Area (Map 24/B1)
Found on the shores of Rock Island Lake, this recreation area has a 51 unit campground, as well as a boat launch for anglers and trails for hikers. Fishing is by far the most popular activity here.

Tangent Park (Map 46/G6)
This is a rather large campground, with 68 sites (some with power and water and a few others with power only) near the Shaftesbury Ferry. Amenities include washrooms with flush toilets and showers, laundry facilities, a playground, picnic shelter, concession stand and store and wheelchair accessibility. In July, there is a popular music jamboree held here. Visitors will find a ball diamond, horseshoes and some short hiking trails along the river. There is also a separate group use area.

Trapper Lea's Cabin Recreation Area (Map 7/G5)
Trapper George Lea is a historical figure in the Swan Hills, albeit a relatively recent one. He lived at this very spot until the 1960s. The district of Swan Hills maintains this site, which is located just off the quiet Highway 33. Of the 18 campsites, the outside loop provides the more private sites, as they are pushed into the bush and away from everybody else. There's a picnic shelter and pit toilets on site as well. This is the main staging area for the Swan Hills Snow Goers Snowmobile Trail system which can be used by ATVs in the summer.

Tourangeau Park (Map 86/G4)
Found 2.5 km west of La Crete, Tourangeau Lake is home to a small day use park with picnic tables and a boat launch. Visitors to the area will find a few private campsites near town as well as Tomkins Landing Ferry, one of two operating ferries in Alberta (the other one is also found in this book south of Grimshaw).

Twin Lakes Recreation Area (Map 74/B3)
Located 65 km north of Manning on Highway 35, there are 49 rustic campsites at this popular recreation area with a playground, cook shelters and pit toilets. Anglers will appreciate the pier, fish cleaning stations and hand launch. The east lake is stocked annually with rainbow trout. Other activities include hiking, mountain biking, swimming, paddling, boating with electric motors only and wildlife viewing. There is a 3 km trail loop from the one lake to the other.

Two Lakes Recreation Area (Map 1/D4)
There are actually three campsites at Two Lakes, one at Gunderson Meadows, one at Pine Hollows and one at Stetson Flats. Between the three, there is space for 86 camping groups. Amenities include a boat launch, fish cleaning stations and pit toilets. This is the farthest most vehicles can make it towards Kakwa Falls (some cannot even make it this far, depending on road conditions) and many groups hike or bike to the spectacular cascade. Fishing in the lakes is also a popular pursuit here year round.

Valhalla Centre Park (Map 30/B6)
Found along Highway 59 near the community of Valhalla Centre, this is an informal day use picnic area with 5 spots. The site is user maintained and is located next to a museum, Heritage Garden, and troll park.

Wadlin Lake District Park (Map 87/C7)
Operated by the Municipal District, this small park offers what you would expect: camping on the lake, with access to the water for swimming, boating, waterskiing or fishing. The 33 campsites, 8 of which are seasonal, are popular with anglers heading out onto the lake, but it is also popular with people just looking to get away for the weekend. Amenities include a picnic shelter, playground, park store, flush toilets, boat launch and fish cleaning stations. The lake is home to a nesting colony of rare white pelicans. During winter the area is a popular staging area for the Polar Cats Snowmobile Trails.

Waskahigan River Recreation Area (Map 5/A2)
Located between Valleyview and Fox Creek, this sprawling, open site has space for 20 groups to camp. Most of the sites are around the edge of the field that forms the centre of the site, but there are a few private sites. The amenities are rustic including cook shelters, fish cleaning stations, pit toilets and a picnic shelter. The Waskahigan River flows into the Little Smoky River just across the highway from the site. There is an advisory not to eat whitefish caught in either river.

Whitemud Falls Wildland Park (Map 70/F7)
This park, along with the Whitemud Falls Ecological Reserve, protects a stretch of the Clearwater River Valley. This section of the Clearwater has been designated a Canadian Heritage River. There are no roads to the park, but it is possible to canoe the Clearwater from Saskatchewan to Fort McMurray or even run up the river in winter. The key feature of the park is Whitemud Falls.

Williamson Provincial Park (Map 18/E4)
The day use area of Williamson Lake is big and (mostly) open. It is the focus of most of the attention at this small park. Oh, sure, there are 67 campsites, 31 of which have power, set back in the bush, but the lake is the thing here. There is a beach at the north end of the main campground and amenities include a picnic shelter, cook shelters, change rooms, pit toilets, a horseshoe pit and playground. There is a boat launch and fish cleaning stations, while water sports (like power boating, sailing, windsurfing and waterskiing) are popular. Fishing is also popular on Sturgeon Lake year round, where you will find big northern pike and walleye. In winter there is off site snowmobiling.

Winagami Lake Provincial Park (Map 33/F4–34/A5)
Winagami Lake is a big lake and very popular with anglers. Wildlife (especially bird) watching is also a popular activity and the Window on the Lake Interpretive Trail provides a good place to see some of the many species of birds. There are 66 campsites spread out across three areas, 35 with electrical hook-ups, as well as a reservable group use site with power that can accommodate up to 12 units. Amenities include a boat launch and pier, cook shelters, washrooms with flush toilets and showers, a playground with spray park and wading pool and wheelchair accessibility. Other summer activities include paddling, hiking, sailing, volleyball, windsurfing and waterskiing. The park is open year-round, with cross-country skiing and snowshoeing being a common winter pursuits. At certain times, the lake lives up to its name, in that Winagami means "stinking water" due to the strong hydrogen sulphate odor. Group site reservations are available.

Winagami Wildland Park (Map 33/G6–34/B4)
The Winagami Wildlands are prime bird habitat. More than 200 bird species stay in or migrate through the park, from gulls and grebes to bald eagles and merlins. The wildland protects a portion of the South Heart River Valley, which serves as a wildlife corridor and is home to many great blue heron and bald eagle nests. There are no developed facilities in the area, but bird watchers utilize the old roads and trails through the eastern section of the park. Backcountry camping, ATV riding on designated trails, mountain biking, hiking and hunting is permitted in the park.

Wolf Lake Recreation Area (Map 13/E4)
Found in the middle of nowhere, this lake is 30 km north of Highway 55 between Lac La Biche and Cold Lake. It makes for a nice and quiet spot for fishing and canoeing, which is what most of its visitors come here for. There are 65 rustic, non-reservable campsites, some of which are double sites. There are also fish cleaning stations, a playground, boat launch and pier at this recreation area.

Wood Buffalo National Park (Maps 88–90, 95, 96)
Canada's largest National Park, Wood Buffalo protects an area larger than Switzerland. Much of this area is roadless wilderness; however, access from Fort Smith in the Northwest Territories is possible on the Pine Lake Road. The Pine Lake Campground and day use area is located 60 km south of Fort Smith and offers a playground, pit toilets and a couple of wheelchair accessible campsites. There is a group campground at Kettle Point with pit toilets, a log shelter, beach and playground, while the more adventurous can find semi-formal camping areas at Rainbow Lakes and at Sweetgrass Landing. Otherwise, random camping is allowed throughout the park. A popular way to access the park is by jetboat, which are allowed on the park's main waterways: the Athabasca River, Rivière des Rochers, Quatre Fourches River, Peace River and Slave River. In addition to many wood bison and other large mammals, the park is also an internationally recognized bird watching area. There are few formal trails and adventurers need to be very self-sufficient when travelling here.

Worsley Campground (Map 58/G6)
The village of Worsley offers travellers a 16 unit campground. Full facilities make this a popular site for RV's. No tenting is permitted at this site.

Young's Point Provincial Park (Map 18/E4)
This is a large, sprawling park with 124 campsites, 78 of which have power, in two distinct areas, one close to the lake, one set farther back into the bush. There is also a group campsite that can accommodate up to 25 units. Park amenities include fish cleaning stations, washrooms with flush toilets and showers, a horseshoe pitch, life jacket loaner station and a picnic shelter. In addition to a small beach with a reedy swimming area, the boat launch and pier provides good access to the lake. Fishing (for pike, perch or walleye) is one of the more common activities at the park, as are water sports like boating, sailing, paddling, windsurfing and waterskiing. Bird watchers can look for over 150 species of birds here as well. In the winter there is a warm-up shelter while ice fishing and skating on the lit rink are popular. Snowmobiles can access the lake from the boat launch parking lot when ice conditions permit. Reservations are available.

Trail
Adventures

While there are trails in northern Alberta, they are not found in the same number as points farther south. Part of it has to do with the fact that there just isn't the same number of destinations as you will find elsewhere. There are few mountains and most of the really interesting lakes and rivers are inaccessible by road or can't be accessed at all, other than by air. There are vast areas of muskeg or of untracked boreal forest.

And, of course, there are fewer people in northern Alberta, so there is less pressure to build new, more and better trails.

The most notable hiking trail development in the region is the Trans Canada Trail. The majority of the TCT will follow a historical route from Fort Assiniboine to Lesser Slave Lake before continuing north to Peace River. Many sections of this historical route can still be found, although most of it has yet to be cleared. The truly adventurous can try and hike the old route—just don't say we didn't warn you.

There are some hotspots where an avid hiker can try many trails in a small area. There are also towns that are working hard to make themselves known for their trail networks. In Fort McMurray the Birchwood Trail System offers multiple hikes within the city. Fort Smith also offers multiple trails and Wood Buffalo National Park has good options for novice to advanced hikers. Although these hotspots are quite north, for the adventure seeker this may be the perfect place to vacation.

Still, this section is the shortest trail section of any of our mapbooks. We welcome your feedback to add more trails for people to enjoy. Please drop us a note at updates@backroadmapbooks.com or call us at 1-877-520-5670.

On the following pages we have included icons beside the names of each trail and on the maps to show what user groups can use the trail. To help you select the trail which best suits your abilities, we have also included elevation gain, return distance and special features whenever possible. Please note that all distances and times are for round trip hikes unless otherwise noted.

Difficulty is given for hikers, unless noted or unless the trail is a bike/horse trail only. An easy trail is a is a gentle grade excellent for family excursions, while trails marked as moderate are fairly strenuous, often with climbing involved. These trails will challenge most trail users and should not be underestimated. Finally, trails marked as difficult should be left for experienced users, as the trails are often rough and/or unmarked.

African Lake Loop (Map 14/E7)

This trail can be found 2 km east of Highway 55/28, on 50th Avenue in Cold Lake. This trail is approximately 8 km (5 mile) in length and forms a loop around African Lake. The trail winds through a forested area just south of the Cold Lake Provincial Park. The multi-use route can be enjoyed by hikers, mountain bikers or cross-country skiers, in the winter. There is beautiful scenery and views of Cold Lake from multiple spots along the trail.

Athabasca Dunes Ecological Reserve (Map 90/C5)

The hike into these dunes is only a couple kilometres from the Fort Chipewyan Winter Road, but the obstacles are many. The first issue to overcome is getting there. It is about a 70 km ATV ride along the winter road just to get to the edge of the Maybelle River Wildland Park. Once there, ATVs are not allowed into the Wildland Park or the Ecological Reserve, so you will have to walk in. The second issue is there are no trails in the reserve, nor could there be, as the tower dunes are constantly shifting. However, the destination is certainly special since the reserve protects the largest sand dune complex in the area.

Athabasca Landing Trail [TCT] (Map 10/B6–C4)

This section of the Trans Canada Trail follows the historic Athabasca Landing Trail from Edmonton to the Athabasca River. The trail follows a mix of road allowances, old railbeds and newly built trail as it makes its way 32 km (19.9 miles) from Athabasca south to Perryville. There are some boggy sections in spring and a section of the trail is missing and routed along the highway.

Birchwood Trail System (Map 68/G7)

This trail system can be found right in the heart of Fort McMurray. The Ptarmigan Nordic Ski Club maintains these trails yearround. In the winter, these trails are groomed for snowmobiles and cross-country skiing, in the summer, they are open to hiking and mountain biking. Trail distances vary from the shorter Arctic Winter Games, Cougar, Moose, Squirrel and Wolf Trails (all less than 2 km long), to the longer trails like the Bear, Deer, Lynx and Beaver Trails (all 4 to 5 km long). There are expert trails with steep hills and easy trails for novice hikers, cyclists or skiers. Also in the area is the 3 km interpretive Suncor Nature Trail that treks through the former mine site.

Buffalo Head Hills (Map 86/G6–87/A6)

A road leads to the old Buffalo Tower, which is near the top of the Buffalo Head Hills. From here, a number of trails head into the hills. The trails are mostly unmaintained and random. The area has not been surveyed, so no one is quite sure how many trails there are or how long the trails are, but suffice it to say there are trails here. The Buffalo Head Hills are about 600 metres (2,000 feet) tall.

Canfor Trail [TCT] (Map 59/D6)

This section of the Trans Canada Trail is so named because it lies right beside the main haul Canfor Road between Hines Creek and Worsley. Fortunately for summer travellers, the road is little used in summer and traffic shouldn't be an issue. The route is 75 km (46 miles) long and hooks up to the St. John's Trail.

Cassette Rapids (Map 96/G2)

Found 24 km south of Fort Smith near Fort Fitzgerald, this trek follows the road to the river and the Smith's Landing First Nations area. Once at the river head north and look for signage to the rapids. It is a 3.5 km (2 mile) loop through thick woods to the first lookout jutting into the current. There are a few other lookouts on the route before following a sandy road back to your vehicle.

Centre of Alberta Trail (Map 8/A6)

You will have to watch the north side of Highway 33 very carefully or you may miss the start of this trail. If you are coming from Swan Lake, you will come across the trailhead a few minutes after passing Trapper Leas Recreation Area. The location marks the geographical centre of Alberta, but to get here you must first hike the 5 km (3 mile) in. The trail is a relatively easy stroll through the boreal forest to a clearing with a cairn that has a grizzly cub on it.

Cold Lake Provincial Park (Map 14/F4–F7)

There are 13 km (8 miles) of trails in Cold Lake Provincial Park. The longest trail–South Trail– starts at the day-use area and circumnavigates the peninsula that the campsite is built on, covering a distance of 5.4 km (3.3 miles). The rest wind their way through the forests around the campsite, creating short loop trails that are mostly less than a kilometre in length.

Cummings Lake Trail (Map 45/F5)

The elevation does not change very much on this 11 km (6.8 mile) trail that wanders through the town of Fairview. It goes through wetlands, forests, campgrounds, past the golf course and north to Cummings Lake. It is an easy trail, with a number of access points to make your hike shorter, if you so desire. Look for the many varieties of birds and other wildlife spotted along the trail.

Don Nicholson Trail (Map 5/D6)

This is a scenic 8 km (5 mile) stroll following Fox Creek in between the campground and the tourist information centre in the town of Fox Creek. The plan is to eventually have the trail run past the golf course and circumnavigate the town.

Dunes Trails (Map 17/B3)

Just southeast of Grande Prairie is a large area, defined by the Resource Road in the west, Bear Creek to the north and the Wapiti River to the south. This area of rolling sand dunes is a popular multi-use area. So popular, in fact, that there is a move afoot to have it turned into a provincial park. Hikers, Bikers and ATVers share this sprawling area. Recent development includes a paved trail network in the Dunes. Phase 1 of the trail starts south of the County Industrial Park and runs for nearly 6 km (3.7 miles).

Fort Assiniboine Sandhills Wildland Park (Map 8/E7)

This 66 square km (40.3 sq. mile) park offers plenty of trails that can be stitched together into a full day or overnight trip. About two thirds of the park is covered by the sand dunes from whence it takes its name. All the trails in the park are closed to motorized use, except the snowmobile access to the Timeu Off-Highway Vehicle Area. The longest trail in the park is the Wagon Trail, at 13.7 km (8.4 miles), which weaves its way across the park and provides access to other trails. Other trails include the 7.3 km (4.5 mile) Klondike Trail, the 7.7 km (4.7 mile) Migration Trail and the 6.6 km (4 mile) River Valley Trail. Random backcountry camping is allowed in the park.

Fort Vermilion Nature Trail (Map 87/B3)

This easy trail is a hike along the river shore through a forested area with a great view of the Peace River. The trail is signed and can be found off River Road in Fort Vermilion. It can be hiked in about an hour.

Freighter Lakeshore Trail [TCT] (Map 22/C1–D2)

Freighter Lakeshore Trail runs through Lesser Slave Lake Provincial Park from Devonshire Beach in the South to Marten Creek in the north, a distance of 23 km (14mile) return. It is not a tough trail and there are four main access points; Devonshire Beach, North Shore, Lily Creek and the Marten River Campground. The trail passes the Lesser Slave Lake Bird Observatory and avid bird watchers can expect to see all manner of song birds, as well as shore birds and waterfowl along the trail. The trail is also part of the Trans Canada Trail and it is possible to continue on, along an unimproved (probably overgrown) historical route that circles around the lake to Hilliard's Bay Provincial Park.

Friendship Trail [TCT] (Map 46/F4–47/B4)

The Friendship Trail is an officially designated section of the Trans Canada Trail, connecting Lac Cardinal to the towns of Grimshaw and Peace River. The 28.9 km (18 mile) route follows a mix of backroads and newly constructed trail (about 16 km/10 miles in all), as it makes its way from Queen Elizabeth Provincial Park to Grimshaw, through the wilderness park, past the Mighty Peace Golf and Country Club and Misery Mountain Ski Hill.

Gregoire Lake Provincial Park (Map 55/C3)

There is a trio of trails in this provincial park. The longest of these is the Long Loop, an easy 4.8 km (2.9 mile) route that skirts the edge of the lake. The second longest trail is the Short Loop, at 3.4 km, followed by the 1.2 km interpretive Woodland Trail. The trailheads for all three trails are accessed from the group camping area.

Grouard Trail [TCT] (Map 34/E7–35/D7)

Also known as the Peace River Road, the Grouard Trail took travellers from Lesser Slave Lake to the Peace River area. The route was a continuation of the Chalmers Trail and followed an old native trading route that was used up until the early 1900s. Today the trail is being rediscovered and converted into the Trans Canada Trail. Currently 55 km (34 mile) of signed and maintained trail exist from the hamlet of Grouard to Big Point on Lesser Slave Lake. When it is completed, this section of trail will be 100 km (60 miles) long and connect the town of Slave Lake to Peace River.

Gunderson Trail (Map 1/D4)
The Gunderson Trail runs about 6 km southeast of North Lake from the Gunderson Meadows Campground. It also loops southwest and joins the Two Lakes Interpretive Trail. Across the Two Lakes Road, on the west side, the Pine Hollow Trail can be found as well.

Harmon Valley Park Trail (Map 47/G5)
At the east end of Township Road 830 this trail follows the Harmon Valley Park roadway for about 1 km. There is a slight elevation change around 35 m (120 ft), but overall the trail is easy. Along the way there are likely to be fallen trees, offshoots to access the creek and beaver dams to look for on the creek.

Hat Mountain [Gunderson] Trail (Map 1/D4)
There are three scenic hikes in the area. An unimproved trail climbs to the top of Hat Mountain from Site 14 of the Gunderson Meadows Campsite in Two Lakes Recreation Area. The 3 km (1.8 mile) trail climbs 489 m (1,589 ft) to a ridge and nice viewpoint. There is also an Interpretive Trail that is around 3.6 km (2.2 mile) long and joins the South and North Lake from Moberly Flats to the Pine Hollow Campground. Be bear aware and watch for osprey and loons that nest in the area.

Hilliard's Bay: Boreal Forest Interpretive Trail (Map 34/G7)
From the shower area at the Hilliard's Bay Campground, a trail crosses the access road into the park. From the far side of the road, the trail loops and then loops again to form a figure eight. The easy trail is designed to introduce visitors to the vast boreal forest that surround the lake and forms much of the flora of northern Alberta.

Hilliard's Bay: Lakeshore Trail [TCT] (Map 34/G7)
A 2.2 km (1.3 mile) trail along the shoreline of Lesser Slave Lake connects the camping area of Hilliard's Bay Provincial Park to the boat launch and day-use area. This trail is part of the Trans Canada Trail and can be extended along a slowly degenerating route (also known as the Grouard Trail) along the northern shores of Lesser Slave Lake. From all reports, the route beyond the boat launch is hard to follow and mostly overgrown.

The most notable hiking trail development in the region is the Trans Canada Trail. The majority of the TCT will follow a historical route from Fort Assiniboine to Lesser Slave Lake before continuing north to Peace River.

Horn Ridge Trail (Map 1/B6)
This old road heads pretty steeply up Horn Ridge to the top, gaining 366 m (1200 ft) in about 9 km (5.5 miles). From here, the route follows the ridge for another 15 km (9 miles). ATVs must stay on the main trail, although hikers and equestrians can wander the alpine meadows. Access is 4 km (2.4 miles) past Stinking Creek; watch for the old road heading west off the Two Lakes Road.

Ike's Hill Trail [TCT] (Map 58/F6)
This easy 6 km (3.6 mile) trail—currently under development—is part of the Trans Canada route through this area. It will wind across the community pasture, through the forest to Ike's Hill, a popular picnic spot with the locals. The trail follows the historic St. John's Trail, an old route to Fort St. John.

Iosegun Lake Trails (Map 5/D6)
Found northwest of Whitecourt, in Fox Creek, there is a popular hiking trail located between the boat launch and south loop of the campsite. The trail follows the edge of Iosegun Lake and links to a longer route that extends south to the inlet. The easy hike should take no more than an hour, return.

Kakwa River Trail (Map 1/B7)
From Dead Horse Meadows, a trail cuts overland to intersect the Kakwa River, then follows the river downstream. The multi-use trail leaves the Kakwa Valley and heads south, to follow the South Kakwa River Trail. This latter trail also hooks up with the Famm/Trench Creek Trail into Willmore Wilderness Park.

From the Dead Horse Meadows Trailhead it is 5 km (3 miles) to the Kakwa River, 12 km (7.3 miles) to where the trail leaves the Kakwa and 17 km (10.4 miles) to the South Kakwa River.

La Crete Walking Trail (Map 86/G4)
This is an easy 3 km (1.8 mile) one-way out and back trail in the town of La Crete. The trail is paved, with two painted lanes allowing for hikers, bikers and even roller bladers to share the trail. The local walking club is working on extending the paved section deeper into town, as well as adding another 3 km to the other end of the trails.

Lac La Biche Trail (Map 12/B3)
The 16 km (10 mile) Lac La Biche Walking and Biking Trail follows the Lac La Biche shoreline and then the access road to Sir Winston Churchill Provincial Park. It can be accessed from a variety of locations around the town of Lac La Biche.

Lakeland Provincial Park/Recreation Area (Map 12, 13)
With dozens of lakes and trails to discover in the area, the intrepid explorer could spend many days roaming the area. In addition to the many trails, there are short portage trails and a well-established network of ATV and snowmobile trails. In fact, this area is an oddity among provincial parks since snowmobile and ATV/OHV travel is actively encouraged. Trails like the Air Weapons Range Boundary, Dabbs Lake, East & West Wishbone and Pinehurst Trails are mainly used by OHV. Here are a few of the more popular hiking/biking trails:

Amisk Trail (Map 12/F2)
Starting from the Jackson Lake Staging Area, this trail continues 8.7 km (5.3 miles) south to connect up with the Mosquito Lake Trail and Jackson Lake Isthmus. It is open to hikers, mountain bikers and skiers.

Black Duck Lake/Dabbs Lake Trail (Map 12/G3)
From the eastern shore of Black Duck Lake to the eastern shore of Dabbs Lake, this 6 km (3.6 mile) trail was historically used as a portage trail. Few people lug their boats that far anymore, but the trail is open to hiking and biking and connects up with the Dabbs Lake Trail. Note that the trail has been closed to ATVs until further notice.

Blackett Lake Trail (Map 12/F4)
This trail came about due to the closure of the Black Duck Lake/Dabbs Lake Trail to ATV traffic. The 10 km (6 mile) trail connects up with the Kinnaird Lake Trail and starts from the trailhead 3.3 km west of Pinehurst Lake Campground.

Jackson Lake Trail (Map 12/F3)
This 3.2 km (2 mile) trail is mostly used as a portage trail for canoeists to get to the lake, but hikers and bikers can follow the easy trail, too. There is good wildlife watching around Jackson Lake and many people make the hike just to see what they can find.

Mosquito Lake Trail (Map 12/E3)
Beginning from the Shaw Lake Staging Area, this 14 km (8.5 mile) hike and ski trail leads east from the cross-country ski trails that surround Shaw Lake, through mature boreal forest and hilly terrain to McGuffin Lake. The trail skirts the shore for a ways then continues on to connect with Amisk Lake Trail at Jackson Lake Isthmus. You can also use this trail to connect to the west shore of Kinnaird Lake.

Shaw Lake Cross-Country Trail System (Map 12/E3)
Made up of six loop trails that range from 1 km to 11 km in length, the trail difficulty generally becomes more challenging on the longer trails. A seventh trail follows the shores of Shaw Lake and is 26.5 km (16.5 miles) in length—this is the most popular hiking trail. There is a cabin and picnic area at the parking lot.

Spencer Lake Trail (Map 13/A3)
Starting across the lake from Touchwood Lake Campground, this trail connects to the west shore of Spencer Lake after 3.5 km (2.2 miles).

Leddy Lake Trail (Map 47/A2)
This interpretive trail winds its way through the boreal forest north of Peace River. There is an interpretive brochure that identifies plant species you will see along the way. In winter, it is possible to cross country ski the easy 2 km (1.2 mile) trail. It is located 24 km northwest of Peace River on Secondary Highway 743 (Weberville Road).

Lesser Slave Lake Park Trails (Map 22/C1–D2)

Along with the Trans Canada Trail (see Freighter Lakeshore Trail above) coursing through the park, there are a series of short trails to explore. In addition to the 1.8 km long Jack Pine Trail that runs from Marten River Campground to the Marten River Group Use Area and the 600 metre interpretive Songbird Trail, visitors can try these popular trails:

Marten Mountain Trail (Map 22/D1)

Found 23 km north of Slave Lake (the town), off Highway 88, this trail heads up Marten Mountain to a viewpoint with a breathtaking panoramic view of Slave Lake and the surrounding forest. This is also the trailhead for the Lily Lake Trail.

Lily Lake Trail (Map 22/D1)

The Lily Lake Trail is unique in this part of the world. Whereas most trails in this neck of the woods are relatively flat, following lakeshores or meandering through the boreal forest, this 3 km (1.8 mile) trail has a 119 m (387 ft) elevation change. Give yourself about three hours return to hike this route, which accesses a stocked fishing lake. The trailhead is found at the viewpoint of the Marten Mountain Trail. Be sure to visit the Walk Through Time Trail, a short 500 metre side trail leading through a magnificent old growth forest, which starts 300 metres down the Lily Lake Trail.

Whispering Sands Trail (Map 22/D3)

This easy trail is actually a small section of the much larger Trans Canada Trail. Located at the south end of Lesser Slave Lake Provincial Park, access can be found at the Devonshire Beach parking lot. The 1.5 km (0.9 mile) interpretive hiking trail passes through a fragile environment, traversing 1500 year old dunes. Users are asked to stay on the trail.

Little Fisheries Trail (Map 68/G7)

This mountain bike trail winds through the boreal forest southwest of Fort McMurray, following a combination of single-track, ATV trails, cutlines and muddy, abandoned roads. The trailhead can be found at the end of Real Martin Drive near the Fort McMurray Golf Club. The 12 km (7.4 mile) trail starts with a steady 400 m (1,310 ft) climb to a plateau, with a loop trail that overlooks the Athabasca River.

Machesis Lake Trails (Map 86/F3)

There is an unmaintained horse camp at Machesis Lake. From here, there are a number of trails including a newly developed trail that goes into the sand hills. Another hooks up with the old Peace River Wagon Road and follows the edge of the valley to Prairie Point Road. By horse, it is about four hours out and back to the Peace River and about eight hours to Prairie Point.

Mill Brown Park Trail (Map 47/D6)

Mill Brown Park is located in the town of Nampa. A short, easy walking trail wanders through the woods at the backside of the park and down to the river. The trail is about 2 km (1.2 miles) long.

Moonshine Provincial Park Trails (Map 44/E7)

The big trail at Moonshine Lake is a 7 km (4.8 mile) trail around the lake. It is an interpretive trail and chances of seeing some sort of wildlife (birds, usually, but sometimes deer and moose) are good. The lake also has a series of cross-country ski trails carved through the bush at the south end of the lake. Only some of these are accessible in the summer.

Mountain Portage Rapids Trail (Map 96/F1)

About 8 km south of the town of Fort Smith, just past the golf course, look for a dirt road heading towards the Slave River. Here it is a quick walk down a sandy trail through the dense boreal forest to a sandy beach on the river. This is a great spot to launch a kayak it you want to play in the rapids, hikers can continue along the shore, up a small hill, where you can see the powerlines. Follow the powerlines along the narrow ridge that drops off on both sides to an interpretive sign for 'The White Pelican Study Area'. You can watch Canada's northernmost pelicans nesting from this spot.

Muskeg Creek Park Trails (Map 10/C4)

This 17.5 km (10.7 mile) series of trails is located in Muskeg Creek Park in the town of Athabasca. The trails cut through a steep-sided, heavily wooded ravine providing a good chance to see wildlife that ranges from birds to deer and even moose. In the winter, these trails are groomed for classic and skate skiing.

Muskoseepi Park (Map 17/A2)

Bear River runs through the heart of Grande Prairie and this urban park bisects the city from north to south along the river valley. (Muskoseepi is Cree for Bear Creek). A trail system follows the stream and offers easy, peaceful walking through the heart of the rapidly growing city. There are 18 km (11 miles) of trails in the park, many of which are paved. In the winter, some of the trails are designated for cross-country skiing. A portion of the park also protects Crystal Lake, in the northeast corner of the city.

Nose Lake Trail (Map 1/E2)

Nose Lake is a popular fishing lake found 117 km south of Grande Prairie. The Nose Mountain Road heads just west of the lake, so anyone wanting to get to lake and the campsite on the shores of the lake must walk 3.6 km (2.2 miles). Despite the 70 metre (230 ft) elevation drop into the lake area, it is a fairly easy hike.

O'Brien Provincial Park Trails (Map 16/G3)

A trail network in O'Brien Provincial Park follows along the bank of the Wapiti River and through the mixed boreal forest that surrounds it. The 12 km (7.5 mile) trail network is easy to hike and well maintained. The park is found 12 km south of Grande Prairie off Secondary Highway 666.

Old Peace River Trail [TCT] (Map 10/C1–23/E4)

This 60.2 km (36.7 mile) section of the Trans Canada Trail takes travellers from the trailhead, northwest of Athabasca off of Secondary Highway 813, through Calling Lake Provincial Park to the end of the trail near Moose Portage. The trail generally skirts the top of the Athabasca River Valley along a historical trail. The trail is generally easy to follow, over rolling terrain with some creek valleys to hike through.

Pat's Creek Interpretive Trail (Map 47/C4)

Highway 2 used to follow Pat's Creek into Peace River, but was abandoned due to severe landslides. The 3 km (1.8 mile) section of old road is now an interpretive trail high above Pat Wesley (Pat's) Creek. The major attraction here are the slides, or rather, the glacial landscape that caused the slides. Follow 100 Street out of town until you reach the parking area.

Pelican Rapids (Map 96/F1)

This multi-use trail can be a 60 minute hike or a great bike ride from the Halfway Meadows to the rapids nearby. Follow the old railway for about 1 km until it ends at the river and then look for a footpath that branches over the creek and up the other side. The trail ends on a peninsula of pink granite overlooking the powerful rapids below.

Pine Hollow Trail (Map 1/D4)

A steep trail starts at the Pine Hollow Campsite, which is found at the south end of North Lake in Two Lakes Recreation Area and climbs to the top of a knoll. From here, you have great views out over the lakes, Hat Mountain and the surrounding area.

Queen Elizabeth Provincial Park Trail (Map 46/F4)

Located about 8 km northwest of Grimshaw off Highway 35, this trail offers great birdwatching with over 160 different species in the area. The trail is a fairly easy 4.5 km (2.8 mile) hike around the lake.

Rocky Lane Ski Trails (Map 86/G2–87/A3)

Located in the small community of Rocky Lane, the ski trails can be explored in the summer on foot or horseback. (The trails are open to mountain biking, too, but few people actually ride them). There are 13 km (8 miles) of easy walking on both sides of the Ponton River. In winter, the frozen river can be crossed, but in summer, you will have to pick a side. The trails start at either the Skate Shack or the Arena.

Saskatoon Island Provincial Park (Map 16/E1)

Four interconnecting loop trails create about 4 km (2.5 miles) of wheelchair-accessible trails within the park. The longest trail is only 1.8 km long and loops past Little Lake (the aptly named Little Lake Trail). The 1.2 km Saskatoon Trail loops near the lake through a large patch of Saskatoon berry shrubs and is a popular destination in mid-summer when the berries ripen. The easiest trail is the 1.2 km Parkland Trail, a paved trail that leads to a viewing platform on Little Lake. The final trail–the 1.7 km Beach Trail–links the other three trails with the camping area and the beach.

Sir Winston Churchill Park Trails (Map 12/B2)
This provincial park is set on an island allowing for some good views of Lac La Biche. Trails include the Boardwalk Trail, which is a 1.2 km interpretive trail through a unique old-growth boreal forest. The Interior Trails start from the centre of the island along a number of utility corridors that spread outward, ultimately connecting up with the main park road. There is about 3.5 km (2.1 miles) of trail in the interior system that allows for good bird watching opportunities. The Long Point Trail is a scenic 2.5 km trail that also offers great bird watching opportunities. Following the perimeter of the island is Old Growth Alley, a 6 km (3.7 miles) loop that connects to all the above trails.

Spring Lake Recreation Site (Map 30/A4)
There are 6 km (3.6 miles) of nature trails around the recreation site that can be hiked in the summer. In winter the area comes alive with a downhill ski area and about 26 km (15.6 miles) of groomed cross-country ski trails to enjoy.

St. John's Trail [TCT] (Maps 58/E5–59/A6)
Part of the historic St. John's Trail, this easy 6 km (3.6 mile) section of trail is part of the Trans Canada Trail. It follows unused road allowances, connecting the Ike's Hill Trail with the Canfor Trail.

Stetson [Moberly Flats] Trail (Map 1/C4)
A moderate trail leads from the road west of SouthLake to the top of a knoll for a great panoramic view. The 1.5 km (0.9 mile) trail climbs 244 m (793 ft) to the top. The trailhead is just north of the Moberly Flats Campground.

Sulphur Mountain Route (Map 1/C6)
This difficult, unimproved trail climbs 580 m (1,902 feet) in about 5.5 km (3.3 miles) up into the Sulphur Mountain alpine. There is no real route above treeline; rather, any of a number of ridges or peaks can be accessed, so distance and elevation will vary, depending on your destination. It will take hikers about 2.5 hours to hike above the treeline from Stinking Springs off the Two Lakes Road.

Torrens Chute Trail (Map 1/C5)
This unmaintained trail drops steeply down to the Torrens Chutes, a dramatic rapid on the Torrens River. Don't get too close to the edge, as you wouldn't want to fall in. The moderately difficult trail is 3 km (1.8 km) to the falls, but those willing to ford the river can follow an indistinct trail leading up the hill for a number of kilometres more.There is a small parking area and a small sign at the start of the trail south of Two Lakes Recreation Area.

Torrens Lookout Route (Map 1/C5)
From the south end of Two Lakes Recreation Area, a steep, rough gravel road climbs to the Torrens Lookout. The road to the lookout is fairly long (about 15 km/9.3 miles one-way) and doesn't make for the most interesting hiking, but mountain bikers and ATVers do enjoy it.

Trans Canada Trail [TCT] (Maps 10, 22–24, 34–36, 45–47, 58–59)
The Northern Section of the Trans Canada Trail through Alberta heads north from Calgary through Edmonton and into Northern Alberta, passing through Athabasca, Peace River and on into Northern BC. While the southern section of the Trans Canada Trail is less than half done, the sections north of Wetaskiwin (see Central Alberta Mapbook) are 80% done and nice stretches of trail grace these maps. However, don't expect one unbroken trail running from Edmonton to BC. There are still large sections where the route has been designated along roads and gaps in the existing pieces. From south to north, look for these trail segments: the Athabasca Landing Trail, the Old Peace River Trail, the Freighter Lakeshore Trail, the Grouard Trail, the Friendship Trail, the Canfor Trail, the St. John's Trail and Ike's Hill Trail. All of these sections are written in more detail in this section of the book.

Two Lakes Interpretive Trail (Map 1/D4)
This 4 km (2.4 mile) trail runs between North Two Lake and South Two Lake, passing through three distinct sections. Brochures are available, explaining the 27 stops along the way. The easy trail can be accessed from all three campgrounds. Wildlife is a common site along the trail.

Vega Natural Area (Map 8/E7)
Part of a large complex of protected areas in the Athabasca River Sandhills, the Vega Natural Area is a small area just south of the ferry crossing. While the main recreational feature here is a viewpoint over the river, there is also an old wagon road that snakes along the top of the escarpment above the river. The road does not currently connect with the parking lot, but plans are in place to connect the two.

Wapiti Nordic Ski Trails (Map 16/G3)
This is one of the best cross-country ski areas in north central Alberta, with over 35 km (21.7 miles) of groomed trails in winter (see winter for more information) . In summer, this area is open to hikers and mountain bikers. Mountain bikers have, of course, added a few extra trails to the system. One of the key hiking trails in the area is the Forest Trail, a 5 km (3 mile) trail with an extensive interpretive brochure.

> *The northern landscape can be very difficult to navigate and hikers should carry a map, compass and GPS and know how to use all three.*

Wood Buffalo National Park (Maps 89, 96)
Wood Buffalo National Park is a World Heritage Site and Canada's largest national park.In addition to the shorter trails, like the 750 metre long Karstland Interpretive Trail that visits unique karst landscape, there are several longer trails to explore. Registration is required if you are planning to complete an overnight trail.

Lakeside Trail (Map 96/D4)
The Lakeside Trail follows the lakeshore from the Pine Lake Recreation Area to the Kettle Point Group Camp. It is an easy 6.4 km (4 mile) hike through aspen and spruce forests. There is a sandy beach for swimming and the trail also connects to a trailhead for Lane Lake.

Lane Lake Trail (Map 96/D4)
Following a chain of sinkhole lakes this moderate 13 km (8 mile) trail winds deep into the mature boreal forest. There is a variety of waterfowl and beavers along the route, which terminates at Lane Lake, a large clear sinkhole lake.

North Loop Trail (Map 96/D2)
Featuring sinkholes, scenic views and geological formations, this 7.5 km (6.5 mile) long trail climbs to the top of an escarpment. It is a moderate hike with access from the trailhead roughly 2.4 km (1.5 mile) past the Salt River Day Use Area.

Rainbow Lakes Trail (Map 96/E2)
Rainbow Lake is a deep sinkhole lake surrounded by spruce trees. The trail follows a cutline from Pine Lake Road for 6 km (3.6 mile) to the lake. There is a primitive lakeshore campsite for backcountry tenting.Keep an eye out for bison along the way.

South Loop Trail (Map 96/E2)
The South Loop is a relatively easy 9 km (5.6 mile) trail that meanders through open meadows and peaceful forests. The highlight of the trail is Grosbeak Lake and the boulder-strewn salt flats. Access is found across from the Salt River Day Use Area east of Pine Lake Road. The Salt River Meadows is an easy 1.3 km side trail.

Sweetgrass Station Trail (Map 96/E1–89/E1)
This 12 km (7.2 mile) trail used to be a road from Sweetgrass Landing to Sweetgrass Station, where there was a bison management station in the 1950s and 60s. Today, the road is gone, leaving a rough, difficult trail that sees more bison than humans. The trail starts at the campsite on the south bank of the Peace Riverthat can only be accessed by water, either by canoe or floatplane. The station is located in the Peace-Athabasca Delta, a wildlife hot spot near Lake Claire. Over the past few years, Parks Canada has been restoring the area and you will find a trio of historical buildings: the old Warden's Cabin, the old visitor's cabin and a historical warehouse.

ATV [OHV]
Adventures

The varied terrain of Northern Alberta is a playground for the OHV (off-highway vehicle) enthusiast. Whether kicking up mud on your ATV (all-terrain vehicle) on a summer day, or blazing trails on your snowmobile, you will discover uncharted territory.Just hop on, and joyride the sand dunes or cruise the backcountry. On an ATV you can explore untamed wilderness from abandoned railways, epic lakes, muddy forest trails and endless views of the Rockies. Just be sure to plan ahead.

Like any good explorer you will want to map a route and be prepared. Due to the remote nature of most of the trails, conditions can vary depending on the time of year. Expect snow and cold temperatures from October to April, and dress or pack accordingly. Stock up on good equipment like GPS units and two-way radios to cover those areas without cellular reception. And check with the Alberta Sustainable Resource Development Office for trail closures due to weather or wildlife considerations before heading out.

The Alberta Off-Highway Vehicle Association is a great place to find ATV and snowmobile clubs, as well as information on local laws. While the expanse of Northern Alberta offers enough room for the adventurer to roam, there are some restrictions from provincial parks, municipal boundaries, and unbroken boreal forest and muskeg with no accessible routes. Riders must obey private property postings, and should respect hikers, bikers and horseback riders on multi-use trails. Be prepared for unkempt areas as you ride, and have provisions in place.

With all systems go you can hit the trails with confidence. Northern Alberta contains a few designated OHV areas including Lakeland Provincial Recreation Area, and Timeu Creek OHV Recreation Area (near Vega Ferry). A great deal of ATV riding happens off the beaten path, however, with thousands of kilometres of backroads, cutlines, pipelines, corridors, cleared routes and abandoned trails all available for you to wheel along and explore.

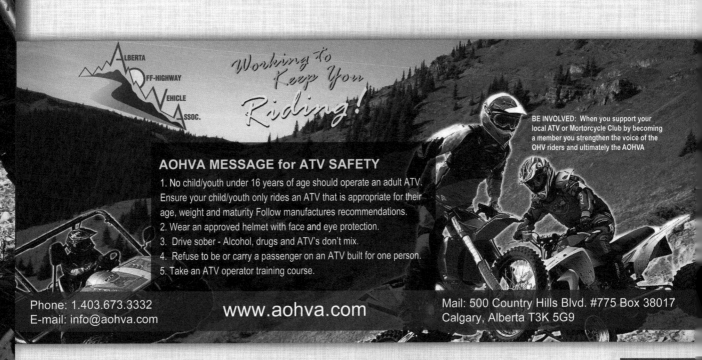

Working to Keep You Riding!

BE INVOLVED: When you support your local ATV or Mortorcycle Club by becoming a member you strengthen the voice of the OHV riders and ultimately the AOHVA

AOHVA MESSAGE for ATV SAFETY

1. No child/youth under 16 years of age should operate an adult ATV. Ensure your child/youth only rides an ATV that is appropriate for their age, weight and maturity Follow manufactures recommendations.
2. Wear an approved helmet with face and eye protection.
3. Drive sober - Alcohol, drugs and ATV's don't mix.
4. Refuse to be or carry a passenger on an ATV built for one person.
5. Take an ATV operator training course.

Phone: 1.403.673.3332
E-mail: info@aohva.com

www.aohva.com

Mail: 500 Country Hills Blvd. #775 Box 38017
Calgary, Alberta T3K 5G9

Abasands OHV Area (Map 55/A1)

Abasands is one of the most popular staging areas for OHVs around Fort McMurray. It is found just across from the school on the west side of the Aba-sands subdivision. From here, there are hundreds of kilometres of riding to be had. The riding here can be challenging, with lots of mud, cutlines, wooded trails, some creek crossings and other features. However, there is usually an easy way for those looking for an easier ride.

Big Mountain ATV Route (Map 17/A6–E3)

Also known as the Smoky/Jackpine Area, Big Mountain is located 40 km south of Grande Prairie off Highway 40. From the Big Mountain Recreation Area, a series of roads and cutlines radiate out in every direction, which can be followed as far north as the Wapiti River and as far east as the Smoky. Down on the banks of the Smoky you will find a grave for Smoky Mike. Mike Vasselifs was a trapper who died in 1932 and dug his own grave on the banks of the river. His grave site is an archeological site and should be protected. In 1996, the South Peace ATV Club put a headstone marking the gravesite.

The use of off-highway vehicles in any OHV designated area requires vehicle registration, valid insurance, lights and a muffler. It is the responsibility of all off-road riders to know if the trail they are on is open and/or designated for OHV use.

Bistcho Lake OHV Route (Map 92/E4–F2)

Folks planning on making the epic 15 hour ATV/snowmobile ride from Zama City to Bistcho Lake need to put in some research on this route, as well as bring along extra gas. There are outfitter camps at the lake, which can be used if they are not already occupied, but make sure to bring a tent, just in case. This is a difficult overnight trip. Access is approximately 24 km east of Zama City off Township Road 1170A. There is also a route up to Thurston Lake from the east side of Bistcho Lake as well.

Copton Airstrip OHV Route (Map 1/G7)

Starting from the Beaverdam Road about 8 km north of Grande Cache (see Central Alberta mapbook), it is about 40 km (25 miles) to the Copton Airstrip or 80 km (50 miles) to the Porcupine Cabin. Of course there are dozens of side roads and trails along the way including the trail to Caw Ridge. Caw Ridge is about 30 km (18.6 miles) to the turnoff, then another 8 km to the top. This spectacular alpine ridge is one of the most popular places around Grande Cache to see large mammals. Access to the ridge is along a rough 4wd road, which can be used by ATVers.

Chisholm OHV Trails (Map 9/B1–23/C7)

North of Chisholm between the Athabasca River and Highway 44, you will find a good riding area with plenty of trails and random camping. Chisholm has a bylaw to allow ATVs along township roads (at reduced speeds).

Cutbank Falls (Map 3/A2)

To get to Cutbank Falls first head south from Grande Prairie for approximately 68 km. After crossing the Cutbank River there is a staging area, providing some camping and fishing areas. The trail to the falls is at the back of the staging area. Travel about 3 km along the powerline trail until it heads into the trees. The trail is often well traveled with steep sections and large ruts.

Fawcett Lake (Map 23/E3)

Fawcett Lake is about 18 km north of the town of Smith, off Range Road 12A. There is a staging area and a few different choices for camping nearby. For more formal camping there is the Fawcett Lake Provincial Recreation Area offering plenty of fishing, boating and mountain bike trails. The OHV trails are found off the north side of the lake and follow a series of cutlines and old roads.

Fort Chipewyan Winter Road (Map 81/F4–90/C6)

In the winter, this is a road, used to access Fort Chipewyan and points north of Fort McMurray. In the summer the road is usable by ATVers to access a number of popular backcountry destinations, such as the Richardson River Sand Dunes and the Six Lakes Area. The road itself can be driven as far as Richardson Lake before disappearing into the muskeg and lakes. To get here look for signs off the winter road heading west to Embarrass Portage, there is a trail west of the Richardson River that follows the eastern side of the Richardson River Dunes Wildland Park. The park is a protected area so watch the boundary. It is quite an adventure trying to access the Athabasca Dunes located nearby.

Horn Ridge Trail (Map 1/B6)

The Horn Ridge Trailhead is accessed from the Lick Creek Staging area between Two Lakes Provincial Park and Kakwa Wildland Provincial Park. Beyond Two Lakes, the road is quite rough and riders might just want to start there. There is a fork in the road where taking the east (or left) trail will cross Stinking Creek and continue to Kakwa Falls. The west trail or the Horn Ridge Trail follows Torrens Creek steeply up to the ridge, which spans the BC/Alberta boundary. The ride down is steep!

Kakwa Wildland Provincial Park (Map 1)

As with most provincial parks riding is limited to designated trails only; however, this wildland park offers quite a few nice riding areas. The park is located at the end of Two Lakes Road towards the boundary of British Columbia. This can be a rough 4wd access road when the conditions are wet. In fact, some prefer to ride the road as opposed to drive it to access the area. Once in the core area of the park, there are many trails to ride. Some of the more popular trails are the trail to Kakwa Falls, which is about 20 km (12 miles), or the Kakwa Lake Trail leading over the border.

Lakeland Provincial Park/Recreation Area (Maps 12–13)

With well over 140 km of shared motorized and non-motorized trails this area offers some beautiful backcountry wilderness riding. Off highway vehicle riding is allow only on the designated trails of which there are many. Some trails are clearly marked, some are multi-purpose and some are season specific. In fact, many of the trails are designed for use once the lakes freeze solid enough to be driven over. When there is enough snow, these become snowmobile trails, but when there is not enough snow, this area sees a lot of ATV use in the winter.

There are a few options for staging areas: at the north end of Horne Lake, at the south end of Seibert Lake, west of Pinehurst Lake campground, at the Mile 10 Trailhead, and at the Jackson Lake Trailhead. In addition to the trails listed below, other popular options include the Snug Cover Trail (6.3 km), the Spencer Crossing Trail (3.3 km), and the Trans Canada Pipeline Trail (27 km). Allow for a weekend or longer to truly enjoy this area.

Air Weapons Range Boundary Trail (Map 13/A2)

This a 24 km multi-use trail that runs from Heart Lake Tower Road to the north shore of Seibert Lake. Most of the trail runs the boundary between the recreation area and the Air Weapons Range immediately east of the area.

Blackett Lake Trail (Map 12/F4)

Resulting from the closure of the Black Duck Lake/Dabbs Lake Trail to ATV traffic, this 9.6 km trail connects up with the Kinnaird Lake Trail. The trailhead is 3.3 km west of Pinehurst Lake Campground.

Dabbs Lake Trails (Map 12/G2)

There are three Dabbs Lake Trails. The West Trail was originally the main access road to the Lakeland Provincial Recreation Area during the winter months and now leads to the main trail. The Dabbs Lake East Trail can be found off Touchwood Lake Road, approximately 0.6 km west of the Touchwood Lake Campground. The trail is rated as moderately difficult and offers access to the main Dabbs Lake Trail. The main trail provides access to the West Wishbone Trail and is 8.9 km one-way.

East Wishbone Trail (Map 13/B4)

This moderately difficult trail starts along the Snug Cove Road, 6.6 km west of the Siebert Lake Road. The 21.4 km trail ends at the Dore Bridge, where it becomes the West Wishbone Trail. A trio of winter trails cut off from this one to access Siebert Lake and Pinehurst Lake.

Helena Lake Trail (Map 12/F5)

A short, relatively easy 3.3 km trail accesses Helena Lake from the trailhead found 3.6 km west of the Pinehurst Lake Campsite. A 2.4 km winter-only trail connects the northeast shore of Helena Lake with the southwest short of Blackett Lake.

Mile 10 Trail (Map 12/F2)

This moderate 5.3 km trail runs through a mixture of mature forest trails and heads towards Jackson Lake. The trail is primarily used for car-top boat access via quads.

Pinehurst South and West (Map 12/F5)

The Pinehurst South Trail is a 10.5 km trail that goes south from Pinehurst Lake to the Trans Canada Pipeline. The Pinehurst West Trail is found 1.8 km west of the Pinehurst Lake Campground and heads north to the West Wishbone Trail.

Puller Lake South and West (Map 13/B4)

The Puller South Trail is found 2.5 km east of the Dore Bridge on the West Wishbone trail. This trail will take you to the west shores of Seibert Lake. The Puller West Trail heads north at the same junction east of the Dore Bridge, taking this trail will also give you access to Seibert Lake while passing by three other smaller lakes.

Tchir Road (Map 13/B4)

Located in Lakeland Provincial Recreation Area, this road is 13 km in length and is mostly used by ATVers and mountain bikers in summer. Snowmobilers also use this road in winter.

West Wishbone Trail (Map 12/F5)

Another recreation area trail that appeals mainly to ATV's and mountain bikers, there is approximately 18 km of trail to explore that is ideal for off road enthusiasts. The main trailhead is found on Pinehurst Lake Road, 4.2 km west of Pinehurst Lake Campground. This backcountry trail leads up to the Dore Bridge area.

Musreau Lake Area (Map 3/A3)

Located about 80 km south of Grande Prairie off Highway 40 towards Grande Cache, Musreau Lake has lots of informal and unmaintained trails. Pack accordingly as there may be occasional obstacles to go around or cut through. There is a recreation area campground at the north end of the lake where no off highway vehicles are allowed. It is only a 4 km ride east of Highway 40 on a gravel road to the campground if you are looking to explore other trails in the area.

Narraway OHV Trails (Map 1/C1)

This popular ATV trail has recently been converted to a logging road and large areas along Chinook Ridge have been logged. But this route, which starts off of the Two Lakes Road and leads over the Narraway River, is still a gorgeous trip. There are a series of cutlines and trails that you can follow to within eyeshot of the BC Boundary.

Nose Mountain OHV Trails (Map 1/E2–G4)

While it is possible to make it to the trailhead that leads to Nose Lake with a good 2wd vehicle, further south the road is nearly impassable for about 32 km to all but ATVs. Here, a Weyerhaeuser Road joins the Nose Mountain Road and heads southeast to the Kakwa River and some great ATVing along the Kakwa. Those trying to access Lower Kakwa Falls should leave this route until late summer since the route crosses the Kakwa five times. There are also a number of logging roads and cutlines in the Nose Mountain area, including the Wapiti and Sherman ATV Routes, to explore.

Rainbow Lake Trails (Map 85/A3)

From the campground at Rainbow Lake, ATVers can head out onto literally hundreds of kilometres of unmaintained, unmapped trails. The town of Rainbow Lake is approximately 136 km west of High Level and Highway 35. There was once around 300 km (186 miles) of maintained snowmobile trails here but they have since been abandoned. ATV riders can still have fun trying to explore this old system.

Richardson River Sand Dunes OHV Area (Map 90/A5–C6)

The Richardson River Sand Dunes is a popular destination for ATVs and motorcyclists about two hours north of Fort McMurray. The dunes are located north of the Richardson River Dunes Wildland Park and just getting there is an off-road trip along the Fort Chipewyan Winter Road of nearly 100 km (60 miles) from the staging area outside of town. Watch for the access route (Embarras Portage Road) into the sand dunes, which leaves the winter road before it crosses the Richardson River. Note that off-highway vehicles are not allowed in any of the wildland parks in the area and the trail has kilometre markers.

Six Lakes OHV Area (Map 90/B6)

The so-called Six Lakes area is located just south of the Richardson River Dunes Wildland Park. Access into the area is along the Fort Chipewyan Winter Road. Watch for ATV trails that string the lakes together, accessed from the winter road. There are a number (nine) semi-formal camping areas in this region, scattered around the lakes.

Shuttler Flats (Map 15/G6)

Located southwest of Grande Prairie, off Two Lakes Road, this area offers many kilometres of informal ATV trails. You can even ride into British Columbia from here. The Shuttler Flats Recreation Area offers camping, but no riding is allowed in the actual campsite itself.

Simonette River Area (Map 17/F3)

Found east of Grande Prairie, this riding area is found off the Forestry Trunk Road (Secondary Highway 734) near the Simonette River Recreation Area. Most base their stay at the campsite where there is limited quading available. But if you continue south to Economy Creek there is a groomed gravel road that heads east. This will take you to a staging area and some OHV trails including the 25 km (15.5miles) trail to the Simonette River. There are also powerlines in the area that provide a dry and flat route to travel for about 30 km (18.6 miles)

Swan Hills OHV Trails (Map 7/D3–G4)

While these trails were designed specifically for snowmobiles, they have been upgraded to handle ATV traffic in the summer as well. From Krause Lake, trails head east to hook up with the Trapper Leas Trails. Trails heading south and east help form a series of loops, ranging from the 20 km Freeman Loop to the much longer Tamarack and Marigold Loops.

Thickwood Trails (Map 68/E6)

Just outside Fort McMurray there is a staging area off Tower Road near where the powerlines cross the road. Generally the powerline trail is easy riding, but there are some side trails that will offer more of a challenge. It is also possible to ride up the road to the fire lookout for a nice view of town and surrounding area.

Timeu OHV Area (Map 8/E6)

In the summer, Timeu Off-Highway Vehicle Area is one of this region's only designated Off Highway Vehicle riding areas. As such, it sees heavy use from ATVers, motorbikers and other off road vehicles. The trails are found in an area of sand dunes just west of the Athabasca River and literally across the road from the Fort Assiniboine Sandhills Wildland Park.

Trapper Leas Trails (Map 7/G5)

In the summer, the Swan Hills Snowmobile Trails can be used by ATVers. There are two loops north of Trapper Leas Cabin Recreation Area—Trapper Leas' Loop and the Swan Dive Loop and more trails to the south, including the Morse Loop, as well as the Golden Triangle Route. The main trails are signed and groomed allowing for easy riding.

Tucker Lake OHV Area (Map 14/A6)

Found just west of Cold Lake, the area north of Tucker Lake offers lots of opportunity to explore. You can head north up to Bourque Lake, which is approximately 20 km from Tucker Lake, or northwest to Marguerite Lake. The series of old roads and cutlines in the area allow for unlimited riding; just be careful not to venture too far north and into the Cold Lake Air Weapons Range. You can easily spend the day exploring this area.

Waterways OHV Area (Map 55/C1–E3)

This is one of a handful of staging areas found near Fort McMurray. From here, an easy trail loops around to Saprae Creek. The main trail is about 50 km (31 miles) long, but there are countless side trails to explore. For an extended ride, it is possible to continue south up the Christina River Valley. If the water is low enough, you can also cross the Christina River and follow the Clearwater River upstream. This area also features some old railroad tracks connecting to the trail behind Gregoire and Rotary Park.

Wapiti River Valley (Map 17/B3)

The Wapiti River Valley southeast of Grande Prairie is used by many different people; from horseback riders to off road vehicles and ATVs. It is a sandy forested area with some grassy and muskeg sections. There is a network of inter-connecting trails that are well travels but not mapped. Ride carefully as it is very likely you will encounter other people on the trails.

Snowmobile
Adventures

Recreational Off-Highway Vehicles are broadly divided into two categories: vehicles that are used in summer, which include ATVs and dirt bikes; and vehicles that are used in winter, which are primarily snowmobiles. While there is typically some overlap of areas, this is not always the case. Areas that are popular with snowmobilers in winter may be too wet to ride in summer (for instance, it's tough to take an ATV out onto the ice when there isn't any). And some popular ATV areas just don't get that much snow.

Thankfully, Alberta has some well-organized clubs for both ATVing and snowmobiling. They resulted from the rash of trail closures about a decade ago where many popular riding areas were closed to motorized vehicles. In response, the Alberta Off-Highway Vehicle Association and the Alberta Snowmobile Association began organizing riders and lobbying the government to keep certain areas open. As a result, riders in the province are in a much better position than in many other provinces. Show your support to local clubs by purchasing trail passes to help these clubs groom and maintain the trails. For more information and to find your local club, check out the Alberta Snowmobile Association at www.altasnowmobile.ab.ca.

With an ever expanding trail and club system, we have tried to list most of the formal riding areas and some of the more popular unmaintained areas. However, this is only the tip of the iceberg. Any logging road or oil and gas road that is not ploughed in winter can become a prime snowmobile route, while the endless seismic or cutlines in the region also offer possible snowmobile routes. In fact there are many parts of the north that are better accessed on a snowmobile. The only real limitations are restrictions in most provincial parks and many municipal boundaries as well as the vast swaths of unbroken boreal forest and muskeg where there are no roads or routes to follow.

Many of the major settlements have a snowmobile club that looks after a patch of snowmobile trails. These areas draw the majority of riders, but, as with ATVing, there are literally thousands upon thousands of kilometres of informal riding areas.

As always, caution must be exercised when riding informal areas, especially when crossing lakes or venturing into private land. Riding on ice brings with it its own set of dangers and should not be undertaken lightly. Avalanches are also a common hazard when travelling through mountains in the winter. Always carry an avalanche beacon and never travel alone. When in doubt, stick to groomed routes.

Snowmobile Adventures

Anzac Snowmobile Area (Map 55/C1–D4)
Found mostly south of Secondary Highway 881 near Anzac, there is up to 80 km (50 miles) worth of trails in this area that forms a nice loop. The trails are groomed and offer easy riding, with a pair of shelters, complete with fire pits along the way. The terrain is good for novice riders and allows for many nice rest areas along the route. The northern access is found at the staging area within the Fort McMurray city limits about 2 km from the airport.

Big Mountain Snowmobile Area (Map 17/A6–E3)
The Swan City Snowmobile Club maintains the Big Mountain Creek Recreation Area, which has a group campground and signed staging area about 32 km south of Grande Prairie and 6 km east of Highway 40. The recreation area is the start of 118 km (73 miles) of signed but ungroomed snowmobile trails. The area offers all levels of riders a variety of terrain ranging from rolling hills, to forests, to open meadows.

Bistcho Lake Snowmobile Route (Map 92/F2–F5)
This unmaintained and often-unused route will take snowmobilers from a Microwave Tower northeast of Zama City to Jackfish Point on Bistcho Lake. This is a wilderness trip and should not be undertaken lightly. It takes about two hours to get to the lake. Talk to the Watt Mountain Wanderers in High Level for more information.

Buffalo Head Hills Trail System (Map 76/B2–86/G6)
Located southeast of La Crete, this series of hills reach a height of 600 metres (2,000 feet). There is a series of loops and trails that head through the area, connecting to Wadlin Lake and Talbot Lake. The La Crete Polar Cats keep 280 km (175 miles) of trails groomed. They also maintain a warm-up cabin due west of Wadlin Lake.

Caribou Mountains Snowmobile Route (Map 88/D1–95/C6)
Using old cutlines and fire access lines, it is about a six hour snowmobile ride to Caribou Lake through the Caribou Mountains. This is a wilderness trip along an unmaintained and often untraveled route. Talk to the Watt Mountain Wanderers in High Level for more information.

Cold Lake Snowmobile Trails (Map 14)
The Cold Lake area has seemingly unlimited potential for riders to explore. The Cold Lake Snowmobile Club maintains about 60 km of groomed trails around Cold Lake, but these trails connect to a portion of the Iron Horse/Trans-Canadian Snowmobile Trail, which links to the Meadow Lake Club Trails in Saskatchewan. Another trail is a moderate trail from English Bay on Cold Lake to the club's cabin on Crane Lake. This area offers good variety form dense forests to riverbank riding and meadows and cutlines.

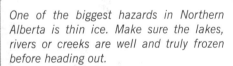

One of the biggest hazards in Northern Alberta is thin ice. Make sure the lakes, rivers or creeks are well and truly frozen before heading out.

Draper Rail Bed Trail (Map 55/B1)
Found along Draper Road on the south side of the Clearwater River near Fort Mac, this easy trail is 16.5 km (10 miles) long, about half of it following the old rail bed from which the trail gets its name. The trail hooks up with the Anzac Trails at its southeast end. Most riders start in the northwest, stringing together the two shorter trails into a much longer ride. The Draper Rail Trail was closed for the 2013 season due to damages from heavy rains, check with the McMurray Sno-Drifters for any updates.

Golden Triangle Snowmobile Route (Maps 5–7)
This is some of the best rides in Alberta! The trails throughout this 350 km (224 mile) loop are full of varied terrain including flat stretches and rolling hills, tons of creeks, rivers and small lakes to cross and hundreds of kilometres of cut-lines, pipelines and forestry roads to ride. It will take most riders two or three days to ride the entire triangle, which runs between Fox Creek's Iosegun Lake, Swan Hills' Krause Lake and Whitecourt's Eagle River snowmobiling areas. The Eagle River Staging Area is found south of these maps in the Central Alberta Backroad Mapbook. This is a very popular route with trail riders and it forms part of the Trans-Canadian Snowmobile Trail.

High Level North East Loop (Map 86/D2–F2)
Approximately 13 km north of High Level this trail heads east for about 47 km before turning south towards Highway 58. Look for the trail crossing Highway 35 north of Footner Lake. In total this section runs for about 63 km (39 miles), following mostly cutlines. You can cross Highway 58 and continue on the Machesis Route if you wish to extend the outing. Both systems are maintained by the Watt Mountain Wanderers out of High Level; be sure to support your local club.

Iosegun Lake Snowmobile Trails (Map 5/D6)
Iosegun Lake area has over 80 km (50 miles) of marked and brushed snowmobile trails. The system officially begins at the Iosegun Lake Recreation Area, but you can also access the trails from Fox Creek. There are a number of loops that can be followed like the Raspberry Run, Iosegun Lane, Heavysound and West Heavysound Loops. There are also a few one-way trails; the longest is the Eagle Run, which takes you to the Eagle Lookout where there is a warm up shack. The Eagle Run Trail continues to Swan Hills along the Golden Triangle/Trans-Canadian Snowmobile Route.

Kakwa Area (Map 1/B7–D4)
The Kakwa area is accessible from the Lick Creek Staging Area, about 160 km (100 miles) south of Grande Prairie. It is a sprawling area spanning two provinces, tied together by a groomed snowmobile trail from Lick Creek to Kakwa Lake in BC, via Kakwa Falls. Along the way, sledders set up shelter in an area known informally as Bordertown. The trail itself is about 50 km (31 miles) long and it accesses a huge network of trails, alpine bowls and old roads. On the Alberta side of the boundary, snowmobiles must stick to the groomed trails, while riding in BC is more open. However, camping is only permitted in Alberta. Other trails are from Dead Horse Meadows to the BC Boundary and from the east park boundary to Lower Kakwa Falls.

La Crete Snowmobile Route (Map 86/D2–F4)
La Crete is about 135 km southeast of High Level and riders can day trip it from the Watt Mountain Wanderers system. There are groomed trails from the popular Watt Mountain Riding Area as well as Highways 35 and 58 that connect to the La Crete Polar Cats Trail System. There are more groomed trails about 55 km south of La Crete that are maintained by the Polar Cats club. If crossing the Peace River, be sure to ensure the ice is safe.

Lakeland Provincial Park/Recreation Area (Maps 12, 13)
Trails in the park will take you all over this backcountry wilderness area, with well over 140 km (87 mile) of shared motorized and non-motorized trails. Snowmobiles are only allowed on the designated motorized trails, these trails are marked however it is recommended that you carry a saw to clear any downed trees. There are several campgrounds from which to base camp, while staging areas include the Jackson Lake Staging Area, Dabbs Lake and Shaw Lake area.

Air Weapons Range Boundary Trail (Map 13/A2)
This is a 24 km multi-use trail that runs from Heart Lake Tower to the north shore of Spencer Lake where there is a small campsite. From here the trail heads around the bay and towards the north shore of Seibert Lake. The trailhead is 9.75 km northeast of the Touchwood Lake Campground.

Blackett Lake Trail (Map 12/D5)
Access is by snowmobile from the north on the Mile 10 Trail off the Touchwood Lake Road or the south from the Blackett Lake and Helena Lake Trails off the Pinehurst Lake Access Road. This 10 km trail connects up with the Kinnaird Lake Trail. The trailhead is 3.3 km west of Pinehurst Lake Campground.

Dabbs Lake Trails (Map 12/G3)
There are three Dabbs Lake Trails. The West Trail was originally the main access road to the Lakeland Provincial Recreation Area during the winter months and now leads to the main trail. The Dabbs Lake East Trail can be found off Touchwood Lake Road, approximately 0.6 km west of the Touchwood Lake Campground. The trail is rated as moderate and offers access to the main Dabbs Lake Trail. The main trail provides access to the West Wishbone Trail.

Helena Lake Trail (Map 12/F5)
A short, relatively easy 3.3 km trail accesses Helena Lake from the trailhead found 3.6 km west of the Pinehurst Lake Campsite. A 2.4 km winter-only trail connects the northeast shore of Helena Lake with the southwest short of Blackett Lake.

Pinehurst South and West (Map 12/E6)

The Pinehurst South Trail is a 10.5 km trail that goes south from Pinehurst Lake to the Trans Canada Pipeline. The Pinehurst West Trail is found 1.8 km west of the Pinehurst Lake Campground and heads north to the West Wishbone Trail.

Puller Lake South and West (Map 13/F5)

The Puller South Trail is found 2.5 km east of the Dore Bridge on the West Wishbone trail. This trail will take you to the west shores of Seibert Lake. The Puller West Trail heads north at the same junction east of the Dore Bridge, taking this trail will also give you access to Seibert Lake while passing by three other smaller lakes.

Tchir Road (Map 12/G5)

This moderate 13 km trail leads you to the northeast shore of Seibert Lake. The trailhead is 1.5 km south of Seibert Lake Campground.

Machesis Lake Area (Map 86/F3)

Another in a series of the Watt Mountain Wanderers trails near High Level, a route heads south from Highway 58, past Machesis Lake, to the Peace River. The trailhead is about 31 km east of High Level on the border of the Child Lake Indian Reserve. From here, the trail follows roads, open areas and cutlines as it runs about 35 km south to the Peace River shore where, if frozen, you can pass over to the La Crete area. It is also possible to access this area from the west. A trail crosses Highway 35 about 10 km south of High Level and follows a cutline east for about 42 km (26 miles) to the Peace. If crossing the Peace River, be sure the ice is safe.

Peden's Point Snowmobile Trails (Map 69/A7)

Found south of the Steepbank Mine area near Fort McMurray, this series of trails (basically a loop) takes riders down to Peden's Point on the Clearwater River. This is a relatively easy 40.4 km (25 mile) ride, although the trail is no longer maintained. The trail can be fairly rough, so snowmobilers should wait for a fair bit of snow before heading out. Note that the trail passes the Suncor Mine Site. Make sure you do not ride onto private property.

Rainbow Lake Snowmobile Trails (Map 85/B3)

The local snowmobile club once maintained 300 km (186 miles) of trails in the surrounding area. Unfortunately, there is a shortage of volunteers and the bush seems to grow back in almost as fast as it can be cleared. There are still hundreds of kilometres of cut lines and old roads in the area that can be ridden, just do not expect to find well-tended trails.

Snye Waterway (Map 69/A7)

The Snye is a quiet waterway that once linked the Athabasca and Clearwater Rivers but has since been dammed. Thick layers of ice cover the water during the winter allowing snowmobilers to access the trail systems across the river and into the boreal forest where there are plenty of cutlines to follow. It goes without saying to be sure the ice is safe before venturing out.

Stony Mountain Snowmobile Area (Map 55/A5)

There are about 46 km (28.5 miles) of signed and groomed trails in the area just north of the Stony Mountain Wildland Park. Access to the staging area can be found just south of Stoney Mountain Road off Range Road 91A. The main trail is a loop trail that passes by a couple of lakes and a fire pit area. This route is very scenic with lots of wild game, including caribou, which are sensitive to disturbances. Please be cautious of industry in the area and be respectful of wildlife when riding.

Swan Hills Snowmobile Trails (Map 7/D3–G4)

This area offers over 65 km (40 miles) of riding including cutlines, logging roads and trails. Some trails are signed, but may or may not be groomed. However heading south via the Golden Triangle Trails it is 115 km (71 miles) to Whitecourt or 112 km (70 miles) to Fox Creek, on groomed and well-marked trails. Camping and staging areas can be found at the southeast corner of Krause Lake, 6 km south of Swan Hills or at the Trapper Leas Recreation Area. In addition to a series of loop trails, these systems join up with the Golden Triangle System to provide over 340 km (211 miles) of trails.

Thickwood Towers Snowmobile Area (Map 68/F6–D7)

The local McMurray Sno-Drifters maintain a number of trails in the Fort McMurray area and this is the largest groomed and signed area. There are approximately 69 km (43 miles) of groomed trails and about another 100 km (62 miles) of ungroomed, unsigned trails. There are two fire pits along the groomed section of trail, which form a series of interconnected loops in the Thickwood Tower area. The longest loop follows the Syncrude Powerline.

Timeu Riding Area (Map 8/F6)

In the summer, Timeu Off-Highway Vehicle Area is one of this region's only designated Off Highway Vehicle riding areas. In the winter, it becomes the heart of the Fort Assiniboine Trails. The riding is informal, with no groomed routes or signed trails, but the most popular routes are usually well tracked. The staging area is found about 40 km north of Barrhead and about 1 km west of Klondyke Crossing Ferry off Secondary Highway 661.

Trans-Canadian Snowmobile Trail (Maps 5–7)

When completed the Trans Canadian Trail will be the world's longest recreational trail, stretching approximately 22,500 km (13,980 mile), and will link over 1,000 communities across Canada. More than 16,500 km of trail has been completed. The Alberta portion is not fully finished, but it is still possible to ride from Saskatchewan through to British Columbia.

The Alberta section runs through the southern section of this mapbook following the Golden Triangle Route around Whitecourt in the west and Alberta's Iron Horse Trail around Cold Lake in the east. North and south the trail continues alongside the highways eventually linking Fox Creek and Little Smoky with Peace River the city and then Fort St John in BC. There are many unofficial trails running up to places like Valleyview and beyond plus water routes, like the Athabasca River Trail that heads north into the Northwest Territories. Plans exist in the near future to link to the Big Mountain area south of Grande Prairie to the trail system near Dawson Creek in BC.

Tucker Lake Area (Map 13/F7)

Found just west of Cold Lake, the area north of Tucker Lake offers lots of opportunity to explore. You can head north up to Bourque Lake, which is approximately 20 km from Tucker Lake, or northwest to Marguerite Lake. The series of old roads and cutlines in the area allow for unlimited riding; just be careful not to venture too far north and into the Cold Lake Air Weapons Range. You can easily spend the day exploring this area.

Many of the major settlements have a snowmobile club that looks after a patch of snowmobile trails. For more information and to find your local club, check out www.altasnowmobile.ab.ca.

Vista Ridge Snowmobile Area (Map 55/C1)

East of Fort McMurray, about 23.5 km (14.6 miles) of groomed and signed snowmobile trails are found west of the Vista Ridge Ski area, between Highway 69 and the Clearwater River. The main trail is an old railway line that starts at the Waterways Staging area and follows the Draper Trail to Vista Ridge. Further south, there are 72 km (45 miles) worth of groomed and signed cutlines, powerlines and trails that make up this series of loops between Vista Ridge and Anzac. The Vista Ridge to Anzac Snowmobile Route crosses the railway track; caution is needed making this crossing.

Watt Mountain Snowmobile Trails (Map 86/C1)

The Watt Mountain Wanderers Snowmobile Club takes their name from this mountain, found northwest of High Level. There are a number of staging areas off Highway 58 or 35 for this series of trails that lead up and around Mount Watt. The club also maintains a cabin southwest of Hutch Lake. This is a large, sprawling area with well over 350 km (217 miles) of groomed trails to explore.

Wembley Snowmobile Trails (Map 16/D3)

South of the town of Wembley is a riding area that leads around the Wapiti River. South of the river a series of cutlines and old and new roads can be linked with the trails heading north from the Two Lakes Area. The local snowmobile club offers groomed trails and a cabin, as well as poker races here.

Westlock Snowmobile Trails (Map 9/E6)

While Westlock itself is not to be found on these maps (see the Central Alberta Mapbook), its snowmobile trails are. There are 150 km (93 miles) of signed trails found about half an hour north of town on Highway 44. Maintained by the Pembina Drift Busters, there are two warm up shacks along the route system.

Wildlife
Adventures

The north is renowned for its abundant wildlife and is home to many species of animals and birds. Deer, moose and even elk are commonly seen along the sides of highways. Sometimes, especially in the winter and late at night, they are seen standing in the middle of the highway. Be cautious!

There are no specially designated viewing spots for large mammals in this area, with one notable exception.

Wood Buffalo National Park is not only home to many bison, which are commonly seen in the Sweetwater Station area, it is also home to a unique salt flats area, which is accessed off the Pine Lake Road. These salt flats attract a wide variety of animals, especially bison, elk, moose and deer. And where there is prey, there are predators, too. While wolves themselves are not a common sight, they do frequent this area, and it is quite common to find signs of wolf.

Rounding out the list of large mammals are bear, usually black though occasionally grizzly. These big creatures are commonly seen alongside the roads of northern Alberta.

Some wildlife is easy to spot. If you were to go to Hay-Zama Lakes Provincial Park at the right time, you could not turn around without seeing another duck. On the other hand, many birds and animals tend to flee when they hear, see or smell humans. In order to improve your chances of spotting these more elusive creatures, wear natural colours and unscented lotions. Bring along binoculars or scopes so you can observe from a distance and move slowly but steadily. Keep pets on a leash, or better yet, leave them at home, as they will only decrease your chances to spot wildlife. Early mornings and late evenings are usually the best time to see most birds and animals.

Never approach an animal directly and, do not try to bring animals to you by offering them food. Animals can become conditioned to handouts, which may put both of you into harm's way. Rather, figure out what natural foods they prefer, and situate yourself near where these animals will feed.

This list is certainly far from complete list of everywhere you can see a bird or beast. Because the larger mammals are so common, the following areas tend to emphasize bird-watching areas. As most of these areas focus around parks, there is a good chance to see other animals too. For those looking for their wildlife not quite so wild, there are a number of elk and bison farms scattered throughout the Peace (southwest) region.

Wildlife Adventures

Birch Mountains Wildland Provincial Park (Map 79/E2–80/B2)
Besides Wood Buffalo National Park, Birch Mountains is home to one of Canada's only free-roaming herds of wood bison. Access to this park is only for the keen as there are no roads; you will have to charter a floatplane or hike or snowmobile your way in the winter. The diverse ecosystem also provides a home for osprey and bald eagle as well as over 30 species of spider.

Calling Lake Provincial Park (Map 24/D5)
Found about 55 km north of Athabasca, Calling Lake Provincial Park is a birder destination. Visitors will be able to view a wide variety of bird species including, but not limited to, American white pelican and great blue heron along with a number of other waterfowl.

Chinchaga Wildland Provincial Park (Map 71/B2)
The Chinchaga Wildland Provincial Park, located near the headwaters of the Chinchaga River, is the habitat of grizzly bear, woodland caribou and trumpeter swan. The area here is not easily accessible by road as it's mainly a very poor soft, muddy and rut filled 4wd trail.

Cold Lake (Map 14/F7)
Cold Lake is a barrier to migration as birds fly around the edge of the lake, concentrating their numbers. About 200 species of birds have been seen in the area. Look for teal, loon, mallard, flycatcher, sparrow, thrush wood warbler, solitary vireo, western tanger, golden-crowned kinglet, brown creeper, blackburnian and Cape May and bay-breasted warbler. Also keep your eyes peeled for mink along the shoreline. The park at the south end of the lake has an observation platform overlooking Hall's Lagoon, while one of the largest colonies of western grebes is found at Centre Bay.

Colin-Cornwall Lakes Wildland Park (Map 97/C3)
Located in the far northeastern corner of the province, this park is about 340 km north of Fort McMurray in the northeastern corner of the province and only accessed by air. Birding is very popular as the park is home to a number of bird species due to the large number of lakes. Some species include the provincially rare mew gull and semipalmated plover.

Cotillion Park (Map 44/A3)
Located north of Grand Prairie, this park is located close to the BC/Alberta border. Visitors will be able to see unusual geographic features like hoodoos and high cliffs along with beaver, black bear, moose and bald eagle.

Cross Lake Provincial Park (Map 9/F4)
The fish ladder at the west end of Steele Lake is a great place to watch spawning northern pike. The park is also home to a large population of birds of prey, including osprey and great blue heron, both of which nest around Steele Lake. The wooded uplands are home to a wide variety of birds and mammals. Visitors will see red squirrel, snowshoe hare, moose, bear and deer. Birders can spot ruffed grouse, sparrow and several warbler species. In the winter, it is a great place to see Bohemian waxwing, white-winged crossbill and pine grosbeak.

Cummings Lake (Map 45/F5)
While not as prolific a birding site as some other lakes in this region (like Kimiwan or Winigami), the 75 species of various birds found here—songbirds, shorebirds and waterfowl—are nothing to sneeze at.

Fort Assiniboine Sandhills Wildland Park (Map 8/E7)
There are an abundance of birds and animals to see in this large area. The open forests of the sandhills make for good habitat for mule and white-tailed deer and moose, while the trees host great gray owl, Cooper's hawk, sandhill crane and pileated woodpecker. The wetlands are also home to beaver, mink, muskrat and river otter.

George Lake Campground (Map 45/E3)
The area surrounding this popular campsite, located off Highway 64 near Hines Creek, provides prime wildlife viewing for birders. There are a recorded 28 species of birds, including three different types of owl, 19 different mammals and 5 amphibians/reptiles including three species of frog. There are merlin, raven, great blue heron as well as different types of ducks, coots and swans.

Goose Mountain Ecological Reserve (Map 6/F2)
The draw to Goose Mountain is more flora than fauna. At 1,180 metres (3,835 feet) above sea level, the Swan Hills area is the highest point in Canada, east of the Rockies. Goose Mountain is 45 km north of town and the 5,780 hectare area is home to unique plant life, including 16 plant species that are rare to Alberta; even some orchids. The area is highly sensitive, but is open to people on foot. Wildlife in the region includes mule and white-tailed deer, elk, moose, black bear and cougar.

Hay-Zama Lakes Wildland Park (Map 92/B7)
Established in 1999, this wildland park protects a large wetland complex which is good habitat for Woodland Caribou and one of the few wild populations of wood bison outside of Wood Buffalo National Park. However, the real reason this area is notable is that it is on the migration route for three of four North American Flyways, and it can see up to a million birds during the fall migration. Most notably are the ducks and geese, with upwards of 200,000 of each species passing through here in a peak year. Other birds include gulls, terns, raptors, and songbirds. All tolled, more than 100 species pass through this area. However, the area is not people-friendly and birders will have to either be content with watching from dry land outside the park, or be willing to make a very wet trek into the park. This park has also been targeted as a reintroduction place for the wood bison which are being kept apart from the herds of Wood Buffalo National park who have been having some disease issues.

Heart River Dam Recreation Area (Map 34/B6)
The recreation area located next to the dam and pond of its name sake is a popular birding location. Similar to the wildland park, visitors can find shorebirds and waterfowl like pipers, gulls, grebes and ducks. Also look for great blue herons and bald eagles.

Hubert Lake Wildland Park (Map 8/G5–9/B6)
A mix of small lakes, wetlands and sand dunes make up this wildland providing great habitat for wildlife. It is an important nesting area for sandhill crane and blue heron. Also a small herd of woodland caribou come in and out of the park on occasion.

Jackbird Pond (Map 44/F7)
Jackbird Pond is a part of Moonshine Lake Provincial Park, although it is not actually connected to the main body of the park itself. The pond is an important feeding area for trumpeter swan. There are two bird-viewing platforms connected by an interpretative trail where you will have a great vantage point to see all types of waterfowl, birds and mammals like beaver.

Kakwa Wildland Provincial Park (Map 1/B7)
Close to Grand Prairie, this wildland park encompasses the last part of the Canadian Rockies before the BC border. It's not a well frequented park, but has many wildlife viewing possibilities. Species include bighorn sheep and mountain goat; woodland caribou, elk, mule and white-tailed deer and moose; black and grizzly bear; lynx, wolverine, wolf and red fox.

Kimiwan Lake (Map 33/E3)
The town of McLennan, at the south end of Kimiwan Lake, is the self-proclaimed Bird Capital of Canada. As you might expect, there are great viewing opportunities here, especially during the migrations. There are literally thousands of waterfowl and migratory shorebirds, including the rare cinnamon teal. Predatory birds in the area include Merlin and northern goshawk.

The north is renowned for its abundant wildlife and is home to many species of animals and birds. Deer, moose and even elk are commonly seen along the sides of highways.

Kleskun Hill Natural Area (Map 17/C1)
This 65 hectare natural area is developed around a hill that stands 100 metres (325 feet) above the surrounding plains. It is the most northern occurrence of a badlands landscape in Alberta. Northern saw-whet owls, American kestrels, black terns and sharp-tailed grouse are typical birds that you may see here.

La Saline Natural Area (Map 68/G2)
This natural area is found north of Fort McMurray on the east side of the Athabasca River. It is best accessed by boat. Visitors will not only find a calcium carbonate Tufa cone, but Saline Lake is also one of the most important waterfowl lakes in the area. Species include thousands of ducks and geese that nest on the Peace-Athabasca Delta each year specifically mallard, bufflehead and green-winged teal, coots and widgeons.

Lesser Slave Lake Provincial Park (Map 22/D2–36/C7)

Lesser Slave Lake is a huge lake, and most birds fly around, rather than over the lake. As well, nearby Marten Mountain is too high to fly over, resulting in birds that are funnelled along the Slave Lake shoreline. The park is home to the Lesser Slave Lake Bird Observatory, and the viewing list they provide includes over 220 species of birds. The big draw here is the songbirds, and the area is designated an Important Bird Area by Canada Birdlife Partners for its songbirds. In addition, the large forested areas east of the highway are home to black and grizzly bear, deer, marten, and in the winter, lynx and gray wolf are frequently seen.

Many Islands Park (Map 44/F2)

Located on the shores of the Peace River south of Highway 64, birders can enjoy both the spring and fall bird migrations from this location. Birders will see many species of geese, including Canada goose, and ducks.

Muskoseepi Park (Map 17/A2)

Bear River runs through the heart of Grande Prairie and this long, thin park stretches along the ravine. A trail follows the creek, offering a view of wildlife in the city including small mammals, amphibians and reptiles. Crystal Lake, located in the northeast section of the city, also offers excellent bird watching opportunities.

Notikewin Provincial Park (Map 74/F3)

On the banks of the mighty Peace River lies this pretty park. It is home to sandhill cranes, raptors, moose, elk and deer. Black and grizzly bear can also be found here on occasion. The wooded upland area is home to songbirds. Cross the Notikewin River (which offers good fishing at its mouth) and hike through the southern end of the park where lodgepole and jack pine predominate. The open understory is a great place to spot birds and other woodland creatures.

Ole's Lake Recreation Area (Map 43/G1)

Located near the British Columbia border, this recreation area has many wildlife viewing opportunities. Species include beaver, moose, blue heron, loon and osprey.

Otauwau and Salteaux Natural Areas (Map 22/G4–23/B5)

The University of Alberta utilizes these two natural areas which are part of a trio of natural areas mainly used for botany research. The access is limited and the most interesting features here are the plants.

Peace River Wildland Provincial Park (Maps 31–32; 45–47)

Stretching out along the Peace River and Smoky River Valleys, this wildland park was formed to help protect the prime wildlife habitat in the area. Visitors will find wildlife like black bear, deer, elk and wolf to be abundant in the area.

Police Point Natural Area (Map 34/E6)

Birding is the main wildlife activity in this natural area that is found at the west end of Lesser Slave Lake on Buffalo Bay. The area is covered with wetlands and home to amphibians, reptiles, waterfowl, birds and small mammals like otter and beaver.

Poplar Creek (Map 68/G6)

A large gravel pit north of Fort McMurray provides good habitat for a variety of species. The shrub and open grasslands create forage for a deer that use the nearby stands of aspen and spruce to bed down. The area is also visited by Canada goose, great blue heron and sandhill crane.

Queen Elizabeth Provincial Park (Map 46/F4)

Over one hundred and sixty species of birds have been seen in this park including song birds and waterfowl. A bird-viewing platform with spotting scope is provided to help you see how many you can spot. Species include the common coot, red winged blackbird, ruffed grouse, great blue heron, northern oriole, robin, snipe and yellowlegs.

Saskatoon Island Provincial Park (Map 16/E2)

The park includes several habitats, including the best remaining example of Saskatoon scrublands in Northern Alberta. The dense shrubbery is loaded with berries come July. Bird watchers will enjoy viewing the large numbers of grassland, forest and lakeside birds. There is even a bird-viewing platform by Little Lake, complete with telescope. In autumn, hundreds of trumpeter and tundra swans converge on Saskatoon Lake for three weeks before their migration south. The area is designated by Canada Birdlife Partners as an Important Bird Area because of its globally significant swan habitat. There are also many smaller mammals here, including snowshoe hare, weasel, muskrat and beaver, as well as deer.

Saskatoon Mountain Natural Area (Map 16/C1)

Once a military base, this natural area is now a location for bird and wildlife viewing. Species include warblers, flycatchers and other song birds as well as coyote, mule deer, moose, snowshoe hare and Columbian ground squirrel.

Sir Winston Churchill Provincial Park (Map 12/B2)

Home to some grand stands of old-growth white and black spruce, balsam, birch and poplar, this provincial park is also home to the birds that inhabit these boreal forests. There are twenty species of wood warblers alone along with boreal owl, white-winged crossbill, Swainson's and hermit thrush and barred and Northern saw-whet owl. As you might expect, Pelican Viewpoint is a great place to observe American white pelican as well as California gull and double-crested cormorant. The best trail on which to find birds is the Long Point Trail. In the picnic area there are also Franklin's ground squirrels.

For people looking for their wildlife not quite so wild, there are a number of elk and bison farms scattered throughout the Peace region.

Slave River-Mountain Rapids (Map 96/F1)

Mountain Rapids are found right before the Slave River flows north out of Alberta. It is located at the junction of two ecosystems. The area is unusually diverse in flora and fauna, but the real draw here for bird watchers is a nesting island in the Slave River for American white pelican. The unique and perilous location is located in the heart of the thundering rapids. There is a viewpoint over the island.

Wadlin Lake (Map 87/C7)

This lake, found south of Fort Vermillion, is home to a colony of American white pelican.

Winagami Lake Provincial Park (Map 33/F4–34/A5)

More than 200 species of birds have been recorded at Winagami Lake Provincial Park. From the boat launch parking area, a short trail leads to a raised viewing platform, where you can watch the nesting grebes, sandpipers, ducks and gulls.

Winagami Wildland Provincial Park (Map 33/G6–34/B4)

While not as easy to access as Winagami Lake Provincial Park, this wildland park protects much the same habitat for birds, which include shorebirds and waterfowl like pipers, gulls, grebes and ducks. Great blue heron and bald eagle nest in large shoreline trees while white pelican forage on water bodies.

Wood Buffalo National Park (Maps 88–90, 94–97)

This huge, sprawling park protects much of the huge, sprawling Peace Athabasca delta. All four major migratory flyways converge on this area, and it is one of the world's greatest birding sites. Along with the only nesting area for the extremely rare whooping crane, Wood Buffalo the only park in Canada with two RAMSAR sites, an international designation given to critical habitat for migrating birds. (Only 37 RAMSAR sites have been designated in Canada). There is no public access to the nesting grounds. Of course, the park is also home to the largest herd of wood bison in Canada. These can frequently be seen in the salt plains (along with other large mammals), as well as in the open delta around Sweetgrass Station.

Young's Point Provincial Park (Map 18/E4)

Over 150 bird species nest in or pass through this park, which offers about 7 km (4.4 miles) of shoreline habitat for shorebirds and waterfowl. The nearby boreal forest provides a great home for songbirds. Moose and deer are frequently seen in the park as well.

Winter
Adventures

Winter recreation is big in northern Alberta, and it's no wonder—winter takes up almost half the year. Rather than hide away and wait for summer, Albertans face winter head-on, seeing it as an opportunity for excitement and not just that long, cold stretch between autumn and spring.

There's a whole lot to do outdoors in the winter, but the most popular pursuits by far are skiing (cross-country or Nordic) and snowmobiling. There are also a few small downhill ski areas in northern Alberta, including one near Grande Prairie and another near Fort McMurray.

For cross-country skiers, most of the developed ski systems appear around parks and recreation areas, but there are also many old roads and cutlines that make great winter getaways on skis. Even if there is no maintained trail system, most provincial parks offer some form of cross-country skiing, either along snow-covered hiking trails or out on frozen lakes. Most of the larger communities also maintain some sort of cross-country skiing area. Where there are no local ski clubs, cross-country skiers head over to the nearest community, or explore local trails, cutlines and snow-covered logging roads.

Snowshoeing has increased in popularity over the past few years. Many trails that once sat unused during winter are seeing use by snowshoers, who can go most anywhere there is a trail – and many places where there aren't. Folks will even go snowshoeing on frozen lakes and rivers, just for fun. While we can't say we recommend this, be sure that the waterbody is fully and thoroughly frozen should you choose to go. Because snowshoeing can be done anywhere, there are no areas in northern Alberta set aside specifically for snowshoers. In fact, about the only place that snowshoers shouldn't go is onto groomed cross-country ski trails. Check out the trails section for some possibilities.

As always, avalanches are a hazard when travelling through the mountains in winter. Although this applies only to folks riding in the southwestern corner of this book, it is a good idea to always carry an avalanche beacon and never travel alone in these areas. More problematic in northern Alberta are rivers and creeks, which are not always as solid as one might think. Always make sure of ice thickness before heading out. Remember: when in doubt, stick to groomed routes.

The most important thing to bear in mind when exploring the winter landscapes of northern Alberta is safety. In addition to checking for ice thickness, wear proper winter gear, and don't forget the sunscreen. Once you're suited up and well-prepared, northern Alberta becomes a frozen playground. You'll never want to hibernate again.

Cold Lake Provincial Park (Map 14/F6)

Cold Lake Provincial Park is a beautiful setting in the winter, set on a peninsula jutting into Cold Lake, with rolling hills covered in a mixed-wood forest. There are 13 km (7.9 miles) of mostly short trails here that are groomed fairly regularly. While the trails are groomed for skate and classic skiing, you may need to share them with snowshoers. There is no fee to use this area.

Dunvegan Nordic Ski Club (Maps 45/D4, 45/F5)

The Dunvegan Nordic Ski and Bike Club is based out of Fairview and volunteers groom classic and free trails near the town as well as the Sand Hills Lake area (snow permitting) throughout the winter months. Closer to town, the trails around Cummings Lake are usually packed and groomed by early December. Getting to the Sand Lake area depends on how far the road is ploughed, although the road itself is usually track set if it is not ploughed. If you contact the club when you are in the area, they would be happy to provide you with current trail information.

Fairview Ski Hill (Map 45/D6)

Located 13 km south of Fairview on Highway 2, then 6 km west, this is a small but surprisingly vibrant ski area with 15 runs, four lifts and all manner of features like a Terrain Park and all the amenities you would expect, including rentals and a cafeteria. No, it's not going to be mistaken for Mount Norquay with the mere 153 metre (505 foot) vertical elevation, but it is lit for night skiing and a day pass is quite inexpensive. The ski hill also offers a hill for tobogganing and tubing at no charge. Watch out for the moose, who occasionally wander through the property.

Figure Eight Lake Recreation Area (Map 46/D3)

There are 5 km (3 miles) of ungroomed trails that can be enjoyed by skiers and snowshoers at Figure Eight Lake. The recreation site is located 25 km west of Peace River off Secondary Highway 737.

Fort McMurray Ski Trails (Maps 68, 69)

Fort McMurray has a good selection of cross-country ski trails to explore. From city greenbelts to the more established Birchwood Trail System, there is something here for all levels of skiers.

Birchwood Trail System (Map 68/G7)

The Ptarmigan Nordic Club maintains a 35 km (21.8 mi) trail system consisting of ten named trails located in Fort McMurray. The trails offer something for all levels of skier, from beginner to expert, with the longest of the groomed trails is the Deer Trail, at 5.5 km (3.3 miles). The parking area and the Doug Barnes Ski Cabin, is located just off Thickwood Boulevard, although access can be found at other spots throughout the residential community which surrounds the forest. There are dozens of kilometres of ungroomed trails in the area.

Central Reserve Ski Trail (Map 68/G7)

This 3.5 km (2.1 mi) cross-country ski trail designed for beginners in Fort McMurray runs from Hillcrest Drive to Hinge Road.

Little Fisheries Creek (Map 68/G7)

This set of trails is accessed off Real Martin Drive in Fort McMurray. The 15 km (9 mile) set of ungroomed trails is a little challenging and is best left to experienced skiers.

McDonald Island (Map 69/A7)

This 7 km (4.2 mile) series of trails is located at the Miskanaw Golf Course in Fort McMurray. The trails are set and groomed for Nordic style skiing and open during daylight hours. Skiers are asked to check in with guest services before entering the golf course.

Ross Haven Loop Trail (Map 69/A7)

This easy 2 km (1.25 mi) trail follows the greenbelt on Ross Haven Drive in Fort McMurray.

Timberline Drive Loop Trail (Map 69/A7)

The Timberline Drive Loop in Fort McMurray offers a 3 km (1.9 mi) double track that follows the greenbelt and joins the Birchwood Trail System via a cut line on Tamarack Way.

Fort Smith Area (Map 96/G1)

Although located in the Northwest Territories, Fort Smith does sit right on the border of Alberta and is adjacent to Wood Buffalo National Park. Summer hiking trails, along with gravel roads and frozen rivers, become cross-country ski routes in the winter months. The frozen Slave River becomes the main access route to and from town. The Fort Smith Ski Club maintains a network of trails, groomed for classic and skate skiing, which travel through boreal forests and offer great panoramic views of the Slave River. The club also organizes the Fitz-Loppet each March. Skiers of all levels can take part in the event. The trail follows an old portage route that bi-passes the Slave River and is part of the Trans-Canada Trail.

Those who wish to strap on a pair of snowshoes will find there aren't too many places they can't go in the backcountry around Fort Smith.

Gregoire Lake Provincial Park (Map 55/C3)

Located 29 km southeast of Fort McMurray on Secondary Highway 881, there are 10 km (6 miles) of groomed ski trails in this popular provincial park. Snowmobilers use the boat launch area to access the lake (when the ice is safe) and there is also ice fishing.

Grizzly Ridge Nordic Ski Area (Map 22/C5)

This area once featured both downhill and cross-country skiing, but the downhill area is closed. Cross-country skiers can still utilize the trail system here, which features over 25 km (15.5 miles) of trails.

Hilliard's Bay Provincial Park (Map 34/F7)

There are 10 km (6.2 miles) of groomed trails in this park, which is found on the shores of Lesser Slave Lake. There are two main trails, the Beach Ridge Trail and the Spruce Bay Trail. The Spruce Bay Trail is the more difficult of the two since it traverses the rolling terrain along the lake. One of the loops is kept open for winter camping and there is a warm-up shelter.

For cross-country skiers, most of the developed ski systems are found around parks and recreation areas, but there are also many old roads and cutlines that make great winter getaways on skis.

Iosegun Lake Provincial Recreation Area (Map 5/D5)

This recreation area north of the town of Fox Creek offers cross-country skiing in the winter months. If venturing out on the lake, please ensure the ice is safe.

Kinosoo Ridge Ski Area (Map 14/G4)

There are ten named runs at Kinosoo Ridge on French Bay, next to Cold Lake Provincial Park. Once you get to the top with either the triple chair or T-bar, the hill offers skiers an interesting choice: heading left brings you into Saskatchewan, while staying right keeps you in Alberta. The full-service resort has a total elevation of 183 metres (600 feet), natural and man-made snow, night skiing, a snow tube area, and a terrain park.

Lesser Slave Lake Provincial Park (Map 22/D1)

There is a warm up shelter and 17.8 km (11 miles) of groomed trails at this large provincial park. Trails include the easy 600 metre Songbird Trail, the 4 km BCBC to Lily Creek Trail and the 8.4 Northshore to BCBC Trail. The difficult 4.8 km Devonshire Beach to Northshore Trail travels behind ancient sand dunes and through a Jack pine forest. Watch for bison in this area during the winter months. The parking area is found off Highway 88 north of the town of Slave Lake.

Little Smoky Ski Hill (Map 33/B7)

Found near where Highway 43 crosses the Little Smoky River, this small community hill has seven downhill runs, a T-bar and a bunny hill. You will also find a skating rink and a tube park in the area. For cross-country enthusiasts, there are 10 km (6 miles) of ski trails in and around the Little Smoky River valley that start from the ski hill.

Manning and District Ski Club (Map 61/B2)

Not to be confused with BC's Manning Park Resort, this smaller hill is located 8 km east of Manning on Highway 691, then 5 km north on Range Road 224. The ski hill features a T-bar and five different runs. There is a chalet and ski rentals available.

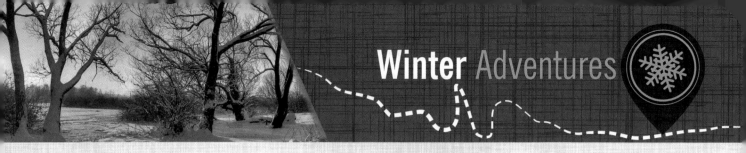

Misery Mountain Ski Hill (Map 47/B4)

Calling this a mountain is perhaps a bit of an overstatement, as the ski area is located on the west side of the Peace River and is less a hill than it is a valley. It is found in the town of Peace River and is off Shaftsbury Trail (Secondary Highway 684). It features a tee-bar and a handful of mostly easy to moderate runs. There is also a terrain park. Snowshoers can enjoy the trails in the ski area or make their own.

Moonshine Lake Provincial Park (Map 44/E7)

There are a number of cross-country ski trails at the south end of Moonshine Lake, the longest of which is Logger's Lane, at 3.1 km (1.9 miles) long. The trails run through a mix of meadows, shrubs and an open aspen forest. Other trails include Moose Meadows and the Muskeg Mile, which passes through small spruce and aspen. All told, there are 21 km (13 miles) of groomed ski trails here offering a range of easy to more difficult trails.

Nitehawk Ski Area (Map 16/G4)

Located south of Grande Prairie, just across the Wapiti River, this small downhill ski area is built on the banks of the river. There are nine runs, one triple chair and a bunny hill. There are also two terrain parks and all the trails are fully lit for night skiing. The runs are broken up evenly between novice, intermediate and expert terrain.

O'Brien Provincial Park (Map 16/G3)

There are no groomed trails at O'Brien and the gates are closed in the winter. Most area skiers head for the groomed Wapiti Nordic Trails across the river, but it is possible to ski or snowshoe into the park along the untrammelled road or follow the 4 km (2.5 mi) O'Brien Park Trail, a summer hiking trail through the park.

Police Point Natural Area (Map 34/F6)

The Police Point Natural Area is located off Secondary Road 750 on the eastern shore of Buffalo Bay of Lesser Slave Lake. The area contains a section of the Grouard Trail, which was a major route for traders, missionaries and settlers travelling to the Peace Country. The area has a fair bit of wildlife and the trails that wind through the area can be used for cross-country skiing and snowshoeing in the winter months. There are no facilities at the site so those wishing to enjoy the area are advised to plan ahead.

Queen Elizabeth Provincial Park (Map 46/F4)

There are 4.5 km (2.8 miles) of groomed trails maintained in the woods of this park on the shores of Lac Cardinal. Snowshoers are asked to stay off the ski tracks.

Rocky Lane Ski Trails (Map 87/A2)

Located in the small community of Rocky Lane, these easy trails travel through the Ponton River Valley. There are two main areas; one on the flats above the river, one in the valley itself. When the river is frozen, the two areas can be connected by crossing the river. All told, there are 13 km (8.1 miles) of mostly easy and intermediate skiing in the area, groomed for both classic and skate skiing. The Oxbow Loop offers skiers a backcountry skiing experience. Skis can be rented at the Skate Shack, which is located at the trailhead and open Friday afternoons and weekends. There is usually enough snow to ski from December to March and dogs are allowed on all the trails.

Sand Lakes Natural Area (Map 45/D4)

This natural area is found 15 km northwest of Fairview and home to a couple of cross-country ski trails. The longest trail is the 7 km (3.6 mile) long Sand Lake Loop. The other trail is the 2.5 km (1.5 mile) Overhill-Underhill Loop. The Dunvegan Nordic Ski Club maintains these trails, although care needs to be taken in low snow years, as there are places, usually under larger trees, where there may be bare patches. Access depends on how far the road is ploughed, although the club does track set the road for classic skiing too. Once on the trails, please follow the signs and remember to ski the loops counter clockwise.

Saskatoon Island Provincial Park (Map 16/E2)

There is 6.4 km (4 miles) of groomed trails at Saskatoon Island Park. These scenic trails are often less busy than those found closer to Grande Prairie. The trails are great for beginner to intermediate skiers and feature many bird species.

Saskatoon Mountain Natural Area (Map 16/C1)

Found west of Grande Prairie, there is an ungroomed network of ski and snowshoe trails through this natural area.

Shaw Lake Trails (Map 12/E3)

Maintained by the Lac La Biche Nordic Ski Club, the main trail in the Lakeland Provincial Park is a 26.5 km (16.5 mile) long trail that follows the shores of Shaw Lake. There are a variety of other trails in the area, from 1–11 km (0.6–6.7 miles) long. The trails are groomed for cross-country skiing and snowshoeing is also popular here. There is a warming hut at the trailhead and no trail fees.

Sir Winston Churchill Park Trails (Map 12/B2)

In the winter, this park is open to cross-country skiing. All tolled, there are 8 km (5 miles) of ungroomed trails/roadway to ski. The park is located 13 km northeast of the town of Lac La Biche on Secondary Highway 881.

Spring Lake Recreation Area (Map 30/A4)

Spring Lake was built in 1974 by Proctor and Gamble as a year round recreation area. In winter, there is a downhill ski area and 26 km (15.6 miles) of groomed cross-country ski trails to enjoy.

Swan Hills Cross-Country Trails (Map 7/D3)

Just south of Swan Hills, there are 8 km (5 miles) of groomed cross-country ski trails, ranging from easy to moderately tough. The trails go through a variety of landscapes including mature timber stands, lowlands, muskeg and the site of a 1972 forest fire. There is a warm-up shelter at the trailhead.

Vista Ridge Ski Area (Map 55/D1)

Located just east of Fort McMurray, this small ski hill has one quad chair, a rope tow and eight named runs. In fact, it's not really a ski hill, as the parking area is at the top and you ski into the Clearwater River Valley. There is a terrain park, a halfpipe, a tubing park and even a luge track. As an added bonus, there is snowmaking equipment and lights for night skiing.

Wapiti Nordic Centre (Map 16/G3)

Found 6 km (3.7 miles) south of Grande Prairie on Highway 40, this is a full service area run by the Wapiti Nordic Ski Club. There are over 35 km (21.7 miles) of ski trails for both classic and skate skiing in the dunes above the Wapiti River. 4 km (2.4 miles) of trail is lit for night skiing and rentals are available at the lodge. There is even a biathlon range to help train future Olympians.

Whispering Pines Ski Hill (Map 58/D5)

A family-oriented ski hill found northeast of Worsley, it is not uncommon to see deer, moose and fox run across the runs. In total there over 19 runs for downhill skiers and snowboarders to enjoy, a terrain park as well as a connecting series of cross-country ski trails. The view from the top of the hill and the lack of crowds makes this a nice hill to visit.

Winagami Lake Provincial Park (Map 33/G5)

Winagami Lake Provincial Park features 12.5 km (7.8 mi) of groomed trails for classic skiing. The two shorter, 1 km and 2 km, trails are designed for beginners while the more difficult 9 km (5.6 mi) trail has more hills and will challenge most. Snowshoers are welcome to explore parks virgin snow but are asked to refrain from travelling on the groomed ski trails. Look for access to the system off the north side of Secondary Highway 679.

Wood Buffalo National Park (Maps 88–90, 94–97)

For those rugged, self-sufficient outdoor adventurers, a winter trip to Wood Buffalo can offer a great experience. There are no tracked trails in the park so a compass and map will be required by those wishing to ski and snowshoe here. Temperatures can dip to -40°C at night but the area offers spectacular viewing of the Aurora Borealis (Northern Lights) and is growing as a winter destination. A winter road, open from mid-December to mid-March depending on conditions, runs from Fort McMurray up to Fort Chipewyan where it continues through the park to Fort Smith offers a southern access route. Alternatively, a year round road off the MacKenzie Highway allows access to the park headquarters at Fort Smith from the north. It is recommended that visitors plan their trips between late-March through April when the temperatures are slightly warmer and the days longer.

Young's Point Provincial Park (Map 18/E4)

There are 12.5 km (7.8 miles) of groomed trails to explore here. Much like Winagami, there are two short trails of 2.5 km and 3 km for beginners and a longer 7 km trail for intermediate skiers. In addition to skiing, there is a lit rink to skate on, ice-fishing and even the option to snowmobile across the lake from the boat launch area…just make sure the ice is safe first.

Industry Resource

Central Alberta

Map 3

Gas Plants

Canadian Natural Resources Limited ....
.... 03/E3
LSD...............10-10-065-02W6
City.................................Grande Prairie
Phone#..........................780 831-7475

Paramount Resources Ltd 03/A4
LSD...............08-13-063-05W6
City.................................Grande Prairie
Phone#..........................780 882-6635

Seven Generations Energy Ltd...........03/E4
LSD...............01-21-063-02W6
City.................................Drayton Valley
Phone#..........................780 515-9190

Twin Butte Energy Ltd.......................03/C6
LSD...............06-08-062-03W6
City..Calgary
Phone#..........................403 215-2045

Map 4

Gas Plants

ARC Resources Ltd 04/D2
LSD...............10-36-065-25W5
City.......................................Valleyview
Phone#..........................780 524-4355

Canadian Natural Resources Limited ....
.... 04/E4
LSD...............15-07-064-23W5
City.......................................Valleyview
Phone#..........................780 524-5496

Canadian Natural Resources Limited ....
....04/F2
LSD...............10-04-066-23W5
City.......................................Valleyview
Phone#..........................780 524-5496

Canadian Natural Resources Limited ....
.... 04/G6
LSD...............06-05-063-22W5
City.......................................Valleyview
Phone#..........................780 524-5496

Keyera Energy Ltd 04/B5
LSD...............09-06-063-25W5
City.................................Drayton Valley
Phone#..........................780 894-7000

Trilogy Resources Ltd 04/C5
LSD...............01-15-063-25W5
City..Fox Creek
Phone#..........................780 622-3739

Work Camps

DJ Catering Open Camps....................04/C5
LSD...............12-10-063-25W5
City...Swan Hills
Phone#..........................877 212-3391

Horizon North Camp & Catering Partnership
.... 04/B4
LSD...............09-22-064-26W5
City.......................................Valleyview
Phone#..........................403 990-3633

Map 5

Gas Plants

Firenze Energy Ltd..............................05/A6
LSD...............10-24-062-22W5

SemCAMS ULC 05/D7
LSD...............01-12-062-20W5
City.......................................Whitecourt
Phone#..........................780 778-7800

Sinopec Daylight Energy Ltd 05/G7
LSD...............05-36-061-18W5
City.......................................Whitecourt

Phone#..........................780 778-5052

Trilogy Resources Ltd 05/B4
LSD...............06-16-064-21W5
City..Fox Creek
Phone#..........................780 622-3739

Trilogy Resources Ltd 05/E5
LSD...............08-09-064-19W5
City..Fox Creek
Phone#..........................780 622-3739

Well Disposal

CCS Midstream Services....................05/C6
LSD...............03-29-062-20W5
City..Fox Creek
Phone#..........................780 622-3355

Secure Energy Services......................05/C6
LSD...............09-22-062-20W5
City..Fox Creek
Phone#..........................780 622-8277

Map 6

Gas Plants

AltaGas Ltd...06/D7
LSD...............01-15-062-15W5
City...Athabasca
Phone#..........................780 675-1249

Apache Canada Ltd.............................06/F5
LSD...............10-17-064-13W5
City.......................................Whitecourt
Phone#..........................780 369-7100

Penn West Petroleum Ltd 06/D6
LSD...............06-12-063-15W5
City.......................................Whitecourt
Phone#..........................780 778-8502

Trilogy Resources Ltd 06/B6
LSD...............07-04-063-16W5
City..Fox Creek
Phone#..........................780 622-3739

Map 7

Gas Plants

Pengrowth Energy Corporation...........07/C5
LSD...............15-25-064-11W5
City..Calgary
Phone#..........................403 233-0224

Second Wave Petroleum Inc 07/D6
LSD...............08-24-063-10W5
City..Calgary
Phone#..........................403 451-0165

Well Disposal

CCS Midstream Services....................07/B7
LSD...............04-05-063-11W5
City.......................................Whitecourt
Phone#..........................780 778-1970

Map 8

Gas Plants

Apache Canada Ltd.............................08/F4
LSD...............05-27-065-04W5
City.......................................Whitecourt
Phone#..........................780 369-7100

TAQA North Ltd 08/F7
LSD...............12-25-062-04W5
City.......................................Whitecourt
Phone#..........................780 778-4694

Trident Exploration (Alberta) Corp......08/B6
LSD...............11-17-063-06W5
City..................................Fort Assiniboine
Phone#..........................780 584-2102

Trident Exploration (Alberta) Corp......08/C7
LSD...............07-25-062-06W5
City..................................Fort Assiniboine
Phone#..........................780 584-2102

Map 9

Gas Plants

Canadian Natural Resources Limited ....
.... 09/D3
LSD...............13-36-066-27W4
City...Slave Lake
Phone#..........................780 849-2910

Husky Oil Operations Limited 09/D7
LSD...............08-35-062-27W4
City...Athabasca
Phone#..........................780 675-4950

Husky Oil Operations Limited 09/E5
LSD...............04-26-064-26W4
City...Athabasca
Phone#..........................780 675-4950

Map 10

Gas Plants

Sinopec Daylight Energy Ltd 10/B2
LSD...............08-18-068-23W4
City..St Albert
Phone#..........................780 458-0599

Well Disposal

Duniece Bros Trucking Ltd.................10/F1
LSD...............07-28-068-20W4
City...Athabasca
Phone#..........................780 525-2262

Work Camps

Athabasca Open Camp Ltd...............10/G4
LSD.......................SW 21-066-20W4
City...Athabasca
Phone#..........................780 499-3670

Map 15

Gas Plants

Conocophillips Canada Energy Partnership..
....15/F1
LSD...............04-19-072-11W6
City.................................Grande Prairie
Phone#..........................780 539-3007

CONOCOPHILLIPS CANADA OPERATIONS
LTD 15/G3
LSD...............SE-08-070-11W6
City.................................Grande Prairie
Phone#..........................780 539-3007

Map 16

Gas Plants

Devon Canada 16/C6
LSD...............16-36-067-09W6
City.................................Grande Prairie
Phone#..........................780 402-8871

Devon Canada 16/D5
LSD...............04-08-069-08W6
City.................................Grande Prairie
Phone#..........................780 402-8871

Well Disposal

Newalta Corporation 16/G3
LSD...............06-02-071-06W6
City.................................Grande Prairie
Phone#..........................780 539-1845

Secure Energy Services......................16/G5
LSD...............06-36-068-06W6
City.................................Grande Prairie
Phone#..........................866 206-5395

Map 17

Gas Plants

Birchcliff Energy Ltd...........................17/D3
LSD...............01-18-071-03W6
City..Spirit River

Phone#..........................780 864-4633

Canadian Natural Resources Limited ....
.... 17/A6
LSD...............13-26-067-05W6
City.................................Grande Prairie
Phone#..........................780 831-7475

Well Disposal

CCS Midstream Services....................17/A5
LSD...............15-13-069-06W6
City.................................Grande Prairie
Phone#..........................780 539-6917

Newalta Corporation 17/A1
LSD...............16-35-072-06W6
City..Clairmont
Phone#..........................780 539-1845

Newalta Corporation 17/A3
LSD...............06-02-071-06W6
City.................................Grande Prairie
Phone#..........................780 539-1845

Wapiti Waste Management Inc..........17/A4
LSD...............15-07-070-05W6
City..Clairmont
Phone#..........................780 876-2094

Map 18

Gas Plants

AltaGas Ltd...18/D6
LSD...............02-26-068-25W5
City....................................Fort St John
Phone#..........................250 785-9655

Barrick Energy Inc..............................18/B2
LSD...............03-03-072-26W5
City.......................................Valleyview
Phone#..........................780 524-3341

Harvest Operations Corp 18/A3
LSD...............02-30-071-26W5
City.................................Grande Prairie
Phone#..........................780 833-4037

NAL Resources Limited 18/D6
LSD...............13-07-069-24W5
City..Eckville
Phone#..........................403 746-2222

Well Disposal

Newalta Corporation 18/G6
LSD...............04-21-069-22W5
City.......................................Valleyview
Phone#..........................780 524-4336

Map 19

Gas Plants

AltaGas Ltd...19/G3
LSD...............06-24-072-18W5
City...Athabasca
Phone#..........................780 675-1249

Barrick Energy Inc 19/A6
LSD...............02-02-069-22W5
City.......................................Valleyview
Phone#..........................780 524-3341

Longview Oil Corp 19/D5
LSD...............06-22-070-20W5
City..Calgary
Phone#..........................403 718-8000

Well Disposal

CCS Midstream Services....................19/A6
LSD...............09-16-069-22W5
City.......................................Valleyview
Phone#..........................780 524-3336

Newalta Corporation 19/A6
LSD...............04-21-069-22W5
City.......................................Valleyview

Resource Index

City..High Level
Phone#................................780 841-3456
Long Run Exploration Ltd...................32/G3
LSD..................................04-21-078-23W5
City..High Level
Phone#................................780 841-3456
Sinopec Daylight Energy Ltd.............32/A6
LSD..................................01-16-075-01W6
City...Grande Prairie
Phone#................................780 538-0840

Map 33

Gas Plants

Long Run Exploration Ltd....................33/C5
LSD..................................06-01-077-21W5
City...Redwater
Phone#................................780 942-3300

Map 34

Gas Plants

Canadian Natural Resources Limited ....
....34/C2
LSD..................................08-26-079-16W5
City...Valleyview
Phone#................................780 524-5496

Map 35

Gas Plants

Celtic Exploration ULC........................35/F1
LSD..................................13-15-081-09W5
Pengrowth Energy Corporation...........35/G3
LSD..................................04-08-079-08W5
City..Calgary

Phone#................................403 233-0224
Penn West Petroleum Ltd..................35/F1
LSD..................................12-28-080-09W5
City..Slave Lake
Phone#................................780 849-7900

Map 36

Gas Plants

AltaGas Ltd..36/E6
LSD..................................10-02-077-05W5
City..Athabasca
Phone#................................780 675-1249

Canadian Natural Resources Limited ....
....36/A2
LSD..................................02-11-080-08W5
City..Slave Lake
Phone#................................780 849-2910

Map 37

Gas Plants

AltaGas Ltd..37/G2
LSD..................................16-36-080-25W4
City..Athabasca
Phone#................................780 675-1249

Apache Canada Ltd..............................37/E7
LSD..................................12-18-076-25W4
City..Slave Lake
Phone#................................780 805-3600

Work Camps

Canada North Open Camps................37/F2
LSD......................................26-80-024W4
City..Wabasca

Phone#................................780 891-3391
Jennifer's Open Camp Ltd..................37/F2
LSD..................................NW 23-80-25W4
City..Wabasca
Phone#................................780 891-2267
Noralta Lodge Ltd................................37/F2
LSD..................................SW 26-080-24W4
City..Wabasca
Phone#................................780 891-3962

Map 38

Gas Plants

Canadian Natural Resources Limited ....
....38/C2
LSD..................................13-01-081-23W4
City..Slave Lake
Phone#................................780 891-4200

Map 40

Work Camps

Clean Harbors Lodging Services........40/D1
LSD..................................NE17-20-82-12W4
City...Fort McMurray
Phone#................................888 228-2220
Clean Harbors Lodging Services........40/E1
LSD..................................NW 13-24-082-12W4
City...Fort McMurray
Phone#................................888 228-2220
PTI Open Camp Services......................40/B2
LSD..................................10-04-081-13W4
City..Conklin
Phone#................................877 234-8983

Map 41

Work Camps

Black Diamond Camps and Logistics ....
....41/E7
LSD..................................SE 12-76-07W4
City..Conklin
Phone#................................780 623-0383
Clean Harbors Lodging Services........41/C6
LSD..................................10-03-077-08W4
City..Conklin
Phone#................................888 228-2220
Northgate Contractors Inc.................41/C6
LSD..................................SE 02-77-08W4
City..Conklin
Phone#................................800 207-9818
PTI Open Camp Services.....................41/C6
LSD..................................NW 10-77-08W4
City..Conklin
Phone#................................877 234-8983

Map 42

Gas Plants

Canadian Natural Resources Limited 42/A3
LSD..................................11-19-080-04W4
City...Fort McMurray
Phone#................................780 714-6161

Map 43

Gas Plants

AltaGas Ltd..43/F5
LSD..................................03-03-081-13W6
City..Fort St John
Phone#................................250 785-9655

ARC RESOURCES LTD.................43/A4
LSD...................SW-09-081-16W6
City...........................Bonanza
Phone#................780 353-3766

ARC RESOURCES LTD.................43/D6
LSD...................SE-34-079-14W6
City...........................Bonanza
Phone#................780 353-3766

ARC Resources Ltd 43/G6
LSD...................11-34-079-12W6
City...........................Bonanza
Phone#................780 353-3766

Birchcliff Energy Ltd.................43/F6
LSD...................07-08-080-12W6
City........................Spirit River
Phone#................780 864-4633

CANADIAN NATURAL RESOURCES LIMITED
...............................43/C2
LSD...................SE-34-083-15W6
City.........................Fort St John
Phone#................250 785-3085

CANADIAN NATURAL RESOURCES LIMITED
...............................43/F5
LSD...................SW-03-081-13W6
City.........................Fort St John
Phone#................250 785-3085

CROCOTTA ENERGY INC 43/C5
LSD...................NW-24-080-15W6
City...........................Calgary
Phone#................403 538-3737

IMPERIAL OIL RESOURCES LIMITED .. 43/E1
LSD...................SE-02-085-14W6
City.........................Fort St John
Phone#................250 781-3315

SPECTRA ENERGY MIDSTREAM CORPORA-
TION...........................43/C5
LSD...................SE-25-080-15W6
City........................Spirit River
Phone#................780 864-3125

Spectra Energy Midstream Corporation ......
...............................43/F6
LSD...................05-23-080-13W6
City........................Spirit River
Phone#................780 864-3125

SUNCOR ENERGY INC 43/B4
LSD...................SW-29-081-15W6
City.........................Fort St John
Phone#................250 787-8200

SUNCOR ENERGY INC 43/D1
LSD...................NW-24-084-15W6
City.........................Fort St John
Phone#................250 787-8200

TOURMALINE OIL CORP 43/B5
LSD...................NW-25-080-16W6
City...........................Calgary
Phone#................403 261-3008

WESTCOAST ENERGY INC.................43/E6
LSD...................SW-07-080-13W6

Well Disposal

CCS Midstream Services.................43/E1
LSD...................15-26-084-14W6
City...........................Goodlow
Phone#................250 781-3171

Secure Energy Services.................43/C7
LSD...................16-05-079-14W6
City......................Dawson Creek
Phone#................877 612-9119

Map 44

Gas Plants

AltaGas Ltd.................................44/A7

LSD...................16-31-078-11W6
City.........................Fort St John
Phone#................250 785-9655

Barrick Energy Inc.................44/G6
LSD...................09-07-081-07W6
City...........................Valleyview
Phone#................780 524-3341

Canadian Natural Resources Limited ....
...............................44/D3
LSD...................09-01-083-10W6
City.........................Fort St John
Phone#................250 785-3085

Devon Canada 44/F1
LSD...................16-04-085-08W6
City...........................Fairview
Phone#................780 835-2247

Devon Canada 44/F2
LSD...................08-15-084-08W6
City...........................Fairview
Phone#................780 835-2247

Spectra Energy Midstream Corporation ......
...............................44/B7
LSD...................11-24-079-11W6
City........................Spirit River
Phone#................780 864-3125

Spectra Energy Midstream Corporation ......
...............................44/D7
LSD...................11-26-079-09W6
City........................Spirit River
Phone#................780 864-3125

Spectra Energy Midstream Corporation ......
...............................44/E4
LSD...................16-11-082-09W6
City........................Spirit River
Phone#................780 864-3125

Well Disposal

Four Winds Midstream Solutions.......44/B7
LSD...................16-12-079-11W6
City...........................Gordondale
Phone#................780 864-5996

Four Winds Midstream Solutions.......44/C7
LSD...................08-18-079-09W6
City...........................Silver Valley
Phone#................780 864-8559

Newalta Corporation 44/C7
LSD...................10-10-079-10W6
City...........................Gordondale
Phone#................780 353-3770

Map 45

Gas Plants

Cequence Energy Ltd 45/C5
LSD...................09-07-082-05W6
City...........................Calgary
Phone#................403 229-3050

Delphi Energy Corp.....................45/D4
LSD...................12-13-083-05W6
City...........................Calgary
Phone#................403 265-6171

Devon Canada 45/E6
LSD...................15-03-081-04W6
City...........................Fairview
Phone#................780 835-2247

XGEN Ventures Inc 45/B1
LSD...................03-28-085-06W6

Map 46

Gas Plants

Devon Canada 46/E7
LSD...................16-20-080-24W5
City...........................Eaglesham
Phone#................780 359-2650

Penn West Petroleum Ltd 46/F7
LSD...................13-29-080-23W5
City...........................Peace River
Phone#................780 624-2222

Weigh Scale

Weigh Scale 46/G4
LSD...................06-07-084-23W5
City...........................Grimshaw
Phone#................780 332-2243

Map 47

CCS Midstream Services 47/G2
LSD...................12-24-085-19W5
City...........................Coronation
Phone#................403 575-3911

Map 48

Penn West Petroleum Ltd 48/F4
LSD...................09-15-084-14W5
City...........................Peace River
Phone#................780 624-2222

Map 49

Harvest Operations Corp 49/D2
LSD...................04-36-086-11W5
City...........................Red Earth Creek
Phone#................780 649-2402

Penn West Petroleum Ltd 49/D2
LSD...................07-01-087-11W5
City...........................Peace River
Phone#................780 624-2222

Weigh Scale

Weigh Scale Mobile Inspection Station ....
...............................49/G1
LSD...................07-12-087-09W5
City...........................Red Earth Creek

Well Disposal

Newalta Corporation 49/G1
LSD...................12-13-087-09W5
City...........................Red Earth
Phone#................780 649-3793

Work Camps

Jennifer's Open Camp Ltd................49/G1
LSD...................SE 14-87-09W5
City...........................Red Earth Creek
Phone#................780 649-2221

Red Earth Lodge Ltd.....................49/G1
LSD...................08-23-087-09W5
City...........................Red Earth Creek
Phone#................780 649-2422

Map 51

Husky Oil Operations Limited 51/F6
LSD...................02-33-083-25W4
City...........................Slave Lake
Phone#................780 849-2276

Perpetual Energy Operating Corp.......51/D2
LSD...................06-10-087-01W5
City...........................Athabasca
Phone#................780 675-9252

Map 52

Horizon North Camp & Catering Partnership
...............................52/C7
LSD...................12-06-83-22W4
City...........................Wabasca
Phone#................780 891-2907

Map 53

Gas Plants

Perpetual Energy Operating Corp.......53/B1
LSD...................05-08-088-18W4
City...........................Athabasca
Phone#................780 675-9252

Perpetual Energy Operating Corp.......53/B3
LSD...................08-36-086-19W4
City...........................Athabasca
Phone#................780 675-9252

Map 54

Work Camps

Clean Harbors Lodging Services........54/D7
LSD...................NE17-20-82-12W4
City...........................Fort McMurray
Phone#................888 228-2220

Clean Harbors Lodging Services........54/E7
LSD...................NW 13-24-082-12W4
City...........................Fort McMurray
Phone#................888 228-2220

Great White Energy Services/ LLC 54/F5
LSD...................SW 04-07-85-10W4
City...........................Fort McMurray
Phone#................780 713-1969

Map 55

Gas Plants

Canadian Natural Resources Limited ....
...............................55/G6
LSD...................15-14-083-05W4
City...........................Fort McMurray
Phone#................780 714-6161

Weigh Scale

Weigh Scale Mobile Inspection Station ....
...............................55/B3
LSD...................02-12-087-09W4
City...........................Fort McMurray

Work Camps

PTI Open Camp Services.................55/E5
LSD...................SW 36-84-07W4
City...........................Anzac
Phone#................877 234-8983

PTI Open Camp Services.................55/E6
LSD...................NE-07-84-06W4
City...........................Anzac
Phone#................877 234-8983

Map 57

Gas Plants

AltaGas Ltd.................................57/G4
LSD...................13-07-088-12W6
City.........................Fort St John
Phone#................250 785-9655

Canadian Natural Resources Limited ....
...............................57/G4
LSD...................16-11-088-13W6
City.........................Fort St John
Phone#................250 785-3085

CANADIAN NATURAL RESOURCES LIMITED
...............................57/G4
LSD...................NE-11-088-13W6
City.........................Fort St John
Phone#................250 785-3085

Canadian Natural Resources Limited ....
...............................57/G7
LSD...................01-14-085-13W6
City.........................Fort St John
Phone#................250 785-3085

CANADIAN NATURAL RESOURCES LIMITED
...............................57/G7
LSD...................SE-14-085-13W6

City ....Fort St John
Phone# 250 785-3085
CHINOOK ENERGY (2010) INC.......... 57/E7
LSD..................SE-25-085-14W6
City..................................Calgary
Phone# 403 261-6883
Penn West Petroleum Ltd 57/G6
LSD....................15-13-086-13W6
City...........................Fort St John
Phone# 250 785-8363
SUNCOR ENERGY INC 57/E7
LSD..................NW-10-085-14W6
City...........................Fort St John
Phone# 250 787-8200
TAQA NORTH LTD 57/G6
LSD....................NE-13-086-13W6
City.................................Goodlow
Phone# 250 781-3502

Map 58

Gas Plants

AltaGas Ltd 58/A2
LSD....................07-33-090-12W6
City...........................Fort St John
Phone# 250 785-9655
Birchcliff Energy Ltd 58/E5
LSD....................08-21-087-09W6
City.............................Spirit River
Phone# 780 864-4633
Iteration Energy.............................. 58/B7
LSD....................10-33-085-11W6
City..................................Calgary
Phone# 403 261-6883
Terra Energy Corp........................... 58/B6
LSD....................10-19-086-11W6
City...........................Fort St John
Phone# 250 261-5442
Terra Energy Corp........................... 58/D6
LSD....................16-36-086-10W6
City...........................Fort St John
Phone# 250 261-5442

Work Camps

Clear Prairie Open Camp.................. 58/C5
LSD....................NE 20-87-10W6
City..................................Worsley
Phone# 780 685-0006
Moffat's Open Camp....................... 58/G6
LSD....................NE 35-086-08W6
City..................................Worsley
Phone# 780 685-3000

Map 59

Gas Plants

Canadian Natural Resources Limited 59/A5
LSD....................14-28-087-07W6
City...........................Fort St John
Phone# 250 785-3085
Sydco Energy Inc........................... 59/A6
LSD....................11-22-087-07W6
City..................................Calgary
Phone# 403 261-3008

Map 61

Gas Plants

Bonavista Energy Corporation 61/A4
LSD....................04-22-090-23W5
City.....................Yellowhead County
Phone# 780 693-7300

Map 63

Gas Plants

Penn West Petroleum Ltd 63/B3

LSD.....................12-29-091-12W5
City.................................Manning
Phone# 780 836-3448

Map 64

Gas Plants

Devon Canada 64/A3
LSD....................03-32-091-08W5
City........................Red Earth Creek
Phone# 780 649-3698
Penn West Petroleum Ltd 64/B7
LSD....................02-23-088-08W5
City.............................Peace River
Phone# 780 624-2222

Map 66

Gas Plants

Canadian Natural Resources Limited..66/F3
LSD....................03-29-092-20W4
City.........................Fort McMurray
Phone# 780 714-6161

Map 68

Work Camps

ATCO Structures & Logistics Ltd 68/F1
LSD....................SW 31-94-10W4
City.........................Fort McMurray
Phone# 780 743-2579
ATCO Structures & Logistics Ltd 68/F1
LSD....................NW 31-94-10W4
City.........................Fort McMurray
Phone# 780 788-2310
Clean Harbors Lodging Services 68/F1
LSD....................SW 32-94-10W4
City.........................Fort McMurray
Phone# 888 228-2220
Horizon North Camp & Catering Partnership
....68/F4
LSD....................02-05-092-10W4
City.........................Fort McMurray
Phone# 780 628-3820
Horizon North Camp & Catering Partnership
....68/F4
LSD....................NW 05-92-10W4
City.........................Fort McMurray
Phone# 780 628-3805
Horizon North Camp & Catering Partnership
....68/G4
LSD....................09-28-091-10W4
City.........................Fort McMurray
Phone# 780 554-3884
Noralta Lodge Ltd........................... 68/G4
LSD....................NE 26-091-10W4
City.........................Fort McMurray
Phone# 780 791-3334
PTI Open Camp Services.................. 68/F2
LSD....................08-01-094-11W4
City...........................Fort MacKay
Phone# 877 234-8983
PTI Open Camp Services.................. 68/F2
LSD....................NE 01-94-11W4
City...........................Fort MacKay
Phone# 877 234-8983
PTI Open Camp Services.................. 68/F3
LSD....................SW 09-93-10W4
City...........................Fort MacKay
Phone# 877 234-8983

Map 69

Work Camps

Horizon North Camp & Catering Partnership
....69/C1
LSD....................00-19-094-07W4

City ....Fort McMurray
Phone# 877 471-5515
Noralta Lodge Ltd........................... 69/E1
LSD....................10-16-095-06W4
City.........................Fort McMurray
Phone# 780 743-0322

Map 71

Gas Plants

APACHE CANADA LTD...................... 71/A2
PNG....................032-H/94-H-08
City............................Dawson Creek
Phone# 250 795-2000
Bonavista Energy Corporation 71/F3
LSD....................08-25-096-10W6
City.....................Yellowhead County
Phone# 780 693-7300
Canadian Natural Resources Limited 71/A4
LSD....................04-30-094-12W6
City...........................Fort St John
Phone# 250 785-3085
Canadian Natural Resources Limited 71/C2
LSD....................12-29-096-11W6
City...........................Fort St John
Phone# 250 785-3085
Devon Canada 71/D2
LSD....................11-14-097-11W6
City...........................Fort St John
Phone# 250 787-0346
TAQA NORTH LTD 71/A2
PNG....................032-H/94-H-08
City.................................Goodlow
Phone# 250 781-3502

Work Camps

Moffat's General Contracting Ltd 71/C2
LSD....................NE 19-096-11W6
City.................................Manning
Phone# 780 836-4091

Map 72

Gas Plants

Baytex Energy Ltd 72/B3
LSD....................10-20-096-07W6
City...........................Fort St John
Phone# 250 262-0015
Canadian Natural Resources Limited .72/F1
LSD....................07-16-098-05W6
City...........................Fort St John
Phone# 250 785-3085
Canadian Natural Resources Limited .72/F3
LSD....................01-24-096-05W6
City...........................Fort St John
Phone# 250 785-3085
Devon Canada 72/A3
LSD....................11-33-096-08W6
City...........................Fort St John
Phone# 250 787-0346
Keyera Energy Ltd 72/B1
LSD....................05-32-098-07W6
City...........................Drayton Valley
Phone# 780 894-7000
Plains Midstream Canada ULC...........72/F3
LSD....................01-24-096-05W6
City...........................Rainbow Lake
Phone# 780 956-3852

Work Camps

Moffat's General Contracting Ltd 72/A5
LSD....................03-21-094-08W6
City.................................Manning
Phone# 780 836-4746

Map 73

Gas Plants

Bonavista Energy Corporation 73/B6
LSD....................07-13-094-03W6
City.....................Yellowhead County
Phone# 780 693-7300
Bonavista Energy Corporation 73/D4
LSD....................15-10-096-01W6
City.....................Yellowhead County
Phone# 780 693-7300
Canadian Natural Resources Limited 73/C6
LSD....................02-35-094-02W6
City...........................Fort St John
Phone# 250 785-3085
Surge Energy Inc 73/D7
LSD....................08-14-093-01W6
City..................................Calgary
Phone# 403 930-1010

Map 74

Gas Plants

Stittco Energy Limited 74/B2
LSD....................01-04-099-22W5

Map 75

Gas Plants

Baytex Energy Ltd 75/A6
LSD....................16-28-094-18W5
City...........................Fort St John
Phone# 250 262-0015
Lone Pine Resources Canada Ltd 75/E6
LSD....................15-05-095-15W5
City...........................Grande Prairie
Phone# 780 532-8024

Map 77

Gas Plants

Gas Plant...................................77/D6
LSD....................12-06-096-06W5
City...........................Peerless Lake

Map 81

Work Camps

Clean Harbors Lodging Services 81/E7
LSD....................SW 04-096-11W4
City.........................Fort McMurray
Phone# 888 228-2220

Map 82

Work Camps

Clean Harbors Lodging Services 82/C6
LSD....................NE 19-096-07W4
City.........................Fort McMurray
Phone# 888 228-2220
PTI Open Camp Services................... 82/D7
LSD....................E 29-95-07W4
City.........................Fort McMurray
Phone# 877 234-8983

Map 84

Gas Plants

CONOCOPHILLIPS CANADA OPERATIONS
LTD...84/D5
PNG....................049-B/94-H-16
City...........................Fort St John
Phone# 250 785-4887
CONOCOPHILLIPS CANADA OPERATIONS
LTD...84/E6
PNG....................081-I/94-H-09
City...........................Fort St John
Phone# 250 785-4887
CONOCOPHILLIPS CANADA OPERATIONS

Index

Northern Alberta

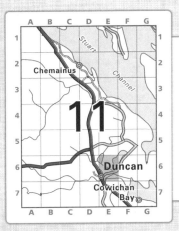

The **Map Index** listings consist of: listing name, page number/coordinates. In the example found on the left, Duncan is found on page 11/E6.

For the **Adventure Index**, the listing also consists of the Reference Page number, where the description of the listing is found. In the example below the Stuart Channel listing description is found on page 89.

Stuart Channel............11/B1-G4,**89** ──▶ **Reference Page**

⎵_____⎵ ⎵_____⎵
   Name   **Map Page/Coordinate**

The grid lines found in the example are used for illustration purposes only. The blue gridlines found on the maps refer to UTM coordinates.

Adventure Index

KAYAKERS PADDLING IN BOW RIVER

WHITE-FACED IBIS IN CRETE POND

Hunting Adventures

Paddling Adventures

TRAINS CANADA TRAIL ON A FOGGY NOVEMBER DAY

Park Adventures

HERD OF PLAINS BISON IN HAY-ZAMA LAKES WILDLAND PARK

Trail Adventures

ATV [OHV] Adventures

Map Index - (Name,Map Page/Coordinates)

A VIEW OF LAKE ATHABASKA FROM FORT CHIPEWYAN

SUNSET OVER FRANK LAKE

WILD FLOWERS IN GRANDE PRAIRIE, ALBERTA

Jernis Lake.....................89/B7
Jenkins Lake....................10/A1
Jeremie Lake....................12/C5
Jessie Lake.......................8/B1
Jim Lake.........................10/F6
Jodoin Creek....................96/A6
John D'Or Prairie............87/E2
Johnson Lake....................83/C2
Johnson Lake....................89/D1
Johnson Lake....................97/F2
Jones Lake.......................30/F6
Joseph Lake.....................10/D6
Josephine Creek.................44/E5
Joslyn Creek....................81/C7
Joussard.......................20/G2
Judah..........................47/E2
Judy Creek.......................7/C6

K

Kakisa River..............Inset 98/A1
Kakut Creek.....................31/D5
Kakut Lake......................31/D4
Kakut Lake Park.................31/D4
Kakwa River................1/A7-3/B4
Kakwa Wildland Provincial Park .. 1/C7
Kamisak Lake....................15/F2
Kamisak Lake Natural Area......15/E2
Kamistikowik Lake...............52/B7
Karr Lake........................3/E3
Kathleen.......................33/F5
Kathryn Lake.....................8/B3
Kaybob.........................5/D7
Keane Creek.....................90/D5
Kearl Lake......................82/B7
Keeping Lake....................29/E5
Keg River......................86/G1
Keg River....................85/F6-86/G1
Keg River Metis Settlement F1
Keg River Natural Area..........86/G1
Keith Lake......................13/C6
Kemp River......................74/C2
Kemp River.................73/G1-86/G1
Kennedy Lake....................95/G4
Kenny Creek......................2/A5
Kenny Woods....................90/E1

Kenzie..........................33/F6
Keppler Creek..........61/F1-74/F7
Kerr Lake.......................12/A6
Ketchum Lake....................45/E7
Kettle River....................41/G2
Kidney Lake..........64/G6,65/A6
Kikino.........................12/A7
Kilome Lake.....................95/C1
Kilpatrick Creek.......95/G6-96/A6
Kilsyth Creek....................9/B4
Kilsyth Lake.....................9/B5
Kimiwan Lake....................33/E3
Kimiwan Lake Natural Area.......33/E3
King Lake........................9/B5
Kinikinik......................10/F5
Kinnaird Lake...................12/F3
Kinosis........................55/E5
Kinosis Lake....................55/D5
Kinosiu Lake....................11/F4
Kinuso.........................21/E2
Kirby Lake......................27/G2
Kiskatinaw Lake.................55/D2
Kleskun Hill Natural Area......17/A3
Kleskun Creek...................31/G4
Kleskun Creek Natural Area......31/G5
Kleskun Lake Grazing Reserve......
..........................17/A3,31/G3
Klondike Ferry County Park 8/F7
Knights Creek.........95/F5-96/A6
Konah Lake......................12/C5
Krause Lake......................7/D3
Ksituan........................44/G7
Ksituan Lake....................30/C1
Ksituan River.........30/E1-45/G3

L

L'hirondelle...................48/G2
La Biche River..........11/E1-25/G6
La Biche River Wildland Provincial Park
.........................11/C1,25/G3
La Butte Creek..............97/A-C5
La Butte Creek Wildland Prov Park......
................................97/B4
La Corey.......................13/G7
La Crite.......................86/D7
La Glace.......................30/E6

Lake Gray........................9/D2
Lake May...................Inset 98/A2
Lake St. Germain................47/B1
Lakeland (Buffer) Natural Area ......
.........................12/E3,13/A2
Lakeland Provincial Park........12/F3
Lakeland Provincial Recreation Area ....
.........................12/G4,13/A3
Lakeview Estates...............12/C3
Lakeview Lake....................9/D6
Lalby Creek.....................33/A3
Lambert Creek...................88/F1
Landels River...................42/E3
Lane Lake.......................13/E4
Lane Lake.......................96/E4
Larkspur........................9/F7
Larne Creek.....................93/A4
Larocque Lake...................90/E3
Last Lake......................46/C4
Last Lake.......................46/C4
Lathrop Creek...................58/C5
Latornell.......................3/D2
Latornell River..........3/D5-18/E1
Lattice Creek...................15/C3
Lawrence Lake...................23/G7
Lawrence Lake Recreation Area......
................................23/G7
Lawrence River..................87/E3
Leddy Lake......................47/B1
Leddy Lake Regional Park........47/B1
Lee Lake........................10/D6
Legend Lake.....................80/A5
Leggett Creek.........68/G4-69/A4
Leggo Lake......................97/D2
Leicester......................34/C4
Leicester Lake..................12/C3
Leighmore......................15/F2
Leismer........................41/D5
Leith (little burnt) River......46/A7
Leland Lakes....................97/B1
Leming Lake.....................14/B5
Lemiseau Lake...................25/F4
Lennard Creek.........71/B1-84/D7
Lessard........................14/A7
Lessard Creek.......93/F1-Inset 99/F6

Lindgren Lake...................97/F1
Line Lake.......................83/C1
Lingrell Creek..................15/D7
Lingrell Lake...................15/D7
Linton Lake.....................86/D6
Lister Lake.....................97/F2
Little Bear Lake................14/D6
Little Beaver Lake..............11/F5
Little Buffalo Lake.............48/F2
Little Buffalo River............84/E3
Little Buffalo River....95/E3-96/B2
Little Cadotte River 61/E6-63/A4
Little Clear River..............58/B6
Little Driftpile River....20/G5-21/A3
Little Fishery.................88/B5
Little Fishery River............68/D6
Little Grassey Natural Area.....20/F1
Little Grayling Creek............1/E2
Little Hay River........91/F7-92/A7
Little Horse Creek..............35/C3
Little Horse Lake...............35/B3
Little Johnson Lake.............11/C5
Little Lake.....................16/E2
Little Muddy Creek.......1/F1-15/G7
Little Pine Creek...............10/D5
Little Prairie Creek............20/C5
Little Puskwaskau Lake..........19/A4
Little Puskwaskau River.........32/B6
Little Rapids Creek......93/D3-94/A6
Little Red River...............87/G3
Little Redrock Creek.............2/B4
Little Smoky....................5/A2
Little Smoky Losegun Natural Area......
.................................5/A1
Little Smoky Losegun Natural Area ....
................................13/B3
Little Smoky River.......5/A2-33/D7
Livock River..........52/G5-53/A3
Liege River...........65/F2-79/C6
Lodge Lake......................11/E4
Lofty Lake......................11/D4
Logan Lake......................27/A6
Logan Lake......................97/E1
Logan River.....................26/D4
Lois Lake........................7/E3
Lone Pine Lake..................12/A7
Long End Lake....................8/G5
Long Island Lake.................9/F7
Long Island Lake County Park 9/E7
Long Lake...........9/G5, 10/C5
Long Lake.......................18/F5
Long Lake.......................38/F5
Long Lake.......................64/F6
Long Lake Provincial Park.......11/B7
Loon Creek......................53/B7
Loon Lake......................49/A6
Loon Lake.......................49/A6
Loon Lake.......................95/G3
Loon River...........49/A4-64/C2
Loop Creek......................96/E3
Losegun Lake.....................5/D5
Loseman Lake....................14/C2
Lost Hope Creek.................20/C6
Lothrop........................46/A7
Louise Creek.....................7/B5
Louise River..........80/B2-89/G2
Loutit Lake.....................97/C7
Lovet Creek.....................72/F6
Lowe Lake.......................30/D7
Lowen Lake......................15/G1
Lubicon Lake...................49/C2
Lubicon Lake.........48/G3,49/C1

Lubicon River...................49/B6
Lumba Lake......................12/F7
Lutose.........................93/D3
Lutose Creek....................93/D3
Lyle Lake.......................25/D4
Lylich Lake.....................36/F5
Lymburn........................29/F6
Lynx Creek.......................1/D7
Lynx Lake.......................12/C1
Lynx Lake.......................96/E5

M

Mackay River..........52/F1-68/F1
Majors Lake.....................10/A2
Maloney Lake....................14/C7
Mamawi Creek....................89/C7
Mamawi Lake.........89/B7,90/B1
Mamawi River....................89/C7
Manatokan Creek.................13/E7
Manatokan Lake..................13/E7
Manir..........................31/B4
Manning........................60/G2
Manning........................61/A2
Margaret Lake...................94/D6
Margie.........................27/A2
Marguerite Lake.................13/G5
Marguerite River.......82/D1-90/G5
Marguerite River Wildland Provincial
Park....................70,82,83,90
Maria Lake......................50/G3
Marie Creek.....................14/D2
Marie Lake......................14/D5
Marie-Reine....................47/F2
Marigold Lake....................7/B3
Marina.........................58/G6
Marlow Creek....................93/A1
Marlow Creek..............Inset 99/A5
Marten Creek....................36/C7
Marten Lakes....................36/F6
Marten River...................48/F1
Marten River....................48/D2
Martin Lake.....................30/A5
Martineau River.................14/G4
Martyn Lake.....................97/G2
Mary Lake.......................56/E3
Mastin Lake.....................10/E6
Matthews Lake...................12/D4
Maurice Lake....................12/C5
Maurice Lake....................33/F7
Maxwell Lake....................89/G5
May Lake........................14/C4
May River...........26/A7-41/A7
Maybelle River..................90/E3
Mcallister Creek................46/G5
Mcbernie Lake...................12/B4
Mccarthy Lake...................12/B4
Mcclelland Lake.................82/B4
Mcconachie Lake.................36/D3
Mccowan Lake....................97/F1
Mcdougall Lake..................14/B5
Mcgowan Creek.........19/G6-20/A6
McGrane Estates................12/B2
Mcguffin Lake...................12/F3
Mcinnes Lake....................97/E2
Mcivor River.........80/F1-89/G3
Mckinley Creek..................20/D6
Mclean Creek.........57/G5-58/A6
Mclean Creek....................69/A5
Mcleans Creek...................33/D7
Mclelland Lake..................97/A2
McLennan.......................33/E4
Mclennan Lake...................90/E7

MOOSE IN SLAVE LAKE, ALBERTA

LAC LA BICHE
12/B3

INCORPORATED
1798

AREA (TOTAL)
6.20 km2

ELEVATION
560 m (1,840 ft)

POPULATION (2011)
Total: 2,520

AREA CODE(S)
780

PEACE RIVER
47/D3

INCORPORATED
1781

AREA (TOTAL)
25.92 km2

ELEVATION
330 m (1,080 ft)

POPULATION (2011)
Total: 6,729

AREA CODE(S)
780

PILEATED WOODPECKER IN QUEEN ELIZABETH PROVINCIAL PARK

ABANDONED GRAIN ELEVATOR IN THE SALT PRAIRIES

ADVERTISERS

IMPORTANT NUMBERS

General

Avalanche Information .... www.avalanche.ca | 1-800-667-1105
Government of Alberta ....gov.ab.ca
....................................Outside of Edmonton (Alberta only): 310-0000
....Outside of Alberta: (780) 427-2711
Report a Poacher 1-800-642-3800
Report a Forest Fire 310-FIRE
Road Reports...........www.ama.ab.ca | 511.alberta.ca/map | 511
Tourism Alberta....................1-800-252-3782 | www.travelalberta.com
Alberta North Tourism Destination Region Association ...1-800-756-4351
.... www.travelalbertanorth.com
Updates.................................... www.backroadmapbooks.com
Weather Conditions.................... www.weatheroffice.ec.gc.ca

Fish & Wildlife

Alberta Environment & Sustainable Resource Development ....
.... (780) 524-3567 | esrd.alberta.ca/fish-wildlife/default.aspx
Fishing Regulations ....
.................www.albertaregulations.ca/fishingregs/further-inquiries.html
Hunting Regulations ....
.... www.albertaregulations.ca/huntingregs/inquiries.html
Fish & Wildlife Area Office Contacts............................1-877-944-0313
.... esrd.alberta.ca
/about-esrd/contact-esrd/fish-and-wildlife-area-office-contacts.aspx

Parks

Alberta Parks Campground Reservations 1-877-537-2757
.... reserve.albertaparks.ca
Parks and Protected Areas 1-866-427-3582
....www.albertaparks.ca
Parks Canada (National Parks) 1-800-651-7959
.... www.pc.gc.ca
National Parks Campground Reservations....................1-877-737-3783
.... www.pccamping.ca
Wood Buffalo National Park.............................. (867) 872-7960
.... www.pc.gc.ca/eng/pn-np/nt/woodbuffalo/index.aspx

Clubs & Organizations

Alberta Camping Association .... (403) 453-8570
Alberta Conservation Association 1-877-969-9091
Alberta Resort & Campground Association .... (403) 963-3993
Alberta Trailnet Society ....www.albertatrailnet.com
Alberta Off-Hwy Vehicle Association ....www.aohva.com
Alberta Snowmobile Federation............................... (780) 427-2695
.... www.altasnowmobile.ab.ca
Alpine Club of Canada .... (403) 678-3200
.... www.alpineclubofcanada.ca
Cross Country Alberta .... www.xcountryab.net

British Columbia / Alberta Distance Chart

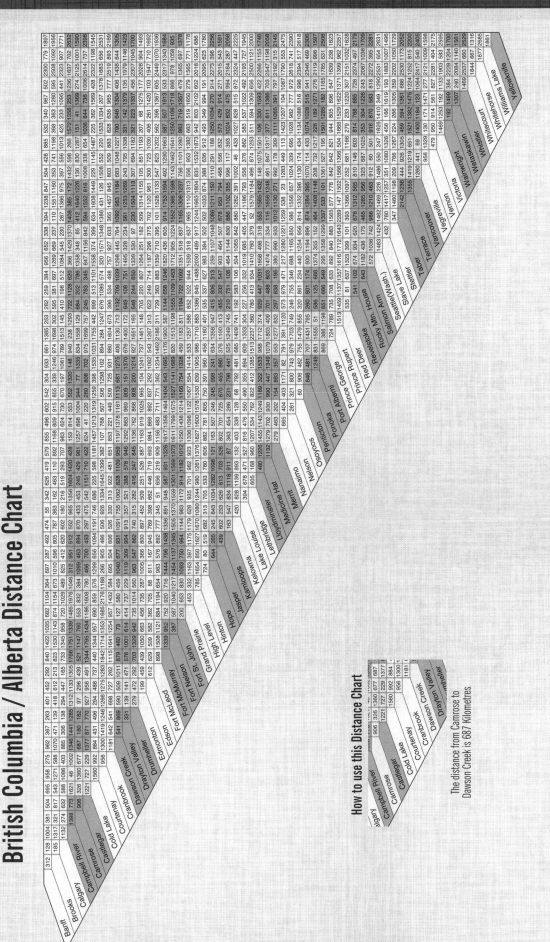

How to use this Distance Chart

The distance from Camrose to Dawson Creek is 687 Kilometres.

1 Kilometre = 0.621 Mile

1 Mile = 1.6 Kilometres

Speed Conversion Chart

WILD & FREE

Photo Contest
Win up to $10,000
in cash & prizes

For complete contest rules & Details
visit BackroadMapbooks.com/contests

#BRMBphoto

f / backroadmapbooks

t @backroadmapbook

g+ /+Backroadmapbooks

o / backroadmapbooks
